Thomson Custom Solutions allows you to:

▶ Create a comprehensive course solution by incorporating your original content such as course notes, handouts, regional or state material, or articles in a professional and attractive format. In addition, our flexible and attractive cover options will help make your project stand apart.

▶ Make technology work for you, utilizing our skilled **Custom Media Solutions** team to match your technology to your text and course.

▶ Enrich your course with selections from one of our **Thomson Custom Solutions Collections** offering additional readings, exercises, and case selections for a wide range of subjects. Use our powerful TextChoice book-building web site, **www.textchoice.com**, to explore the options available to you.

▶ Offer students more choices in their textbook format and delivery.

Thomson Custom Solutions expert editorial team will guide you through each step and work with you to ensure your project meets your goals and objectives.

For more information about your options and our services, visit **www.thomsoncustom.com** or contact your local Thomson representative.

For more information about your options and our services, visit: www.thomsoncustom.com

ISBN: 0-495-22063-9

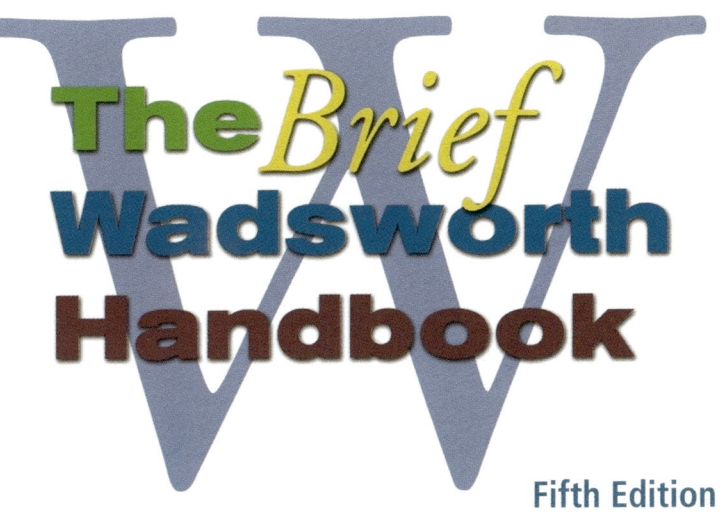

The *Brief* Wadsworth Handbook

Fifth Edition

Laurie G. Kirszner
University of the Sciences in Philadelphia

Stephen R. Mandell
Drexel University

THOMSON
━━━━━━━━★━━ ™
WADSWORTH

Australia • Brazil • Canada • Mexico • Singapore • Spain • United Kingdom • United States

The Brief Wadsworth Handbook, Fifth Edition
Laurie G. Kirszner, Stephen R. Mandell

Publisher: *Michael Rosenberg*
Senior Acquisitions Editor:
  Dickson Musslewhite
Development Editor: *Karen Smith*
Editorial Assistant: *Jonelle Lonergan*
Technology Project Manager: *Tim Smith*
Managing Marketing Manager:
  Mandee Eckersley
Marketing Assistant: *Dawn Giovanniello*
**Associate Marketing Communications
  Manager:** *Patrick Rooney*
**Senior Project Manager, Editorial
  Production:** *Lianne Ames*

Senior Print Buyer: *Mary Beth Hennebury*
Senior Permissions Editor: *Isabel Alves*
Permissions Editor: *Karyn Morrison*
Production Service: *Nesbitt Graphics*
Text Designer: *Nesbitt Graphics*
Photo Manager: *Sheri Blaney*
Photo Researcher: *Sharon Donahue*
Cover Designer: *Brian Salisbury*
Cover Printer: *China Translation and
  Printing Services*
Compositor: *Nesbitt Graphics*
Printer: *China Translation and Printing Services*

Printed in China
1 2 3 4 5 6 7 09 08 07 06

Library of Congress Control Number:
2005937958

ISBN 1-4130-2030-5

Thomson Higher Education
25 Thomson Place
Boston, MA 02210-1202
USA

For more information about our products, contact us at:
Thomson Learning Academic Resource Center
1-800-423-0563
For permission to use material from this text or product, submit a request online at
http://www.thomsonrights.com
Any additional questions about permissions can be submitted by e-mail to
thomsonrights@thomson.com

The Brief Handbook that Meets the Needs of Today's Students ...

The most comprehensive brief handbook available, the fifth edition of **The Brief Wadsworth Handbook** provides students with extensive coverage of rhetorical concerns, the writing and research process, writing and researching with computers, visual rhetoric, the habits of a successful college student and other topics essential for 21st century student writers.

... Accompanied by Interactive Solutions for Today's Instructors

See pages 7 and 8 of this Preview for details!

An Accessible Design that Makes Information Easy to Reference

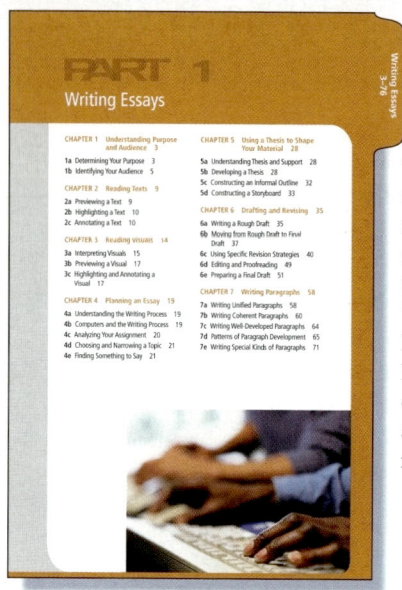

The Brief Wadsworth Handbook features a fresh, inviting design that makes it easy for students to quickly access relevant information. Another trademark of this text, Chapter 21, "Ten Habits of Successful Students," helps students become more active learners, providing them with effective time management strategies and tips on using campus services, resources, and technology.

14 tabbed dividers, corresponding in color to each section of the handbook, provide an overview of the chapters in that section and include *Frequently Asked Questions* on the back of each tabbed divider, with page references directing students to the answers.

In addition, marginal FAQ icons appear beside the answer in the text so students can easily locate the answer.

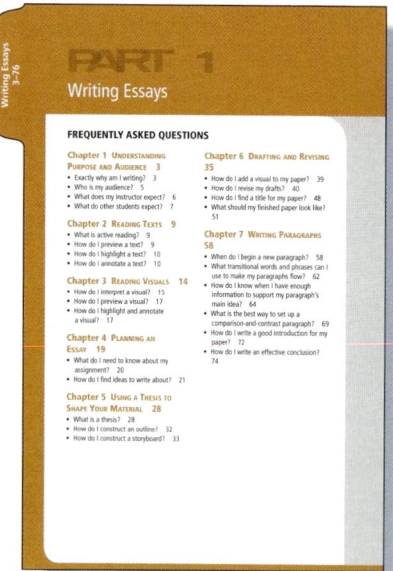

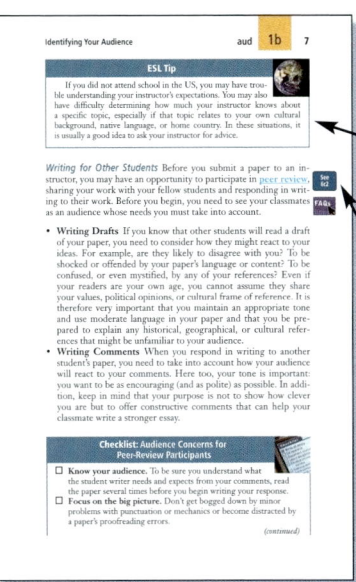

The *Brief Wadsworth Handbook* also features a variety of other innovative and valuable features for students, including:

ESL tips that explain concepts in relation to the unique experiences of bilingual students.

Marginal cross-references that direct students to other sections that treat topics in more detail.

Close-up boxes that provide students with an in-depth look at writing-related issues they'll encounter.

Computer Tips that highlight specific ways in which technology can help students throughout various steps of the writing process.

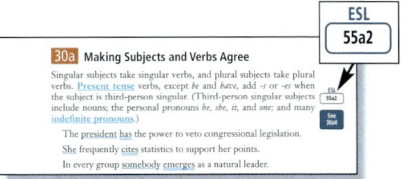

Marginal ESL cross-references that direct students to sections of Part 13, "Resources for Bilingual and ESL Writers," where concepts applicable to second-language writers are explained.

Checklists that summarize key information, as well as guide students through specific writing-related tasks.

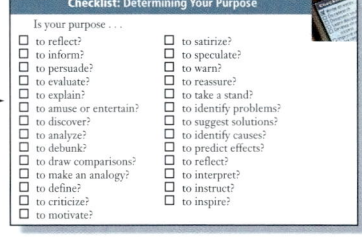

Five New Chapters Focusing on Writing

This new edition features expanded coverage of the writing process; critical thinking; argumentation; writing in an electronic environment; visual rhetoric; and writing in the disciplines. Five new chapters help students adapt to the many challenges of writing in the 21st century:

Chapter 1: "Understanding Purpose and Audience," provides students with a practical approach to classical rhetorical concepts that is integrated throughout the text—showing students how purpose and audience considerations apply to both written and visual texts.

Because visuals inundate everyday culture, **Chapter 3: "Reading Visuals,"** emphasizes the importance of visual rhetoric in the 21st century, offering students advice on how to critically interpret and evaluate visuals in different forms.

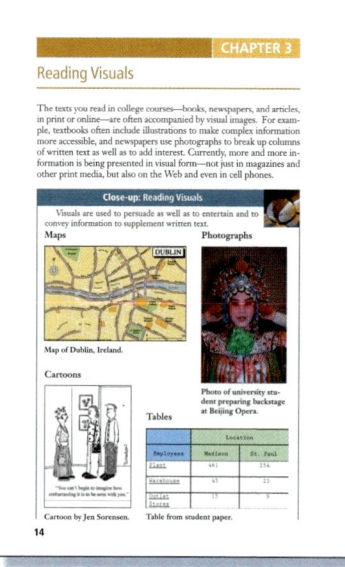

Chapter 11: "Writing Electronic Arguments," helps students unfamiliar with the conventions of electronic writing transition to Internet-based communication such as blogging and e-mail by emphasizing the differences between electronic and print arguments.

Chapter 10: "Using Visuals in Argumentative Essays," shows students how to effectively use different types of visuals to clarify and support the arguments they will construct throughout college, as well as in the workplace.

Grounded in the core rhetorical principles, **Chapter 22, "Writing in the Disciplines,"** supplies students with a practical framework for understanding the conventions for writing in the humanities, social sciences, and natural sciences.

A Reliable and Easy-to-Use Research and Documentation Guide

Parts 4–5 contain the most comprehensive coverage of researching in the disciplines as well as documenting sources in MLA, APA, Chicago, and CSE styles. Designed for easy use, the research sections include specially designed documentation directories that make it easy for students to locate models for various sources.

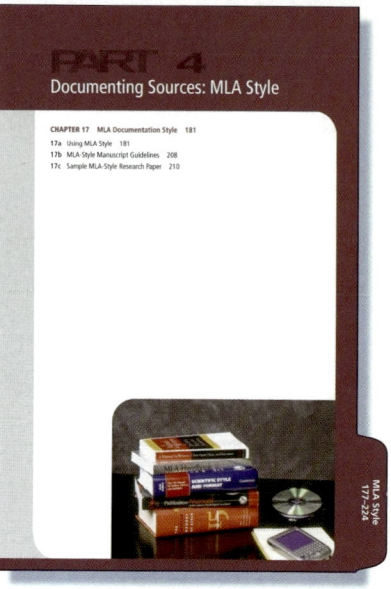

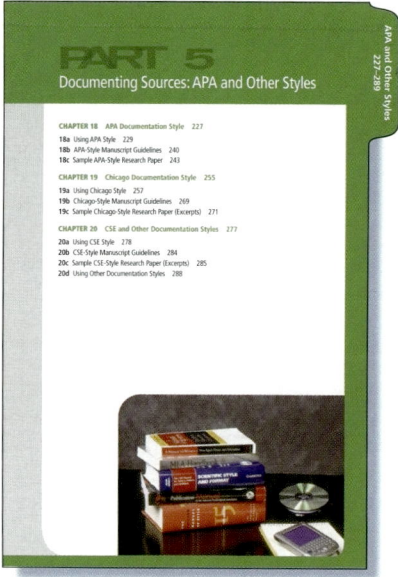

In addition, **Part 3, "Doing Research,"** offers the most extensive example of a student's work through each step of the research process (finding and evaluating appropriate print and electronic sources, formulating a research question, and writing the research paper), including expanded coverage on how to avoid plagiarism in **Chapter 16, "Avoiding Plagiarism."**

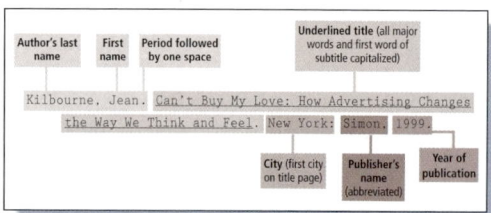

Author's last name | First name | Period followed by one space | Underlined title (all major words and first word of subtitle capitalized)

Kilbourne, Jean. Can't Buy My Love: How Advertising Changes the Way We Think and Feel. New York: Simon, 1999.

City (first city on title page) | Publisher's name (abbreviated) | Year of publication

Diagrams of sample works-cited entries clearly illustrate the elements of proper documentation, and annotated sample student papers demonstrate how the documentation styles are used.

Interactive Solutions for Today's Instructors

Thomson's InSite for Writing and Research™

Finally, life just got easier! Thomson's new **InSite** is a groundbreaking all-in-one course management tool designed specifically for courses that require writing and/or research. From a single site, instructors can manage the flow of papers electronically, check originality using **InSite's** originality-checker powered by Turnitin®, the world's most widely used plagiarism prevention software, allow students to submit papers and conduct peer reviews, and more—all in an interface that's easier to use than any other on the market. To view a demonstration, visit **http://insite.thomson.com.** Ask your Thomson Wadsworth sales representative how to package **InSite** with this text.

ThomsonNOW™ for Kirszner & Mandell's *The Brief Wadsworth Handbook,* Fifth Edition

Offering choice and flexibility, ThomsonNOW for Kirszner & Mandell's *The Brief Wadsworth Handbook,* **Fifth Edition** saves you time through its automatic grading and easy-to-use grade book and provides your students with an efficient way to study. For every chapter, personalized learning plans allow students to focus on what they still need to learn and to select the activities that best match their learning styles (such as videos, animations, visual overviews, web links, and text pages). Ask your Thomson Wadsworth sales representative how to package **ThomsonNOW** with this text.

A service of iParadigms, LLC

This proven online plagiarism-prevention software promotes fairness in the classroom by helping students learn to correctly cite sources and allowing instructors to check for originality before reading and grading papers. **Turnitin** quickly checks student papers against billions of pages of Internet content, millions of published works, and millions of student papers and within seconds generates a comprehensive originality report. To view a demonstration, visit **http://turnitin.thomson.com.** Ask your Thomson Wadsworth sales representative how to package **Turnitin** with this text.

WriteNote

http://writenote.thomsonlearning.com

WriteNote is a web-based research and writing tool that helps students search for and organize references used in their academic papers, so they can focus on the content of their research and the presentation of ideas. Using **WriteNote,** students can format bibliographies instantly because **WriteNote** knows the latest updates for more than 1,000 documentation styles, including such standards as MLA, APA, Chicago, and CSE. Students can also install optional plug-in toolbars that link directly to library resources, annotate and save Web pages for later use, and insert references and format papers instantly in Microsoft®Word documents using the **Cite While You Write**™ feature. Ask your Thomson Wadsworth sales representative how to package **WriteNote** with this text.

Comp21: Composition in the 21st Century for Kirszner & Mandell's *The Brief Wadsworth Handbook,* Fifth Edition ONLINE!

Through interactive instruction, this groundbreaking online tool teaches students how to analyze the various texts that inundate their lives, and demonstrates how to use rhetorical devices in their writing. Using Thomson Wadsworth's unique "Explicator" technology—which guides students in critically analyzing texts and media—students can create useful notes for their work to enhance their inquiry into their chosen topics. This online program includes:

- More than 300 "texts" (essays, images, video clips, and audio clips)
- A wealth of reading selections that reflect many different discourse forms and genres, including traditional essays, academic analyses, editorials from print and online sources, excerpts from books, and texts from a variety of periodicals
- PLUS—access to InfoTrac® College Edition with InfoMarks™
  Ask your Thomson Wadsworth sales representative how to package **Comp21** with this text.

Additional Teaching and Learning Resources

**Instructor Flex-Files for
Kirszner & Mandell's
The Brief Wadsworth Handbook,
Fifth Edition**

Designed to give instructors maximum flexibility in planning and customizing their courses, FLEX-FILES provide an abundance of instructor materials including sample syllabi and activities; "Questions for Teachers," which raises a variety of pedagogical questions with solutions for instructors to consider in teaching with the handbook; an ESL insert aimed at helping instructors teach writing effectively to ESL students; and an insert on disability issues as they relate to teaching first-year composition.

**Exercises for
Kirszner & Mandell's
The Brief Wadsworth Handbook,
Fifth Edition**
1-4130-2197-2

A collection of grammar and composition exercises for students who need reinforcement of basic skills.

**Exercises Answer Key for
Kirszner & Mandell's
The Brief Wadsworth Handbook,
Fifth Edition**
1-4130-2196-4

Answers to the exercises print ancillary.

**Book Companion Web Site for
Kirszner & Mandell's
The Brief Wadsworth Handbook,
Fifth Edition**
http://english.wadsworth.com/wadsworthhb_b5

This robust site provides interactive exercises on the fundamentals of writing, including grammar, mechanics, and punctuation. A student paper library includes sample papers with accompanying editing and revising activities.

Complete & Convenient Handbook— Designed Just for You

Thomson Custom Solutions makes it easier than ever to customize this text or any one of our leading English Composition handbooks to create a highly personalized and convenient course resource for your students.

▶ **Tabbed for Easier Access.** Tabs make it even easier and quicker to locate and find the information you need. Each section of your handbook will be separated by tabs allowing students to quickly reference the needed resources.

▶ **The First Tab Is all Yours!** We have set aside the first tabbed section just for you. Include your syllabus, school policies, writing samples, style guides or other course-specific information. You have up to 16 pages for your content.

▶ **Add a Personal Touch with a Customized Cover.** Personalize the handbook by including your course and instructor information on the front and back cover. Learn more about your available options from your local Thomson Wadsworth representative.

Thomson Custom Solutions' experienced editorial and design teams will be there to guide you through each step to help you create your perfect Composition handbook. For more information about our services, visit **www.thomsoncustom.com**

How to Use This Book

We would like to introduce you to the fifth edition of *The Brief Wadsworth Handbook*, a compact, easy-to-use reference guide for college students that comes out of our years of experience as full-time teachers of writing. This handbook offers concise yet comprehensive coverage of the writing process, critical thinking, argumentation, common sentence errors, grammar and style, word choice, punctuation and mechanics, English for speakers of other languages, and college survival skills. In addition, it includes the most up-to-date information on writing in an electronic environment; visual rhetoric; MLA, APA, Chicago, and CSE documentation; writing in the disciplines; document design; and Web-page design.

Throughout, we balance what is new with tried and true advice that our years in the classroom have taught us that students need. For this reason, despite its compact size, *The Brief Wadsworth Handbook* is more than just a quick reference; it is a complete guide for writing in college and beyond. Most of all, it is a book that writers can depend on for sound, sensible advice about grammar and usage as well as about the electronic tools that define the writing environment of the twenty-first century.

What's New in the Fifth Edition?

In this new edition, we kept what students and instructors told us worked well, and we fine-tuned what we thought could work better. In addition, we expanded our coverage to include the material students need to function in today's classrooms as well as in today's world.

Five New Chapters
- **Chapter 1: Understanding Purpose and Audience**   A new chapter on purpose and audience that explains how these considerations apply to both written and visual texts
- **Chapter 3: Reading Visuals**   A discussion of visual rhetoric focusing on how to interpret and critically evaluate different kinds of visuals

- **Chapter 10: Using Visuals in Argumentative Essays**
  A chapter devoted to using visuals effectively to clarify and
  strengthen arguments
- **Chapter 11: Writing Electronic Arguments**   A discussion of
  the electronic writing environment with emphasis on the differences between electronic and print arguments
- **Chapter 22: Writing in the Disciplines**   A survey of the conventions for writing in the humanities, the social sciences, and
  the natural sciences

Updated and Expanded Coverage

- More coverage of document and Web design in Chapters 24–25
- Thorough coverage of avoiding plagiarism in Chapter 16,
  Avoiding Plagiarism
- Updated and expanded coverage of MLA, APA, Chicago, and
  CSE documentation styles—with special emphasis on document-
  ing electronic sources—in Parts 4–5
- Expanded and enhanced coverage of topics of interest to non-
  native and bilingual speakers in Part 13, Resources for Bilingual
  and ESL Writers

Features of *The Brief Wadsworth Handbook*

Throughout the fifth edition of *The Brief Wadsworth Handbook*, we
have focused on making the text clear, inviting, and easy to navigate.
The book's many innovative pedagogical features, listed below, have
helped us achieve these goals.

FAQs *Frequently Asked Questions (FAQs)* appear at the beginning of
link each part, on the back of the tabbed dividers. Marginal FAQ
icons appear in the chapters beside each answer.

Computer tips highlight specific ways in which technology can help you throughout the writing, revising, and editing processes. Each computer tip includes the URL for the book's companion Web site
<http://kirsznermandell.wadsworth.com>, which contains a
wealth of online resources.

Grammar checker boxes illustrating sample errors show the
advantages and limitations of using a grammar checker.

 *Numerous checklists* summarize key information that you can quickly access as needed.

Close-up boxes provide an in-depth look at some of the more perplexing writing-related issues you will encounter.

 *Parts 4–5* include the most up-to-date documentation and format guidelines from the Modern Language Association, the American Psychological Association, the University of Chicago Press, and the Council of Science Editors. Specially designed documentation directories make it easy for you to locate models for various kinds of sources, including those found online through library subscription services such as InfoTrac® College Edition and LexisNexis™. In addition, annotated diagrams of sample works-cited entries clearly illustrate the elements of proper documentation.

 Marginal cross-references throughout the book allow you to flip directly to other sections that treat topics in more detail.

Marginal ESL cross-references throughout the book direct you to sections of Part 13, "Resources for Bilingual and ESL Writers," where concepts are presented as they apply specifically to second-language writers.

ESL tips are woven throughout the text to explain concepts in relation to the unique experiences of bilingual students.

Acknowledgments

We would like to take this opportunity to thank Jessie Swigger, University of Texas at Austin, for allowing us to reprint her literary analysis. In addition, we thank the following reviewers for their advice, which helped us develop the fifth edition:

James Allen, *College of DuPage*
Richard Battaglia, *California State University, Northridge, and California Lutheran University*
Paul Benson, *Mt. View College*
Gregg Berlie, *Blue Mountain Community College*
Mary Campbell, *Davenport University*
Victoria Wardzinski Cope, *St. Francis University*
T. Allen Culpepper, *Manatee Community College, South Campus*
Adam Davis, *Truman State University*
Wayne Deahl, *Eastern Wyoming College*
Dominique Dieffenbach, *Florida Community College at Jacksonville*
Marie Eckstrom, *Rio Hondo College*
Sharon B. Fellows, *Binghamton University, State University of New York*
Jim Fisher, *Peninsula College*
Marilyn Garrett, *Galveston College*
Elizabeth Hardy, *Mayland Community College*
Michael Harrah
Jaime H. Herrera, *Mesa Community College*
Dan Horner, *Antelope Valley College*
Joanne Jacobs, *Shenandoah University*
Margaret Karsten, *Ridgewater College*
Patti Kurtz, *Minot State University*
Drew Lanier, *University of Central Florida*
Lawana Marlin, *East Georgia College*
Kenneth P. Novak, *Dakota Wesleyan University*
Velvet Pearson, *Long Beach City College*
Beverly A. Reilly, *Rio Hondo College*
Karen Schultz, *Shenandoah University*
Mandy Senn, *University of South Carolina, Aiken*
Mary Soltman, *South Puget Sound Community College*
M. Ellen Syswerda, *Grand Rapids Community College*
Jo Wiley, *Western Michigan University*
Laura L. Young, *Southern Oregon University*
Lucy Zimmerman, *Glen Oaks Community College*

We are very grateful to Michael Rosenberg, Publisher, for his continued commitment to this book as well as for his continued friendship and support. At Wadsworth, we are also grateful to Dickson Musslewhite, Senior Acquisitions Editor, for keeping the project moving along, and to Lianne Ames, Senior Production Project Manager, for her careful attention to detail. Our biggest thanks go to Karen Smith, our wonderful Development Editor; it has been a pleasure to work with her.

The staff of Nesbitt Graphics did its usual stellar job, led by Project Manager Susan McIntyre, who also did exceptionally careful and thoughtful copyediting. Lisa Adamitis's inviting design is the icing on the cake.

We would also like to thank our families—Mark, Adam, and Rebecca Kirszner and Demi, David, and Sarah Mandell—for being there when we needed them. And, finally, we each thank the person on the other side of the ampersand for making our collaboration work one more time.

Laurie Kirszner
Steve Mandell
February 2006

PART 1

Writing Essays

PART 1

Writing Essays

FREQUENTLY ASKED QUESTIONS

CHAPTER 1

Understanding Purpose and Audience

Everyone who sets out to write confronts a series of choices. In the writing you do in school, on the job, and in your personal life, your understanding of purpose and audience is essential, influencing the choices you make about content, emphasis, organization, style, and tone.

Every written text you create addresses a particular audience and sets out to achieve one or more specific purposes.

NOTE: Like written texts, <u>visual texts</u>—fine art, charts and graphs, photographs, maps, advertisements, and so on—are also created with specific purposes and audiences in mind.

See
Ch. 3,
24d

1a   Determining Your Purpose

In simple terms, your **purpose** for writing is what you want to accomplish. For instance, your purpose may be to **reflect,** to express private feelings, as in the introspective or meditative writing that appears in personal journals, diaries, and memoirs. Or your purpose may be to **inform,** to convey factual information as accurately and as logically as possible, as in the informational or expository writing that appears in reports, news articles, encyclopedias, and textbooks. At other times, your purpose may be to **persuade,** to convince your readers, as in advertising, proposals, editorials, and some business communications. Finally, your purpose may be to **evaluate,** to make a judgment about something, as in a recommendation report or a comparative analysis.

(1) Writing to Reflect

In diaries and journals, writers explore ideas and feelings to make sense of their experiences; in autobiographical memoirs and in personal correspondence, they communicate their emotions and reactions to others.

> At the age of five, six, well past the time when most other children no longer easily notice the difference between sounds uttered at home and words spoken in public, I had a different experience. I lived in a world magically compounded of sounds. I remained a child longer than most; I lingered too long, poised at the edge of language—often frightened by the sounds of *los gringos,* delighted by the sounds of Spanish at home. I

shared with my family a language that was startlingly different from that used in the great city around us. (Richard Rodriguez, *Aria: A Memoir of a Bilingual Childhood*)

(2) Writing to Inform

In newspaper articles, writers report information, communicating factual details to readers; in reference books, instruction manuals, textbooks, and the like (as well as in catalogs, cookbooks, and government-sponsored Web sites), writers provide definitions and explain concepts or processes, trying to help readers see relationships and understand ideas.

> Most tarantulas live in the tropics, but several species occur in the temperate zone and a few are common in the southern U.S. Some varieties are large and have powerful fangs with which they can inflict a deep wound. These formidable-looking spiders do not, however, attack man; you can hold one in your hand, if you are gentle, without being bitten. Their bite is dangerous only to insects and small mammals such as mice; for man it is no worse than a hornet's sting. (Alexander Petrunkevitch, "The Spider and the Wasp")

(3) Writing to Persuade

In proposals and editorials, as well as in advertising, writers try to convince readers to accept their positions on various issues.

> Testing and contact tracing may lead to a person's being deprived of a job, health insurance, housing and privacy, many civil libertarians fear. These are valid and grave concerns. But we can find ways to protect civil rights without sacrificing public health. A major AIDS-prevention campaign ought to be accompanied by intensive public education about the ways the illness is *not* transmitted, by additional safeguards on data banks and by greater penalties for those who abuse HIV victims. It may be harsh to say, but the fact that an individual may suffer as a result of doing what is right does not make doing so less of an imperative. (Amitai Etzioni, "HIV Sufferers Have a Responsibility")

(4) Writing to Evaluate

In reviews of books, films, or performances and in reports, critiques, and program evaluations, writers assess the validity, accuracy, and quality of information, ideas, techniques, products, procedures, or services, perhaps assessing the relative merits of two or more things.

★★★★★ **One of Grisham's Best,** April 29, 2003

Reviewer: **CHARLES H. PETERSON** from METAIRIE, LOUISIANA, United States

> Grisham is not going to win any prizes for literature, but when he tries, he can sure win a prize for page turners. This one was better thought out than most of his recent efforts. He

clearly knew how he was going to end it before he started writing, which is not always the case with Grisham. While there may be literary flaws in his character development, the book proceeds at a lively and generally logical pace. It also sheds some light on the problems associated with the "class action" mentality in our legal system these days.

It is what it is, and it is an excellent read. (Amazon.com customer review of John Grisham's *The King of Torts*)

Although writers write to reflect, to inform, to persuade, and to evaluate, these purposes are certainly not mutually exclusive, and writers may have other purposes as well. And, of course, in any piece of writing a writer may have a primary aim and one or more secondary purposes. In fact, a writer may even have different purposes in different sections—or different drafts—of a single document.

Checklist: Determining Your Purpose

Is your purpose . . .

- ☐ to reflect?
- ☐ to inform?
- ☐ to persuade?
- ☐ to evaluate?
- ☐ to explain?
- ☐ to amuse or entertain?
- ☐ to discover?
- ☐ to analyze?
- ☐ to debunk?
- ☐ to draw comparisons?
- ☐ to make an analogy?
- ☐ to define?
- ☐ to criticize?
- ☐ to motivate?

- ☐ to satirize?
- ☐ to speculate?
- ☐ to warn?
- ☐ to reassure?
- ☐ to take a stand?
- ☐ to identify problems?
- ☐ to suggest solutions?
- ☐ to identify causes?
- ☐ to predict effects?
- ☐ to reflect?
- ☐ to interpret?
- ☐ to instruct?
- ☐ to inspire?

1b Identifying Your Audience

When you are in the early stages of a writing project, staring at an empty computer screen or a blank sheet of paper, it is easy to forget that what you write will have an audience. But except for diaries and private journals, you always write for an **audience,** a particular reader or group of readers. In this sense, writing is a public rather than a private activity.

(1) Writing for an Audience

At different times, in different roles, you will address a variety of audiences.

- **In your personal life,** you may send notes, emails, or text messages to friends and family.
- **As a citizen,** consumer, or member of a community, civic, political, or religious group, you may respond to pressing social, economic, or political issues by writing letters or emails to newspapers, public officials, or representatives of special interest groups.
- **As an employee,** you may write letters, memos, and reports to your superiors, to staff members you supervise, or to coworkers; you may also be called on to address customers or critics, board members or stockholders, funding agencies or the general public.
- **As a student,** you write essays, reports, and other papers for your instructors, and you may also participate in **peer review,** writing evaluations of classmates' essays and writing responses to their comments about your own work.

As you write, you shape your writing in terms of what you believe your audience needs and expects. Your assessment of your readers' interests, educational level, **biases**, and expectations determines not only the information you include but also what you emphasize and how you arrange your material.

See
8c

(2) The College Writer's Audience

FAQs
links

Writing for Your Instructor As a student, you usually write for an audience of one: the instructor who assigns the paper. Instructors want to know what you know and whether you can express what you know clearly and accurately. They assign written work to encourage you to **think critically**, so the way you organize and express your ideas can be as important as the ideas themselves.

See
Ch. 8

As a group, instructors have certain expectations. Because they are trained as careful readers and critics, your instructors expect accurate information, standard grammar and correct spelling, logically presented ideas, and a reasonable degree of stylistic fluency. They also expect you to define your terms and to support your generalizations with specific examples. Finally, every instructor expects you to draw your own conclusions and to provide full and accurate **documentation** for ideas that are not your own.

See
Pts.
4–5

If you are writing in an instructor's academic field, you can omit long overviews and basic definitions. Remember, however, that outside their areas of expertise, most instructors are simply general readers. If you think you may know more about a subject than your instructor does, be sure to provide background and to supply the definitions, examples, and analogies that will make your ideas clear.

ESL Tip

If you did not attend school in the US, you may have trouble understanding your instructor's expectations. You may also have difficulty determining how much your instructor knows about a specific topic, especially if that topic relates to your own cultural background, native language, or home country. In these situations, it is usually a good idea to ask your instructor for advice.

Writing for Other Students Before you submit a paper to an instructor, you may have an opportunity to participate in **peer review**, sharing your work with your fellow students and responding in writing to their work. Before you begin, you need to see your classmates as an audience whose needs you must take into account.

See
6c2

FAQs
link

- **Writing Drafts** If you know that other students will read a draft of your paper, you need to consider how they might react to your ideas. For example, are they likely to disagree with you? To be shocked or offended by your paper's language or content? To be confused, or even mystified, by any of your references? Even if your readers are your own age, you cannot assume they share your values, political opinions, or cultural frame of reference. It is therefore very important that you maintain an appropriate tone and use moderate language in your paper and that you be prepared to explain any historical, geographical, or cultural references that might be unfamiliar to your audience.
- **Writing Comments** When you respond in writing to another student's paper, you need to take into account how your audience will react to your comments. Here too, your tone is important: you want to be as encouraging (and as polite) as possible. In addition, keep in mind that your purpose is not to show how clever you are but to offer constructive comments that can help your classmate write a stronger essay.

Checklist: Audience Concerns for Peer-Review Participants

- ☐ **Know your audience.** To be sure you understand what the student writer needs and expects from your comments, read the paper several times before you begin writing your response.
- ☐ **Focus on the big picture.** Don't get bogged down by minor problems with punctuation or mechanics or become distracted by a paper's proofreading errors.

(continued)

Audience concerns for peer-review participants (continued)

☐ **Look for a positive feature,** zeroing in on what you think is the paper's greatest strength.

☐ **Be positive throughout.** Try to avoid words like *weak, poor,* and *bad;* instead, try using a compliment before delivering the "bad news": "Paragraph 2 is very well developed; can you add this kind of support in paragraph 4?"

☐ **Show respect.** It is perfectly acceptable to tell a student that something is confusing or inaccurate, but don't go on the attack.

☐ **Be specific.** Avoid generalizations like "needs more examples" or "could be more interesting"; instead, try to offer helpful, focused suggestions: "You could add an example after the second sentence in paragraph 2"; "Explaining how this process operates would make your discussion more interesting."

☐ **Don't give orders.** Ask questions, and make suggestions.

☐ **Include a few words of encouragement,** emphasizing the paper's strong points.

CHAPTER 2

Reading Texts

Central to developing effective reading skills is learning the techniques of **active reading.** Being an active reader means being actively involved with the text: reading with pen in hand and physically marking the text in order to identify parallels, question ambiguities, distinguish important points from not-so-important ones, and connect causes with effects and generalizations with specific examples. The understanding you gain from active reading prepares you to think (and write) critically about a text.

ESL Tip

When you read a text for the first time, don't worry about understanding every word. Instead, just try to get a general idea of what the text is about and how it is organized. Later on, you can use a dictionary to look up any unfamiliar words.

2a Previewing a Text

Before you actually begin reading a text, you should **preview** it—that is, skim it to get a sense of the writer's subject and emphasis.

When you preview a **book,** start by looking at its table of contents; then, turn to its index. A quick glance at the index will reveal the amount of coverage the book gives to subjects that may be important to you. As you leaf through the chapters, look at pictures, graphs, or tables and the captions that appear with them.

When you preview a **periodical article,** scan the introductory and concluding paragraphs for summaries of the writer's main points. (Journal articles in the sciences and social sciences often begin with summaries called **abstracts.**) Thesis statements, topic sentences, repeated key terms, transitional words and phrases, and transitional paragraphs can also help you to identify the points a writer is making. In addition, look for the **visual cues**—such as headings—that writers use to emphasize ideas.

See
24b

Close-up: Visual Cues

When you preview a text, don't forget to note its use of color and of various typographical elements—typeface and type size, boldface and italics—to emphasize ideas.

2b Highlighting a Text

When you have finished previewing a work, you should **highlight** it, using a system of graphic symbols and underlining to identify the writer's key points and their relationships to one another. (If you are working with library material, photocopy the pages before you highlight them.) Be sure to use symbols that you will understand when you reread your material later on.

Checklist: Using Highlighting Symbols

- ☐ Underline to indicate information you should read again.
- ☐ Box or circle key words or important phrases.
- ☐ Put question marks next to confusing passages, unclear points, or words you need to look up.
- ☐ Draw lines or arrows to show connections between ideas.
- ☐ Number points that are discussed in sequence.
- ☐ Draw a vertical line in the margin to set off an important section.
- ☐ Star especially important ideas.

2c Annotating a Text

After you have read through a text once, read it again—this time, more critically. At this stage, you should **annotate** the pages, recording your responses to what you read. This process of recording notes in the margins or between the lines will help you understand the writer's ideas and your own reactions to those ideas.

ESL Tip

You may find it useful to use your native language when you annotate a text.

Some of your annotations may be relatively straightforward. For example, you may define new words, identify unfamiliar references, or jot down brief summaries. Other annotations may be more personal: you may identify a parallel between your own experience and one described in the reading selection, or you may record your opinion of the writer's position.

Close-up: Reading Critically

See
Ch. 8

When you start to **think critically** about a text, your annotations may identify points that confirm (or dispute) your own ideas, question the appropriateness or accuracy of the writer's support, uncover the writer's biases, or even question (or challenge) the writer's conclusion.

The following passage illustrates a student's highlighting and annotations on an article about the decline of American public schools.

One of the most compelling arguments about <u>the Vietnam War</u> is that it lasted as long as it did because of its "classist" nature. The central thesis is that because neither the decision makers in the government *nor anyone they knew* had children fighting and dying in Vietnam, they had no personal incentive to bring the war to a halt. The government's generous college-deferment system, steeped as it was in class distinctions, allowed the white middle class to avoid the tragic consequences of the war. <u>And the people who did the fighting and dying in place of the college-deferred were those whose voices were least heard in Washington: the poor and the disenfranchised.</u>

Is this comparison valid? (seems forced)

I bring this up because <u>I believe that the decline of the public schools is rooted in the same cause</u>. Just as with the Vietnam War, as soon as the middle class no longer had a stake in the public schools, the surest pressure on school systems to provide a decent education instantly disappeared. Once the middle class was gone, no mayor was going to get booted out of office because the schools were bad. No incompetent teacher had to worry about angry parents calling for his or her head "downtown." No third-rate educationalist at the local teachers college had to fear having his or her methods criticized by anyone that mattered.

bias

Who are these people? Does he really represent them?

The analogy to the Vietnam War can be extended even to the extent of the denial. <u>It amuses me sometimes to hear people like myself decry the state of the public schools</u>. We bemoan the lack of money, the decaying facilities, the absurd credentialism, the high foolishness of the school boards. We applaud the

Is this "one small example" enough to support his claim?*

bias

Oversimplification—Do all parents have the same motives?

burgeoning reform movement. And everything we say is deeply, undeniably true. We can see every problem with the schools clearly except one: the fact that our decision to abandon the schools has helped create all the other problems. One small example: In the early 1980s, Massachusetts passed one of those tax cap measures, called Proposition 2 1/2, which has turned out to be a force for genuine evil in the public schools. Would Proposition 2 1/2 have passed had the middle class still had a stake in the schools? I wonder. I also wonder whether 20 years from now, in the next round of breast-beating memoirs, the exodus of the white middle class from the public schools will finally be seen for what it was. Individually, every parent's rationale made impeccable sense—"I can't deprive my children of a decent education"—but collectively, it was a deeply destructive act.

Is this a valid assumption?

Why does he assume intent was "good" + "moral"? Is he right?

The main reason the white middle class fled, of course, is race, or more precisely, the complicated admixture of race and class and good intentions gone awry. The fundamental good intention—which even today strikes one as both moral and right—was to integrate the public classroom, and in so doing, to equalize the resources available to all school children. In Boston, this was done through enforced busing. In Washington, it was done through a series of judicial edicts that attempted to spread the good teachers and resources throughout the system. In other big city districts, judges weren't involved; school committees, seeing the handwriting on the wall, tried to do it themselves.

?

However moral the intent, the result almost always was the same. The white middle class left. The historic parental vigilance I mentioned earlier had had a lot to do with creating the two-tiered system—one in which schools attended by the kids of the white middle class had better teachers, better equipment, better everything than those attended by the kids of the poor. This did not happen because the white middle-class parents were racists, necessarily; it happened because they knew how to manipulate the system and were willing to do so on behalf of their kids. Their neighborhood schools became little havens of decent education, and they didn't much care what happened in the other public schools.

Interesting point—but is it true?

Slanted language (over-emotional)

In retrospect, this behavior, though perfectly understandable, was tragically short-sighted. When the judicial fiats made those safe havens untenable, the white middle class quickly discovered

[marginal annotations:] neralization • anted guage /er- otional) • her/or acy? Were ere other oices? • ersimpli- ation? No ceptions?

what the poor had always known: There weren't enough good teachers, decent equipment, and so forth to go around. For that matter, there weren't even enough good students to go around; along with everything else, middle-class parents had to start worrying about whether their kids were going to be mugged in school.

Faced with the grim fact that their children's education was quickly deteriorating, middle-class parents essentially had two choices: They could stay and pour the energy that had once gone into improving the neighborhood school into improving the entire school system—a frightening task, to be sure. Or they could leave. Invariably, they chose the latter. And it wasn't just the white middle class that fled. The black middle class, and even the black poor who were especially ambitious for their children, were getting out as fast as they could too, though not to the suburbs. They headed mainly for the parochial schools, which subsequently became integration's great success story, even as the public schools became integration's great failure. (Joseph Nocera, "The Case Against Joe Nocera: How People Like Me Helped Ruin the Public Schools")

Checklist: Reading Texts

As you read a text, consider the following questions:

☐ Does the writer provide any information about his or her background? If so, how does this information affect your reading of the text?

☐ Are there parallels between the writer's experiences and your own?

☐ What is the writer's **purpose**? How can you tell?

☐ What **audience** is the text aimed at? How can you tell?

☐ What is the text's most important idea? What support does the writer provide for that idea?

☐ What information can you learn from the text's introduction and conclusion?

☐ What information can you learn from the **thesis statement** and **topic sentences**?

☐ What key words are repeated? What does this repetition tell you about the writer's purpose and emphasis?

☐ How would you characterize the writer's tone?

☐ Where do you agree with the writer? Where do you disagree?

☐ What, if anything, is not clear to you?

See Ch. 1

See 5b

See 7a

CHAPTER 3

Reading Visuals

The texts you read in college courses—books, newspapers, and articles, in print or online—are often accompanied by visual images. For example, textbooks often include illustrations to make complex information more accessible, and newspapers use photographs to break up columns of written text as well as to add interest. Currently, more and more information is being presented in visual form—not just in magazines and other print media, but also on the Web and even in cell phones.

Close-up: Reading Visuals

Visuals are used to persuade as well as to entertain and to convey information to supplement written text.

Maps

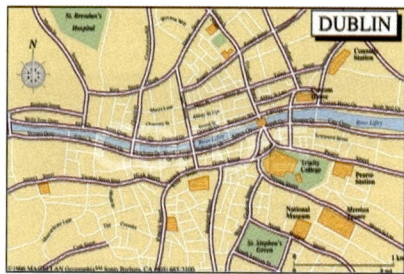

Map of Dublin, Ireland.

Photographs

Photo of university student preparing backstage at Beijing Opera.

Cartoons

"You can't begin to imagine how embarrassing it is to be seen with you."

Cartoon by Jen Sorensen.

Tables

Employees	Location	
	Madison	St. Paul
Plant	461	254
Warehouse	45	23
Outlet Stores	15	9

Table from student paper.

Fine Art

Advertisements

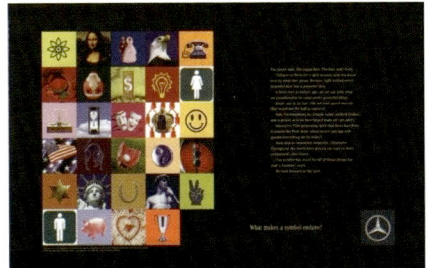

Mercedes-Benz ad.

Profile of a Woman Wearing a Jabot (pastel on paper) by Mary Stevenson Cassatt (1844–1926).

Scientific Diagrams

Bar Graphs

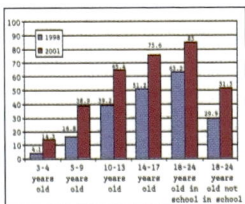

Bar graph from student's MLA research paper.

Plant engineering diagram.

3a Interpreting Visuals

Because the world audience is becoming increasingly visual, it is important for you to acquire the skills needed to read and interpret visuals as well as to use them in your own written work. (For information on incorporating visuals into your own writing, **see 6b3.**)

The powerful newspaper photograph shown in Figure 3.1 on page 16, which depicts a Marine in front of the Vietnam Veterans Memorial, uses a variety of techniques to convey its message. To **interpret** this photograph, you need to determine what strategies it uses to achieve its effect.

You might notice right away that contrasts are very important in this picture. In the background is the list of soldiers who died in the war; in the foreground, a lone member of a Marine honor guard stands in silent vigil, seemingly as static as the names carved in granite. Still, those who view this photo know that the Marine is motionless only in the picture; when the photographer puts the camera down, the Marine lives on, in contrast to those whose names are listed behind him. The large close-up of the Marine set against the smaller names in the background also suggests that the photographer's purpose is at least in part to capture the contrast between the past and the present, the dead and the living. Thus, the photograph has a persuasive purpose: it suggests, as its title states, that "the whole world is watching" (and, in fact, *should* be watching) this scene in order to remember the past and honor the dead.

The whole world is watching

Member of Marine honor guard passes the Vietnam memorial on which names of casualties of the war are inscribed

Figure 3.1 Newspaper photograph taken at the Vietnam Veterans Memorial.

To convey their ideas, visuals often rely on contrasting light and shadow and on the size and placement of individual images (as well as on the spatial relationship of these images to one another and to the whole). In addition, visuals often use words (captions, slogans, explanatory text), and they may also include color, animation, audio narration, and even musical soundtracks. Given the complexity of most visuals and the number of individual elements each one uses to convey its message, analyzing (or "reading") visual texts can be challenging. This task will be easier, however, if you follow the same **active reading** process you use when you read a written text.

3b Previewing a Visual

Just as with a written text, the first step in analyzing a visual text is to preview it, scanning it to get a sense of its subject and emphasis. At this stage, you may notice little more than the visual's major features: its central image, its dominant colors, its use of empty space, and the most prominent blocks of written text. Still, even these elements can give you a general idea of what the focus of the visual is and what purpose it might have.

For example, the New Balance ad shown in Figure 3.2 shows two large images—a foot and a shoe—both with the distinctive NewBalance "N" logo. This logo also appears in the slogan "N is for fit," which has a prominent central position. The slogan is allowed to speak for itself, with the text that explains the visual message appearing in very small type at the bottom of the page. Yellow is used to highlight the logo, the shoe's tread, and the word *fit*.

Figure 3.2 Magazine ad for New Balance sneakers.

3c Highlighting and Annotating a Visual

When you highlight a visual text, you mark it up to help you identify key images and their relationship to one another. You might, for example, use arrows to point to important images, or you might circle key words or details. When you annotate a visual text, you record your reactions to the images and words you see. (If a visual's background is dark, or if you are not permitted to write directly on it, you can do your highlighting and annotating on small self-stick notes.)

A student in a composition class was asked to analyze the magazine advertisement for Mercedes-Benz automobiles shown in Figure 3.3 on page 18. When she visited the company Web site, she saw that Mercedes was appealing not just to those who value performance and safety but also to those interested in owning a classic, a car whose reputation is well established and well known. Moreover, with the slogan "Imagine the possibilities," the company was also appealing to those who dream of owning a luxury automobile. The student's highlighting and annotating focus on how the ad's written text and visuals work together to present the company's message: that Mercedes symbolizes safety, style, and status.

Many small, colorful pictures make readers look closely at each image

Light type on dark background

Short 9s set off points

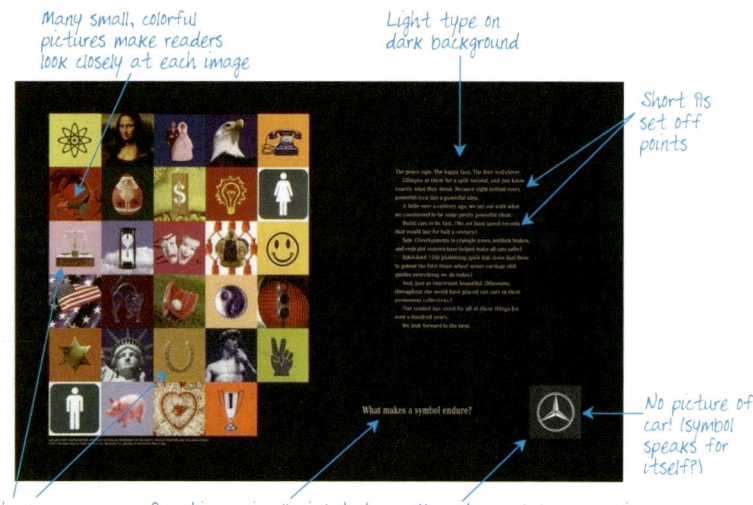

Symbols all have positive connotations

Question = visually isolated; larger type than other text.

Mercedes symbol = same size as others but set apart and isolated against contrasting background

No picture of car! (symbol speaks for itself?)

Figure 3.3 Mercedes-Benz ad.

Checklist: Reading Visuals

See 1a

- ☐ Who has created the visual?
- ☐ For what **purpose** was the visual created? For example, does it seem to be designed primarily to inform? To persuade? To entertain or amuse?

See 1b

- ☐ Where did the visual originally appear? What is the target **audience** for this publication?
- ☐ What scene does the visual depict?
- ☐ What individual images are included in the visual? What associations do these images have for you?
- ☐ Do any people appear in the visual? What do they suggest about its target audience? What is their relationship to the scene and to one another? What are they doing?
- ☐ How would you describe the people's facial expressions? Their positions? Their body language?
- ☐ Does the visual include a lot of blank space?
- ☐ How large are the various elements (words and images)?
- ☐ Is the background light or dark? Clear or blurred? What individual elements stand out most clearly against this background?
- ☐ What general mood is suggested by the visual's use of color and shadow?
- ☐ Does the visual include any written text? What is its purpose?
- ☐ In general terms, what is the visual's message? How do its individual elements help to communicate this message?
- ☐ How would the visual's message or impact be different if something were added? If something were deleted?

CHAPTER 4

Planning an Essay

4a   Understanding the Writing Process

Writing is a complex process of decision making—of selecting, deleting, and rearranging material.

Close-up: The Writing Process

The writing process includes the following stages:

Planning: Consider your purpose, audience, and tone; choose your topic; discover ideas to write about.

Shaping: Decide how to organize your material.

Drafting: Write your first draft.

Revising: "Re-see" what you have written; write additional drafts.

Editing: Check grammar, spelling, punctuation, and mechanics.

Proofreading: Reread every word, checking for any remaining errors.

The neatly defined stages listed above communicate neither the complexity nor the flexibility of the writing process. These stages actually overlap: as you look for ideas, you begin to shape your material; as you shape your material, you begin to write; as you write a draft, you reorganize your ideas; as you revise, you continue to discover new material. Moreover, these stages may be repeated again and again throughout the writing process. During your college years and in the years that follow, you will develop your own version of the writing process and use it whenever you write, adapting it to the audience, purpose, and writing situation at hand.

ESL Tip

In many high school and college writing classes in the US, classroom activities and homework are organized around the stages of the writing process outlined in this text.

4b   Computers and the Writing Process

Computers have changed the way we write and communicate in both academic and <u>workplace</u> settings. In addition to using

See Ch. 26

See
27d
word-processing applications for typical writing tasks, writers may rely on programs such as *__PowerPoint__*® for presentations, *Publisher*® for creating customized résumés or brochures, and Web-page authoring software such as *FrontPage*® for creating Internet-accessible documents that include images, movies, and a wide range of visual effects.

With the expanding role of the Internet in professional, academic, and personal communication, it is becoming increasingly likely that the feedback you receive on your writing will be electronic. For example, you may receive email from your instructor about a draft that you have submitted to a digital drop box, a tool often associated with course management software such as *WebCT*™ or *Blackboard*™. Or, you may use discussion boards for attaching or sharing your documents with other students. Chat room and Net meeting software also allow you to discuss ideas collaboratively and to offer and receive feedback on drafts. Although the tools you use may be course- or workplace-specific, your writing process will be similar.

4c Analyzing Your Assignment

Planning your essay—thinking about what you want to say and how you want to say it—begins well before you actually start recording your thoughts in any organized way. This planning is as important a part of the writing process as the writing itself. During this planning stage, you determine your **purpose** for writing and identify your **audience**. Then, you go on to focus on your assignment, choose and narrow your topic, and gather ideas.

See
Ch. 1

Before you begin writing, be sure you understand the exact requirements of your **assignment**. Ask questions, and be sure you understand the answers.

FAQs

Checklist: Analyzing Your Assignment

☐ Has your instructor assigned a specific topic, or can you choose your own?

☐ What is the word or page limit?

☐ How much time do you have to complete your assignment?

☐ Will you get feedback from your instructor? Will you have an opportunity to participate in **peer review**?

See
6c2

☐ Does your assignment require research?

See
Ch. 17

☐ What format (for example, **MLA**) are you supposed to follow? Do you know what its conventions are?

☐ If your assignment has been given to you in writing, have you read it carefully and highlighted key words?

Kimberly Romney, a first-year composition student, was given the following assignment.

> College broadens your horizons and exposes you to new people, places, and experiences. At the same time, it can also create problems. Write an essay (about 5–7 pages long) about a problem you (and perhaps others) have encountered since coming to college. Be sure that your essay has a clearly stated thesis and that it helps readers to understand your problem.

The class was given two weeks to complete the assignment. Students were expected to do some research and to have the instructor and other students read and comment on at least one draft.

4d   Choosing and Narrowing a Topic

Sometimes your instructor will allow you to choose your own topic; more often, however, you will be given a general assignment, which you will have to narrow to a **topic** that suits your purpose and audience.

Narrowing a Topic		
Course	**Assignment**	**Topic**
American History	Analyze the effects of a social program on one segment of American society.	How did the GI Bill of Rights affect American servicewomen?
Psychology	Write a three- to five-page paper assessing one method of treating depression.	Animal-assisted therapy for severely depressed patients
Composition	Write an essay about a problem you have encountered since coming to college.	Overcoming my computer illiteracy

4e   Finding Something to Say

Once you have a topic, you can begin to collect ideas for your paper, us-ing one (or several) of the strategies discussed in the pages that follow.

> ### ESL Tip
> Don't use all your time making sure you are writing gram-matically correct sentences. Remember, the purpose of writing is to communicate ideas. If you want to write an interesting, well-devel-oped essay, you will need to devote plenty of time to the activities de-scribed in this section.

(1) Reading and Observing

As you read textbooks, magazines, and newspapers and browse the Internet, be on the lookout for ideas that relate to your topic. Films, television programs, interviews, telephone calls, letters, emails, and questionnaires can also provide material. But be sure your instructor permits such research—and remember to **document** ideas that are not your own. If you do not, you will be committing plagiarism.

See
Ch. 16

(2) Keeping a Journal

Many professional writers keep print or electronic **journals,** writing in them regularly whether or not they have a specific project in mind. Journals, unlike diaries, do more than simply record personal experiences and reactions. In a journal, you explore ideas, ask questions, and draw conclusions. You might, for example, analyze your position on a political issue, try to solve an ethical problem, or trace the evolution of your ideas about an academic assignment. Kimberly Romney's journal entry appears below.

Journal Entry

I'm not really comfortable writing about my own poor computer skills, but I have to admit it's a good topic for a paper about a problem I have. What I really want to focus on, though, is the ways in which computer illiteracy is a big problem not just for me but for many college students. I don't want to write about the hours it took me to register for classes online or the fact that it took me an hour to figure out how to email my professor and then save that email. I don't want this paper to be about me and my problems. What I want to do is write about the difficulties students with weak computer skills have and mention a few things about my own life to illustrate these general ideas.

(3) Freewriting

When you **freewrite,** you write nonstop about anything that comes to mind, moving as quickly as you can. Give yourself a set period of time—say, five minutes—and don't stop to worry about punctuation, spelling, or grammar, or about where your freewriting takes you. This strategy encourages your mind to make free associations; thus, it helps you to discover ideas you probably aren't even aware you have. When your time is up, look over what you have written, and underline, circle, bracket, or star the most promising ideas. You can then use one or more of these ideas as the center of a focused freewriting exercise.

When you do **focused freewriting,** you zero in on your topic. Here too you write without stopping to reconsider or reread, so you have no time to be self-conscious about style or form, to worry about the relevance of your ideas, or to count how many words you have (and panic about how many more you think you need). At its best, focused freewriting can suggest new details, a new approach to your topic, or even a more interesting topic. Excerpts from Kimberly's freewriting and focused freewriting exercises appear below.

Freewriting (Excerpt)

```
        This isn't so bad because I finally don't have to worry
about typing perfectly. I can make mistakes, and I won't have to
stop writing and then correct myself. That's how I feel using
computers: anxious. We had a few computers at my high school, but
we didn't have to take a computer class, or even a typing class.
Maybe we should have! When I got to college, I felt like such an
idiot. Everyone else seemed to have no trouble using the Internet
for research, creating PowerPoint presentations for class
projects and even creating their own Web sites. All of a sudden I
was expected to use computers to register, for research, and to
communicate with my professors. It was horrible! Most other
students didn't ever have to ask a question about computers. It's
like there are two groups when you get to college: the people who
are computer literate and those who aren't.
```

Focused Freewriting (Excerpt)

```
        The first day of orientation we were told to use the
computers to register. It's not like I'd never used a computer
before or seen the Internet. Still, I had to raise my hand and
get the proctor in the computer room to come help me click on
the right icon. And then I had to ask a lot of questions to
figure out how to access two Web sites at the same time so that
I could look at both the online course catalog and the
registration program. Meanwhile, most of the other students
```

were already finished and on their way to dinner. When I asked
if I could get a copy of the course schedule on paper, the
proctor told me that the university had recently gone
"paperless." I realized then and there that I was going to have
to do a lot of extra work to make myself computer literate.

(4) Brainstorming

One of the most useful ways to accumulate ideas is by brainstorming
(either on your own or in a group). This strategy enables you to recall
bits of information and to see connections among them.

When you **brainstorm,** you list all the points you can think of that
seem pertinent to your topic, recording ideas—comments, questions,
single words, symbols, or diagrams—as quickly as you can, without
pausing to consider their relevance or trying to understand their significance. An excerpt from Kimberly's brainstorming notes appears below.

Brainstorming Notes (Excerpt)

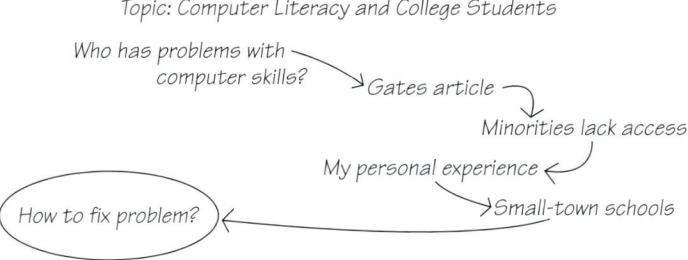

Topic: Computer Literacy and College Students

Who has problems with computer skills?
Gates article
Minorities lack access
My personal experience
Small-town schools
How to fix problem?

(5) Clustering

Clustering—sometimes called *webbing* or *mapping*—is similar to
brainstorming. However, clustering encourages you to explore your
topic in a more systematic (and more visual) manner.

Begin your cluster diagram by writing your topic in the center of a
sheet of paper. Then, surround your topic with related ideas as they
occur to you, moving outward from the general topic in the center
and writing down increasingly specific ideas and details as you move
toward the edges of the page. Following the path of one idea at a time,
draw lines to create a diagram (often lopsided rather than symmetrical) that arranges ideas on spokes or branches radiating out from the
center (your topic). Kimberly's cluster diagram appears on the facing
page.

Cluster Diagram

Understanding basic word processing   Minorities

Internet savvy   Small-town students

Assumptions that all are computer literate   My problems

Topic: Computer Literacy and College Students

Ways of fixing the problem

Programs at school

High school?

http://kirsznermandell.wadsworth.com

Computer Tip: Finding Ideas

You can use your computer to help you find material to write about:

- When you **freewrite**, try turning down the brightness of the monitor, leaving the screen dark to eliminate distractions and encourage spontaneity. When you reread what you have written, you can boldface or underline important ideas (or highlight them in color).
- When you **brainstorm**, type your notes randomly. Later, after you print them out, you can add more notes and graphic elements (arrows, circles, and so on) by hand to indicate parallels and connections.

---

(6) Asking Journalistic Questions

Journalistic questions offer an orderly, systematic way of finding material to write about. Journalists ask the questions *Who? What? Why? Where? When?* and *How?* to ensure that they have explored all angles of a story, and you can use these questions to make sure you have considered all aspects of your topic. Kimberly's list of journalistic questions appears below.

Journalistic Questions

- <u>Who</u> is familiar with computers and the Internet, and <u>who</u> is not?

- <u>What</u> is computer literacy? <u>What</u> are the effects of weak computer skills? <u>What</u> kinds of programs exist to help college students improve computer skills?

- <u>When</u> did computers become essential for college students?

- <u>Where</u> are students most likely to learn computer skills?

- <u>Why</u> is familiarity with the Internet so important in college? <u>Why</u> are some students' computer skills so much better than others'?
- <u>How</u> can we help students who lag behind?

ESL Tip

Using your native language for planning activities has both advantages and disadvantages. On the one hand, if you do not have to contend with the strain of trying to think in English, you may be able to come up with better ideas. Additionally, using your native language may help you record your ideas more quickly and keep you from losing your train of thought. On the other hand, using your native language while planning may make it more difficult for you to move from the planning stages of your writing to drafting. After all, you will eventually have to write your paper in English.

---

(7) Asking In-Depth Questions

If you have time, you can ask a series of more focused questions about your topic. These in-depth questions not only can give you a great deal of information but also can suggest ways for you to eventually shape your ideas into paragraphs and essays.

In-Depth Questions

What happened? When did it happen? Where did it happen?	Suggest <u>narration</u> (an account of your first day of school; a summary of Emily Dickinson's life)
What does it look like? What does it sound like, smell like, taste like, or feel like?	Suggest <u>description</u> (of the Louvre; of the electron microscope; of a Web site)
What are some typical cases or examples of it?	Suggests <u>exemplification</u> (three infant day-care settings; four popular fad diets)
How did it happen? What makes it work? How is it made?	Suggest <u>process</u> (how to apply for financial aid; how a bill becomes a law)
Why did it happen? What caused it? What does it cause? What are its effects?	Suggest <u>cause and effect</u> (the events leading to the Korean War; the results of global warming; the impact of a new math curriculum on slow learners)

How is it like other things? How is it different from other things?	Suggest comparison and contrast (of the popular music of the 1970s and 1980s; of two paintings)
What are its parts or types? Can they be separated or grouped? Do they fall into a logical order? Can they be categorized?	Suggest division and classification (components of the catalytic converter; kinds of occupational therapy; kinds of dietary supplements)
What is it? How does it resemble other members of its class? How does it differ from other members of its class?	Suggest definition (What is Marxism? What is photosynthesis? What is a MOO?)

An excerpt from Kimberly's list of in-depth questions appears below.

In-Depth Questions (Excerpt)

What causes the gap between those who are computer savvy and those who are not? Differences in family income, parents' education level, quality of public education, regional differences.

What are the effects of the gap? Differences in achievement in college and performance on the job; differences in access to information; differences in earning power.

Once you have gathered ideas for your essay—and perhaps begun to see the direction these ideas are taking—you are ready to decide how to **shape** your material.

See
Ch. 5

CHAPTER 5

Using a Thesis to Shape Your Material

After you have collected possible ideas for your essay, you start to sift through these ideas and choose those you can use. As you do this, you begin to **shape** your material into a thesis-and-support essay.

5a Understanding Thesis and Support

FAQs

Your **thesis** is the main idea of your essay, the central point your essay supports. The concept of **thesis and support**—stating the thesis and then supplying information that explains and develops it—is central to much of the writing you will do in college.

See 7e2–3

As the following diagram illustrates, the essays you will write will consist of an **introductory paragraph**, which opens your essay and states your thesis; a **concluding paragraph**, which reviews your essay's major points and gives it a sense of closure, perhaps restating your thesis; and a number of **body paragraphs,** which provide the support for your thesis statement.

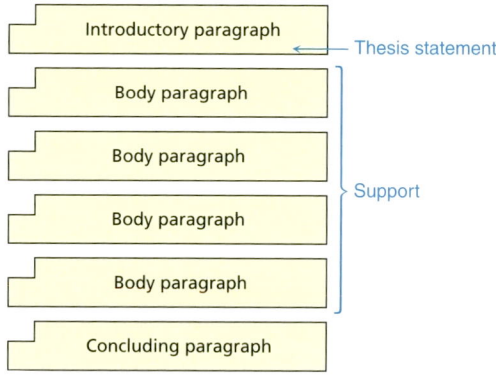

```
Introductory paragraph      ← Thesis statement

Body paragraph

Body paragraph              ┐
                            ├ Support
Body paragraph

Body paragraph              ┘

Concluding paragraph
```

5b Developing a Thesis

(1) Stating Your Thesis

An effective **thesis statement** has four characteristics:

1. **An effective thesis statement clearly communicates your essay's main idea.** It tells readers what your essay's topic is and

suggests what you will say about it. Thus, your thesis statement reflects your essay's **purpose**.

See
1a

2. **An effective thesis statement is more than a general subject, a statement of fact, or an announcement of your intent.**

Stating Your Thesis

Subject	**Statement of Fact**	**Announcement**
The Military Draft	The United States currently has no military draft.	In this essay, I will reconsider our country's need for a draft.

Thesis statement   Although today's all-volunteer force has replaced the draft, a draft may eventually be necessary.

---

3. **An effective thesis statement is carefully worded.** Because it communicates your paper's main idea, your thesis statement should be clearly and accurately worded. Your thesis statement—usually expressed in a single concise sentence—should be direct and straightforward, including no vague or abstract language, overly complex terminology, or unnecessary details that might confuse or mislead readers. Moreover, effective thesis statements should not include phrases such as "I hope to demonstrate" and "It seems to me," which weaken your credibility by suggesting that your conclusions are tentative or are based solely on opinion rather than on reading, observation, and experience.

4. **Finally, an effective thesis statement suggests your essay's direction, emphasis, and scope.** Your thesis statement should not make promises that your essay will not fulfill. It should suggest how your ideas are related, in what order your major points will be discussed, and where you will place your emphasis, as the following thesis statement does.

Effective Thesis Statement

Widely ridiculed as escape reading, romance novels are important as a proving ground for many never-before-published writers and, more significantly, as a showcase for strong heroines.

This thesis statement is effective because it tells readers that the essay to follow will focus on two major roles of the romance novel: providing markets for new writers and (more important) presenting strong female characters. It also suggests that the essay will briefly treat the role of the romance novel as escapist fiction. As the diagram below shows, this effective thesis statement also indicates the order in which the various ideas will be discussed.

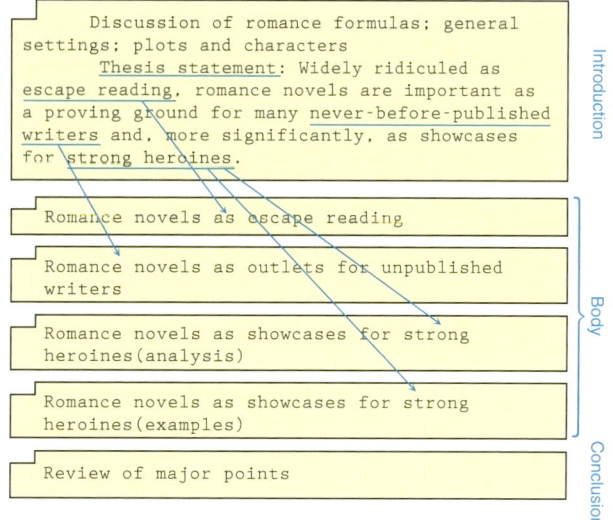

```
        Discussion of romance formulas; general
    settings; plots and characters
        Thesis statement: Widely ridiculed as
    escape reading, romance novels are important as
    a proving ground for many never-before-published
    writers and, more significantly, as showcases
    for strong heroines.
```
Introduction

```
    Romance novels as escape reading
```

```
    Romance novels as outlets for unpublished
    writers
```

```
    Romance novels as showcases for strong
    heroines(analysis)
```

```
    Romance novels as showcases for strong
    heroines(examples)
```
Body

```
    Review of major points
```
Conclusion

Close-up: Avoiding Vague Wording

Try to avoid vague, wordy phrases—*centers on, deals with, involves, revolves around, has a lot to do with, is primarily concerned with*, and so on. Be direct and forceful.

```
                                    is
The real problem in our schools does not
revolve around the absence of nationwide goals
and standards; the problem is primarily
concerned with the absence of resources with
which to implement them.
```

Checklist: Stating Your Thesis

☐ Does your thesis statement clearly communicate your essay's main idea? Does it suggest the approach you will take toward your material? Does it reflect your essay's purpose?

☐ Is your thesis statement more than a subject, a statement of fact, or an announcement of your intent?

☐ Is your thesis statement carefully worded?

☐ Does your thesis statement suggest your essay's direction, emphasis, and scope?

---

(2) Revising Your Thesis Statement

At this point, the thesis statement that you develop is only **tentative.** As you write and rewrite, you may modify your essay's direction, emphasis, and scope several times; if you do so, you must reword your thesis statement to reflect these modifications.

Notice how the following thesis statement changed as the student writer moved through successive drafts of his essay.

Tentative Thesis Statement (rough draft)	Revised Thesis Statement (final draft)
Professional sports can easily be corrupted by organized crime.	Although some people argue that organized crime cannot make inroads into professional sports, the way in which underworld figures fixed the 1919 World Series suggests the opposite.

Close-up: Using a Thesis Statement to Shape Your Essay

The wording of your thesis statement often suggests not only a possible order and emphasis for your essay's ideas, but also a specific pattern of development—*narration, description, exemplification, process, cause and effect, comparison and contrast, division and classification*, or *definition*. (These familiar patterns of development may also shape individual paragraphs of your essay.)

See 7d

Thesis Statement	Pattern of Development
As the months went by and I grew more and more involved with the developmentally delayed children at the Learning Center, I came to see how important it is to treat every child as an individual.	Narration
Looking around the room where I spent my childhood, I realized that every object I saw told me I was now an adult.	Description
The risk-taking behavior that has characterized recent years can be illustrated by the increasing interest and involvement in such high-risk sports as mountain biking, ice climbing, sky diving, and bungee jumping.	Exemplification
Armed forces basic training programs take recruits through a series of tasks designed to build camaraderie as well as skills and confidence.	Process
The gap in computer literacy between rich and poor has had many significant social and economic consequences.	Cause and Effect

(continued)

Using a thesis statement to shape your essay (continued)

Thesis Statement	Pattern of Development
Although people who live in cities and people who live in small towns have some similarities,their views on issues like crime, waste disposal, farm subsidies, and educational vouchers tend to be very different.	Comparison and Contrast
The section of the proposal that recommends establishing satellite health centers is quite promising; unfortunately, however, the, sections that call for the creation of alternative educational programs, job training, and low-income housing are seriously flawed.	Division and Classification
Many people once assumed that rape was an act perpetrated by a stranger, but today's definition is much broader.	Definition

5c Constructing an Informal Outline

 Once you have decided on a thesis statement, you may want to construct an informal outline to guide you as you write. An **informal outline** arranges your essay's main points and major supporting ideas in an orderly way. Kimberly's informal outline appears below.

Informal Outline

Thesis statement: I was at a real disadvantage when I entered

college because I lacked important computer skills.

Students' computer needs

   • Basic word-processing programs

   • Internet

   • Email

Unprepared students

   • No access at home

   • No access at school

Consequences of computer illiteracy

   • Difficulty with everyday tasks

- Embarrassment
- Missed opportunities

Possible solutions to problem
- Classes
- ??????

Personal experience
- Poor computer skills
- Classes in computer lab

Checklist: Constructing an Informal Outline

☐ Copy down the most important ideas from your notes.
☐ Arrange the notes into categories and subcategories in the order in which you plan to discuss them.
☐ Expand the outline with additional material from your notes, adding any new ideas that come to mind.

NOTE: Sometimes—particularly when you are writing a long or complex essay—you will need to construct a **formal outline**, which indicates both the exact order and the relative importance of all the ideas you will explore.

See 6c4

5d   Constructing a Storyboard

Storyboarding is a way of graphically organizing material into a series of boxes or panels. This technique has long been used for outlining scenes and plot developments in films and commercials, and it can be adapted, with some modifications, into a useful outlining tool for an essay or a Web site.

Unlike a strictly text-based outline, which uses words, phrases, or sentences to plot the organization of material in a linear way, a storyboard uses pictures and diagrams, either electronically generated or drawn by hand, to map out an arrangement of material. As a tool for shaping an essay, a storyboard can use blocks of text as well as pictures.

Storyboarding can help you plan the placement of your ideas; in addition, it can help you visualize the placement of potential source information and illustrations. Kimberly's storyboard appears on the following page.

Storyboard

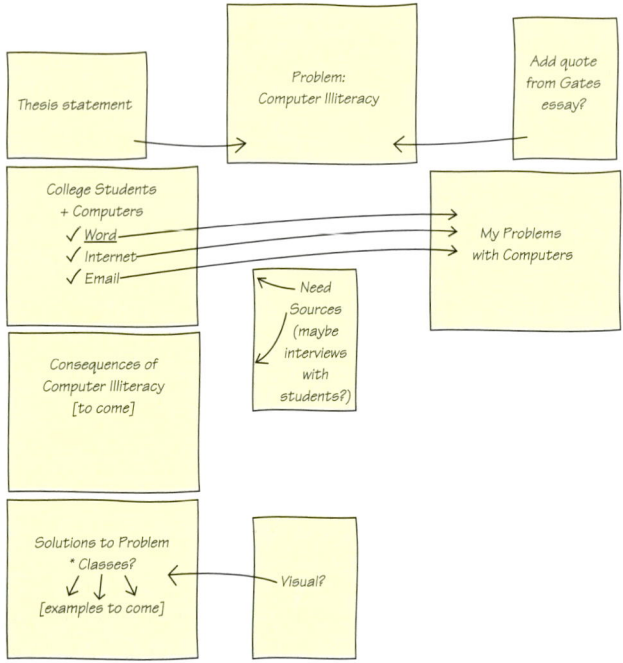

Checklist: Constructing a Storyboard

☐ Use a large sheet of paper to represent your essay.
☐ On the paper, draw a box to represent each major section of the paper; or, use self-stick notes or index cards as boxes.
☐ Fill in each box with a combination of words, shapes, and symbols to represent key ideas, sources, and visuals.
☐ If you like, use the visuals themselves—such as printouts of clip art or images cut from magazines—in your boxes.
☐ Leave blank space (or even a blank box) for undeveloped sections; label blank spaces "to come."
☐ Rearrange boxes on the page if necessary.
☐ Number the boxes if necessary.
☐ Use arrows to indicate possible relocation of elements within boxes.

Once you are able to see a clear order for your ideas, you are ready to write a **rough draft** of your paper.

See 6a

CHAPTER 6

Drafting and Revising

6a Writing a Rough Draft

A **rough draft** is far from perfect; in fact, it usually includes false starts, irrelevant information, and unrelated details. At this stage, though, the absence of focus and order is not a problem. You write your rough draft simply to get your ideas down so that you can react to them. You should expect to add or delete words, to reword sentences, to rethink ideas, and to reorder paragraphs. You should also expect to discover some new ideas—or even to take an unexpected detour.

When you write your rough draft, concentrate on the body of your essay, and don't waste time mapping out an introduction and conclusion. (These paragraphs are likely to change substantially in subsequent drafts.) For now, focus on drafting the support paragraphs of your essay.

> ### ESL Tip
>
> Using your native language occasionally as you draft your paper may keep you from losing your train of thought. However, writing most or all of your draft in your native language and then translating it into English is generally not a good idea. This process will take a long time, and the translation into English may sound awkward.

Using her informal outline and her storyboard to guide her, Kimberly Romney wrote the rough draft that appears below. Notice that she included boldfaced and bracketed notes to remind herself to add or check information later.

Rough Draft

                    College Students and Computer Literacy

     Today, most colleges expect their entering students to
be familiar with computers. From registering for courses to
contacting professors, students are required to use computers
on a daily basis. I was at a real disadvantage when I entered
college because I lacked important computer skills. [Add more
here? Maybe use Gates?]

Computers have become increasingly important on college campuses. When I arrived at school, I was asked to use Microsoft Word to type my papers. I was also encouraged to use the Internet for research. [Do I document this?] In fact, many professors posted their syllabi on Web pages. I also quickly learned the importance of email. Although I'd been exposed to email in high school, I'd never had to learn how to use an email program like Eudora or how to download it to my computer. I had to call the help desk and it was really embarrassing. All of my friends seemed to have few problems doing this.

If you don't have high computer literacy skills, there are many consequences. Students have a lot of difficulty completing everyday tasks. It may take them a long time to email a professor or register for a course simply because they are unfamiliar with the software being used. Students who feel uncomfortable using computers also feel embarrassed. They may not want to admit that they don't understand how to use particular software programs. If they don't seek help, they miss out on a lot of opportunities. Computers are so important in school that students who don't understand them may avoid taking exciting classes that require a working knowledge of specific computer programs.

The reality is that a lot of students don't have a lot of experience with computers. Students who do understand computers are usually math and science people. If you're interested in English, you probably aren't familiar with computers. Even if they are familiar with computers, he or she may have never used the Internet. In small towns, students probably don't have access to a computer at home. Many high schools also have trouble providing their students with computer access, which is a big problem for many students. [Need more/better support here]

Our school does provide students with several opportunities to improve their computer skills, but most students don't know about them. The library offers several classes that teach students how to access useful information online. The computer lab also holds classes on how to use software programs like Microsoft Word and Microsoft Publisher. Students can even learn how to design their own Web pages. Unfortunately, these classes are not well advertised. Course listings appear on the Information Technology Web site, but for those students who avoid using the Internet, finding out when and where to take classes is difficult. Ironically, students who need these classes will probably not be using the Internet a lot to get information about the university. [Check on all of this to make sure]

When I arrived at college, I had very few computer skills. Our high school had a couple of computers, but we didn't have Internet access. My first required class was a writing course and was held in a computer lab. I was forced to learn how to use computers and the Internet to write my papers. After a few weeks of pretending to know what I was doing, I decided to try to find some help. I was too embarrassed to ask my professor where to go for help, so it took me a few days to find out when and where the classes were. I ended up going to the library and asking the librarian. She was really helpful and I enrolled in a couple of them. After a course on Microsoft Word and the Internet, I felt much more comfortable using computers.

It is important to remember that some students arrive at college with few computer skills and that they are at a significant disadvantage. [Add more!]

6b Moving from Rough Draft to Final Draft

As you **revise** successive drafts of your essay, you should narrow your focus from larger elements, such as overall structure and content, to increasingly smaller elements, such as sentence structure and word choice. (You can see how this revision process operates in the drafts of Kimberly Romney's essay that appear in Chapters 4–6.)

(1) Revising Your Rough Draft

After you finish your rough draft, set it aside for a day or two if you can. When you return to it, focus on only a few areas at a time. As you review this first draft, begin by evaluating the thesis-and-support structure of your essay and your paper's general organization. Once you feel satisfied that your thesis statement says what you want it to say and that your essay's content supports this thesis and is logically arranged, you can turn your attention to other matters. For example,

See 7b2

you can make sure that you have included all the **transitional words and phrases** that readers will need to follow your discussion.

(2) Writing and Revising Additional Drafts

After you have read over your rough draft several times, making notes about your plans for revision, you are ready to write a second draft.

Because it can be more difficult to read text on the computer screen than on hard copy, you should print out every draft. This will enable you to make revisions by hand on printed drafts and then return to the computer to type these changes into your document. (As you type your draft, you may want to triple-space. This will make any errors or inconsistencies more obvious and at the same time give you plenty of room to write questions, add new material, or try out new versions of sentences.)

If you write your revisions by hand on hard copy, you will find it helpful to develop a system of symbols. For instance, you can box groups of words (or even entire paragraphs) that you want to relocate, using an arrow to indicate the new location. When you want to add words, use a caret like ^*this*^. An excerpt from one of Kimberly's drafts, with her handwritten revisions, appears below.

Draft with Handwritten Revisions (Excerpt)

Despite the necessity of a strong working knowledge of computers and the Internet, many students arrive at college with very little to no experience of either.

^The reality ~~is that a lot of students don't have a lot of~~
might not, for example, have had access to a computer in their home.
experience with computers. Students ^who ~~do understand~~
~~computers are usually math and science people. If you're~~
~~interested in English, you probably aren't familiar with~~
~~computers.~~ Even if they are familiar with computers, ^*they* ~~he or she~~ may have never used the Internet.

> ## Computer Tip: Revising
>
>
>
> As you revise, it is important to manage your files carefully:
>
> - First, be sure to save your drafts. Using the Save option in your word processor's file menu saves only your most recent draft. If you prefer to save every draft you write (so you can return to an earlier draft to locate a different version of a sentence or to reconsider a section you have deleted), use the Save As option instead.
> - Also, be sure to label your files. To help you keep track of different versions of your paper, label every file in your folder by content and date (for example, `first draft, 10/20`).
> - Finally, if you revise directly on the computer, be very careful not to delete material that you may need later; instead, move this material to the end of your document so that you can assess its usefulness later on and retrieve it if necessary.

(3) Adding Visuals

As you write and revise, you should consider whether one or more **visuals** might enhance your paper. Sometimes you may want to use a visual that appears in one of your sources; at other times, you may be able to create a visual (for example, a photograph or a chart) yourself; at still other times, you may need to search a clip-art database to find an appropriate visual.

Once you have decided to add a particular visual to your paper, the first step is to determine where to insert it. (In general, you should place the visual in the part of the essay where it will have the greatest impact in terms of conveying information or persuading your audience.) Then, you need to format the visual. (Within *Microsoft Word*, you can double-click on an image to call up a picture-editing menu that allows you to alter the size, color, and position of the image within your essay—and even permits you to wrap text around the image.) Next, you should make sure that the visual stands out in your paper: surround it with white space, add ruled lines, or enclose it in a box.

Once the visual has been inserted where you want it, you need to integrate it into your paper. You can include a sentence that introduces the visual (`The following table illustrates the similarities between the two health plans`), or you can refer to it in your text (`Figure 1 shows Kennedy as a young man`) to give it some context and explain why you are using it. You should also identify the visual by labeling it (`Fig. 1. Photo of John F. Kennedy, 1937`). In addition, if the visual is not one you have created yourself, you must **document** it. In most academic disciplines, this means including full

See Pts. 4–5

source information directly below the image and sometimes in the list of references as well. (For an example of a visual in the final draft of Kimberly's paper, **see 6e.**)

Checklist: Inserting Visuals

To add a visual to your paper, follow these steps:

☐ Select an appropriate visual.
☐ Place the image in a suitable location.
☐ Format the image, and make sure it is clearly set off from the written text.
☐ Introduce the visual with a sentence (or refer to it in the text).
☐ Label the visual.
☐ Document the visual (if necessary).

6c Using Specific Revision Strategies

Everyone revises differently, and every writing task calls for a slightly different process of revision. Five strategies in particular can help you revise at any stage of the writing process.

(1) Using Word-Processing Tools

Your word-processing program includes a variety of tools designed to make the revision process easier. For example, *Microsoft Word*'s **Track Changes** feature allows you to make changes to a draft electronically and to see the original version of the draft and the changes simultaneously. Changes appear in color as underlined text, and writers have the option of viewing the changes on the screen or in print. This feature also allows you to accept or reject all changes or just specific changes.

Another useful revision tool is the **Compare Drafts** feature. Whereas Track Changes allows you to keep track of changes to a single document, Compare Drafts allows you to analyze the changes in two completely separate versions of a document, usually an original and its most recent update. Changes appear in color as highlighted text.

Kimberly used Track Changes as she revised her rough draft. An excerpt from her rough draft, along with her changes, appears below.

Rough Draft with Track Changes (Excerpt)

Computers have become increasingly important ~~on college campuses~~ in today's society. Consequently, many scholars and public officials are concerned that those without access to computers will be at a disadvantage. Henry Louis Gates Jr., for example, argues in "One Internet, Two Nations" that the content on the Internet, which is primarily aimed at whites, threatens to leave African Americans behind. Similarly, college students who arrive with low computer literacy skills are at a disadvantage.

When I arrived at school, I was asked to use computers in several ways. First, I was required to use Microsoft Word when typing~~to type~~ my papers. I was also encouraged to use the Internet for research. In fact, many professors posted their syllabi on Web pages. I also quickly learned the importance of email. Although I'd been exposed to email in high school, I'd never had to learn how to use an email program like Eudora or download it to my computer. I had to call the help desk and it was really embarrassing. All of my friends seemed to have few problems doing this.

(2) Participating in Peer Review

Peer review—a collaborative revision strategy that enables you to get feedback from your classmates—is another useful activity. With peer review, instead of trying to imagine an audience for your paper, you address a real audience, exchanging drafts with classmates and commenting on their drafts. Such collaborative work can be formal or informal, conducted in person or electronically. For example, you and a classmate may email drafts back and forth, perhaps using *Word*'s Comment feature (see p. 42), or your instructor may conduct the class as a workshop, assigning students to work in groups to critique other students' essays.

http://kirsznermandell.wadsworth.com

Computer Tip: Peer Review

Certain features in word-processing programs are particularly useful for peer review. For example, the Comment tool allows several readers to insert comments at any point or to highlight a particular portion of the text they would like to comment on and then insert annotations. To write comments, a reviewer clicks the Insert menu and selects Comment.

A particular advantage of this function for peer-review groups is that a single paper can receive comments from multiple readers. Comments are identified by the initials of the reviewer and by a color assigned to the reviewer.

An excerpt from Kimberly's second draft with peer reviewers' comments appears on the following page.

Second Draft with Peer Reviewers' Comments (Excerpt)

When I arrived at school, I was asked to use computers |in several ways| First, I was required to use <u>Microsoft Word</u> when typing my papers. I was also encouraged to use the Internet for research. In fact, many professors posted their syllabi on Web pages. I also quickly learned |the importance of email| Although I'd been exposed to email in high school, I'd never had to learn how to use an email program like <u>Eudora</u> or download it to my computer. I had to call the help desk and it was really embarrassing. All of my friends seemed to have few problems doing this|

> **Comment [KL1]:**
> That's for sure ☺!

> **Comment [KL2]:**
> Talking w/profs. is an-
> other imp. use of email.

> **Comment [BR1]:**
> Yes! I emailed Prof.
> Wilson when I couldn't
> make office hrs.

> **Comment [CB1]:**
> There's a lot more to
> talk about here. What
> about listservs? <u>Power-</u>
> <u>Point</u>?

Checklist: Questions for Peer Review

The following questions can help guide you through the peer-review process:

☐ What is the essay about? Does the topic fulfill the requirements of the assignment?

☐ What is the essay's main idea? Is the thesis clearly worded? If not, how can the wording be improved?

☐ Is the essay arranged logically? Do the body paragraphs appear in an appropriate order?

☐ What ideas support the thesis? Does each body paragraph develop one of these ideas?

☐ Is any necessary information missing? Identify any areas that seem to need further development. Is any information irrelevant? If so, suggest possible deletions.

☐ Can you think of any ideas or examples from your own reading, experience, or observations that would strengthen the writer's essay?

☐ Can you follow the writer's ideas? If not, would clearer connec-tions between sentences or paragraphs be helpful? Where are such connections needed?

☐ Is the introductory paragraph interesting to you? Would another opening strategy be more effective?

☐ Does the conclusion leave you with a sense of closure? Would another concluding strategy be more effective?

☐ Is anything unclear or confusing?

☐ What is the essay's greatest strength?

☐ What is the essay's greatest weakness?

(3) Using Instructors' Comments

Instructors' comments—in correction symbols, in marginal comments, or in conferences—can also help you revise. (Some instructors may prefer to record their comments electronically, perhaps using the Comment tool described in **6c2**.)

Correction Symbols Your instructor may indicate concerns about style, grammar, mechanics, or punctuation by using the correction symbols listed on the inside back cover of this book. Instead of correcting a problem, the instructor will simply identify it and supply the number of the section in this handbook that deals with the error. After reading the appropriate pages, you should be able to make the necessary corrections on your own. For example, the symbol and number beside the following sentence referred a student to **40e2**, the section in this handbook that discusses sexist usage.

> **Instructor's Comment:** Equal access to jobs is a
> _Sxt—see 40e2_
> desirable goal for all (mankind.)

After reading the appropriate section in the handbook, the student made the following change.

> **Revised:** Equal access to jobs is a desirable goal for
> everyone.

Marginal Comments Instructors frequently write marginal comments on your essays to suggest changes in content or structure. Such comments may ask you to add supporting information or to arrange paragraphs differently within the essay, or they may recommend stylistic changes, such as more varied sentences. Marginal comments may also question your logic, suggest a more explicit thesis statement, ask for clearer transitions, or propose a new direction for a discussion. In some cases, you can consider these comments to be suggestions rather than corrections. You may decide to incorporate these ideas into a revised draft of your essay, or you may not. In all instances, however, you should take your instructor's comments seriously.

An excerpt from Kimberly's second draft, along with her instructor's comments, appears below. (Note that her instructor used _Microsoft Word_'s Comment tool to insert comments.)

Second Draft with Instructor's Comments (Excerpt)

> When I arrived at school, I was asked to use computers in
> several ways. First, I was required to use Microsoft Word when
> typing my papers. I was also encouraged to use the Internet
> for research. In fact, many professors posted their syllabi on
> Web pages. I also quickly learned the importance of email.

Although |I'd| been exposed to email in high school,
|I'd| never had to learn how to use an email program
like <u>Eudora</u> or download it to my computer. I
had to call the help desk and it was really
|embarrassing.| All of my friends seemed to
have few problems doing this.

> **Comment [PW1]:** In your final draft, edit out all contractions. (Contractions are too informal for most college writing.) See 40a.

> **Comment [PW2]:** Consider making this point less personal. Use this paragraph to talk about all of the reasons a student might use a computer in college. Remember, you are moving from general to specific. See 7b1.

Conferences Many instructors require or encourage one-on-one conferences, and you should certainly schedule a conference if you can. During a conference, you can respond to your instructor's questions and ask for clarification of marginal comments. If a certain section of your paper presents a problem, use your conference time to focus on it, perhaps asking for help in sharpening your thesis or choosing more accurate words.

Checklist: Getting the Most Out of a Conference

☐ **Make an appointment.** If you are unable to keep your appointment, be sure to call or email your instructor to reschedule.

☐ **Review your work carefully.** Before the conference, reread your notes and drafts and go over all your instructor's comments and suggestions. Make all the changes you can on your draft.

☐ **Bring a list of questions.** Preparing a list in advance will enable you to get the most out of the conference in the allotted time.

☐ **Bring your paper-in-progress.** If you have several drafts, you may want to bring them all, but be sure you bring any draft that has your instructor's comments on it.

☐ **Take notes.** As you discuss your paper, write down any suggestions that you think will be helpful so you won't forget them when you revise.

☐ **Participate actively.** A successful conference is not a monologue; it should be an open exchange of ideas.

---

http://kirsznermandell.wadsworth.com

Computer Tip: Online Conferences

Conferences can also take place online—most commonly, through email. If you send emails to your instructor or to members of your peer-review group, include a specific subject line that clearly identifies the message as coming from a student writer (for example, "question about assignment"). This is especially important if your email address does not include your name. And when you attach a document to an email and send it to your instructor for comments, mention the attachment in your subject line (for example, "first draft—see attachment")—and be sure your name appears on the attachment itself, not just on the email.

(4) Constructing a Formal Outline

Outlining can be helpful early in the revision process, when you are reworking the larger structural elements of your essay, or later on, when you are checking the logic of a completed draft. A **formal outline** reveals at once whether points are irrelevant or poorly placed—or, worse, missing. It also reveals the hierarchy of your ideas—which points are dominant and which are subordinate.

Close-up: The Conventions of Outlining

Formal outlines conform to specific conventions of structure, content, and style. If you follow the conventions of outlining carefully, your formal outline can help you make sure that your paper presents all relevant ideas in an effective order, with appropriate emphasis.

Structure
- Outline format should be followed strictly.

    I. First major point of your paper
      A. First subpoint
      B. Next subpoint
         1. First supporting example
         2. Next supporting example
            a. First specific detail
            b. Next specific detail
    II. Second major point

- Headings should not overlap.
- No heading should have a single subheading. (A category cannot be subdivided into one part.)
- Each entry should be preceded by an appropriate letter or number, followed by a period.
- The first word of each entry should be capitalized.

Content
- The outline should include the paper's thesis statement.
- The outline should cover only the body of the essay, not the introductory or concluding paragraphs.
- Headings should be concise and specific.
- Headings should be descriptive, clearly related to the topic to which they refer.

Style
- Headings of the same rank should be grammatically parallel.
- A **sentence outline** should use complete sentences, with all sentences in the same tense.
- In a sentence outline, each entry should end with a period.
- A **topic outline** should use words or short phrases, with all headings of the same rank using the same parts of speech.
- In a topic outline, entries should not end with periods.

As part of her revision process, Kimberly made the following topic outline to help her check her paper's organization.

Topic Outline

<u>Thesis statement:</u> I was at a real disadvantage when I entered college because I lacked important computer skills.

    I. Importance of computers
        A. Those with access to Internet vs. those without
           (Gates)
        B. "Digital divide" among college students
   II. College students' computer needs
        A. Running basic programs
        B. Using the Internet
        C. Using email
  III. Reasons for some students' poor computer skills
        A. Lack of access to computers at home
        B. Limited access to computers in elementary or high
           school
   IV. Consequences for students with poor computer skills
        A. Difficulty with everyday tasks, such as
           registering for classes or contacting professors
           or classmates
        B. Embarrassment
        C. No access to Internet or sophisticated software
    V. Possible solutions on our campus
        A. Classes
        B. More publicity
   VI. My personal experience
        A. Weak computer skills
        B. Writing class in computer lab
        C. Classes on <u>Word</u>, email, and the Internet
  VII. Future
        A. High schools
        B. Colleges

(5) Using Checklists

The four revision checklists that follow are keyed to sections of this text. Moving from global to specific concerns, they parallel the actual revision process. As your understanding of the writing process increases and you become better able to assess the strengths and weaknesses of your writing, you may want to add items to (or delete items from) these checklists. You can also use your instructors' comments to tailor the checklists to your own needs.

Checklist: Revising the Whole Essay

- ☐ Do you understand your essay's purpose? (**See 1a.**)
- ☐ Have you taken your audience's needs into account? (**See 1b.**)
- ☐ Are thesis and support logically related, with each body paragraph supporting your thesis statement? (**See 5a.**)
- ☐ Is your thesis statement clearly and specifically worded? (**See 5b1.**)
- ☐ Have you discussed everything promised in your thesis statement? (**See 5b1.**)
- ☐ Have you presented your ideas in a logical sequence? Can you think of a different arrangement that might be more appropriate for your purpose? (**See 5c–d.**)

Checklist: Revising Paragraphs

- ☐ Does each body paragraph have one main idea? (**See 7a.**)
- ☐ Are topic sentences clearly worded and logically related to your thesis? (**See 7a1.**)
- ☐ Does each body paragraph have a clear organizing principle? (**See 7b1.**)
- ☐ Are the relationships between sentences within your paragraphs clear? (**See 7b2–4.**)
- ☐ Are your body paragraphs developed fully enough to support your points? (**See 7c.**)
- ☐ Does your introductory paragraph arouse reader interest and prepare readers for what is to come? (**See 7e2.**)
- ☐ Are your paragraphs arranged according to familiar patterns of development? (**See 7d.**)
- ☐ Have you provided transitional paragraphs where necessary? (**See 7e1.**)
- ☐ Does your concluding paragraph sum up your main points? (**See 7e3.**)

Checklist: Revising Sentences

☐ Have you used correct sentence structure? **(See Chs. 28 and 29.)**
☐ Have you avoided potentially confusing shifts in tense, voice, mood, person, or number? **(See 31a1–4.)**
☐ Are your sentences constructed logically? **(See 31b–d.)**
☐ Have you placed modifiers clearly and logically? **(See Ch. 32.)**
☐ Are your sentences varied? **(See Ch. 36.)**
☐ Have you combined sentences where ideas are closely related? **(See 36b.)**
☐ Have you used emphatic word order? **(See 37a.)**
☐ Have you used sentence structure to signal the relative importance of clauses in a sentence and their logical relationship to one another? **(See 37b.)**
☐ Have you strengthened your sentences with repetition, balance, and parallelism? **(See 37c–d, 39a.)**
☐ Have you eliminated nonessential words and unnecessary repetition? **(See 38a–b.)**
☐ Have you avoided overloading your sentences with too many words, phrases, and clauses? **(See 38c.)**

Checklist: Revising Words

☐ Is your level of diction appropriate for your audience and your purpose? **(See 40a–b.)**
☐ Have you selected words that accurately reflect your intentions? **(See 40b1.)**
☐ Have you chosen words that are specific, concrete, and unambiguous? **(See 40b3–4.)**
☐ Have you enriched your writing with figures of speech? **(See 40c.)**
☐ Have you eliminated jargon, neologisms, pretentious diction, clichés, and offensive language from your writing? **(See 40d–e.)**

Close-up: Choosing a Title

When you are ready to decide on a title for your essay, keep these criteria in mind:

• A title should be descriptive, giving an accurate sense of your essay's focus. Whenever possible, use one or more of the key words and phrases that are central to your paper.
• A title can echo the wording of your assignment, reminding you (and your instructor) that you have not lost sight of it.
• Ideally, a title should arouse interest, perhaps by using a provocative question or a quotation or by taking a controversial position.

Assignment: Write about a problem faced on college campuses today.

Topic: Free speech on campus
Possible titles:

Free Speech: A Problem for Today's Colleges (echoes wording of assignment and includes key words of essay)

How Free Should Free Speech on Campus Be? (provocative question)

The Right to "Shout 'Fire' in a Crowded Theater" (quotation)

Hate Speech: A Dangerous Abuse of Free Speech on Campus (controversial position)

6d Editing and Proofreading

Once you have revised your drafts to your satisfaction, two final tasks remain: **editing** and **proofreading**.

http://kirsznermandell.wadsworth.com

Computer Tip: Editing and Proofreading

- As you edit and proofread, try looking at only a small portion of text at a time. Reduce the size of your window so that you can see only one or two lines of text at a time. By using this technique, you can dramatically reduce the number of surface-level errors in your paper.
- Use the Search or Find command to look for usage errors you commonly make—for instance, confusing *it's* with *its*, *lay* with *lie*, *effect* with *affect*, *their* with *there*, or *too* with *to*. You can also uncover sexist language by searching for words like *he*, *his*, *him*, or *man*.
- Finally, keep in mind that neatness does not equal correctness. The clean text that your computer produces can mask flaws that might otherwise be apparent; for this reason, it is up to you to make sure spelling errors and typos do not slip by.

See
40e2

Editing When you **edit,** you concentrate on grammar and spelling, punctuation and mechanics. Although you have dealt with these issues as you revised previous drafts of your paper, editing is now your primary focus. As you edit, read each sentence carefully, consulting the items on the Editing Checklist below. Keep your preliminary notes and drafts and your reference books (such as this handbook and a dictionary) nearby as you work.

Checklist: Editing

Grammar

- ☐ Do subjects and verbs agree? (**See 30a.**)
- ☐ Do pronouns and antecedents agree? (**See 30b.**)

(continued)

Editing (continued)

☐ Are verb forms correct? (**See 33a.**)
☐ Are tense, mood, and voice of verbs logical and appropriate? (**See 33b–d.**)
☐ Have you used the appropriate case for each pronoun? (**See 34a–b.**)
☐ Are pronoun references clear and unambiguous? (**See 34c.**)
☐ Are adjectives and adverbs used correctly? (**See Ch. 35.**)

Punctuation

☐ Is end punctuation used correctly? (**See Ch. 43.**)
☐ Are commas used correctly? (**See Ch. 44.**)
☐ Are semicolons used correctly? (**See Ch. 45.**)
☐ Are apostrophes used correctly? (**See Ch. 46.**)
☐ Are quotation marks used where they are required? (**See Ch. 47.**)
☐ Are quotation marks used correctly with other punctuation marks? (**See 47e.**)
☐ Are other punctuation marks—colons, dashes, parentheses, brackets, slashes, and ellipses—used correctly? (**See Ch. 48.**)

Spelling

☐ Are all words spelled correctly? (**See Ch. 49.**)

Mechanics

☐ Is capitalization consistent with standard English usage? (**See Ch. 50.**)
☐ Are italics used correctly? (**See Ch. 51.**)
☐ Are hyphens used where required and placed correctly within and between words? (**See Ch. 52.**)
☐ Are abbreviations used where convention calls for their use? (**See Ch. 53.**)
☐ Are numerals and spelled-out numbers used appropriately? (**See Ch. 54.**)

Proofreading After you have completed your editing, print out a final draft and **proofread,** rereading every word carefully to make sure neither you nor your computer missed any typos or other errors. Finally, make sure the final typed copy of your paper conforms to your instructor's format requirements.

Close-up: Proofreading Strategies

To help you proofread more effectively, try using these strategies:

- Read your paper aloud.
- Have a friend read your paper aloud to you.
- Read silently word by word, using your finger or a sheet of paper to help you keep your place.
- Read your paper's sentences in reverse order, beginning with the last sentence.

http://kirsznermandell.wadsworth.com

Computer Tip: Using Spell Checkers and Grammar Checkers

Although spell checkers and grammar checkers can make the process of editing and proofreading your papers easier, they have limitations. For this reason, neither a spell checker nor a grammar checker is a substitute for careful editing and proofreading.

- **Spell Checkers** A spell checker simply identifies strings of letters it does not recognize; it does *not* distinguish between homophones or spot every typographical error. For example, it does not recognize *there* in "They forgot <u>there</u> books" as incorrect, nor does it identify a typo that produces a correctly spelled word, such as *word* for *work* or *thing* for *think*. Moreover, a spell checker may not recognize every technical term, proper noun, or foreign word you may use.
- **Grammar Checkers** Grammar checkers scan documents for certain features (the number of words in a sentence, for example); however, they are not able to read a document to see if it makes sense. For this reason, grammar checkers are not always accurate. For example, they may identify a long sentence as a run-on when it is in fact grammatically correct, and they generally advise against using passive voice—even in contexts where it is appropriate. Moreover, grammar checkers do not always supply answers; often, they ask questions—for example, whether *which* should be *that* or whether *which* should be preceded by a comma—that you must answer. In short, grammar checkers can guide your editing, but you must be the one who decides when a sentence is (or is not) correct.

6e　Preparing a Final Draft

The annotated essay that follows is the final draft of Kimberly Romney's essay, which you first saw on pages 35–37. It incorporates the suggestions that her peer reviewers and her instructor made on her second draft (pages 42 and 43–44).

This final draft is very different from the rough draft of the essay. As she revised, Kimberly moved from a focus on her own problems to a broader view of the issue, and she revised her thesis statement accordingly. She also added specific information from sources to support her points, including parenthetical documentation and a works-cited list that conform to **MLA** documentation style. Finally, she added a **visual** (accompanied by a caption) to illustrate the progress made in her high school since she graduated.

FAQs
links

See Ch. 17

See 6b3

Kimberly Romney

Professor Wilson

English 101

10 November 2005

                    Computer Illiteracy: A Problem for
                          College Students

Introduction   Today, most colleges expect entering students
          to be familiar with computers. From registering for
          courses to contacting professors, students are
          required to use computers on a daily basis. For
          this reason, students who enter college with weak
Thesis
statement   computer skills are at a significant
          disadvantage.

Importance   Computers are increasingly important in today's
of computers
in society society. As Henry Louis Gates Jr. writes in his
          article "One Internet, Two Nations," many people are
          concerned that there is a division between those who
          have access to the Internet and those who do not. He
          writes, "Today we stand at the brink of becoming two
          societies, one largely white and plugged in and the
          other black and unplugged" (500). The gap between
          those who are technologically literate and those who
          are not extends beyond race and ethnicity to include
          the elderly, the disabled, and those who live in rural
          areas. This "digital divide" is particularly obvious
          among college students.

Importance of   Entering college students are expected to be
computers in
college   familiar with a variety of software programs. Most
          professors, for example, require their students to use
          Microsoft Word to write their papers, and many
          instructors expect their students to use PowerPoint to
          present their papers or research projects.

Romney 2

Students are also expected to be familiar with
the Internet. For example, registration for classes is
often conducted online. Professors and administrators
use the Internet to post information about campuswide
events, and many professors create their own Web pages
where they post their syllabi and class assignments.
Finally, professors expect their students to use the
Internet when conducting research.

Importance of the Internet

A good understanding of how email works is also
necessary for college success. Discussion questions
for class are often posted on listservs. If a student
wants to communicate with someone in the class, email
is one of the most efficient ways to do so. Email is
also vital for communicating with professors. For
example, if a student cannot attend office hours, he
or she can still ask the professor a question.

Importance of email

Despite the importance of a strong working
knowledge of computers and the Internet, many students
arrive at college with very little experience with
either. In fact, computer illiteracy is a real problem
for entering college students. Some students have poor
computer skills because they did not have access to a
computer at home. Some families cannot afford
computers, and others simply do not see a computer as
a necessity.

Reason for students' poor skills: lack of access at home

Other students may not have been taught computer
skills in elementary or high school. A recent study of
efforts to bridge the "digital divide" in elementary
and high schools reported that although many schools
are improving their access to computers, teachers
still might not use them in the classroom:

Reason for students' poor skills: lack of access at school

Romney 3

These results paint an alarming picture:
despite the expenditure of literally billions
of dollars in classroom technology, fully 14%
of U.S. K-12 teachers make no use whatsoever
of computers for instructional purposes, and
nearly half (45%) use it with their students
less than 15 minutes per week—equivalent to
just 3 minutes per day! (Norris et al. 17-18)

Those students who arrive at college with weak
computer skills face serious consequences. For
example, registering for classes on the Internet and
contacting professors or other students via email
become time-consuming (rather than timesaving) tasks.
Students may be so embarrassed by their weak computer
skills that they do not ask for help. Without help,
they have difficulty improving their skills. As a
result, they do not benefit from the opportunities
offered by the Internet (such as faster and more
thorough research) or by sophisticated software
programs (such as professional-looking papers and
presentations).

Colleges and universities recognize the problems
these students face and offer programs to help them.
For example, our campus has an outreach program aimed
at students with sub-par computer skills. Once a week,
the computer lab offers classes on software programs
such as <u>Microsoft Word</u>, <u>PowerPoint</u>, and <u>Dreamweaver</u>. A
class about email not only gives students basic
information (such as how to send and open
attachments), but also tells them how to use programs
(such as <u>Outlook Express</u>) to track their daily

Problems caused by weak computer skills

Possible solution to problems: classes

Romney 4

schedules and appointments. The library also offers several classes, both general and more discipline-specific, about how to use the Internet for research.

However, while this outreach program can provide students with opportunities to improve their skills, many do not know about it. Students are not given information about these classes at orientation, and they are not well advertised in the student newspaper, or even in the computer lab and library. The administration is also not very sensitive to the embarrassment that many students feel about having poor computer skills. Many students might avoid asking a librarian or computer lab proctor for help, and this is a problem that a good advertising campaign would remedy.

As a student from a small town where computer classes were not a part of the high school curriculum, I have personal experience with this problem. I came to college with very limited computer skills. Although I had some knowledge of Microsoft Word and had used the Internet and email, I was not very comfortable using computers. One of my first classes here was a writing class that was held in a computer lab. I was confronted with my problem every Monday, Wednesday, and Friday, and because I was embarrassed about my poor computer skills, I did not want to ask the professor for help. Trying to find help on my own was difficult. It took me two weeks to figure out when and where classes on Microsoft Word and the Internet were held. However, after taking these classes, my skills were greatly improved.

Limitations of classes

Personal experience: problems in college

Romney 5

             Through my own experience, I have come to realize

Personal experience: changes in high school   that more efforts need to be made at the high school level to educate students about technology. In my own hometown, such efforts are already underway: the school district instituted a computer literacy class for all high school freshmen the year after I graduated.

Fig. 1. Student in the Woodrow Wilson High School computer lab, personal photograph by Vicky Wellborn, 5 Oct. 2005.

    According to my high school English teacher, Vicky Wellborn, students really enjoy this class: they go to the new computer lab during breaks or after school, and the lab is frequently full. In addition, the district now requires teachers to take a computer literacy class so that they are better prepared to answer students' questions (Wellborn).

Romney 6

Despite my own frustrating experiences, I am optimistic about the future. As high schools continue to make efforts to incorporate technology into the classroom, students entering college will be better prepared for the technological challenges they will face. And as they become more computer literate, the "digital divide" will close.

Conclusion

Romney 7

Works Cited

Gates, Henry Louis Jr. "One Internet, Two Nations." The Blair Reader. 4th ed. Ed. Laurie G. Kirszner and Stephen R. Mandell. Upper Saddle River: Prentice, 2002. 499-501.

Norris, Cathleen, et al. "No Access, No Use, No Impact: Snapshot Surveys of Educational Technology in K-12." Journal of Research on Technology in Education 36.1 (2003): 15-27. Expanded Academic ASAP. Gale Group Databases. U of Texas Lib. System. 15 Oct. 2005 <http://www.galegroup.com>.

Wellborn, Vicky. "Re: Computer Literacy." Email to the author. 23 Oct. 2005.

CHAPTER 7

Writing Paragraphs

A **paragraph** is a group of related sentences, which may be complete in itself or part of a longer piece of writing.

Checklist: When to Begin a New Paragraph

- ☐ Begin a new paragraph whenever you move from one major point to another.
- ☐ Begin a new paragraph whenever you move your readers from one time period or location to another.
- ☐ Begin a new paragraph whenever you introduce a new step in a process or sequence.
- ☐ Begin a new paragraph when you want to emphasize an important idea.
- ☐ Begin a new paragraph every time a new person speaks.
- ☐ Begin a new paragraph to signal the end of your introduction and the beginning of your conclusion.

7a Writing Unified Paragraphs

A paragraph is **unified** when it develops a single main idea. The **topic sentence** states the main idea of the paragraph, and the other sentences in the paragraph support that idea.

(1) Using Topic Sentences

A topic sentence usually comes at the beginning of a paragraph. Occasionally, a topic sentence may occur at the end of a paragraph, particularly if a writer wants to present an unexpected conclusion.

Topic Sentence at the Beginning A topic sentence at the beginning of a paragraph tells readers what to expect and helps them to understand your paragraph's main idea immediately.

> I was a listening child, careful to hear the very different sounds of Spanish and English. Wide-eyed with hearing, I'd listen to sounds more than words. First, there were English (*gringo*) sounds. So many words

were still unknown that when the butcher or the lady at the drugstore said something to me, exotic polysyllabic sounds would bloom in the midst of their sentences. Often the speech of people in public seemed to me very loud, booming with confidence. The man behind the counter would literally ask, "What can I do for you?" But by being so firm and so clear, the sound of his voice said that he was a *gringo*; he belonged in public society. (Richard Rodriguez, *Aria: A Memoir of a Bilingual Childhood*)

Topic Sentence at the End A topic sentence at the end of a paragraph is useful if you are presenting an unusual or hard-to-accept idea. By presenting a logical chain of reasoning before you state your conclusion in your topic sentence, you are more likely to convince readers that your conclusion is reasonable.

> These sprays, dusts and aerosols are now applied almost universally to farms, gardens, forests, and homes—nonselective chemicals that have the power to kill every insect, the "good" and the "bad," to still the song of birds and the leaping of fish in the streams, to coat the leaves with a deadly film, and to linger on in soil—all this though the intended target may be only a few weeds or insects. Can anyone believe it is possible to lay down such a barrage of poisons on the surface without making it unfit for life? <u>They should not be called "insecticides," but "biocides."</u> (Rachel Carson, "The Obligation to Endure," *Silent Spring*)

(2) Testing for Unity

Each sentence in a paragraph should support the main idea that is stated in the topic sentence. The following paragraph is not unified because it includes sentences that do not support the main idea.

Paragraph Not Unified

> <u>One of the first problems I had as a college student was learning to use a computer.</u> All students were required to buy a computer before school started. Throughout the first semester, we took a special course to teach us to use a computer. My laptop has a lot of memory and can do word processing and spreadsheets. It has a large screen and a DVD drive. My parents were happy that I had a computer, but they were concerned about the price. Tuition was high, and when they added in the price of the computer, it was almost out of reach. To offset expenses, I got a part-time job in the school library. I am determined to overcome "computer anxiety" and to master my computer by the end of the semester. (student writer)

Sentences do not support main idea

When he revised, the writer deleted the sentences about his parents' financial situation and the computer's characteristics and added details related to the main idea.

Revised Paragraph

One of the first problems I had as a college student was learning to use a computer. All first-year students were required to buy a computer before school started. Throughout the first semester, we took a special course to teach us to use the computer. In theory this system sounded fine, but in my case it was a disaster. In the first place, I had never owned a computer before. The closest I had ever come to a computer was the computer lab in high school. In the second place, I could not type well. And to make matters worse, many of the people in my computer orientation course already knew everything there was to know about operating a computer. By the end of the first week, I was convinced that I would never be able to keep up with them.

Sentences now support main idea

7b Writing Coherent Paragraphs

A paragraph is **coherent** when all its sentences are logically related to one another. You can create coherence by arranging details according to an organizing principle, by using transitional words and phrases, by using parallel structure, and by repeating key words and phrases.

(1) Arranging Details

Even if all its sentences are about the same subject, a paragraph lacks coherence if the sentences are not arranged according to a general organizing principle—that is, if they are not arranged *spatially*, *chronologically*, or *logically*.

Spatial order establishes the way in which readers will "see" details. For example, an object or scene can be viewed from top to bottom or from near to far. Spatial order is central to descriptive paragraphs.

See 7d2

Chronological order presents events in sequence, using transitional words and phrases to establish the time order of events—*at first*, *yesterday*, *later*, *in 1930*, and so on. Chronological order is central to narrative paragraphs and process paragraphs.

See 7d1, 4

Logical order presents details or ideas in terms of their logical relationships to one another. Transitional words and phrases such as *first*, *second*, and *finally* establish these relationships and lead readers through the paragraph. For example, the ideas in a paragraph may move from *general to specific*, as in the conventional topic-sentence-at-the-beginning paragraph, or the ideas may progress from *specific to general*, as they do when the topic sentence appears at the end of the paragraph. A writer may also choose to begin with the *least important* idea and move to the *most important*. Logical order is central to <u>exemplification paragraphs</u> and <u>comparison-and-contrast paragraphs</u>.

See
7d3, 6

(2) Using Transitional Words and Phrases

Transitional words and phrases clarify the relationships between sentences by identifying the spatial, chronological, and logical organizing principles discussed above. The following paragraph, which has no transitional words and phrases, illustrates just how important these words and phrases are.

Paragraph without Transitional Words and Phrases

> Napoleon certainly made a change for the worse by leaving his small kingdom of Elba. He went back to Paris, and he abdicated for a second time. He fled to Rochefort in hope of escaping to America. He gave himself up to the English captain of the ship *Bellerophon*. He suggested that the Prince Regent grant him asylum, and he was refused. All he saw of England was the Devon coast and Plymouth Sound as he passed on to the remote island of St. Helena. He died on May 5, 1821, at the age of fifty-two.

In the narrative paragraph above, the topic sentence states the main idea of the paragraph, and the rest of the sentences support this idea. However, the paragraph is not only choppy, but also difficult to understand. Because of the absence of transitional words and phrases, readers cannot tell exactly how one event in the paragraph relates to another in time. Notice how much easier it is to read this passage once transitional words and phrases (such as *after, finally, once again*, and *in the end*) have been added.

Paragraph with Transitional Words and Phrases

> Napoleon certainly made a change for the worse by leaving his small kingdom of Elba. <u>After</u> Waterloo, he went back to Paris, and he abdicated for a second time. A hundred days <u>after</u> his return from Elba, he fled to Rochefort in hope of escaping to America. <u>Finally</u>, he gave himself up to the English captain of the ship Bellerophon. <u>Once again</u>, he suggested that the Prince Regent grant him asylum, and <u>once again</u>, he was refused. <u>In the end</u>, all he saw of England was the Devon coast and Plymouth Sound as he passed on to the remote island of St. Helena. <u>After</u> six years of exile, he died on May 5, 1821, at the age of fifty-two. (Norman Mackenzie, *The Escape from Elba*)

Frequently Used Transitional Words and Phrases

To Signal Sequence or Addition

again	in addition
also	moreover
besides	one . . . another
first . . . second . . . third	too
furthermore	

To Signal Time

afterward	later
as soon as	meanwhile
at first	next
at the same time	now
before	subsequently
earlier	soon
finally	then
in the meantime	until

To Signal Comparison

also	likewise
by the same token	similarly
in comparison	

To Signal Contrast

although	nevertheless
but	nonetheless
despite	on the contrary
even though	on the one hand . . . on the other hand
however	
in contrast	still
instead	whereas
meanwhile	yet

To Introduce Examples

for example	specifically
for instance	thus
namely	

To Signal Narrowing of Focus

after all	in particular
indeed	specifically
in fact	that is
in other words	

To Introduce Conclusions or Summaries

as a result	in summary
consequently	therefore
in conclusion	thus
in other words	to conclude

To Signal Concession

admittedly   naturally
certainly   of course
granted

To Introduce Causes or Effects

accordingly   since
as a result   so
because   then
consequently   therefore
hence

(3) Using Parallel Structure

Parallelism—the use of matching words, phrases, clauses, or sentence structures to emphasize similar ideas—can increase coherence in a paragraph. Note in the following paragraph how parallel constructions beginning with *He was* link Thomas Jefferson's accomplishments.

> Thomas Jefferson was born in 1743 and died at
> Monticello, Virginia, on July 4, 1826. During his
> eighty-four years, he accomplished a number of things.
> Although best known for his draft of the Declaration of
> Independence, Jefferson was a man of many talents who had
> a wide intellectual range. He was a patriot who was one
> of the revolutionary founders of the United States. He
> was a reformer who, when he was governor of Virginia,
> drafted the Statute for Religious Freedom. He was an
> innovator who drafted an ordinance for governing the West
> and devised the first decimal monetary system. He was a
> president who abolished internal taxes, reduced the
> national debt, and made the Louisiana Purchase. And,
> finally, he was an architect who designed Monticello and
> the University of Virginia. (student writer)

See 37c, 39a

(4) Repeating Key Words and Phrases

Repeating **key words and phrases**—those essential to meaning—throughout a paragraph connects the sentences to one another and to the paragraph's main idea. The following paragraph repeats the key word *mercury* to keep readers focused on the subject. (Notice that to avoid monotony the writer sometimes refers indirectly to the subject of the paragraph with phrases such as *similarly affected* and *this problem*.)

```
    Mercury poisoning is a problem that has long been
recognized. "Mad as a hatter" refers to the condition
prevalent among nineteenth-century workers who were exposed
to mercury during the manufacturing of felt hats. Workers
in many other industries, such as mining, chemicals, and
dentistry, were similarly affected. In the 1950s and 1960s,
there were cases of mercury poisoning in Minamata, Japan.
Research showed that there were high levels of mercury
pollution in streams and lakes surrounding the village. In
the United States, this problem came to light in 1969, when
a New Mexico family got sick from eating food tainted with
mercury. Since then, pesticides containing mercury have been
withdrawn from the market, and chemical wastes can no longer
be dumped into the ocean. (student writer)
```

7c　Writing Well-Developed Paragraphs

**FAQs
links**

A paragraph is **well developed** when it includes all the **support**—examples, statistics, expert opinion, and so on—that readers need to understand and accept its main idea. Keep in mind that length alone does not determine whether a paragraph is well developed. To determine the amount and kind of support you need, consider your audience, your purpose, and your paragraph's main idea.

The following paragraph is not adequately developed because it does not include enough support to convince readers that the topic sentence's assertion is correct.

Underdeveloped Paragraph

```
    From Thanksgiving until Christmas, children and their
parents are bombarded by ads for violent toys and games. Toy
manufacturers persist in thinking that only toys that appeal
to children's aggressiveness will sell. Despite claims that
they (unlike action toys) have educational value, video
games have escalated the level of violence. The real
question is why parents continue to buy these violent toys
and games for their children. (student writer)
```

When the student writer revised her paragraph, she added specific examples to support her topic sentence.

Revised Paragraph (Examples Added)

```
    From Thanksgiving until Christmas, children and their
parents are bombarded by ads for violent toys and games. Toy
manufacturers persist in thinking that only toys that appeal
```
Examples
```
to children's aggressiveness will sell. One television
commercial praises the merits of a commando team that
attacks and captures a miniature enemy base. Toy soldiers
wear realistic uniforms and carry automatic rifles, pistols,
```

knives, grenades, and ammunition. Another commercial shows laughing children shooting one another with plastic rocket launchers and tanklike vehicles. Despite claims that they (unlike action toys) have educational value, video games have escalated the level of violence. The most popular video games involve children in strikingly realistic combat simulations. One game lets children search out and destroy enemy fighters on the ground and in the air. Other best-selling games graphically simulate hand-to-hand combat on city streets and feature dismembered bodies and the sound of breaking bones. The real question is why parents continue to buy these violent toys and games for their children.

Examples

7d Patterns of Paragraph Development

Patterns of paragraph development—*narration, exemplification,* and so on—reflect the way a writer arranges material to express ideas most effectively.

(1) Narration

A **narrative** paragraph tells a story by presenting events in chrono-logical (time) order. Most narratives move in a logical, orderly se-quence from beginning to end, from first event to last. Clear transi-tional words and phrases (*later, after that*) and time markers (*in 1990, two years earlier, the next day*) establish the chronological sequence.

My academic career almost ended as soon as it began when, three weeks after I arrived at college, I decided to pledge a fraternity. By midterms, I was wearing a pledge cap and saying "Yes, sir" to every fraternity brother I met. When classes were over, I ran errands for the fraternity members, and after dinner I socialized and worked on projects with the other people in my pledge class. In between these activities, I tried to study. Somehow I managed to write papers, take tests, and attend lectures. By the end of the semester, though, my grades had slipped, and I was exhausted. It was then that I began to ask myself some

Topic sentence identifies subject of narrative

Sequence of events

important questions. I realized that I wanted to be popular, but not at the expense of my grades and my future career. At the beginning of my second semester, I dropped out of the fraternity and got a job in the biology lab. Looking back, I realize that it was then that I actually began to grow up. (student writer)

Figure 7.1 Student in pledge cap; one event in narrative sequence.

(2) Description

A **descriptive** paragraph communicates how something looks, sounds, smells, tastes, or feels. The most natural arrangement of details in a description reflects the way you actually look at a person, scene, or object: near to far, top to bottom, side to side, or front to back. This arrangement of details is made clear by transitions that identify precise spatial relationships: *next to, near, beside, under, above,* and so on.

NOTE: Sometimes a descriptive paragraph does not have an explicitly stated topic sentence. In such cases, it is unified by a **dominant impression**—the effect created by all the details in the description.

Details convey dominant impression

When you are inside the jungle, away from the river, the trees vault out of sight. It is hard to remember to look up the long trunks and see the fans, strips, fronds, and sprays of glossy leaves. Inside the jungle you are more likely to notice the snarl of climbers and creepers round the trees' boles, the flowering bromeliads and epiphytes in every bough's crook, and the fantastic silk-cotton tree trunks thirty or forty feet across, trunks buttressed in flanges of wood whose curves can make three high walls of a room—a shady, loamy-aired room where you would gladly live, or die.

Figure 7.2 Vividly detailed close-up of Blue Morpho butterfly in Costa Rican rainforest.

Butterflies, iridescent blue, striped, or clear-winged, thread the jungle paths at eye level. And at your feet is a swath of ants bearing triangular bits of green leaf. The ants with their leaves look like a wide fleet of sailing dinghies—but they don't quit. In either direction they wobble over the jungle floor as far as the eye can see. I followed them off the path as far as I dared, and never saw an end to ants or to those luffing chips of green they bore. (Annie Dillard, "In the Jungle")

(3) Exemplification

An **exemplification** paragraph supports a topic sentence with a series of specific examples (or, sometimes, with a single extended example). These examples can be drawn from personal observation or experience or from research.

Topic sentence identifies paragraph's main idea

Series of examples

Illiterates cannot travel freely. When they attempt to do so, they encounter risks that few of us can dream of. They cannot read traffic signs and, while they often learn to recognize and to decipher symbols, they cannot manage street names which they haven't seen before. The same is true for bus and subway stops. While ingenuity can sometimes help a man or

Figure 7.3 Street signs illustrate one area of confusion for illiterates.

woman to discern directions from familiar landmarks, buildings, cemeteries, churches, and the like, most illiterates are virtually immobilized. They seldom wander past the streets and neighborhoods they know. Geographical paralysis becomes a bitter metaphor for their entire existence. They are immobilized in almost every sense we can imagine. They can't move up. They can't move out. They cannot see beyond. Illiterates may take an oral test for drivers' permits in most sections of America. It is a questionable concession. Where will they go? How will they get there? How will they get home? Could it be that some of us might like it better if they stayed where they belong? (Jonathan Kozol, *Illiterate America*)

(4) Process

Process paragraphs describe how something works, presenting a series of steps in strict chronological order. The topic sentence identifies the process, and the rest of the paragraph presents the steps involved. Transitional words such as *first, then, next, after this,* and *finally* link steps in the process.

<u>Members of the court have disclosed, however, the general way the conference is conducted</u>. It begins at ten A.M. and usually runs on until late afternoon. At the start each justice, when he enters the room, shakes hands with all others there (thirty-six handshakes altogether). The custom, dating back generations, is evidently designed to begin the meeting at a friendly level, no matter how heated the intellectual differences may be. The conference takes up, first, the applications for review—a few appeals, many more petitions for certiorari. Those on the Appellate Docket, the regular paid cases, are considered first, then the pauper's applications on the Miscellaneous Docket. (If any of these are granted,

Topic sentence identifies process

Steps in process

Figure 7.4 US Supreme Court justices after final step in process (handing down opinion in *Gideon v. Wainwright*, November 1962).

they are then transferred to the Appellate Docket.) After this the justices consider, and vote on, all the cases argued during the preceding Monday through Thursday. These are tentative votes, which may be and quite often are changed as the opinion is written and the problem thought through more deeply. There may be further discussion at later conferences before the opinion is handed down. (Anthony Lewis, *Gideon's Trumpet*)

Close-up: Instructions

When a process paragraph presents instructions to enable readers to actually perform the process, it is written in the present tense and in the imperative mood— "*Remove* the cover . . . and *check* the valve."

(5) Cause and Effect

A **cause-and-effect** paragraph explores causes or predicts or describes results; sometimes a single cause-and-effect paragraph does both. Clear, specific transitional words and phrases such as *one cause*, *another cause*, *a more important result*, *because*, and *as a result* convey the cause-and-effect relationships.

Some paragraphs examine causes.

Figure 7.5 Baby sucking thumb (effect).

Topic sentence establishes major cause

> The main reason that a young baby sucks his thumb seems to be that he hasn't had enough sucking at the breast or bottle to satisfy his sucking needs. Dr. David Levy pointed out that babies who are fed every 3 hours don't suck their thumbs as much as babies fed every 4 hours, and that babies who have cut down on nursing time from 20 minutes to 10 minutes . . . are more likely to suck their thumbs than babies who still have to work for 20 minutes. Dr. Levy fed a litter of puppies with a medicine dropper so that they had no chance to suck during their feedings. They acted just the same as babies who don't get enough chance to suck at feeding time. They sucked their own and each other's paws and skin so hard that the fur came off. (Benjamin Spock, *Baby and Child Care*)

Cause explored in detail

Other paragraphs focus on effects.

Topic sentence establishes major effect

> On December 8, 1941, the day after the Japanese attack on Pearl Harbor in Hawaii, my grandfather barricaded himself with his family— my grandmother, my teenage mother, her two sisters and two brothers— inside of his home in La'ie, a sugar plantation village on Oahu's North Shore. This was my maternal grandfather, a man most villagers called by his last name, Kubota. It could mean either "Wayside Field" or else "Broken Dreams," depending on which ideograms he used. Kubota ran La'ie's general store, and the previous night, after a long day of bad news on the radio, some locals had come by, pounded on the front door, and made threats. One was said to have brandished a machete. They were angry and shocked, as the whole nation was in the aftermath of the surprise attack. Kubota was one of the few Japanese Americans in the village and president of the local Japanese language school. He had become a target for their rage and suspicion. A wise man, he locked all his doors and windows and did not open his store the next day, but stayed closed and waited for news from some official. (Garrett Hongo, "Kubota")

Discussion of other effects

Figure 7.6 Headline announcing attack on Pearl Harbor (cause of US entry into World War II).

(6) Comparison and Contrast

Comparison-and-contrast paragraphs examine the similarities and differences between two subjects. **Comparison** focuses on similarities; **contrast** emphasizes differences.

Comparison-and-contrast paragraphs can be organized in one of two ways. Some paragraphs, **point-by-point** comparisons, discuss two subjects together, alternating points about one subject with comparable points about the other.

> <u>There are two Americas.</u> One is the America of Lincoln and Adlai Stevenson; the other is the America of Teddy Roosevelt and the modern superpatriots. One is generous and humane, the other narrowly egotistical; one is self-critical, the other self-righteous; one is sensible, the other romantic; one is good-humored, the other solemn; one is inquiring, the other pontificating; one is moderate, the other filled with passionate intensity; one is judicious and the other arrogant in the use of great power. (J. William Fulbright, *The Arrogance of Power*)

Topic sentence establishes comparison

Alternating points about the two subjects

Figure 7.7 Abraham Lincoln (left) and Theodore Roosevelt (right) symbolize the contrast between the two Americas.

Other paragraphs, **subject-by-subject** comparisons, treat one subject completely and then move on to the other subject. In the following paragraph, notice how the writer shifts from one subject to the other with the transitional word *however*.

Figure 7.8 Man using mute button to halt conversation (illustrates contrast between conversation styles of men and women).

> <u>First, it is important to note that men and women regard conversation quite differently.</u> For women it is a passion, a sport, an activity even more important to life than eating because it doesn't involve weight gain. The first sign of closeness among women is when they find themselves engaging in endless, secretless rounds of conversation with one another. And as soon as a woman begins to relax and feel comfortable in a relationship with a man, she tries to have that type of conversation with him as

Topic sentence establishes comparison

First subject discussed

Second subject introduced

well. <u>However,</u> the first sign that a man is feeling close to a woman is when he admits that he'd rather she please quiet down so he can hear the TV. A man who feels truly intimate with a woman often reserves for her and her alone the precious gift of one-word answers. Everyone knows that the surest way to spot a successful long-term relationship is to look around a restaurant for the table where no one is talking. Ah . . . now that's real love. (Merrill Markoe, "Men, Women, and Conversation")

An **analogy** is a special kind of comparison that explains an unfamiliar concept or object by likening it to a familiar one. In the following paragraph, the writer uses the behavior of people to explain the behavior of ants.

Topic sentence establishes analogy

Analogy explained in detail

<u>Ants are so much like human beings as to be an embarrassment</u>. They farm fungi, raise aphids as livestock, launch armies into wars, use chemical sprays to alarm and confuse enemies, capture slaves. The families of weaver ants engage in child labor, holding their larvae like shuttles to spin out the thread that sews the leaves together for their fungus gardens. They exchange information ceaselessly. They do everything but watch television. (Lewis Thomas, "On Societies as Organisms")

Figure 7.9 Tailor ants sewing leaves together illustrates analogy between ants and people.

(7) Division and Classification

Division paragraphs take a single item and break it into its component parts.

Topic sentence identifies categories

Categories discussed

<u>The blood can be divided into four distinct components: plasma, red cells, white cells, and platelets</u>. One component, plasma, is ninety percent water and holds a great number of substances in suspension. It contains proteins, sugars, fat, and inorganic salts. Plasma also contains urea and other by-products from the breaking down of proteins, hormones, enzymes, and dissolved gases. The red cells, another component of blood, give blood its distinctive color. The red cells are most numerous; they get oxygen from the lungs and release it in the tissues. The less numerous white cells are a component of blood that defends the body against invading organisms. Finally, the platelets, which occur in almost the same number as white cells, are responsible for clotting. (student writer)

Figure 7.10 Components of blood—blood cells and platelets—in vein.

Classification paragraphs take many separate items and group them into categories according to qualities or characteristics they share.

Charles Babbage, an English mathematician, reflecting in 1830 on what he saw as the decline of science at the time, distinguished among three major kinds of scientific fraud. He called the first "forging," by which he meant complete fabrication—the recording of observations that were never made. The second category he called "trimming"; this consists of manipulating the data to make them look better, or, as Babbage wrote, "in clipping off little bits here and there from those observations which differ most in excess from the mean and in sticking them on to those which are too small." His third category was data selection, which he called "cooking"—the choosing of those data that fitted the researcher's hypothesis and the discarding of those that did not. To this day, the serious discussion of scientific fraud has not improved on Babbage's typology. (Morton Hunt, *New York Times Magazine*)

Topic sentence establishes categories

Categories discussed

Figure 7.11 The FeJee mermaid illustrates "forging," one of three categories of scientific fraud.

(8) Definition

Definition paragraphs develop a definition by means of other patterns—for instance, defining *happiness* by telling a story (narration) or defining a diesel engine by telling how it works (process).

The following definition paragraph is developed by means of exemplification: it begins with a straightforward definition of *gadget* and then cites an example.

Figure 7.12 Rural mailbox with semaphore (term defined by exemplification).

A gadget is nearly always novel in design or concept and it often has no proper name. For example, the semaphore which signals the arrival of the mail in our rural mailbox certainly has no proper name. It is a contrivance consisting of a piece of shingle. Call it what you like, it saves us frequent frustrating trips to the mailbox in winter when you have to dress up and wade through snow to get there. That's a gadget! (*Smithsonian*)

Topic sentence gives general definition

Definition expanded with an example

7e   Writing Special Kinds of Paragraphs

So far, this chapter has focused on **body paragraphs,** the paragraphs that carry the weight of your essay's discussion. Other kinds of paragraphs—*transitional paragraphs, introductory paragraphs*, and *concluding paragraphs*—have special functions in an essay.

(1) Transitional Paragraphs

A **transitional paragraph** connects one section of the essay to another. Writers often use transitional paragraphs to present concise summaries of what they have already said before they move on to a new point. The following transitional paragraph uses a series of questions to sum up some of the ideas the writer has been discussing. In the next part of his essay, he goes on to answer these questions.

> Can we bleed off the mass of humanity to other worlds? Right now the number of human beings on Earth is increasing by 80 million per year, and each year that number goes up by 1 and a fraction percent. Can we really suppose that we can send 80 million people per year to the Moon, Mars, and elsewhere, and engineer those worlds to support those people? And even so, nearly remain in the same place ourselves? (Isaac Asimov, "The Case against Man")

(2) Introductory Paragraphs

An **introductory paragraph** prepares readers for the essay to follow. It typically introduces the subject, narrows it, and then states the essay's thesis.

> Christine was just a girl in one of my classes. I never knew much about her except that she was strange. She didn't talk much. Her hair was dyed black and purple, and she wore heavy black boots and a black turtleneck sweater, even in the summer. She was attractive—in spite of the ring she wore through her left eyebrow—but she never seemed to care what the rest of us thought about her. Like the rest of my classmates, I didn't really want to get close to her. It was only when we were assigned to do our chemistry project together that I began to understand why Christine dressed the way she did. (student writer)

To arouse their audience's interest, writers may vary this direct approach by using one of the following introductory strategies.

Strategies for Effective Introductions

Quotation or Series of Quotations

> When Mary Cassatt's father was told of her decision to become a painter, he said: "I would rather see you dead." When Edgar Degas saw a show of Cassatt's etchings, his response was: "I am not willing to admit that a woman can draw that well." When she returned to Philadelphia after twenty-eight years abroad, having achieved renown as an Impressionist painter and the esteem of Degas, Huysmans, Pissarro, and Berthe Morisot, the *Philadelphia Ledger* reported: "Mary

---

Cassatt, sister of Mr. Cassatt, president of the Pennsylvania Railroad, returned from Europe yesterday. She has been studying painting in France and owns the smallest Pekingese dog in the world." (Mary Gordon, "Mary Cassatt")

Question or Series of Questions

Of all the disputes agitating the American campus, the one that seems to me especially significant is that over "the canon." What should be taught in the humanities and social sciences, especially in introductory courses? What is the place of the classics? How shall we respond to those professors who attack "Eurocentrism" and advocate "multiculturalism"? This is not the sort of tedious quarrel that now and then flutters through the academy; it involves matters of public urgency. I propose to see this dispute, at first, through a narrow, even sectarian lens, with the hope that you will come to accept my reasons for doing so. (Irving Howe, "The Value of the Canon")

Definition

```
    Moles are collections of cells that can
appear on any part of the body. With occasional
exceptions, moles are absent at birth. They
first appear in the early years of life,
between ages two and six. Frequently, moles
appear at puberty. New moles, however, can
continue to appear throughout life. During
pregnancy, new moles may appear and old ones
darken. There are three major designations of
moles, each with its own unique distinguishing
characteristics.
```
(student writer)

Controversial Statement

Something had to replace the threat of communism, and at last a workable substitute is at hand. "Multiculturalism," as the new menace is known, has been denounced in the media recently as the new McCarthyism, the new fundamentalism, even the new totalitarianism—take your choice. According to its critics, who include a flock of tenured conservative scholars, multiculturalism aims to toss out what it sees as the Eurocentric bias in education and replace Plato with Ntozake Shange and traditional math with the Yoruba number system. And that's just the beginning. The Jacobins of the multiculturalist movement, who are described derisively as P.C., or politically correct, are said to have launched a campus reign of terror against those who slip and innocently say "freshman" instead of "freshperson," "Indian" instead of "Native American" or, may the Goddess forgive them, "disabled" instead of "differently abled." (Barbara Ehrenreich, "Teach Diversity—with a Smile")

Close-up: Introductory Paragraphs

An introductory paragraph should make your readers want to read further. For this reason, you should avoid introductions that begin by simply announcing your subject ("In my paper, I will talk about Lady Macbeth") or by undercutting your credibility ("I don't know much about alternative energy sources, but I would like to present my opinion about the subject").

---

(3) Concluding Paragraphs

FAQs link

A **concluding paragraph** often begins with specifics—reviewing the essay's main points, for example—and then moves to more general statements. Whenever possible, it should end with a sentence that readers will remember.

> As an Arab-American, I feel I have the best of two worlds. I'm proud to be part of the melting pot, proud to contribute to the tremendous diversity of cultures, customs and traditions that makes this country unique. But Arab-bashing—public acceptance of hatred and bigotry—is something no American can be proud of. (Ellen Mansoor Collier, "I Am Not a Terrorist")

Writers may use any of the following concluding strategies.

Strategies for Effective Conclusions

Prediction

Looking ahead, [we see that] prospects may not be quite as dismal as they seem. As a matter of fact, we are not doing so badly. It is something of a miracle that creatures who evolved as nomads in an intimate, small-band, wide-open-spaces context manage to get along at all as villagers or surrounded by strangers in cubicle apartments. Considering that our genius as a species is adaptability, we may yet learn to live closer and closer to one another, if not in utter peace, then far more peacefully than we do today. (John Pheiffer, "Seeking Peace, Making War")

Warning

The Internet is the twenty-first century's talking drum, the very kind of grassroots communication tool that has been such a powerful source of education and culture for our people since slavery. But this talking drum we have not yet learned to play. Unless we master the new information technology to build and deepen the forms of social connection that a tragic history has eroded, African-Americans will face a form of cybersegregation in the next century as devastating to our aspirations as Jim Crow segregation was to those of our ancestors. But this time, the fault will be our own. (Henry Louis Gates Jr., "One Internet, Two Nations")

Recommendation for Action

Computers have revolutionized learning in ways that we have barely begun to appreciate. We have experienced enough, however, to recognize the need to change our thinking about our purposes, methods, and outcome of higher education. Rather than resisting or postponing change, we need to anticipate and learn from it. We must harness the technology and use it to educate our students more effectively than we have been doing. Otherwise, we will surrender our authority to those who can. (Peshe Kuriloff, "If John Dewey Were Alive Today, He'd Be a Webhead")

Quotation

When we let freedom ring, when we let it ring from every village and every hamlet, from every state and every city, we will be able to speed up that day when all of God's children, black men and white men, Jews and Gentiles, Protestants and Catholics, will be able to join hands and sing in the words of the old Negro spiritual, "Free at last! Free at last! Thank God almighty, we are free at last!" (Martin Luther King Jr., "I Have a Dream")

Close-up: Concluding Paragraphs

Because a dull conclusion can weaken an otherwise strong essay, try to make your conclusion as interesting as you can. Don't waste time repeating your introduction in different words or apologizing or undercutting your credibility ("I may not be an expert" or "At least, this is my opinion"). And remember, your conclusion should not introduce any new points or go off in new directions.

PART 2

Critical Thinking and Argumentation

PART 2

Critical Thinking and Argumentation

FREQUENTLY ASKED QUESTIONS

CHAPTER 8

Thinking Critically

As you read (and write) essays, you should carefully consider the strengths and weaknesses of the ideas they present. This is especially true in **argumentative essays**—those that take a stand on a debatable topic. Although many writers try their best to be fair, others are less scrupulous. They attempt to manipulate readers by using emotionally charged language, by unfairly emphasizing certain facts over others, and by intentionally using flawed logic. For this reason, it is important that you **think critically** when you read (and when you write). Specifically, you need to learn to distinguish fact from opinion, evaluate supporting evidence, detect bias, evaluate visuals, and understand the basic principles of inductive and deductive reasoning.

 See Ch. 9

8a Distinguishing Fact from Opinion

A **fact** is a verifiable statement that something is true or that something occurred. An **opinion** is a personal judgment or belief that can never be substantiated beyond any doubt and is, therefore, debatable.

> **Fact:** Measles is a potentially deadly disease.
>
> **Opinion:** All children should be vaccinated against measles.

An opinion may be *supported* or *unsupported.*

> **Unsupported Opinion:** All children in Pennsylvania should be vaccinated against measles.
>
> **Supported Opinion:** Despite the fact that an effective measles vaccine is widely available, several unvaccinated Pennsylvania children have died of measles each year since 1992. States that have instituted vaccination programs have had no deaths in the same time period. For this reason, all children in Pennsylvania should be vaccinated against measles.

As the examples above show, supported opinion is more convincing than unsupported opinion. Remember, however, that support can only make a statement more convincing; it cannot turn an opinion into a fact.

Opinions can be supported with **examples, statistics,** or **expert opinion.**

Examples

The American Civil Liberties Union is an organization that has been unfairly characterized as left wing. It is true that it has opposed prayer in the public schools, defended conscientious objectors, and challenged police methods of conducting questioning and searches of suspects. However, it has also backed the antiabortion group Operation Rescue in a police brutality suit and presented a legal brief in support of a Republican politician accused of violating an ethics law.

Statistics

A recent National Institute of Mental Health study concluded that mentally ill people account for more than 30 percent of the homeless population (Young 27). Because so many homeless people have psychiatric disabilities, the federal government should expand the state mental hospital system.

Expert Opinion

No soldier ever really escapes the emotional consequences of war. As William Manchester, noted historian and World War II combat veteran, observes in his essay "Okinawa: The Bloodiest Battle of All," "the invisible wounds remain" (72).

8b   Evaluating Supporting Evidence

The examples, statistics, or expert opinion that a writer uses to support a statement is called **evidence.** The more reliable the supporting evidence, the more willing readers will be to accept a statement.

All evidence—no matter what kind—must be *accurate, sufficient, representative,* and *relevant.*

- Evidence is likely to be **accurate** if it comes from a trustworthy source. Such a source quotes exactly and does not present remarks out of context. It also presents examples, statistics, and expert testimony fairly, drawing them from other reliable sources.
- Evidence is likely to be **sufficient** if a writer presents an adequate amount of information. It is not enough, for instance, for a writer to cite just one example in an attempt to demonstrate that most poor women do not receive adequate prenatal care. Similarly, the opinions of a single expert, no matter how reputable, are not enough to support this position.
- Evidence is likely to be **representative** if it reflects a fair range of sources and viewpoints. Writers should not just choose evidence that supports their position and ignore evidence that does not. In other words, they should not permit their biases to gov-

ern their choice of evidence. For example, a writer who is making the point that Asian immigrants have had great success in achieving professional status in the United States must draw from a range of Asian immigrant groups—Vietnamese, Chinese, Japanese, Indian, and Korean, for example—not just one.

- Finally, evidence is likely to be **relevant** if it specifically applies to the case being discussed. For example, a writer cannot support the position that the United States should send medical aid to developing nations by citing examples that apply only to our own nation's health-care system.

8c   Detecting Bias

Bias is the tendency to base conclusions on preconceived ideas rather than on evidence. As a critical reader, you should be aware that bias may sometimes lead writers to see what they want to see and therefore to select only that evidence that supports their own positions. (And don't forget that your own biases can also affect your response to a text. When you read, it is important to remain aware of your own values and beliefs and to be alert to how they may affect your reactions.)

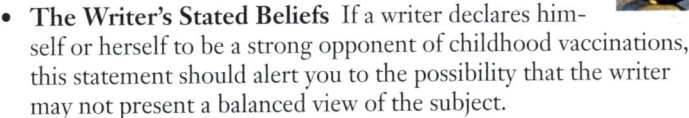

Close-up: Detecting Bias   FAQs

When you read, look for the following kinds of bias:

- **The Writer's Stated Beliefs** If a writer declares himself or herself to be a strong opponent of childhood vaccinations, this statement should alert you to the possibility that the writer may not present a balanced view of the subject.

- **Sexist or Racist Statements** A writer who assumes all engineers are male or all nurses are female reflects a clear bias. A researcher who assumes certain racial or ethnic groups are intellectually superior to others is also likely to present a biased view.

- **Slanted Language** Some writers use **slanted language**—language that contains value judgments—to influence readers' reactions. For example, "The politician gave an impassioned speech" gives one impression; "The politician delivered a diatribe" gives another.

- **Tone** The tone of a piece of writing indicates a writer's attitude toward readers or toward his or her subject. An angry or sarcastic tone might indicate that the writer is not presenting his or her case fairly.

(continued)

See
Ch. 9

Detecting bias (continued)

- **Choice of Evidence** The examples or statistics cited in a piece of writing may reveal the writer's bias. For example, a writer may include only examples that support a point and leave out examples that may contradict it.
- **The Writer's Choice of Experts** A writer should cite experts who represent a fair range of opinion. If, for instance, a writer assessing the government's policy on stem-cell research includes only statements by experts who vehemently oppose this procedure, he or she is presenting a biased case.

8d   Understanding Inductive and Deductive Reasoning

Argumentative essays rely primarily on **logic**. Logical reasoning enables you to construct arguments that reach conclusions in a persuasive and systematic way. Before you can evaluate or write arguments, you need to understand the basic principles of **inductive** and **deductive** reasoning.

(1) Understanding Inductive Reasoning

Inductive reasoning moves from specific facts, observations, or experiences to a general conclusion. Writers use inductive reasoning when they address a skeptical audience that requires a lot of evidence before it will accept a conclusion. You can see how inductive reasoning operates by studying the following list of specific statements that focus on the relationship between SAT scores and admissions at one liberal arts college:

- The SAT is a requirement for all applicants.
- High school grades and rank in class are also examined.
- Nonacademic factors, such as sports, activities, and interests, are taken into account as well.
- Special attention is given to the applications of athletes, minorities, and children of alumni.
- Fewer than 52 percent of applicants for a recent class with SAT verbal scores between 600 and 700 were accepted.
- Fewer than 39 percent of applicants with similar math scores were accepted.
- Approximately 18 percent of applications with SAT verbal scores between 450 and 520 and about 19 percent of applicants with similar SAT math scores were admitted.

After reading the statements above, you can use inductive reasoning to reach the general conclusion that although they are important, SAT scores are not the one single factor that determines whether or not a student is admitted.

Close-up: Making Inferences

Keep in mind that no matter how much evidence is presented, an inductive conclusion is never certain, only probable. You arrive at an inductive conclusion by making an **inference**, a statement about the unknown based on the known. In order to bridge the gap that exists between your specific observations and your general conclusion, you have to make an **inductive leap.** If you have presented enough specific evidence, this gap will be relatively small, and your readers will readily accept your conclusion. If the gap is too big, your readers will accuse you of making a <u>hasty generalization</u> and will not accept your conclusion.

See
8e

---

(2) Understanding Deductive Reasoning

Deductive reasoning moves from a generalization believed to be true or self-evident to a more specific conclusion. Writers use deductive reasoning when they address an audience that is more likely to be influenced by logic than by evidence. The process of deduction has traditionally been illustrated with a **syllogism**, a three-part set of statements or propositions that includes a **major premise,** a **minor premise,** and a **conclusion.**

Major Premise: All books from that store are new.

Minor Premise: These books are from that store.

Conclusion: Therefore, these books are new.

The major premise of a syllogism makes a general statement that the writer believes to be true. The minor premise presents a specific example of the belief that is stated in the major premise. If the reasoning is sound, the conclusion should follow from the two premises. (Note that these two premises contain all the information expressed in the conclusion; that is, the conclusion introduces no terms that have not already appeared in the major and minor premises.) The advantage of a deductive argument is that if readers accept the premises, they usually grant the conclusion.

When you write an <u>argumentative essay</u>, you can use a syllogism during the planning stage (to test the validity of your points), or you can use it as a revision strategy (to test your logic). In either case, the syllogism enables you to express your deductive argument in its most basic form and to see whether it makes sense.

See
Ch. 9

A syllogism is **valid** (or logical) when its conclusion follows from its premises. A syllogism is **true** when it makes accurate claims—that is, when the information it contains is consistent with the facts. To be **sound,** a syllogism must be both valid and true. However, a syllogism may be valid without being true or true without being valid. The following syllogism, for example, is valid but not true.

Major Premise: All politicians are male.

Minor Premise: Barbara Boxer is a politician.

Conclusion: Therefore, Barbara Boxer is male.

As odd as it may seem, this syllogism is valid. In the major premise, the phrase *all politicians* establishes that the entire class *politicians* is male. After Barbara Boxer is identified as a politician, the conclusion that she is male automatically follows—but, of course, she is not. Because the major premise of this syllogism is not true, no conclusion based on it can be true. Even though the logic of the syllogism is correct, its conclusion is not.

8e   Recognizing Logical Fallacies

Fallacies are flawed arguments. A writer who inadvertently uses logical fallacies is not thinking clearly or logically; a writer who intentionally uses them is trying to deceive readers. Learn to recognize fallacies—to challenge them when you read and to avoid them when you write.

Close-up: Logical Fallacies

- **Hasty Generalization** Drawing a conclusion based on too little evidence

  The person I voted for is not doing a good job in Congress. Therefore, voting is a waste of time. (One disappointing experience does not warrant the statement that you will never vote again.)

- **Sweeping Generalization** Making a generalization that cannot be supported no matter how much evidence is supplied

  Everyone should exercise. (Some people, for example those with severe heart conditions, might not benefit from exercise.)

- **Equivocation** Shifting the meaning of a key word or phrase during an argument

  It is not in the public interest for the public to lose interest in politics. (Although clever, the shift in the meaning of the term *public interest* clouds the issue.)

- **Non Sequitur (Does Not Follow)** Arriving at a conclusion that does not logically follow from what comes before

  Kim Williams is a good lawyer, so she will make a good senator. (Kim Williams may be a good lawyer, but it does not necessarily follow that she will make a good senator.)

- **Either/Or Fallacy** Treating a complex issue as if it has only two sides

  Either we institute universal health care, or the health of all Americans will decline. (Good health does not necessarily depend on universal health care.)

- **Post Hoc** Establishing an unjustified link between cause and effect

  The United States sold wheat to Russia. This must be what caused the price of wheat to rise. (Other factors, unrelated to the sale, could have caused the price of wheat to rise.)

- **Begging the Question** (circular reasoning) Stating a debatable premise as if it were true

  Stem-cell research should be banned because nothing good can come from something so inherently evil. (Where is the evidence that stem-cell research is "inherently evil"?)

- **False Analogy** Assuming that because things are similar in some ways, they are similar in other ways

  When forced to live in crowded conditions, people act like rats. They turn on each other and act violently. (Both people and rats might dislike living in crowded conditions, but unlike rats, people do not necessarily resort to violence in this situation.)

- **Red Herring** Changing the subject to distract readers from the issue

  Our company may charge high prices, but we give a lot to charity each year. (What does charging high prices have to do with giving to charity?)

- **Argument to Ignorance** Saying that something is true because it cannot be proved false, or vice versa

  How can you tell me to send my child to a school where there is a child who has AIDS? After all, doctors can't say for sure that my child won't catch AIDS, can they? (Just because a doctor cannot prove the speaker's claim to be false, it does not follow that the claim is true.)

- **Bandwagon** Trying to establish that something is true because everyone believes it is true

  Everyone knows that eating candy makes children hyperactive. (Where is the evidence to support this claim?)

(continued)

Logical fallacies (continued)

- **Argument to the Person** (*Ad Hominem*) Attacking the person and not the issue

  Of course the congressman supports drilling for oil in the Arctic wildlife preserve. He worked for an oil company before he was elected to Congress. (By attacking his opponent, the speaker attempts to sidestep the issue.)

- **Argument to the People** Appealing to people's prejudices

  Because foreigners are attempting to overrun our shores, we should cut back on immigration. (By introducing prejudice, the speaker attempts to distract the audience.)

ESL Tip

In many cultures, people present arguments in order to persuade others to believe something. However, the rules for constructing such arguments are different in different cultures. In US academic settings, writers are discouraged from using the types of arguments outlined in section 8e because they are not considered fair.

Checklist: Thinking Critically

- ☐ Are the writer's points supported primarily by fact or by opinion? Does the writer present opinion as fact?
- ☐ Does the writer offer supporting evidence for his or her statements?
- ☐ What kind of evidence is provided? How convincing is it?
- ☐ Is the evidence accurate? sufficient? representative? relevant?
- ☐ Does the writer display any bias? If so, is the bias revealed through language, tone, or choice of evidence?
- ☐ Does the writer omit pertinent examples?
- ☐ Does the writer present a balanced picture of the issue?
- ☐ Are any alternative viewpoints overlooked?
- ☐ Does the writer use valid reasoning?
- ☐ Does the writer use any logical fallacies?
- ☐ Does the writer oversimplify complex ideas?
- ☐ Does the writer make reasonable inferences?
- ☐ Does the writer represent the ideas of others accurately? fairly?

CHAPTER 9

Writing Argumentative Essays

For most people, the true test of their critical thinking skills comes when they write an **argumentative essay,** one that takes a stand on an issue and uses logic and evidence to convince readers. When you write an argument, you follow the same process you use when you write any essay. However, because the purpose of an argument is to change the way readers think, you need to use some additional strategies to present your ideas to your audience.

See Chs. 4–6

9a Planning an Argumentative Essay

(1) Choosing a Debatable Topic

Because an argumentative essay attempts to change the way people think, it must focus on a **debatable topic,** one about which reasonable people may disagree. **Factual statements**—verifiable assertions about which reasonable people do *not* disagree—are, therefore, not suitable as topics for argument.

> **Fact:** First-year students are not required to purchase a meal plan from the university.

> **Debatable Topic:** First-year students *should be* required to purchase a meal plan from the university.

Your topic should be narrow enough so that you can write about it within your page limit. After all, in your argumentative essay, you will have to develop your own ideas and present convincing support while also pointing out the strengths and weaknesses of opposing arguments. If your topic is too broad, you will not be able to treat it in enough detail.

In addition, your topic should be interesting. Keep in mind that some topics—such as "The Need for Gun Control" or "The Fairness of the Death Penalty"—have been discussed and written about so often that you may not be able to say anything new or interesting about them. Instead of relying on an overused topic, choose one that enables you to contribute something to the debate.

(2) Developing an Argumentative Thesis

After you have chosen a topic, your next step is to state your position in an **argumentative thesis,** one that takes a strong stand. Properly worded, this thesis statement lays the foundation for the rest of your argument.

87

See
5b

One way to make sure that your **thesis statement** actually does take a stand is to formulate an **antithesis,** a statement that takes an arguable position that is the opposite of yours. If you can state an antithesis, your thesis statement takes a stand.

> **Thesis Statement:** Term limits would improve government by bringing people with fresh ideas into office every few years.
>
> **Antithesis:** Term limits would harm government because elected officials would always be inexperienced.

(3) Defining Your Terms

You should always define the key terms you use in your argument—especially those you use in your thesis statement. After all, the soundness of an entire argument may hinge on the definition of a word that may mean one thing to one person and another thing to someone else. For example, in the United States, democratic elections involve the selection of government officials by popular vote; in other countries, the word *democratic* may be used to describe elections in which only one candidate is running or in which all candidates represent the same party. For this reason, if your argument hinges on a key term like *democratic*, you should make sure that your readers know exactly what you mean.

Close-up: Using Precise Language

Be careful to use precise language in your thesis statement. Avoid vague and judgmental words, such as *wrong, bad, good, right,* and *immoral.*

Vague: Censorship of the Internet would be wrong.
Clearer: Censorship of the Internet would unfairly limit free speech.

---

(4) Considering Your Audience

See
1b

As you plan your essay, keep a specific **audience** in mind. Are your readers unbiased observers or people deeply concerned about the issue you plan to discuss? Can they be cast in a specific role—concerned parents, victims of discrimination, irate consumers—or are they so diverse that they cannot be categorized?

Always assume that your audience will question your assumptions. Even if your readers are sympathetic to your position, you cannot assume that they will accept your ideas without question; they will still need to see that your argument is logical and that your evidence is solid. More skeptical readers will need reassurance that you understand their concerns and that you concede some of their points. However, no matter what you do, you may never be able to convince hostile readers that your conclusion is valid. The best you can hope for is that these readers will acknowledge the strengths of your argument even if they reject your conclusion.

(5) Refuting Opposing Arguments

As you develop your argument, you should briefly summarize and then **refute**—that is, disprove—opposing arguments by showing that they are untrue, unfair, illogical, unimportant, or irrelevant. In the following paragraph, a student refutes the argument that Sea World is justified in keeping whales in captivity.

> Of course, some will say that Sea World wants to capture only a few whales, as George Will points out in his commentary in <u>Newsweek</u>. Unfortunately, Will downplays the fact that Sea World wants to capture a hundred whales, not just "a few." And, after releasing ninety of these whales, Sea World intends to keep ten for "further work." At hearings in Seattle last week, several noted marine biologists went on record as condemning Sea World's research program.

If an opponent's position is so strong that it cannot be refuted, concede the point, and then identify its limitations. When you acknowledge an opposing view, be careful not to distort or oversimplify it. This tactic, known as creating a **straw man,** can seriously undermine your credibility.

http://kirsznermandell.wadsworth.com

Computer Tip: Refuting Opposing Arguments

As you formulate an argument, you can use your computer to create a table or chart that organizes all the arguments against your position. Using the Table menu in your word-processing program, create a two-column table. Label the first column "Opposing Arguments" and the second column "Refutations." List the arguments against your position in the first column and your refutations of these arguments in the second column. When you are finished, delete the weakest opposing arguments. When you write your essay, consider only those opposing arguments and refutations that remain.

9b Using Evidence Effectively

(1) Supporting Your Argument

Most arguments are built on **assertions**—statements that you make about your topic—backed by <u>evidence</u>—supporting information, in the form of examples, statistics, or expert opinion. (Keep in mind that all information—words and ideas—that you get from a source requires <u>documentation</u>.)

Only assertions that are **self-evident** ("All human beings are mortal"), **true by definition** (2 + 2 = 4), or **factual** ("The Atlantic Ocean separates England and the United States") need no proof. All other kinds of assertions require support.

NOTE: Remember that you can never prove a thesis conclusively; if you did, there would be no argument. The best you can do is to provide enough evidence to establish a high probability that your thesis is reasonable or valid.

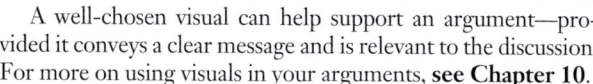

Close-up: Using Visuals as Evidence

A well-chosen visual can help support an argument—provided it conveys a clear message and is relevant to the discussion. For more on using visuals in your arguments, **see Chapter 10**.

(2) Establishing Credibility and Being Fair

In order to convince readers, you must prove that you have **credibility**—in other words, that you are someone they should listen to. Readers will also judge your argument on the basis of its **fairness**.

Checklist: Establishing Credibility

Find Common Ground

☐ Identify the various sides of the issue.
☐ Identify the points on which you and your readers agree, and work these points into your argument.

Demonstrate Knowledge

☐ Include relevant personal experiences.
☐ Include relevant special knowledge of your subject.
☐ Include supporting evidence from research you have done.

Maintain a Reasonable Tone

☐ Avoid talking down to or insulting your readers.
☐ Use moderate language, and qualify your statements, avoiding words like *never*, *all*, and *in every case*.

Checklist: Being Fair

☐ Do not distort evidence.
☐ Do not misrepresent opponents' views by exaggerating them and then attacking this extreme position.
☐ Do not change the meaning of a statement by focusing on certain words and ignoring others.
☐ Do not select only information that supports your case and ignore information that does not.
☐ Do not use inflammatory language calculated to appeal to the emotions or prejudices of your readers.

NOTE: Even if readers see you as credible and fair, they will not accept your argument unless it is logical. Revise carefully to be sure you have avoided <u>logical fallacies</u>.

See
8e

9c   Organizing an Argumentative Essay

In its simplest form, an argument consists of a thesis statement and supporting evidence. However, argumentative essays frequently use <u>inductive and deductive reasoning</u> as well as additional strategies to win audience approval and overcome potential opposition.

See
8d

Close-up: Elements of an Argumentative Essay

FAQs
links

Introduction
   The <u>introduction</u> of your argumentative essay orients your readers to your subject. Here you can show how your subject concerns your audience, establish common ground with your readers, and perhaps explain how your subject has been misunderstood.

See
7e2

Thesis Statement
   Your <u>thesis statement</u> can appear anywhere in your argumentative essay. Most often, you state your thesis in your introduction. However, if you are presenting a highly controversial argument—one to which you believe your readers might react negatively—you may postpone stating your thesis until later in your essay.

See
5b

Background
   In this section, you can briefly present a narrative of past events, an overview of others' opinions on the issue, definitions of key terms, or a review of basic facts.

Arguments in Support of Your Thesis
   Begin with your weakest argument, and work up to your strongest. If all your arguments are equally strong, you might begin with those with which your readers are already familiar and therefore perhaps more likely to accept.

Refutation of Opposing Arguments
   If the opposing arguments are relatively weak, summarize and refute them after you have made your case. However, if the opposing arguments are strong, concede their strengths and then discuss their limitations before you present your own arguments.

Conclusion
   Often, the <u>conclusion</u> restates the major arguments in support of your thesis. Your conclusion can also summarize key points, restate your thesis, remind readers of the weaknesses of opposing arguments, or underscore the logic of your position. Many writers like to end their arguments with a strong last line, such as a quotation or a statement that sums up the argument.

See
7e3

9d Writing and Revising an Argumentative Essay

(1) Writing an Argumentative Essay

The following student essay includes many of the elements discussed in this chapter. The writer, Samantha Masterton, was asked to write an argumentative essay on a topic of her choice, drawing her supporting evidence from her own knowledge and experience as well as from other sources.

Masterton 1

Samantha Masterton

Professor Egler

English 102

4 April 2005

   The Returning Student: Older Is Definitely Better

Introduction
         After graduating from high school, young people must decide what they want to do with the rest of their lives. Many graduates (often without much thought) decide to continue their education uninterrupted, and they go on to college. This group of teenagers makes up what many see as typical first-year college students. Recently, however, this stereotype has been challenged by an influx of older students, including myself, into American colleges and universities. Not only do these students make a valuable contribution to the schools they attend, but they also offer an alternative to young people who go to college simply because they do not know what else to do. A few years off between high school and

Thesis statement
college can give many—perhaps most—students the life experience they need to appreciate the value of higher education and gain more from it.

Background
         The college experience of an eighteen-year-old is quite different from that of an older

Masterton 2

"nontraditional" student. The typical high school graduate is often concerned with things other than cracking books—for example, going to parties, dating, and testing personal limits. However, older students—those who are twenty-five years of age or older—take seriously the idea of returning to college. Although many high school students do not think twice about whether or not to attend college, older students have much more to consider when they think about returning to college. For example, they must decide how much time they can spend getting their degree and consider the impact attending college will have on their families and on their finances.

In the United States, the demographics of college students is changing. According to a 2002 US Department of Education report titled <u>Nontraditional Undergraduates</u>, the percentage of students who could be classified as "nontraditional" has increased over the last decade (see fig. 1). Thus, in spite of the challenges that older students face when they return to school, more and more are choosing to make the effort.

Most older students return to school with well-defined goals. The US Department of Education's <u>Nontraditional Undergraduates</u> report shows that more than one-third of nontraditional students decided to attend college because it was required by their job, and 87 percent enrolled in order to gain skills (10). Getting a college degree is often a requirement for professional advancement, and older students are therefore more likely to take college seriously. In

Background (continued)

Argument in support of thesis

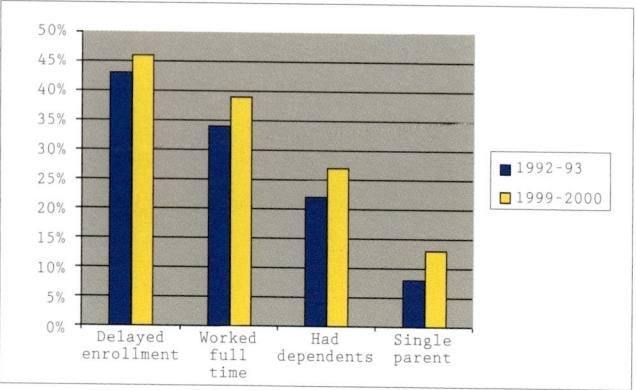

Graph supporting assertion that number of nontraditional students is increasing

Fig. 1. United States, Dept. of Educ., Office of Educ. Research and Improvement, Natl. Center for Educ. Statistics, <u>Nontraditional Undergraduates</u>, NCES 2002-012 (Washington: US Dept. of Educ., 2002) 27 Feb. 2005 <http://nces.ed.gov/pubs2002/2002012.pdf>.

general, older students enroll in college with a definite course of study in mind. For older students, college is an extension of work rather than a place to discover what they want to be when they graduate. A 2001 study by psychologists Eric R. Landrum, Je Taime Hood, and Jerry M. McAdams concluded, "Nontraditional students seemed to be more appreciative of their opportunities, as indicated by their higher enjoyment of school and appreciation of professors' efforts in the classroom" (744). Clearly defining their goals enables older students to take advantage of the opportunities presented by professors as well as to make use of career offices and other services colleges provide.

Older students also understand the actual benefits of doing well in school and successfully

Masterton 4

completing a degree program. Older students I have
known rarely cut lectures or put off studying. This
is because older students are often balancing the   Argument
demands of home and work, and they know how important
it is to do well. The difficulties of juggling
school, family, and work compel older students to be
disciplined and focused—especially concerning their
schoolwork. This pays off; older students tend to
devote more hours per week to studying and tend to
have higher grade point averages than younger
students do (Landrum, Hood, and McAdams 742-43).

My observations of older students have convinced
me that many students would benefit from delaying
entry into college. Given their greater maturity and
experience, older students bring more into the
classroom than younger students do. Eighteen-year-olds   Personal
are immature and inexperienced. They cannot be   experience
used as
expected to have formulated definite goals or   evidence in
developed firm ideas about themselves or about the   support of
thesis
world in which they live. In contrast, older students
have generally had a variety of real-life experiences.
Most have worked for several years, and many have
started families. Their years in the "real world" have
helped them become more focused and more responsible
than they were when they graduated from high school.
As a result, they are better prepared for college than
they would have been when they were young.

Of course, postponing college for a few years is
not for everyone. Certainly some teenagers have a
definite sense of purpose and maturity well beyond
their years, and these individuals would benefit from   Refutation
of opposing
an early college experience, so that they can get a   argument

Masterton 5

head start on their careers. Charles Woodward, a law librarian, went to college directly after high school, and for him the experience was positive. "I was serious about learning, and I loved my subject," he said. "I felt fortunate that I knew what I wanted from college and from life." Many younger students, however, are not like Woodward; they graduate from high school without any clear sense of purpose. For this reason, it makes sense for them to postpone college until they are mature enough to benefit from the experience.

Refutation of opposing argument

Granted, some older students have difficulties when they return to college. Because these students have been out of school so long, they may have difficulty studying and adapting to the routines of academic life. As I have seen, though, these problems disappear after an initial period of adjustment, and older students quickly adapt to college. Of course, it is true that many older students find it difficult to balance the needs of their family with college and to cope with the financial burden of tuition. However, this challenge is becoming easier with the growing number of online courses and the introduction of governmental programs, such as educational tax credits, to ease the financial burden of returning to school (Agbo 164-65).

Conclusion

All things considered, higher education is often wasted on the young, who are either too immature or too unfocused to take advantage of it. Taking a few years off between high school and college would give these students the time they need to make the most of a college education. The increasing number of older students returning to college seems to indicate that many students are taking this path. According to a US

Masterton 6

Department of Education report, <u>Digest of Education Statistics, 2001</u>, 40 percent of students enrolled in American colleges in 2000 were twenty-five years of age or older. Older students such as these have taken time off to serve in the military, to gain valuable work experience, or to raise a family. By the time they get to college, they have defined their goals and made a commitment to achieve them.

Masterton 7

Works Cited

Agbo, S. "The United States: Heterogeneity of the Student Body and the Meaning of 'Nontraditional' in U.S. Higher Education." <u>Higher Education and Lifelong Learners: International Perspectives on Change</u>. Eds. Hans G. Schuetze and Maria Slowey. London: Routledge, 2000. 149-69.

Landrum, R. Eric, Je Taime Hood, and Jerry M. McAdams. "Satisfaction with College by Traditional and Nontraditional College Students." <u>Psychological Reports</u> 89 (2001): 740-46.

United States. Dept. of Educ. Office of Educ. Research and Improvement. Natl. Center for Educ. Statistics. <u>Digest of Education Statistics</u>, 2001. Washington: US Dept. of Educ., 2001. 27 Feb. 2005 <http://nces.ed.gov/pubs2002/digest2001/tables/dt174.asp>.

---. ---. <u>Nontraditional Undergraduates</u>, NCES 2002-012. Washington: US Dept. of Educ., 2002. 27 Feb. 2005 <http://nces.ed.gov/pubs2002/2002012.pdf>.

Woodward, Charles B. Personal interview. 21 Mar. 2005.

Works-cited list begins new page

Two sets of unspaced hyphens indicate that both "United States" and "Dept. of Educ." are repeated from previous entry

(2) Revising an Argumentative Essay

See
6c

When you <u>revise</u> your argumentative essay, you use the same strategies you use for any essay. In addition, you concentrate on some specific concerns, which are listed in the following checklist.

Checklist: Argumentative Essays

☐ Is your topic debatable?
☐ Does your essay have an argumentative thesis?
☐ Have you defined the key terms you use in your argument?
☐ Have you considered the opinions, attitudes, and values of your
  audience?
☐ Have you summarized and refuted opposing arguments?
☐ Have you supported your assertions with evidence?
☐ Have you used relevant visuals to strengthen your argument?
☐ Have you documented all information that is not your own?
☐ Have you established your credibility?
☐ Have you been fair?
☐ Have you avoided logical fallacies?
☐ Have you constructed your argumentative essay logically?
☐ Have you provided your readers with enough background
  information?
☐ Have you presented your points clearly and organized them
  logically?
☐ Have you written an interesting introduction and a strong
  conclusion?

Close-up: Using Transitions in Argumentative Essays

  Argumentative essays should include transitional words and
phrases to indicate which paragraphs are arguments in support of the
thesis, which are refutations of arguments that oppose the thesis, and
which are conclusions.

Arguments in support of thesis	accordingly, because, for example, for instance, in general, given, generally, since
Refutations	although, admittedly, certainly, despite, granted, in all fairness, naturally, nonetheless, of course
Conclusions	all things considered, as a result, in conclusion, in summary, therefore, thus

CHAPTER 10

Using Visuals in Argumentative Essays

10a Using Visuals

Visuals can add a persuasive dimension to your argumentative essays. Because visual images can have such an immediate impact, they can make a good argumentative essay even more persuasive.

See
6b3,
24d

In a sense, visuals are another type of evidence that can support your thesis statement. For example, the addition of a photograph of a roadway work zone choked with traffic (Figure 10.1) could help support your assertion that your township should provide more effective work zone strategies to reduce congestion. In addition, a graph or chart could easily establish the fact that traffic congestion has gotten considerably worse over the past twenty years (Figure 10.2).

Figure 10.1 Traffic jam in a roadway work zone.

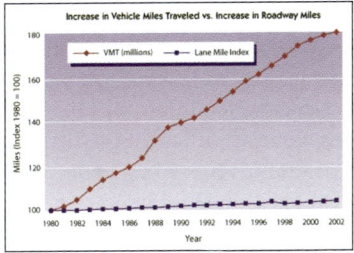

Figure 10.2 Chart showing the increase in vehicle miles traveled versus the increase in roadway miles from 1980 to 2002.

To persuade readers, visuals rely on elements such as images, written text, white space, and color. Consider, for example, the editorial cartoon in Figure 10.3 on page 100. This cartoon was drawn in response to a United States Supreme Court ruling that upheld the Children's Internet Protection Act, which mandated filters on all Internet computers in public libraries. The goal of this law was to prevent children from accessing sexually explicit material online. This cartoon criticizes the Supreme Court's ruling. The two figures (one a child and the other an adult) that dominate the cartoon are staring intently at a computer screen. The use of written text in the cartoon is limited to the labels "Supreme Court" and "Public Library." Thus, with just a few words, this visual forcefully makes the cartoonist's

Figure 10.3 Cartoon from the *Honolulu Advertiser*.

point: that Americans—even minors—do not need the Supreme Court looking over their shoulders and deciding what information they can access in the library. If you were writing an argument that took the same position as this cartoon, it could certainly help you make your point.

Remember, visuals should not be used simply for decoration or to break up the text of your paper. To be effective, they must be useful to your discussion. Irrelevant or inappropriate visuals will not only distract readers but also confuse them. Moreover, visuals that seem misleading or unfair will damage your credibility, thereby undercutting your argument. For this reason, when you select visuals, it is important to remember your purpose and audience and the tone you wish to establish. Just as you would with any other evidence in an argumentative essay, you should **evaluate visuals** to make sure that they are not taken out of context and that they do not make their points unfairly.

See
10b

Checklist: Selecting Visuals

☐ Does the visual clearly support your argument?
☐ In what way do the various elements of the visual reinforce your point?
☐ What point does the visual make?
☐ Is the visual aimed at a particular type of audience?
☐ Could the visual confuse or distract your readers in any way?
☐ Could the visual seem unfair to readers?

10b Evaluating Visuals

FAQs   Just as you have to think critically about the ideas you read, you also have to think critically about the visuals that accompany these texts. Whether they are photographs, advertisements, or statistical charts and graphs, visuals are often designed to influence readers—for example, to encourage them to support a cause or to buy a product. And, like other kinds of evidence, visuals can also distort or misrepresent facts and mislead readers.

(1) Misleading Photographs

Figure 10.4 Elvis sighting.

Almost all photographs that appear in print have been altered in some way. The most common changes involve **cropping** a picture to eliminate distracting background objects, **re-coloring** a background to emphasize subjects in the foreground, and **altering the brightness and contrast** of an image to enhance its overall quality. There is a difference, however, between adjusting an image to make it clearer or more appealing and altering an image for the purpose of misrepresenting facts—for example, in advertisements that show "dramatic" before-and-after weight loss results and in pictures "proving" Elvis is still alive (see Figure 10.4). People usually recognize such photographs for what they are—visual fakes—and do not take them seriously.

Problems arise, however, when an overly zealous editor, reporter, or photographer alters a serious news photograph in order to support a particular point of view or when a scientist alters a photograph to misrepresent data. For example, most people would agree that cropping a photograph of a battle so that it fits within the boundaries of a two-column newspaper article is acceptable. However, cropping the photograph to eliminate wounded civilians on one side of the image—especially when this tactic is used to make a case for or against a war—is more than just misleading; it is dishonest. The same holds true for researchers who write a report in which they include pictures that have been altered to support their conclusions.

Another questionable tactic is the use of **staged photographs,** visual images that purport to be spontaneous when they are actually posed. Even the hint of staging can discredit a visual image. One of the most famous examples of this concerns the flag-raising photograph at the battle of Iwo Jima during World War II (see Figure 10.5 on page 102). Photographer Joe Rosenthal's Pulitzer Prize–winning image is perhaps the most famous war photograph ever taken. When it appeared in newspapers on February 25, 1945, it immediately captured the attention of the American public, so much so that it became the model for the Marine Corps monument in Washington, DC.

Almost immediately, however, people began to question whether or not the photograph was staged. Rosenthal did not help matters when he seemed to admit to a correspondent that it was. Later, however, he said that he had been referring to a posed shot he took the same day (see Figure 10.6), not the famous flag-raising picture. Historians now agree that the flag-raising picture was not staged, but this charge haunted Rosenthal his entire life and is still repeated by some as if it were fact.

Figure 10.5 Soldiers raise a flag at the battle of Iwo Jima, February 1945.

Figure 10.6 Soldiers pose before the camera at Iwo Jima, February 1945.

http://kirsznermandell.wadsworth.com

Computer Tip: Altering Images

With the advent of desktop digital imaging programs, altering images is no longer something only professionals can do. Programs such as *Adobe Photoshop*® give users access to a wide range of digital image editing techniques. If you do decide to alter an image, however, be careful not to distort or misrepresent it.

(2) Misleading Charts and Graphs

Charts and graphs are effective tools for showing relationships among statistical data in science, business, and other disciplines, where they are often used as supporting evidence. However, charts can skew results and mislead readers when their components (titles, labels, and so on) are manipulated—for example, to show just partial or mislabeled data. Whenever you encounter a chart or graph in a document, be sure to examine it carefully to be certain that visual information is labeled clearly and accurately and that data increments are large enough to be significant.

Consider, for example, the potentially misleading nature of the two salary charts on the facing page. At first glance, it appears as if the salaries in the "Salaries Up!" chart (Figure 10.7) rose dramatically and those in the "Salaries Stable!" chart (Figure 10.8) remained almost the same. A closer analysis of the two charts, however, reveals that the salaries in the two charts are nearly identical across the six-year period. The data on the two charts seem to differ so dramatically because of the way each chart displays salary increases: in the first chart, salary increases are given in $500 increments; in the second chart, salary increases are given in $5,000 increments. For this reason, a $1,000 increase on the first chart registers quite visibly, whereas on the second chart it hardly shows at all.

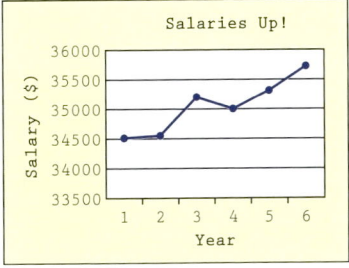

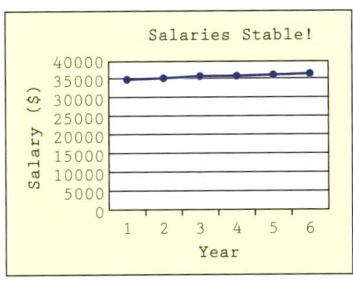

Figure 10.7 Salary chart 1 from the *CPIT Maths2Go* **online tutorial.**

Figure 10.8 Salary chart 2 from the *CPIT Maths2Go* **online tutorial.**

CHAPTER 11

Writing Electronic Arguments

In email, discussion boards, newsgroups, computerized classroom environments, **blogs** and chat rooms, electronic arguments occur daily on a wide variety of topics. Because of the nature of Internet-based communication, these arguments are somewhat different from standard print arguments. In order to write an effective argument for an online audience, you should be aware of the demands of writing in an electronic environment.

NOTE: For a glossary of common computer and Internet terms, go to http://kirsznermandell.wadsworth.com ▶ *The Brief Wadsworth Handbook* ▶ Book Resources ▶ Glossary of Computer and Internet Terms.

11a Considering Audience and Purpose

The most obvious difference between electronic arguments and print arguments is the nature of the **audience.** Audiences for print arguments are relatively passive: they read an argument from beginning to end, form their own ideas about it, and then stop. Depending on the writing situation, however, audiences for electronic arguments can respond differently. In some cases, readers may be passive; in other cases, they can be quite active, posting responses in chat rooms and directly communicating with the writer (sometimes in real time) as well as with one another.

The **purpose** of electronic arguments is also quite different from that of print arguments. Unlike print arguments, which appear as carefully crafted finished products in newspapers and magazines, electronic arguments are frequently written in immediate response to other people's arguments or ideas. In fact, by including links to a writer's email address or to a chat room, many online arguments encourage readers to respond. For this reason, in addition to trying to convince, the purpose of electronic arguments may also be to respond, refute, react, clarify, or instruct.

11b Shaping Electronic Arguments

Because of the dynamic environment of the Internet, electronic arguments are often brief and relatively informal. Much like a con-

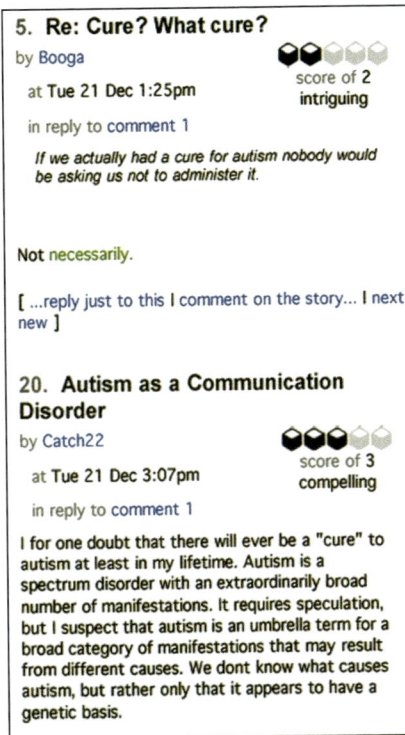

5. Re: Cure? What cure?

by Booga

at Tue 21 Dec 1:25pm

score of 2
intriguing

in reply to comment 1

If we actually had a cure for autism nobody would be asking us not to administer it.

Not necessarily.

[...reply just to this | comment on the story... | next new]

20. Autism as a Communication Disorder

by Catch22

score of 3
compelling

at Tue 21 Dec 3:07pm

in reply to comment 1

I for one doubt that there will ever be a "cure" to autism at least in my lifetime. Autism is a spectrum disorder with an extraordinarily broad number of manifestations. It requires speculation, but I suspect that autism is an umbrella term for a broad category of manifestations that may result from different causes. We dont know what causes autism, but rather only that it appears to have a genetic basis.

Figure 11.1 Plastic.com blog postings.

versation, these arguments frequently begin by making a single point, which they then develop over time as the situation warrants (see Figure 11.1). In order to follow an argument, a reader often has to scroll through page after page of online postings. In this sense, these electronic arguments are more like works in progress than finished products.

Even when electronic arguments physically resemble print arguments (as they do in online journal articles and in newsgroup postings), the way they present information may be different from the way print arguments do. Print arguments are **linear;** that is, readers move in a straight line from the beginning of an argument to the end. Also, in order to be effective, a print argument must be self-contained. It must include all the background information, explanations, supporting evidence, and visuals necessary to make its point. Electronic arguments, however, may not be linear. They often contain **hyperlinks** (design elements or highlighted text that readers can click to access other Web sites) as well as graphics, sound, and video. Because writers of electronic arguments (such as the one shown in Figure 11.2 on page 106) rely on hyperlinks to supplement their discussions, an electronic argument will often address just the main points of an argument. Links then encourage readers to go to other sites that include the facts, statistical data, and even other articles that supplement the discussion. When readers access these sites, they can take in as much or as little information as they want or need. For example, readers of the electronic argument about gun control pictured in Figure 11.2 could link to FBI data about the connection between "concealed carry laws" and violent crime. Once they access this material, they can choose to carefully analyze it, skim it, or ignore it completely.

Link to related book

Links to related articles

Request for email comments

Link to related Web page

Link to FBI data

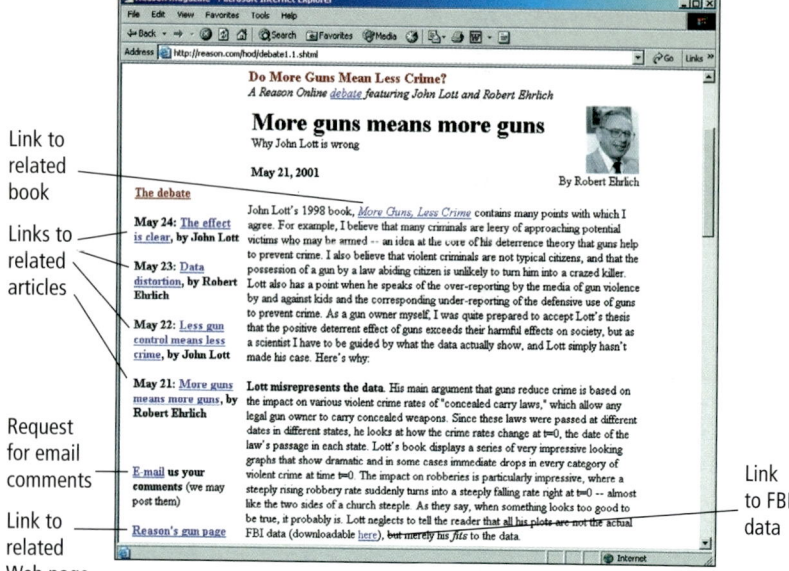

Figure 11.2 Excerpt from "Do More Guns Mean Less Crime? A *Reason Online* Debate."

Checklist: Writing and Revising Electronic Arguments

If you contribute an argument to a Web site or online discussion group, you should be aware of the advantages and challenges of writing in an electronic environment.

☐ Don't overload readers with excess information.

☐ Provide links to Web sites, film clips, articles, and so on.

☐ If a debate is taking place through email, discussion groups, or chat rooms, consider the positions that have been presented.

☐ Consider posting two versions of your argument: a condensed Web-based version for online reading and a longer word-processed version that can be downloaded and read in print form.

☐ Before posting an argument to a discussion group, read through the group's list of Frequently Asked Questions (FAQs) to make sure that you do not inadvertently violate any posting guidelines and damage your credibility with the group.

☐ Use a balanced, reasonable tone rather than one that is dismissive or potentially insulting.

☐ Consider how color, typeface, type size, visuals, and overall design can make your argument clearer.

☐ Consider whether to present any information in the form of tables, charts, or graphs.

☐ Edit and proofread carefully.

PART 3

Doing Research

Doing Research
109–174

PART 3

Doing Research

CHAPTER 12

Writing a Research Paper

Research is the systematic investigation of a topic outside your own knowledge and experience. However, doing research means more than just reading other people's ideas. When you undertake a research project, you become involved in a process that requires you to **think critically**: to evaluate and interpret the ideas explored in your sources and to develop ideas of your own. Your research will be most efficient if you follow a systematic process such as the one outlined below.

See Ch. 8

The Research Process

Activity	Date Due	Date Completed
Move from an Assignment to a Topic, **12a**	_____	_____
Do Exploratory Research and Formulate a Research Question, **12b**	_____	_____
Assemble a Working Bibliography, **12c**	_____	_____
Develop a Tentative Thesis, **12d**	_____	_____
Do Focused Research, **12e**	_____	_____
Take Notes, **12f**	_____	_____
Fine-Tune Your Thesis, **12g**	_____	_____
Outline Your Paper, **12h**	_____	_____
Draft Your Paper, **12i**	_____	_____
Revise Your Paper, **12j**	_____	_____
Prepare Your Final Draft, **12k**	_____	_____

FAQs

12a Moving from Assignment to Topic

(1) Understanding Your Assignment

Every research paper begins with an assignment. Before you can find a direction for your research, you must be sure you understand the exact requirements of this assignment.

Checklist: Understanding Your Assignment

- ☐ When is the completed research paper due?
- ☐ About how long should it be?
- ☐ Will you be given a specific research schedule to follow, or can you set your own schedule?
- ☐ Is your purpose to explain, to persuade, or to do something else?
- ☐ Is your audience your instructor? Your fellow students? Both? Someone else?
- ☐ Is collaborative work permitted? Is it encouraged? If so, at what stages of the research process?
- ☐ Does your instructor expect you to keep your notes on note cards? In a computer file?
- ☐ Does your instructor expect you to prepare a formal outline?
- ☐ Are instructor–student conferences required?
- ☐ Will your instructor review notes, outlines, or drafts with you at regular intervals?
- ☐ Does your instructor require you to keep a research notebook?
- ☐ What manuscript guidelines and documentation style are you expected to follow?
- ☐ What help is available to you—from your instructor, other students, experts on your topic, community resources, your library staff?

In Chapters 4–6 of this text, you followed the writing process of Kimberly Romney as she planned, drafted and revised a short essay for her first-semester composition course. In her second-semester composition class, Kimberly was given the following assignment:

> Write a ten- to fifteen-page research paper that takes a position on any issue related to the Internet. Keep a research notebook that traces your progress.

Throughout this chapter, you will see examples of the work Kimberly did as she completed this assignment.

(2) Choosing a Topic

Once you understand the requirements and scope of your assignment, you need to decide on a topic. In many cases, your instructor will help you choose a topic, either by providing a list of suitable topics or by suggesting a general subject area—for example, a famous trial, an event that happened on the day you were born, a problem on college campuses. Keep in mind, though, that you will still need to narrow your topic to one you can write about: one trial, one event, one problem.

If your instructor prefers that you select a topic on your own, you should consider several possible topics and weigh both their suitability for research and your interest in them. You decide on a topic for your research paper in much the same way you decide on a topic for a short essay: you read, brainstorm, talk to people, and ask questions. Specifically, you talk to friends and family, coworkers, and perhaps your instructor; read magazines and newspapers; take stock of your interests; consider possible topics suggested by your other courses (historical events, scientific developments, and so on); and, of course, browse the Internet. (Your search engine's subject guides can be particularly helpful to you as you look for a promising topic for your research or try to narrow a broad subject area.)

See 14a2

Checklist: Choosing a Research Topic

As you look for a suitable research topic, keep the following guidelines in mind:

- ☐ **Are you genuinely interested in your research topic?**
- ☐ **Is your topic suitable for research?** Topics limited to your personal experience and those based on value judgments are not suitable for research.
- ☐ **Are the boundaries of your research topic appropriate?** A research topic should be neither too broad nor too narrow for your page (and time) limit.

---

(3) Starting a Research Notebook

Keeping a **research notebook,** a combination journal of your reactions and log of your progress, is an important part of the research process. A research notebook maps out your direction and keeps you on track; throughout the research process, it helps you define and redefine the boundaries of your assignment.

In this research notebook, you can record lists of things to do, sources to check, leads to follow up on, appointments, possible community contacts, questions to which you would like to find answers, stray ideas, possible thesis statements or titles, and so on. (Be sure to date your entries and to check off and date work completed.)

Here is an example of an entry from Kimberly's research notebook in which she discusses how she chose a topic for her research paper.

Excerpt from Research Notebook

Last semester, I wrote a personal essay about my
difficulties using computers and the Internet when I arrived

at college. In class, we'd read an essay by Henry Louis
Gates Jr. that confirmed what I thought: not everyone
feels comfortable using computers and the Internet. Gates
says that the Internet threatens to create two societies,
one that is tapped into the digital economy and one that is
not, and he refers to this problem as the "digital divide."
For this paper, I'd like to expand the paper I wrote for my
first-semester composition course and talk more broadly
about the digital divide. I asked my comp professor if I
could, and she gave me permission. (I'll check with
Professor Wilson too.)

12b Doing Exploratory Research and Formulating a Research Question

During **exploratory research,** you develop an overview of your
topic, searching the Internet and looking through general reference
works such as encyclopedias, bibliographies, and specialized dictionaries (either in print or online). Your goal at this stage is to formulate a **research question** that you want your research paper to answer. A research question helps you to decide which sources to seek
out, which to examine first, which to examine in depth, and which to
skip entirely. (The answer to your research question will be your paper's **thesis statement**.)

See
12d

After doing some exploratory research using *Google*—as well as *Info-
Trac College Edition*, a database her library subscribed to (see Figures
12.1 and 12.2)—Kimberly decided on the following research question:
Do all Americans have equal access to the Internet?

12c Assembling a Working Bibliography

During your exploratory research, you begin to assemble a **working
bibliography** for your paper. (This working bibliography will be the
basis for your **works-cited list**, which will include all the sources
you cite in your paper.)

See
17a2

FAQs
links

As you consider each potential source, record full and accurate
bibliographic information in a separate computer file designated
"Bibliography" (or, if you prefer, on individual index cards). Keep
records of interviews (including telephone and email interviews),
meetings, lectures, films, and electronic sources as well as books

Figure 12.1 *Google* search engine.

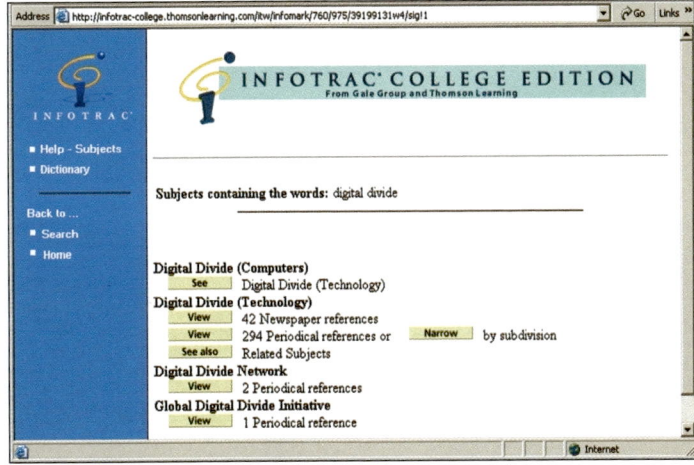

Figure 12.2 *InfoTrac College Edition.*

and articles. For each source, include not only basic identifying details—such as the date of an interview, the call number of a library
book, the URL of an Internet source and the date you downloaded
it, or the author of an article accessed from a database—but also a

brief evaluation that includes comments about the kind of information the source contains, the amount of information offered, its relevance to your topic, and its limitations.

Close-up: Assembling a Working Bibliography

As you record bibliographic information for your sources, include the following information.

Book author(s); title (underlined or in italics); call number (for future reference); city of publication; publisher; date of publication; brief evaluation

Article author(s); title of article (in quotation marks); title of journal (underlined or in italics); volume number; date; inclusive page numbers; URL (if applicable); date downloaded (if applicable); brief evaluation

---

As you go about collecting sources and building your working bibliography, be careful to monitor the quality and relevance of all the materials you examine. Making informed choices early in the research process will save you a lot of time in the long run. For more information on evaluating library sources, **see 13c;** for guidelines on evaluating Internet sources, **see 14c.**

Following are examples of records Kimberly kept for her working bibliography. In the library, she copied her source information on index cards. When she returned to her dorm room, she transferred the information from her cards into a computer file.

Information for Working Bibliography (on Index Card)

Norris, Pippa	—— Author
Digital Divide: Civic Engagement, Information Poverty, and the Internet Worldwide	—— Title
Cambridge: Cambridge UP, 2001	—— Publication information
A book about the digital divide that explains its history and its relationship to economics and class. Published in 2001; may be outdated.	—— Evaluation

Information for Working Bibliography (in Computer File)

Author —	CBS AP
Title —	"Digital Divide Debated"
Publication —	http://www.cbsnews.com/stories/2002/05/30/tech/main510589.shtml
information	May 30, 2002
	Accessed January 2, 2005
Evaluation —	Reports on Bush administration's argument that the digital divide is no longer a significant problem. Cites the findings of the February 2002 Commerce Dept. report.

Close-up: Preparing an Annotated Bibliography

Some instructors require an **annotated bibliography,** a list of all your sources accompanied by a brief summary and evaluation of each source. The following is an excerpt from Kimberly's annotated bibliography.

Young, Jeffrey R. "Does 'Digital Divide' Rhetoric Do More Harm Than Good?" Chronicle of Higher Education 9 Nov. 2001. 10 Jan. 2005 <http://chronicle.com>. This article explains that some scholars feel the focus on the "digital divide" among minorities actually promotes the idea that they are technologically backward. While programs aimed at closing the "digital divide" intend to equalize the technological playing field, the rhetoric used may actually encourage racist stereotypes.

Even though it's several years old, this article made me reconsider my views about programs working to bridge the digital divide. Also, it supports Henry Louis Gates's argument that many minorities are not using the Internet because the content does not appeal to their interests or needs.

12d Developing a Tentative Thesis

Your **tentative thesis** is a preliminary statement of the main point you think your research will support. This statement, which you will eventually refine into your paper's <u>thesis statement</u>, should answer

See 12g

your research question. Kimberly's progress from assignment to tentative thesis is shown below.

Assignment	Topic	Research Question	Tentative Thesis
Issue related to the Internet	Access to the Internet	Do all Americans have equal access to the Internet?	Not all Americans have equal access to the Internet, and this is a potentially serious problem.

Because it suggests the specific direction your research will take as well as the scope and emphasis of your argument, your tentative thesis can help you generate a list of the main points you plan to develop in your paper. This list can help you narrow the focus of your research so you can zero in on a few specific categories to explore as you read and take notes.

Listing Your Points

Tentative Thesis: Not all Americans have equal access to the Internet, and this is a potentially serious problem.
* Give background about the Internet; tell why it's important.
* Identify groups that don't have access to the Internet.
* Explain problems this creates.
* Suggest possible solutions.

12e Doing Focused Research

During exploratory research, you consult general reference works to get an overview of your topic. During **focused research**, however, you consult books, periodical articles, and other sources to find the specific information—facts, examples, statistics, definitions, quotations—you need to support your points. Once you have decided on a tentative thesis and made a list of the points you plan to explore, you are ready to begin your focused research.

(1) Reading Sources

As you look for information, try to explore as many sources as possible. It makes sense to examine more sources than you actually intend to use so you can proceed even if one or more of your sources turns out to be biased, outdated, unreliable, superficial, or irrelevant—in other words, not suitable. You should also explore different viewpoints. After all, if you read only those sources that agree on a particular issue, you will have difficulty understanding the full range of opinion about your topic.

As you explore various sources, quickly evaluate each source's potential usefulness. For example, if your source is a book, skim the table of contents and the index; if your source is a journal article, read the abstract. Then, if an article or a section of a book seems useful, photocopy it for future reference. Similarly, when you find an online source that looks promising, print it out (or send it to yourself as an email attachment) so you can evaluate it further later on. (For information on evaluating print and electronic sources, **see 13c** and **14c**.)

NOTE: Do not paste online source material directly into your paper. This can lead to <u>plagiarism</u>.

See
Ch. 16

See
13b4

(2) Balancing Primary and Secondary Sources

During your focused research, you will encounter both <u>primary sources</u> (original documents and observations) and <u>secondary sources</u> (interpretations of original documents and observations).

For some research projects, primary sources are essential; most research projects, however, rely heavily on secondary sources, which provide scholars' insights and interpretations. Remember, though, that the farther you get from the primary source, the more chances exist for inaccuracies caused by misinterpretations or distortions.

Primary and Secondary Sources	
Primary Source	**Secondary Source**
Novel, poem, play, film	Criticism
Diary, autobiography	Biography
Letter, historical document, speech, oral history	Historical analysis
Newspaper article	Editorial
Raw data from questionnaires or interviews	Social science article; case study
Observation/experiment	Scientific article

12f Taking Notes

As you locate information in the library and on the Internet, take notes (either by hand or on a computer) to create a record of exactly what you found and where you found it.

(1) Recording Source Information

See
Ch. 15
Each piece of information you record in your notes (whether <u>summa-rized</u>, <u>paraphrased</u>, or <u>quoted</u> from your sources) should be accompanied by a short descriptive heading that indicates its relevance to one of the points you will develop in your paper. Because you will use these headings to guide you as you organize your notes, you should make them as specific as possible. For example, labeling every note for a paper on the digital divide `digital divide` or `Internet` will not prove very helpful later on. More focused headings—for instance, `dangers of digital divide` or `government's steps to narrow the gap`—will be much more useful.

Also include brief comments that make clear your reasons for recording the information. These comments (enclosed in brackets so you will know they are your own ideas, not those of your source) should establish the purpose of your note—what you think it can explain, support, clarify, describe, or contradict—and perhaps suggest its relationship to other notes or other sources. Any questions you have about the information or its source can also be included in your comment.

Finally, each note should fully and accurately identify the source of the information you are recording. You do not have to write out the complete citation, but you do have to include enough information to identify your source. For example, `Gates 499` would be enough to send you back to your working bibliography card or file, where you would be able to find the complete documentation for Henry Louis Gates's essay "One Internet, Two Nations." (If you use more than one source by the same author, you need a more complete reference.)

When you take notes, your goal is flexibility: you want to be able to arrange and rearrange information easily and efficiently as your paper takes shape. If you take notes on your computer, type each individual note (accompanied by source information) under a specific heading rather than listing all information from a single source under the same heading, and be sure to divide notes from one another with extra space or horizontal lines. (As you revise, you can move notes around so notes on the same topic are grouped together.)

If you take notes by hand, use the time-tested index-card system, taking care to write on only one side of the card and to use a separate index card for each individual note rather than running several notes together on a single card. (Later, you can enter the information from these notes into your computer file.)

Following are examples of notes that Kimberly kept. For sources that she read in the library, she used index cards to record notes. When she returned to her dorm room, she entered this information into a computer file that she created for this purpose.

Notes (on Index Card)

Short heading   Source

Initiatives questioned   Schwartz, "Lack"

Note —

As a result of the dot.com bust, organizations like PowerUp, which created 1,000 community-based technology centers, have disbanded. According to a PowerUp spokesperson, "The model that was launched in late 1999. . . was a model that had its bloodlines in different economic times. The model isn't necessarily the best one for these economic times."

Comment —

[Is there a new model to replace these organizations?]

Notes (in Computer File)

Short heading — Problems of
digital divide

Source —

Dalton, Knight Ridder/
Tribune, 7/4/04

Note
(quotation) —

"A recent report by the Pew Internet & American Life Project revealed that minorities are slightly more likely than whites to use the Internet at places other than home or work, with 23 percent of blacks and Hispanics using the Internet outside home or work, compared with 19 percent of whites."

Comment —

[Does this mean minorities are less likely to own computers?]

Efforts to close
gap

Dalton, Knight Ridder
Tribune 7/4/04

Note
(paraphrase) —

14 million Americans use the Internet at libraries, and the availability of public-access computers increased library visits by 17 percent between 1996 and 2001.

Comment —

[Are minorities more likely to use library computers to access the Internet?]

(continued)

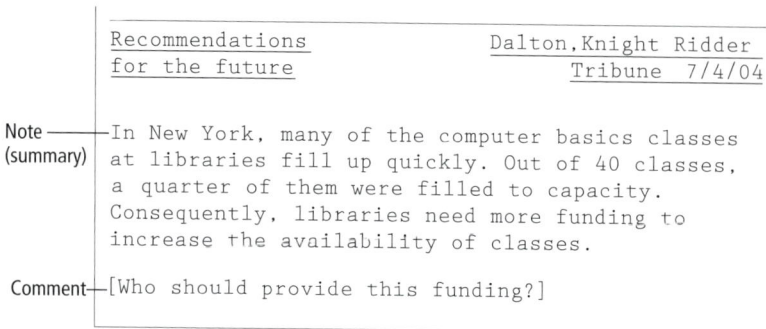

Recommendations
for the future

Dalton,Knight Ridder
Tribune 7/4/04

Note
(summary) — In New York, many of the computer basics classes at libraries fill up quickly. Out of 40 classes, a quarter of them were filled to capacity. Consequently, libraries need more funding to increase the availability of classes.

Comment — [Who should provide this funding?]

http://kirsznermandell.wadsworth.com

Computer Tip: Taking Notes

Note-taking software, such as *WriteNote*, shown below, can make it easy for you to record and organize information, allowing you to create files in which you store notes (quotations, summaries, paraphrases, your own comments), pictures, or tables; to sort and categorize your material; and even to print out the information in order on computerized note cards.

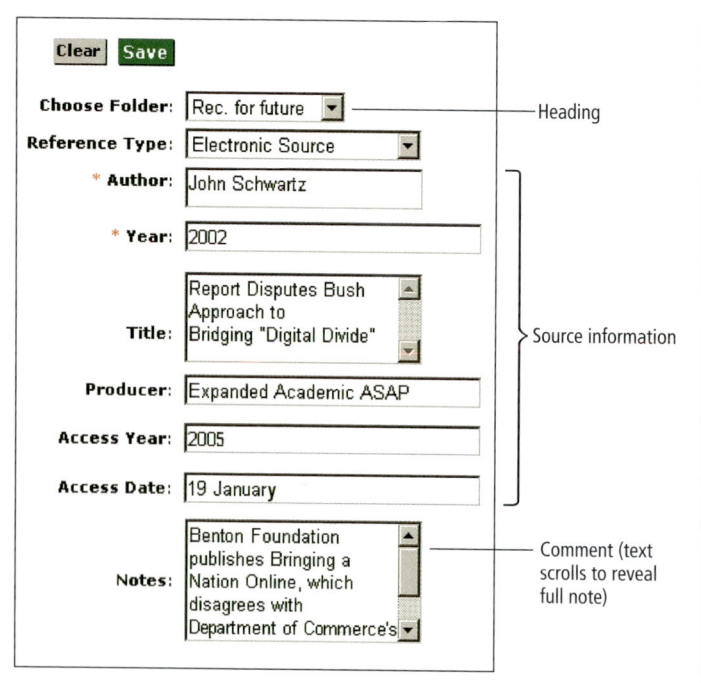

Clear Save

Choose Folder: Rec. for future — Heading

Reference Type: Electronic Source

* Author: John Schwartz

* Year: 2002

Title: Report Disputes Bush Approach to Bridging "Digital Divide"

Producer: Expanded Academic ASAP

Access Year: 2005

Access Date: 19 January

Source information

Notes: Benton Foundation publishes Bringing a Nation Online, which disagrees with Department of Commerce's

Comment (text scrolls to reveal full note)

Checklist: Taking Notes

☐ **Identify the source of each piece of information.**

☐ **Include everything now that you will need later** to understand your note—names, dates, places, connections with other notes—and to remember why you recorded it.

☐ **Distinguish quotations from paraphrases and summaries and your own ideas from those of your sources.** If you copy a source's words, place them in quotation marks. (If you take notes by hand, circle the quotation marks; if you type your notes, put the quotation marks in boldface.) If you write down your own ideas, enclose them in brackets—and, if you are typing, italicize them as well. These techniques will help you avoid accidental plagiarism in your paper.

☐ **Put an author's ideas into your own words whenever possible,** summarizing and paraphrasing material as well as adding your own observations and analyses.

☐ **Copy quoted material accurately,** using the exact words, spelling, punctuation marks, and capitalization.

See Ch. 16

ESL Tip

Taking notes in English (rather than in your native language), will make it easier for you to transfer the notes into a draft of your paper. However, you may find it faster and more effective to use your native language when writing your own comments about each note.

(2) Managing Photocopies and Printouts

Much of the information you gather will be in the form of photocopies (of articles, book pages, and so on) and material downloaded or printed out from the Internet. Learning to manage this source information efficiently will save you a lot of time.

First, be careful not to allow the ease of copying and downloading to encourage you to postpone decisions about the usefulness of your sources. After all, you can easily accumulate so many pages that it will be almost impossible for you to keep track of all your information.

Also keep in mind that making copies of sources is only the first step in the process of taking thorough, careful notes. You still have to evaluate, paraphrase, and summarize your source's ideas and make connections among them.

In addition, photocopies and printouts do not have much flexibility. For example, a single page of text may include information that should be earmarked for several different sections of your paper. This lack of flexibility makes it almost impossible for you to arrange information into any meaningful order.

Remember, you should approach photocopies and material you download or print out just as you approach any other source: as material that you will read, highlight, annotate, and then take notes about.

Close-up: Avoiding Plagiarism

See
Ch. 16

To avoid the possibility of accidental **plagiarism**, be sure to keep all downloaded material in a separate file—not in your Notes file. After you read this material and decide how to use it, you can move the notes you take into your Notes file (along with full source information).

Checklist: Working with Photocopies and Computer Printouts

☐ Record full and accurate source information, including the inclusive page numbers, electronic address (URL), and any other relevant information, on the first page of each copy.

☐ Clip or staple together consecutive pages of a single source.

☐ Do not copy a source without reminding yourself—*in writing*—why you are doing so. In pencil or on removable self-stick notes, record your initial responses to the source's ideas, jot down cross-references to other works or notes, and highlight important sections.

☐ Photocopying can be time-consuming and expensive, so try to avoid copying material that is only marginally relevant to your paper.

☐ Keep photocopies and printouts in a separate file so you will be able to find them when you need them.

12g Fine-Tuning Your Thesis

After you have finished your focused research and note-taking, you should be ready to refine your tentative thesis into a carefully worded statement that expresses a conclusion your research can support. This **thesis statement** should be more precise than your tentative thesis, accurately conveying the direction, emphasis, and scope of your paper.

See
5a–b

Kimberly's tentative thesis and thesis statement are shown on page 123.

Tentative Thesis	Thesis Statement
Not all Americans have equal access to the Internet, and this is a potentially serious problem.	Although the Internet has changed our lives for the better, it threatens to leave many people behind, creating two distinct classes—those who have access and those who do not.

If your thesis statement does not express a conclusion your research can support, you will need to revise it. Reviewing your notes carefully, perhaps grouping information in different ways, may help you decide on a more suitable thesis. Or, you may try other techniques—for instance, using your research question as a starting point for **brainstorming** or **freewriting**.

See 4e3–4

12h Constructing an Outline

Once you have a thesis, you are ready to make an outline to guide you as you write your rough draft.

A formal outline is different from a list of the main points you tentatively plan to develop in your paper. A **formal outline**—which may be either a **topic outline** or a **sentence outline**—includes all the points you will develop. It indicates both the exact order in which you will present your ideas and the relationship between main points and supporting details.

See 6c4

NOTE: The outline you construct at this stage is only a guide for you to follow as you draft your paper. Later on in the writing process, you may want to construct another outline as a revision strategy to help you check the logic of your paper's organization.

Checklist: Constructing a Formal Outline

☐ Write your thesis statement at the top of the page.
☐ Review your notes to make sure each note expresses only one general idea. If this is not the case, recopy any unrelated information, creating a separate note.
☐ Check that the heading for each note specifically characterizes that note's information. If it does not, change the heading.
☐ Sort your notes according to their headings, keeping a miscellaneous file for notes that do not seem to fit into any category. Irrelevant notes, those unrelated to your paper's thesis, should be set aside (but not discarded).
☐ Check your categories for balance. If most of your notes fall into just one or two categories, revise some of your headings to create

(continued)

Constructing a formal outline (continued)

narrower, more focused categories. If you have only one or two notes in a category, you may need to do additional research or treat that topic only briefly (or not at all).

☐ Organize the individual notes within each group, adding more specific subheads to your headings as needed. Arrange your notes in an order that highlights the most important points and subordinates lesser ones.

☐ Decide on a logical order in which to discuss your paper's major points.

☐ Construct your formal outline, using divisions and subdivisions that correspond to your headings.

☐ Review your completed outline to make sure you have not placed too much emphasis on a relatively unimportant idea, ordered ideas illogically, or created sections that overlap with others.

---

http://kirsznermandell.wadsworth.com

Computer Tip: Outlining

Before you begin writing, create a separate file for each major section of your outline. Then, copy your notes into these files in the order in which you intend to use them. You can print out each file as you need it and use it as a guide as you write.

12i Writing a Rough Draft

See 6a When you are ready to write your <u>rough draft</u>, check to be sure you have arranged your notes in the order in which you intend to use them. Follow your outline as you write, using your notes as needed. As you draft, you can write notes to yourself in brackets. In these notes, jot down questions, and identify points that need further clarification and areas that need more development.

As you move along, leave space for material you plan to add, and identify phrases or whole sections that you think you may later decide to move or delete. In other words, lay the groundwork for a major revision.

As your draft takes shape, be sure to supply transitions between sentences and paragraphs to indicate how your points are related. To make it easy for you to revise later on, you might want to triple-space your draft. Be careful to copy source information fully and accurately on this and every subsequent draft, placing the documentation as close as possible to the material it identifies.

Computer Tip: Drafting

You can use a split screen or multiple windows to view your notes as you draft your paper. You can also copy the material that you need from your notes and then insert it into the text of your paper. (As you copy, be especially careful that you do not unintentionally commit **plagiarism**.)

See
16b

(1) Shaping the Parts of the Paper

Like any other essay, a research paper has an introduction, a body, and a conclusion. In your rough draft, as in your outline, you focus on the body of your paper. Don't spend time planning your introduction or conclusion at this stage; your ideas will change as you write, and you will need to revise and expand your opening and closing paragraphs later to reflect those changes.

Introduction In your **introduction**, you identify your topic and establish how you will approach it, perhaps presenting an overview of the problem you will discuss or summarizing research already done on your topic. Your **introduction** also includes your thesis statement, which presents the position you will support in the rest of the paper.

See
7e2

Body As you draft the **body** of your paper, lead readers through your discussion with strong **topic sentences** that correspond to the divisions of your outline.

See
7a1

        In the late 1990s, many argued that the Internet had
    ushered in a new age, one in which instant communication
    would bring people closer together and eventually eliminate
    national boundaries.

You can also use **headings** if they are a convention of the discipline in which you are writing.

See
24b

    Responses to Digital Divide
        In response, the government, corporations, nonprofit
    organizations, and public libraries made efforts to bridge
    the gap between the "haves" and the "have-nots."

Even in your rough draft, carefully worded topic sentences and headings will help you keep your discussion under control.

See 7d

Use different <u>patterns of development</u> to shape the individual sections of your paper, and be sure to connect ideas with clear transitions. If necessary, connect two sections of your paper with a <u>transitional paragraph</u> that shows their relationship.

See 7e1

Conclusion The conclusion of a research paper often restates your thesis. This is especially important in a long paper because by the time your readers get to the end, they may have lost sight of your paper's main idea. Your <u>conclusion</u> can also include a summary of your key points, a call for action, or perhaps an apt quotation. In your rough draft, however, your concluding paragraph is usually very brief.

See 7e3

(2) Integrating Source Material

In the body of your paper, you evaluate and interpret your sources, comparing different ideas and assessing various points of view. As a writer, your job is to draw your own conclusions, blending information from various sources into a paper that coherently and forcefully presents your own original viewpoint to your readers.

See 15d

Be sure to <u>integrate source material</u> smoothly into your paper, clearly and accurately identifying the relationships among various sources (and between those sources' ideas and your own). If two sources present conflicting interpretations, you should be especially careful to use precise language and accurate transitions to make the contrast apparent (for instance, "`Although the Bush administration remains optimistic, some studies suggest . . .`"). When two sources agree, you should make this clear (for example, "`Like Young, McPherson believes . . .`" or "`Department of Commerce statistics confirm Gates's point`"). Such phrasing will provide a context for your own comments and conclusions. If different sources present complementary information about a subject, blend details from the sources carefully, keeping track of which details come from which source.

(3) Integrating Visuals into Your Paper

Photographs, diagrams, graphs, and other <u>visuals</u> can be very useful additions to your research paper because they can provide support for the points you make. You may be able to create a visual on your own (for example, by taking a photograph or creating a bar graph). You may also be able to scan an appropriate visual from a book or magazine or use your browser to access a database that collects images (see Figure 12.3).

Kimberly Rommey searched an image database to find possible visuals to include in her paper.

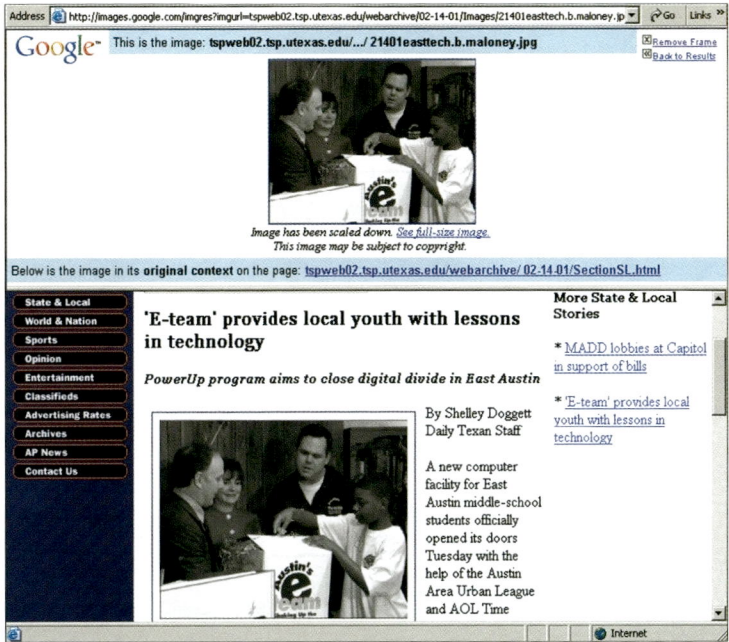

Figure 12.3 *Google* image database.

12j Revising Your Drafts

A good way to begin revising is to make an outline of your draft to
check the logic of its organization and the relationships among sections. The checklists in 6c5 can guide your revisions of your paper's
overall structure and its individual paragraphs, sentences, and words.

As you review your drafts, follow the **revision** procedures that apply to any paper. In addition, focus on the questions in the checklist
on pages 129–30, which apply specifically to research papers.

Of course, you should pay particular attention to your instructor's
revision suggestions, which can come orally (in a conference) or in
handwritten comments on your paper. Alternatively, your instructor
may use *Microsoft Word*'s Comment tool to make comments electronically on your draft. When you revise, you can incorporate these
suggestions, as Kimberly did.

Rough Draft with Instructor's Comments (Excerpt)

The Bill and Melinda Gates Foundation

has provided libraries across the country

with funding that allows them to purchase

Comment [PS1]: You
need a transition sentence
before this one to show
that this paragraph is
about a new idea. See 7b2.

computers and connect to the Internet (Egan). Nonprofit organizations also sponsor Web sites, such as <u>The Digital Divide Network</u>, a site that posts stories about the digital divide from a variety of perspectives. |By posting information on the Web site that they created|, the site's sponsor hopes to raise awareness of the problems that the digital divide causes.

> **Comment [PS2]:** Wordy. See 38a.

Revision Incorporating Instructor's Suggestions

Nonprofit organizations also worked to bridge the digital divide. The Bill and Melinda Gates Foundation, for example, has provided libraries across the country with funding that allows them to purchase computers and connect to the Internet (Egan). Nonprofit organizations also sponsor Web sites, such as <u>The Digital Divide Network</u>, a site that posts stories about the digital divide from a variety of perspectives. By posting information, the site's sponsor hopes to raise awareness of the problems that the digital divide causes.

Feedback you get from **peer review**—other students' comments, handwritten or electronic—can also help you revise. As you incorporate your classmates' suggestions, as well as your own changes and any suggested by your instructor, you can use *Microsoft Word*'s Track Changes tool to help you keep track of the revisions you make on your draft.

Following are two versions of an excerpt from Kimberly's paper. The first version includes comments (inserted with *Microsoft Word*'s Comment tool) from two peer reviewers. The second uses the Track Changes tool to show the revisions Kimberly made in response to these comments.

Rough Draft with Peer Reviewers' Comments (Excerpt)

‖ A recent article| observes that many African-American and other minority groups argue that digital divide rhetoric might actually stereotype minorities. The article says that digital divide rhetoric "could discourage businesses or academics from creating content or services tailored for minority communities—ultimately

> **Comment [TG1]:** You need a transition sentence here!

> **Comment [DL1]:** Ditto, this is really awk.☺

> **Comment [RS1]:** Tell us the name and where this came from.

making the digital divide a self-fulfilling
prophecy." |Many scholars and leaders in the
African-American community fear that a focus on the digital
divide will lead to its being seen as a fact to be accepted
rather than as a problem to be solved.
Tara L. McPherson|says|that "the idea of
challenging the digital divide is not about
denying it's existence. But it is to ensure
that the focus on the digital divide
doesn't naturalize a kind of exclusion of
investment." |

> **Comment [DL2]:** Do you need a p. #?

> **Comment [TG2]:** Use a stronger word—*asserts, claims*, etc. We're not supposed to keep using "says."☺

> **Comment [DL3]:** I think you're supposed to have the author's last name here.

Revision with Track Changes

In other cases, the groups targeted by digital divide
programs argue that they might do more harm than good. A
recent article in the Chronicle of Higher Education observes
that many African-American and other minority groups argue
that digital divide rhetoric might actually stereotype
minorities. The article says that digital divide rhetoric
"could discourage businesses or academics from creating
content or services tailored for minority communities—
ultimately making the digital divide a self-fulfilling
prophecy" (Young). Many scholars and leaders in the African-
American community fear that a focus on the digital divide
will lead to its being seen as a fact to be accepted rather
than as a problem to be solved. Tara L. McPherson agrees,
arguing that "the idea of challenging the digital divide is
not about denying its existence. But it is to ensure that
the focus on the digital divide doesn't naturalize a kind of
exclusion of investment." (qtd. in Young).

Checklist: Revising a Research Paper

☐ Should you do more research to find support for certain points?
☐ Do you need to reorder the major sections of your paper?

(continued)

Revising a research paper (continued)

- ☐ Should you rearrange the order in which you present your points within those sections?
- ☐ Do you need to add section headings? transitional paragraphs?

See 15d

- ☐ Have you **integrated source material** smoothly into your paper?
- ☐ Have you chosen visuals carefully and integrated them smoothly into your paper?
- ☐ Are quotations blended with paraphrase, summary, and your own observations and reactions?

See Ch. 16

- ☐ Have you avoided **plagiarism** by carefully documenting all borrowed ideas?
- ☐ Have you analyzed and interpreted the ideas of others rather than simply stringing those ideas together?
- ☐ Do your own ideas—not those of your sources—define the focus of your discussion?

NOTE: You will probably take your paper through several drafts, changing different parts of it each time or working on one part over and over again. After revising each draft thoroughly, print out a corrected version and make additional corrections by hand on that draft before typing the next version.

http://kirsznermandell.wadsworth.com

Computer Tip: Revising

When you finish revising your paper, copy the file that contains your working bibliography and insert it at the end of your paper. Delete any irrelevant entries, and then create your works-cited list. (Make sure the format of the entries in your works-cited list conforms to the documentation style you are using.)

12k Preparing a Final Draft

See 6d

Before you print out the final version of your paper, **edit and proofread** hard copy of your works-cited list as well as of the paper itself. Next, consider (or reconsider) your paper's **title.** It should be descriptive enough to tell your readers what your paper is about, and it should create interest in your subject. Your title should also be consistent with the **purpose** and tone of your paper. (You would hardly want a humorous title for a paper about the death penalty or world hunger.) Finally, your title should be engaging and to the point—and perhaps even provocative. Often, a quotation from one of your sources will suggest a likely title.

See 1a

When you are satisfied with your title, read your paper through again, proofreading for grammar, spelling, or typing errors you may have missed. Pay particular attention to parenthetical documentation and works-cited entries. (Remember that every error undermines your credibility.) Once you are satisfied that your paper is as accurate as you can make it, print it out one last time. Then, fasten the pages with a paper clip (do not staple the pages or fold the corners together), and hand it in. (For the final draft of Kimberly's research paper, along with her works-cited list, **see 17c.**)

CHAPTER 13

Using and Evaluating Library Sources

See
Ch. 14

A modern, networked college library offers you resources that you cannot find anywhere else—even on the Internet. In the long run, you will save a great deal of time and effort, as well as gain a deeper understanding of your topic, if you begin your research with a survey of the library's print and electronic resources.

Close-up: Advantages of Using the Library

FAQs
links

- Many important and useful publications are available only in print or through the library's subscription databases—and not on the Internet.
- The information in your college library will almost always be more focused and more useful than much of what you will find on the Internet. An Internet search often yields far more information (most of it irrelevant to your topic) than you can reasonably handle or properly evaluate.
- The sites you access on the Internet—unlike the sites in your library's subscription databases—may not be available when you try to access them later on. (For this reason, the Modern Language Association (MLA) recommends that you print out all Internet documents you plan to use in your research.)
- Anyone can publish on the Internet, so sites can vary greatly in quality. Because librarians screen the material in your college library, it will usually meet academic standards of reliability. (Even so, you still

See
14c

have to **evaluate** any information before you use it in a paper.)
- The authorship and affiliation of Internet documents can often be difficult or impossible to determine, but this is not usually the case with the sources in your college library.

13a Doing Exploratory Library Research

During **exploratory research,** your goal is to formulate a **research question**—the question you want your paper to answer. At this stage, you search the library's print and electronic resources to get a general sense of what they contain. (Later, during your **focused re-**

See
13b

search, you will look for specific material to use in your paper.) You can begin this process by searching your college or university library's **online catalog** to see what kind of information is available about your topic. You can then look at general reference works and consult the library's electronic databases.

(1) Using Online Catalogs

Most college and university libraries—and a growing number of regional and community libraries—have abandoned print catalog systems in favor of **online catalogs**—computer databases that list all the books, articles, and other materials held by the library. Figure 13.1 shows the home page of a college library's online catalog.

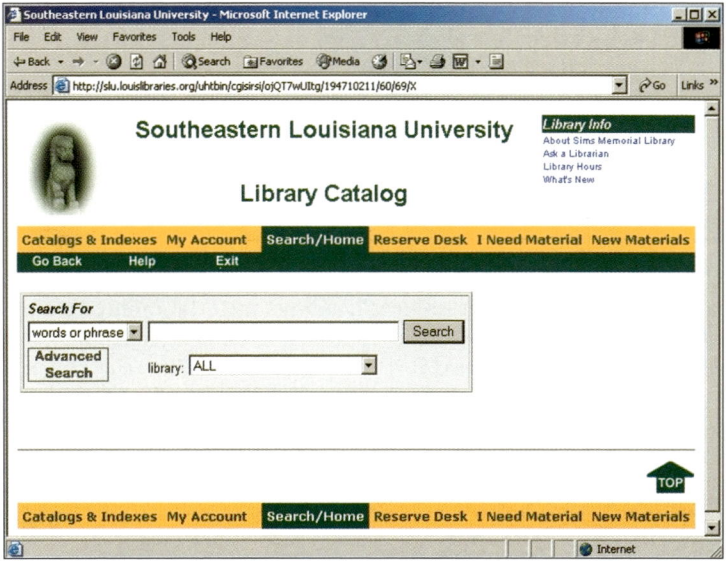

Figure 13.1 Home page of a university library's online catalog.

You access an online catalog (as well as other electronic library resources) by using one of the computer terminals located throughout the library and typing in specific words or phrases that enable you to find the information you need. If you have never used an online catalog, ask your reference librarian for help before you begin.

When you search the online catalog for information about your topic, you may conduct either a *keyword search* or a *subject search*. Later on in the research process, when you know more precisely what you are looking for, you can search for a particular book by entering its title, author, or call number.

Conducting a Keyword Search When you carry out a **keyword search,** you enter into the Search box of the online catalog a word or words associated with your topic. The screen then displays a list of articles that contain those words in their bibliographic citations or abstracts. The more precise your keywords are, the more specific and useful the information you retrieve will be. (Combining keywords

See
14a3

with AND, OR, and NOT allows you to narrow or broaden your search. This technique is called conducting a **Boolean search**.)

Checklist: Keyword Dos and Don'ts

When conducting a keyword search, remember the following hints:

☐ Use precise, specific keywords to distinguish your topic from similar topics.
☐ Enter both singular and plural keywords when appropriate—*printing press* and *printing presses*, for example.
☐ Enter both abbreviations and their full-word equivalents (for example, *US* and *United States*).
☐ Try variant spellings (for example, *color* and *colour*).
☐ Don't use too long a string of keywords. (If you do, you will retrieve large amounts of irrelevant material.)

Conducting a Subject Search When you carry out a **subject search,** you enter specific subject headings into the online catalog. Although it may be possible to guess at a subject heading, your search will be more successful if you consult the *Library of Congress Subject Headings*, held at the reference desk of your library, to help you identify the exact words you need. Figure 13.2 shows the results of a search in an online catalog.

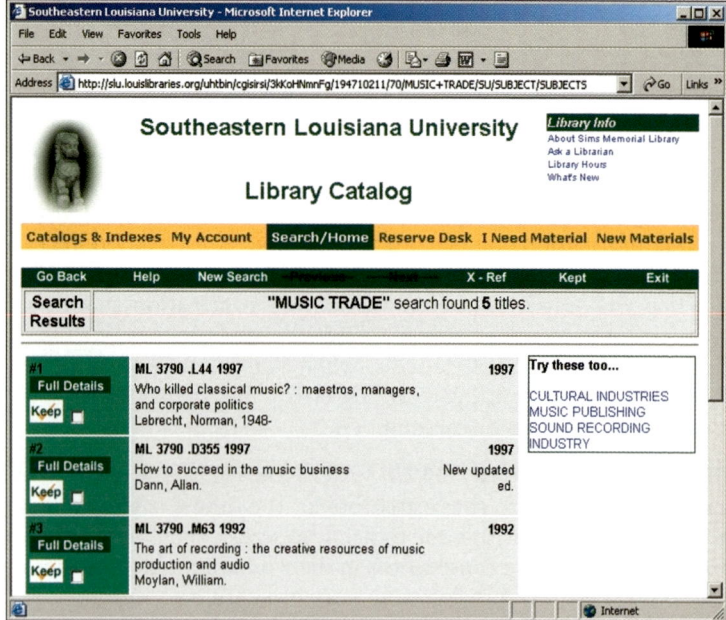

Figure 13.2 Online catalog search results for the subject heading *Music Trade*.

NOTE: Many college and university libraries have Web sites that enable users to access their online catalogs from a dorm room or from any computer connected to the Internet. Ask at your library for the appropriate Web address and password.

Close-up: Keyword Searching versus Subject Searching

Keyword Searching	Subject Searching
• Searches many subject areas	• Searches only a specific subject area
• Any significant word or phrase can be used	• Only the specific words listed in the *Library of Congress Subject Headings* can be used
• Retrieves large number of items	• Retrieves small number of items
• May retrieve many irrelevant items	• Retrieves few irrelevant items

---

(2) Consulting General Reference Works

General reference works—encyclopedias, bibliographies, and so on—which provide broad overviews of particular subjects, can be helpful when you are doing exploratory research. From these sources, you can learn key facts and specific terminology as well as find dates, places, and names. In addition, general reference works often include bibliographies that you can use later on when you do focused research.

NOTE: Articles in general encyclopedias are usually not detailed enough for a college-level research paper. Articles in specialized encyclopedias, dictionaries, and bibliographies, however, are more likely to be appropriate for your research.

Close-up: General Reference Works

General Encyclopedias Many general multivolume encyclopedias are available in electronic format. For example, *The New Encyclopaedia Britannica* is available on CD-ROM and DVD as well as on the World Wide Web at <http://www.britannica.com>.

Specialized Encyclopedias, Dictionaries, and Bibliographies These specialized reference works contain in-depth articles focusing on a single subject area.

General Bibliographies General bibliographies—such as *Books in Print* and *The Bibliographic Index*—list books available in a wide variety of fields.

General Biographical References Biographical reference books—such as *Who's Who in America*, *Who's Who*, and *Dictionary of American Biography*—provide information about people's lives as well as bibliographic listings.

(3) Using Library Databases

The same computer terminals that enable you to access the online catalog also enable you to access a variety of other databases.

Online databases are collections of digital information—citations
of books, reports, and journal, magazine, and newspaper articles (and
sometimes the full text of articles)—arranged for easy access and retrieval by computer. Different libraries offer different databases and
make them available in different ways. Many libraries have implemented Web-based systems that give users remote access to databases (and
online catalogs) beyond the library's walls. Some libraries may have
databases on CD-ROM or DVD, but most subscribe to information
service companies, such as DIALOG or Gale, that provide online access
to hundreds of databases. One of your first tasks should be to determine
what subscription databases your library offers. Visit your library's Web
site, or ask a reference librarian for more information. Figure 13.3
shows a partial list of databases to which one college library subscribes.

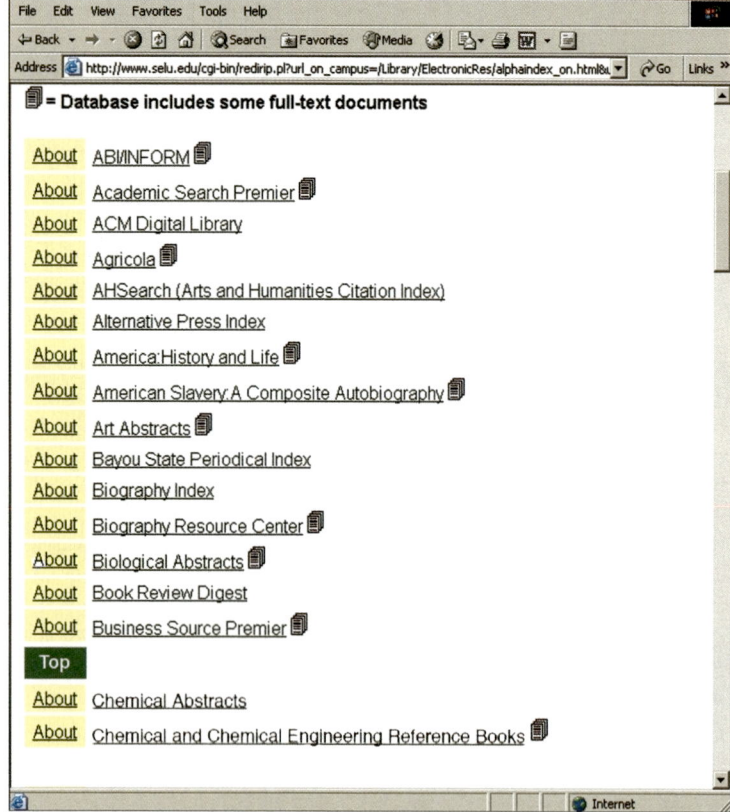

Figure 13.3 Partial list of databases to which one college library subscribes.

General and Specialized Subscription Databases The databases in your college library are likely to be **subscription databases**. This means that the library must subscribe to them in order to make them available to students and faculty. Licensing and copyright agreements restrict the use of these subscription databases; they are not available from outside the library to those who are not affiliated with the school.

Some library databases cover many subject areas (*Expanded Academic ASAP* or *LexisNexis Academic Universe*, for example); others cover just one subject area in great detail (*PsycINFO* or *Sociological Abstracts*, for example). Assuming that your library offers a variety of databases (some libraries subscribe to hundreds), how do you know which ones will be best for your research topic? One strategy is to begin by searching a general database that includes full-text articles and then move on to a more specialized database that covers your subject in more detail. The specialized databases are more likely to include scholarly and professional sources, but they are also less likely to include the full text. They will, however, include **abstracts** (short summaries) that can help you determine the usefulness of a source. If you are in doubt about which databases would be most useful to you, ask a librarian for suggestions. (Figure 13.4 shows a printout from a library subscription database.)

Date   Volume   Issue number   First page of article   Total number of pages

Title: The Supply Side of the Digital Divide: Is There Equal Availability in the Broadband Internet Access Market?

Periodical: *Economic Inquiry,* April 2003 v41 i2 p346(18).

Author: James E. Prieger

Author's Abstract: The newest dimension of the digital divide is access to broadband (high-speed) Internet service. Using comprehensive US data covering all forms of access technology (chiefly DSL and cable modem), I look for evidence of unequal broadband availability in areas with high concentrations of poor, minority, or rural households. There is little evidence of unequal availability based on income or on black or Hispanic concentration. There is mixed evidence concerning availability based on Native American or Asian concentration. Other findings: Rural location decreases availability; market size, education, Spanish language use, commuting distance, and Bell presence increase availability. (JEL L96, J78, L51)

Subjects: Digital Divide (Technology) = Demographic Aspects

Internet = Usage

Features: tables; figures

Figure 13.4 Library subscription database printout.

Searching Databases There are two ways to search library databases for information on a topic: by subject headings and by keyword(s). When you search by **subject headings,** you choose a heading from a list of terms recognized by that database. Sometimes it is easy to choose a subject heading, but sometimes it is harder to choose an appropriate term. For example, what do you call older people? Are they senior citizens? elderly? the aged? (Some databases provide a print or online thesaurus to help you choose subject headings.)

The other option is **keyword searching,** which allows you to type in any significant term likely to be found in the title, subject headings, abstract, or (if the full text is available) text of an article. Keyword searching also allows you to link terms using **boolean operators** (AND, OR, NOT). For example, *elderly* AND *abuse* would identify only articles that mention both elderly people and abuse; *elderly* OR *aged* OR *senior citizens* would identify articles that mention any of these terms. Keyword searching is particularly helpful when you need to narrow or expand the focus of your search.

Both subject heading and keyword searches are useful ways to find information on your topic. The most important thing is to be persistent. One good source often leads to another: abstracts and text may suggest other terms you can use, and references and footnotes may suggest additional sources.

13b Doing Focused Library Research

Once you have completed your exploratory research and formulated your research question, it is time to move to focused research. During **focused research,** you examine the specialized reference works, books, and articles devoted specifically to your topic. At this stage, you may also need to make use of the special services that many college libraries offer.

If your library has a Web site (and most libraries do), you may find it enables you to access more than just the library catalog or the various periodicals to which it subscribes. In fact, many library Web sites are gateways to a vast amount of information, including research guides on a wide variety of topics, electronic journals and newspapers to which the library subscribes, and links to recommended Internet resources.

(1) Consulting Specialized Reference Works

During your exploratory research, you used general reference works to help you narrow your topic and formulate your research question. Now, you can access **specialized reference works**—unabridged dictionaries, special dictionaries, yearbooks, almanacs, atlases, and so on—to find facts, examples, statistics, definitions, and expert opinion.

Close-up: Specialized Reference Works

Unabridged Dictionaries Unabridged dictionaries such as the *Oxford English Dictionary*, are comprehensive works that give detailed information about words.

Special Dictionaries These dictionaries focus on topics such as usage, synonyms, slang and idioms, etymologies, and foreign terms; some focus on specific disciplines such as accounting or law.

Yearbooks and Almanacs A **yearbook** is an annual publication that updates factual and statistical information already published in a reference source. An **almanac** provides lists, charts, and statistics about a wide variety of subjects.

> *World Almanac.* Includes statistics about government, population, sports, and many other subjects. Published annually since 1868.
>
> *Information Please Almanac.* Includes information unavailable in the *World Almanac*. Published annually since 1947.
>
> *Facts on File.* Covering 1940 to the present, this work offers digests of important news stories from metropolitan newspapers.
>
> *Editorials on File.* Reprints important editorials from American and Canadian newspapers.
>
> *Statistical Abstract of the United States.* Summarizes the statistics gathered by the US government. Published annually.

Atlases An **atlas** contains maps and charts as well as historical, cultural, political, and economic information.

> *National Geographic Atlas of the World.* Published by the National Geographic Society. The most up-to-date atlas available.
>
> *Rand McNally Cosmopolitan World Atlas.* A modern and extremely legible medium-sized atlas.
>
> *We the People: An Atlas of America's Ethnic Diversity.* Presents information about specific ethnic groups. Maps show immigration routes and settlement patterns.

Quotation Books A **quotation book**—such as *Bartlett's Familiar Quotations*—contains numerous quotations on a wide variety of subjects. Such quotations can be useful for your paper's introductory and concluding paragraphs.

(2) Consulting Books

The online catalog gives you the information you need—the call numbers—for locating specific titles. A **call number** is like a book's address in the library: it tells you exactly where to find the book you are looking for. (Figure 13.5 on page 140 shows an online catalog entry for a book.)

Once you become familiar with the physical layout of the library and the classification system your library uses, you should find it quite simple to locate the books you need.

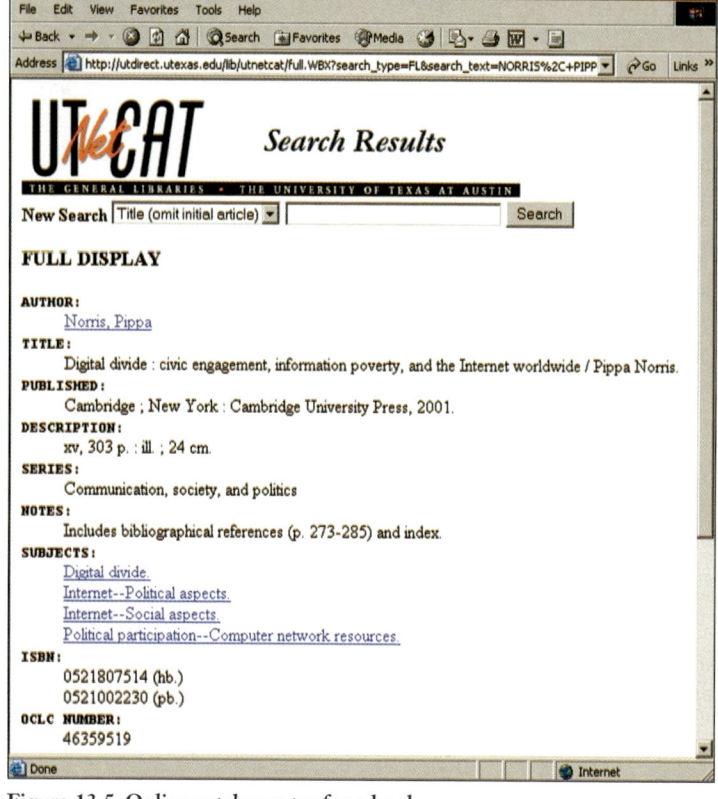

Figure 13.5 Online catalog entry for a book.

Checklist: Tracking Down a Missing Book	
Problem	**Possible Solution**
Book has been checked out of library.	☐ Consult person at circulation desk.
Book is not in library's collection.	☐ Check other nearby libraries.
	☐ Ask instructor if he or she owns a copy.
	☐ Arrange for interlibrary loan (if time permits).
Journal is not in library's collection/article is ripped out of journal.	☐ Arrange for interlibrary loan (if time permits).
	☐ Check to see whether article is available in a full-text database.
	☐ Ask librarian whether article has been reprinted as part of a collection.

(3) Consulting Periodicals

A **periodical** is a newspaper, magazine, scholarly journal, or other publication published at regular intervals (weekly, monthly, or quarterly). Articles in **scholarly journals** can be the best, most reliable sources you can find on a subject; they provide current information and are written by experts on the topic. And, because these journals focus on a particular subject area, they can provide in-depth analysis.

NOTE: You cannot access most scholarly journals on the free Internet. Although you may occasionally find individual articles on the Internet, the easiest and most reliable way to access scholarly journals is through one of the subscription databases in your college library.

Periodical indexes are databases that list articles from a selected group of magazines, newspapers, or scholarly journals. These indexes may be available in bound volumes, on microfilm or microfiche, and on CD-ROM or DVD; however, most libraries now offer them online. They are updated frequently and provide the most current information available.

Close-up: Frequently Used Periodical Indexes

Most academic libraries subscribe to the following periodical indexes. (Be sure to check your library's Web site or ask a librarian about those available to you.)

General Indexes	**Description**
Ebscohost	Database system for thousands of periodical articles on many subjects
Expanded Academic ASAP	A largely full-text database covering all subjects in thousands of magazines and scholarly journals
FirstSearch	Full-text articles from many popular and scholarly periodicals
LexisNexis Academic Universe	Includes full-text articles from national, international, and local newspapers. Also includes large legal and business sections.
Readers' Guide to Periodical Literature	Index to popular periodicals

Specialized Indexes	**Description**
Dow Jones Interactive	Full text of articles from US newspapers and trade journals
ERIC	Largest database of education-related journal articles and reports in the world
General BusinessFile ASAP	A full-text database covering business topics

(continued)

Frequently used periodical indexes (continued)

Specialized Indexes	Description
PubMed (MEDLINE)	Covers articles in medical journals. Some may be available in full text.
PsycINFO	Covers psychology and related fields
Sociological Abstracts	Covers the social sciences

(4) Finding Primary and Secondary Sources

Primary sources give firsthand accounts of topics or events. They include diaries, letters, speeches, manuscripts, memoirs, autobiographies, records of governments or organizations, newspaper articles, and even books written at the time an event occurred. Primary sources also include photographs, maps, films, tape recordings, novels, short stories, poems, and plays.

   Secondary sources are accounts or interpretations of topics, works, or events. In many cases, their purpose is to interpret or analyze primary sources. Secondary sources include textbooks, literary criticism, and encyclopedias.

Checklist: Finding Primary Sources

- ☐ Do a keyword search of your online catalog. Use keywords that combine your topic with additional terms that describe the format of the primary source—for example, *slaves* AND *narratives.*
- ☐ See if the online catalog lists any bibliographies that might include primary sources. For example, a bibliography might list works *by* an author (primary sources) as well as works *about* the author (secondary sources).
- ☐ Check with a reference librarian to see if your library subscribes to any databases that contain full-text primary sources.
- ☐ Check with a reference librarian to see if your library houses government publications that may include primary sources.
- ☐ Check with a reference librarian to see if your library houses any manuscripts.
- ☐ Use the Internet to find digitized collections of primary source materials—for example, documents that relate to US history, transcripts of television shows, or video clips.

Checklist: Finding Secondary Sources

- ☐ Search your library's online catalog for books. Combine a term that describes your topic with terms such as *interpretation, criticism,* or *bibliography.*

- ☐ Search your library's subscription databases for articles in scholarly journals, popular magazines, and newspapers that discuss and interpret the causes and effects of events.
- ☐ Check the notes, bibliographies, and works-cited lists that appear in books and articles.
- ☐ Do a keyword search on the Internet—but be sure to evaluate any information you find.

NOTE: The US Government publishes information on a wide variety of topics, much of it available on the Web—for example, statistical information collected by government agencies; reports issued by government agencies such as the Environmental Protection Agency, the Department of Education, and NASA; US Supreme Court decisions; and presidential papers, political speeches, treaties, and US patents. A good Web site for locating government publications is <http://www.firstgov.gov>.

(5) Using Special Library Services

As you do focused research, consult a librarian if you plan to use any of the following special services.

Close-up: Special Library Services

- **Interlibrary Loans** Your library may be part of a library system that allows loans of books from one location to another.
- **Special Collections** Your library may house special collections of books, manuscripts, or documents.
- **Government Documents** A large university library may have a separate government documents area with its own catalog or index.
- **Vertical File** The vertical file includes pamphlets from a variety of organizations and interest groups, newspaper clippings, and other material collected by librarians.

13c Evaluating Library Sources

Whenever you find a source (print or electronic), take the time to **evaluate** it—to assess its usefulness and its reliability. To determine the usefulness of a library source, ask the following questions:

- **Does the source treat your topic in enough detail?** To be of any real help, a book should include a section or chapter on your topic, not simply a footnote or a brief reference. For articles, either read the abstract or skim the entire article for key facts, looking closely at section headings, information set in boldface type, and topic sentences. An article should have your topic as its central subject (or at least one of its main concerns).

- **Is the source current?** The date of publication tells you whether the information in a book or article is up to date. A source's currency is particularly important for scientific and technological subjects, but even in the humanities, new discoveries and new ways of thinking lead scholars to reevaluate and modify their ideas.

- **Is the source respected?** A contemporary review of a source can help you make this assessment. *Book Review Digest*, available in print and online, lists popular books that have been reviewed in at least three newspapers or magazines and includes excerpts from representative reviews as well as abstracts.

- **Is the source reliable?** Is the source largely fact or unsubstantiated opinion? Does the writer support his or her conclusions? Does the writer include documentation? Is the writer objective, or does he or she have a particular agenda to advance? Compare a few statements with a neutral source—a textbook or an encyclopedia, for instance—to see whether a writer seems to be slanting facts.

- **Is the source a scholarly or a popular publication?** In general, **scholarly publications**—books and journals aimed at an audience of expert readers—are more respected and reliable than **popular publications**—books, magazines, and newspapers aimed at an audience of general readers. However, assuming they are current, written by reputable authors, and documented, articles from some popular publications (such as *Atlantic Monthly* and *Harper's*) may be appropriate for your research. But remember that most popular publications do not have the same rigorous standards as scholarly publications do. For this reason, before you use information from popular sources such as *Newsweek* or *Sports Illustrated*, check with your instructor.

Close-up: Scholarly versus Popular Publications		
Scholarly Publications	**Popular Publications**	
Report the results of research	Entertain and inform	
Are often published by a university press or have some connection with a university or academic organization	Are published by commercial presses	
Are usually **refereed**; that is, a group of expert reviewers determines what will be published	Are usually not refereed	

Scholarly Publications	Popular Publications
Are usually written by someone who is a recognized authority in the field about which he or she is writing	May be written by experts in a particular field, but more often they are written by freelance or staff writers
Are written for a scholarly audience, so they often use technical vocabulary and include challenging content	Are written for general readers, so they usually use an accessible vocabulary and do not include challenging content
Nearly always contain extensive documentation as well as a bibliography of works consulted	Rarely cite sources or use documentation
Are published primarily because they make a contribution to a particular field of study	Are published primarily to make a profit

13d Doing Research Outside the Library

Interviews (conducted in person or by email) often give you material that you cannot always find in a library—for instance, biographical information, a firsthand account of an event, or the opinions of an expert.

The kinds of questions you ask in an interview depend on the information you want. **Open-ended questions**—questions designed to elicit general information—allow a respondent great flexibility in answering: *"Do you think students today are motivated? Why or why not?"* **Closed-ended questions**—questions intended to elicit specific information—enable you to zero in on a particular detail about a subject: *"How much money did the government's cost-cutting programs actually save?"*

Checklist: Conducting an Interview

- ☐ Always make an appointment.
- ☐ Prepare a list of specific questions tailored to the subject matter and the time limit of your interview.
- ☐ Do background reading about your topic. (Do not ask for information that you can easily find elsewhere.)
- ☐ Have a pen and paper with you. If you want to record the interview, get your subject's permission in advance.
- ☐ Allow the person you are interviewing to complete an answer before you ask another question.

(continued)

Conducting an interview (continued)

☐ Take notes, but continue to pay attention as you do so.
☐ Pay attention to the reactions of your interview subject.
☐ Be willing to depart from your prepared list of questions to ask follow-up questions.
☐ At the end of the interview, thank your subject for his or her time and cooperation.
☐ Send a brief note of thanks.

http://kirsznermandell.wadsworth.com

Computer Tip: **Conducting an Email Interview**

Using email to conduct an interview can save you a great deal of time. Before you send your questions, make sure the person is willing to cooperate. If the person agrees, send a short list of specific questions. After you have received the answers, send a response thanking the person for his or her cooperation.

CHAPTER 14

Using and Evaluating Internet Sources

The **Internet** is a vast system of networks that links millions of computers. Because of its size and diversity, the Internet allows people from all over the world to communicate quickly and easily. Furthermore, because it is inexpensive to publish text, pictures, and sound online, businesses, government agencies, libraries, and universities are able to make available vast amounts of information.

> **Close-up: Limitations of Internet Research**
>
> Even with all its advantages, the Internet does not give you access to all the high-quality print and electronic resources found in a typical college library. For this reason, you should consider the Internet to be a supplement to your library research, not a substitute for it. See **13a** for information about library sources.

14a Using the World Wide Web for Research

When most people refer to the Internet, they actually mean the **World Wide Web,** which is just a part of the Internet. The Web relies on **hypertext links,** key words highlighted in blue. By clicking your mouse on these links, you can move easily from one part of a document to another or from one Web site to another.

The Web enables you to connect to a vast number of documents. For example, you can call up a **home page** or **Web page** (an individual document), or a **Web site** (a collection of Web pages). Government agencies, businesses, universities, libraries, newspapers and magazines, journals, and public interest groups, as well as individuals, all operate their own Web sites. Each of these sites contains hypertext links that can take you to other relevant sites.

To carry out a Web search, you need a **Web browser,** a tool that enables you to find information on the Web. Two of the most popular browsers—*Netscape Navigator* and *Microsoft Internet Explorer*—display the full range of text, photos, sound, and video available in Web documents. (Most new computers come with one of these browsers already installed.)

NOTE: Other Web browsers include *Mozilla* and *Safari* (for the Mac). In addition, some browsers are designed specifically for users with disabilities. For example, *MultiWeb* offers screen modification and audio.

See
14a4

Once you are connected to the Internet, you use your browser to access a **search engine**, a program that searches for and retrieves documents available on the Internet. There are three ways to use search engines to find the information you want: *entering an electronic address*, *using subject guides*, and *doing a keyword search*.

(1) Entering an Electronic Address

The most basic way to access information on the Web is to go directly to a specific electronic address, called a **URL** (uniform resource locator). Search engines and Web browsers display a **dialog box** that enables you to enter the URL of a particular Web site. You may also type the URL directly into the **Location field** on your browser's **home page** (the page you see when you open your browser). (Figure 14.1 shows a dialog box and a location field.) Once you type in a URL and click on Open or Search (or hit Enter or the return key), you will be connected to the Web site you want. Make sure to type the URL exactly as it appears—without adding spaces or adding or deleting punctuation marks. Remember that omitting (or adding) just a single letter or punctuation mark will send you to the wrong site—or to no site at all.

Location field

Dialog box

Figure 14.1 Entering an address in *Netscape Navigator*.

Close-up: What to Do If You Cannot Connect

If you cannot connect to a Web site, don't give up. You can use the following strategies to help you connect:

- Wait a short period of time, and try again. If a Web site is extremely busy, it may block users.
- Make sure that you have typed in the URL correctly. Just adding a space or omitting a slash will change the URL.
- If the URL is very long, delete a section from the end—from slash to slash—and try again.
- Try using just the base URL—the part that ends with *.com* or *.gov*. If this abbreviated URL does not take you where you want to go, you have an incorrect address.
- Instead of following a link from one document to another, type the URL of the link into the location field of your search engine and try again.

http://kirsznermandell.wadsworth.com

Computer Tip: Understanding URLs

The first section of a URL indicates the type of file being accessed. In the address <http://www.google.com/images>, *http* indicates that the file is in hypertext transfer protocol. After the colon and the two slashes is the name of the host site where the file is stored (www.google.com). The *www* tells the user that the Web site is on the World Wide Web, *google* is the domain name, and *com* shows that this is a commercial institution. Following this section is the directory path to the file (*images*).

For links to Web sites for exploratory research and focused research, go to http://kirsznermandell.wadsworth.com ▶ *The Brief Wadsworth Handbook* ▶ Chapter 14 ▶ Web Sites for Exploratory and Focused Research.

See 13a–b

(2) Using Subject Guides

You can also use subject guides to help you locate information. Some search engines, such as *Yahoo!*, *About.com*, and *Look Smart*, contain a **subject guide**—a list of general categories (*Arts and Humanities*, *Business*, *Computers*, and so on) from which you can choose. (Figure 14.2 on page 150 shows the home page of the search engine *Yahoo!* with its subject guide.) Each of these categories will lead you to a more specific list of categories and subcategories until, eventually, you get to the topic you want. For example, clicking on *Humanities* would lead you to *History* and then to *American History* and eventually to *Vietnam War*. Although using subject guides is a time-consuming strategy for finding specific information, it can be a useful tool during

See 13a <u>exploratory research</u>, when you want to find or narrow a topic.

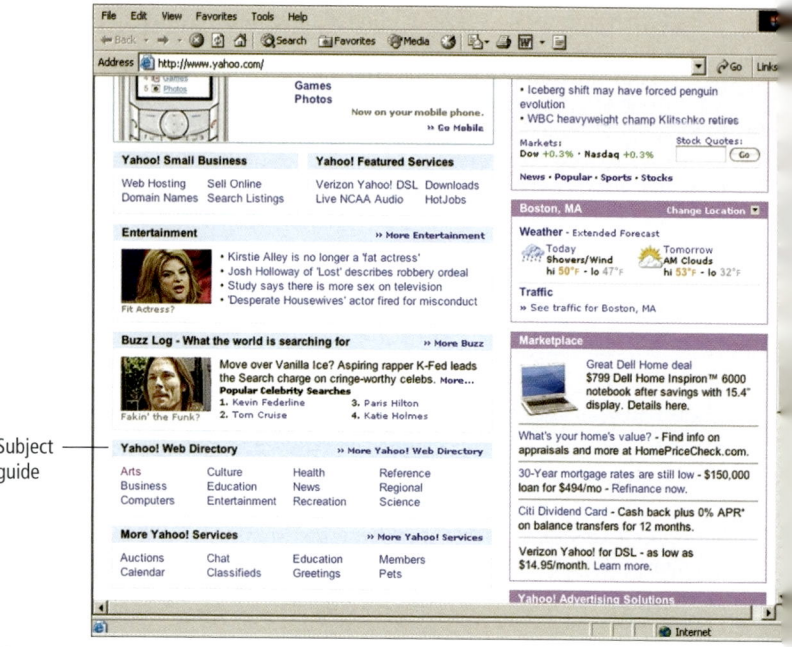

Figure 14.2 *Yahoo!* home page with subject guide. Reproduced with permission of Yahoo! Inc. © 2005 by Yahoo! Inc. YAHOO! and the YAHOO! logo are trademarks of Yahoo! Inc.

(3) Doing a Keyword Search

Finally, you can locate information by doing a **keyword search.** You do this by entering a keyword (or words) into your search engine's search field. (Figure 14.3 shows *Google*'s keyword search page.) The search engine will identify any site in its database on which the keyword (or words) you have typed appears. (These sites are called **hits.**) If, for example, you type *Civil War* in hope of finding information on Fort Sumter during the Civil War, the search engine will generate an enormous list of hits—well over a million. This list will likely include, along with sites that might be relevant to your research, the Civil War Reenactors home page as well as sites that focus on Civil War music.

Because searching this way is inefficient and time consuming, you need to focus your search by using **search operators,** words and symbols that tell a search engine how to interpret your keywords. One way to focus your search is to put quotation marks around your search term (type *"Fort Sumter"* rather than *Fort Sumter*). This will direct the search engine to locate only documents containing this phrase.

Search field

Figure 14.3 *Google* **keyword search page.**

Another way to focus your search is to carry out a **Boolean search,** combining keywords with AND, OR, NOT (typed in all capital letters), or a plus or minus sign to eliminate irrelevant hits from your search. (To do this type of search, you may have to select a search engine's Advanced Search option.) For example, to find Web pages that focus on the battle of Fort Sumter in the Civil War, type *Civil War* AND *Fort Sumter.* Your search will then yield only items that contain *both* terms. (If you type in *Civil War* OR *Fort Sumter,* your search will yield items that contain *either* term.) Some search engines allow you to search using three or more keywords—*Civil War* AND *Fort Sumter* NOT *national monument,* for example. In this case, your search will yield items that contain both the terms *Civil War* and *Fort Sumter,* but not the term *national monument.* By limiting your search in this way, you will get only those items that discuss Fort Sumter and the Civil War and eliminate items that discuss Fort Sumter's current use as a national monument. Focusing your search in this way enables you to avoid irrelevant Web pages.

http://kirsznermandell.wadsworth.com

Computer Tip: Using Search Operators

" " **(quotation marks)** Use quotation marks to search for a specific phrase: *"Baltimore Economy"*

(continued)

Using search operators (continued)

AND Use AND to search for sites that contain both words: *Baltimore* AND *Economy*

OR Use OR to search for sites that contain either word: *Baltimore* OR *Economy*

NOT Use NOT to exclude the word that comes after the NOT: *Baltimore* AND *Economy* NOT *Agriculture*

+ (plus sign) Use a plus sign to include the word that comes after it: *Baltimore + Economy*

− (minus sign) Use a minus sign to exclude the word that comes after it: *Baltimore + Economy − Agriculture*

(4) Choosing the Right Search Engine

FAQs
links
The most widely used search engines are **general-purpose search engines** that focus on a wide variety of topics. Some of these search engines are more user-friendly than others; some allow for more sophisticated searching functions; some are updated more frequently; and some are more comprehensive than others. As you try out various search engines, you will probably settle on a favorite that you will turn to first whenever you need to find information.

Close-up: Popular Search Engines

AllTheWeb <www.alltheweb.com>: This excellent search engine provides comprehensive coverage of the Web. Many users think that this search engine is as good as *Google*. In addition to generating Web page results, *AllTheWeb* has the ability to search for news stories, pictures, video clips, MP3s, and FTP files.

AltaVista <www.altavista.com>: Good, precise engine for focused searches. Fast and easy to use.

Ask Jeeves <www.ask.com>: Good beginner's site. Allows you to narrow your search by asking questions, such as *Are dogs smarter than pigs?*

Excite <www.excite.com>: Good for general topics. Because it searches over 250 million Web sites, you often get more information than you need.

Go <http://infoseek.go.com>: Enables you to access information in a directory of reviewed sites, news stories, and Usenet groups.

Google <www.google.com>: Arguably, the best search engine available. Accesses a large database that includes both text and graphics. It is easy to navigate, and searches usually yield a high percentage of useful hits.

Google recently instituted *Google Scholar*, which searches for scholarly literature, including peer-reviewed papers, books, abstracts, and technical reports from all areas of research. It can be accessed at <www.scholar.google.com>.

HotBot <www.hotbot.com>: Excellent, fast search engine for locating specific information. Good search options allow you to fine-tune your searches.

Lycos <www.lycos.com>: Enables you to search for specific media (graphics, for example). A somewhat small index of Web pages.

Teoma <www.teoma.com>: *Teoma* is a search engine owned by Ask Jeeves. Although it has a smaller index of the Web than *Google* and *AllTheWeb*, it is very effective when it comes to answering questions. It contains a Refine feature that offers suggested topics to explore after you do a search. It also has a Resources section of results that will point you to linked resources about various topics.

WebCrawler <www.webcrawler.com>: Good for beginners. Easy to use.

Yahoo! <www.yahoo.com>: Good for exploratory research. Enables you to search using either subject headings or keywords. Searches its own indexes as well as the Web.

Because even the best search engines search only a fraction of what is on the Web, if you use only one search engine, you will most likely miss much valuable information. It is therefore a good idea to repeat each search with several different search engines or to use one of the **metasearch** or **metacrawler** engines that uses several search engines simultaneously.

Close-up: Metasearch Engines

Dogpile <www.dogpile.com>
Ixquick <www.ixquick.com>
Metacrawler <www.metacrawler.com>
Profusion <www.profusion.com>
Zworks <www.zworks.com>

In addition to the popular general-purpose search engines and metasites, there are also numerous **specialized search engines** devoted entirely to specific subject areas, such as literature, business, sports, and women's issues. Hundreds of such specialized search engines are indexed at *Allsearchengines.com* <www.allsearchengines.com>. These sites are especially useful during **focused research**, when you are looking for in-depth information about your topic.

See 13b

NOTE: *Search Engine Watch* at <www.searchenginewatch.com> maintains an extensive, comprehensive, and up-to-date list of the latest search engines. Not only does this site list search engines by category, it also reviews them.

Close-up: Specialized Search Engines

Voice of the Shuttle (humanities search engine)
   <http://vos.ucsb.edu/>
Pilot-Search.com (literary search engine)
   <http://www.pilot-search.com/>
FedWorld (US government database and report search engine)
   <http://www.fedworld.gov/>
HealthFinder (health, nutrition, and diseases information for
   consumers)
   <http://www.healthfinder.gov/default.htm>
The Internet Movie Database (search engine and database for film
   facts, reviews, and so on)
   <http://www.imdb.com>
SportQuest (sports search engine)
   <http://www.sportquest.com/>
FindLaw (legal search engine)
   <http://www.findlaw.com/>

Checklist: Tips for Effective Searching

☐ **Choose your keywords carefully.** A search engine is only as good as the keywords you use. Use quotation marks and Boolean search operators to make your searches more productive. Review the Computer Tip box on pages 151–52 before you use any search engine.

☐ **Include enough terms.** If you are looking for information on housing, for example, search for several different variations of your keyword: *housing, houses, house buyer, buying houses, residential real estate*, and so on. Some search engines, like *Infoseek*, automatically search plurals; others do not. Some, like *AltaVista*, automatically search variants of your keyword; others require you to think of the variants yourself.

☐ **Choose the right search engine.** No one all-purpose search site exists. Make sure you review the list of a search engines on pages 152–54.

☐ **Use more than one search engine.** Because different search engines index different sites, try several. If one does not yield results after a few tries, switch to another. Also, do not forget to do a metasearch with a search engine like *Metacrawler*.

☐ **Add useful sites to your bookmarks or favorites list.** Whenever you find a particularly useful Web site, **bookmark** it by selecting this option on the menu bar of your browser (with some browsers, such as *Internet Explorer*, this option is called *Favorites*). If you add a site to your bookmark list, you can return to the site whenever you want to by opening the Bookmark menu and selecting it.

14b Using Other Internet Tools

In addition to the World Wide Web, the Internet includes a number of other tools that you can use to gather information for your research.

(1) Using Email

Email can be useful as you do research because it enables you to exchange ideas with classmates, ask questions of your instructors, and even conduct long-distance interviews. You can follow email links in Web documents, and you can also transfer word-processing documents or other files as email attachments from one computer to another.

(2) Using Listservs

Listservs (sometimes called **discussion lists**), electronic mailing lists to which you must subscribe, enable you to communicate with groups of people interested in particular topics. (Many schools, and even individual courses, have their own listservs.) Subscribers to a listserv send emails to a main email address, and these messages are routed to all members of the group. Some listserv subscribers may be experts who can answer your queries. Keep in mind, however, that you must evaluate any information you get from a listserv before you use it in your research.

(3) Using Newsgroups

Like listservs, **newsgroups** are discussion groups. Unlike listserv messages, which are sent to you as email, newsgroup messages are collected on the **Usenet** system, a global collection of news servers, where anyone who subscribes can access them. In a sense, newsgroups function as gigantic bulletin boards where users post messages that others can read and respond to. Thus, newsgroups can provide specific information as well as suggestions about where to look for further information. Just as you would with a listserv, you should evaluate information you get from a newsgroup before you use it.

(4) Using MUDS, MOOS, IRCS, and Instant Messaging

With emails and listservs, there is a delay between the time a message is sent and the time it is received. **MUDS, MOOS, IRCS,** and **instant messaging** enable you to send and receive messages in real time. In other words, communication is **synchronous:** messages are sent and received as they are typed. Synchronous communication programs are being used more and more in college settings—for class discussions, online workshops, and collaborative projects.

Checklist: Observing Netiquette

Netiquette refers to the guidelines that responsible users of the Internet should follow when they communicate. When you use the Internet, especially email and synchronous communication, keep the following guidelines in mind:

☐ **Don't shout.** All-uppercase letters indicate that a person is SHOUTING. Not only is this immature, but it is also distracting and irritating.

☐ **Watch your tone.** Make sure you send the message you actually intend to convey. What may sound humorous to you may seem sarcastic or impolite to someone else.

☐ **Be careful what you write.** Remember, once you hit *Send*, it is often too late to call back your message. For this reason, treat an email message or a posting as you would a written letter. Take the time to proofread and to consider carefully what you have written.

☐ **Respect the privacy of others.** Do not forward or post a message that you have received unless you have permission from the sender to do so.

☐ **Do not flame.** When you **flame**, you send an insulting electronic message. At best, this response is immature; at worst, it is disrespectful.

☐ **Make sure you use the correct electronic address.** Be certain that your message goes to the right person. Nothing is more embarrassing than sending a communication to the wrong address.

☐ **Use your computer facility ethically and responsibly.** Do not use computer labs for personal communications or for entertainment. Not only is this a misuse of the facility, but it also ties up equipment that others may be waiting to use.

14c Evaluating Internet Sites

Web sites vary greatly in reliability. Because anyone can operate a Web site and thereby publish anything, regardless of quality, critical evaluation of Web-based material is even more important than evaluation of more traditional sources of information, such as books and journal articles.

Determining the quality of a Web site is crucial if you plan to use it as a source for your research. If you are using a Web site for personal information or entertainment, it is probably enough just to be aware of what is legal and what is illegal (for example, you should not download copyrighted material, such as software or music, that has been illegally posted on a Web site). However, if you are using the Internet to locate appropriate sources for a research project, you need to be much more careful. For this reason, you should evaluate the content of any Web site for *accuracy, credibility, objectivity* or *reasonableness, currency, coverage* or *scope*, and *stability*.

Accuracy **Accuracy** refers to the reliability of the material itself and to the use of proper documentation. Factual errors—especially errors in facts that are central to the main point of the source—should cause you to question the reliability of the material you are reading. To evaluate a site's accuracy, ask these questions:

- Is the text free of basic grammatical and mechanical errors?
- Does the site contain factual errors?
- Does the site provide a list of references?
- Are links available to other references?
- Can information be verified with print or other resources?

Credibility **Credibility** refers to the credentials of the person or organization responsible for the site. Web sites operated by well-known institutions (the Smithsonian or the Library of Congress, for example) have a high degree of credibility. Those operated by individuals (personal Web pages or **blogs**—Web logs—for example) are often less reliable. To evaluate a site's credibility, ask these questions:

- Does the site list an author? Are credentials (for example, professional or academic affiliations) provided for the author or authors?
- Is the author a recognized authority in his or her field?
- Is the site **refereed?** That is, does an editorial board or a group of experts determine what material appears on the Web site?
- Does the organization sponsoring the Web site exist apart from its Web presence?
- Can you determine how long the Web site has existed?

Objectivity or Reasonableness **Objectivity** or **reasonableness** refers to the degree of bias that a Web site exhibits. Some Web sites make no secret of their biases. They openly advocate a particular point of view or action, or they are clearly trying to sell something. Other Web sites may try to hide their biases. For example, a Web site may present itself as a source of factual information when it is actually advocating a political point of view. To evaluate a site's objectivity, ask these questions:

- Does advertising appear in the text?
- Does a business, a political organization, or a special interest group sponsor the site?
- Does the site express a particular viewpoint?
- Does the site contain links to other sites that express a particular viewpoint?

Checklist: Determining the Legitimacy of an Anonymous or Questionable Web Source

When a Web source is anonymous (or has an author whose name is not familiar to you), you have to take special measures to determine its legitimacy: *(continued)*

> *Determining the legitimacy of a Web source (continued)*
>
> ☐ **Post a query.** If you subscribe to a newsgroup or listserv, ask others in the group what they know about the source and its author.
> ☐ **Follow the links.** Follow the hypertext links in a document to other documents. If the links take you to legitimate sources, you know that the author is aware of these sources of information.
> ☐ **Do a keyword search.** Do a search using the name of the sponsoring organization or the author as keywords. Other documents (or citations in other works) may identify the author.
> ☐ **Look at the URL.** The last part of a Web site's URL can tell you whether the site is sponsored by a commercial entity (*.com*), a nonprofit organization (*.org*), an educational institution (*.edu*), the military (*.mil*), or a government agency (*.gov*). Knowing this information can tell you whether an organization is trying to sell you something (*.com*) or just providing information (*.edu* or *.org*).

Currency **Currency** refers to how up-to-date the Web site is. The easiest way to assess a site's currency is to determine when it was last updated. Keep in mind, however, that even if the date on the site is current, the information that the site contains may not be. To evaluate a site's currency, ask these questions:

- Is the most recent update displayed?
- Are all the links to other sites still functioning?
- Is the actual information on the page up-to-date?
- Does the site clearly identify the date it was created?

Coverage or Scope **Coverage** or **scope** refers to the comprehensiveness of the information on a Web site. More is not necessarily better, but some sites may be incomplete. Others may provide information that is no more than common knowledge. Still others may present discussions that may not be suitable for college-level research. To evaluate a site's coverage, ask these questions:

- Does the site provide in-depth coverage?
- Does the site provide information that is not available elsewhere?
- Does the site identify a target audience? Does this target audience suggest the site is appropriate for your research needs?

Stability **Stability** refers to whether or not the site is being maintained. A stable site will be around when you want to access it again. Web sites that are here today and gone tomorrow make it difficult for readers to check your sources or for you to obtain updated information. To evaluate a site's stability, ask these questions:

- Has the site been active for a long period of time?
- Is the site updated regularly?
- Is the site maintained by a well-known, reliable organization, committed to financing the site?

CHAPTER 15

Summarizing, Paraphrasing, Quoting, and Synthesizing Sources

Simply copying down the words of a source is the least efficient way of <u>taking notes</u>. Experienced researchers know that a better strategy is to take notes that combine summary and paraphrase with direct quotation. By doing so, they make sure they understand both the material and its relevance to their research. This, in turn, makes it possible for them to <u>synthesize sources</u>, combining source material with their own original ideas.

See 12f

See 15d3

15a Writing a Summary

A **summary** is a brief restatement, *in your own words*, of the main idea of a passage or an article. (If you think it is necessary to include a distinctive word or phrase from your source, place it in quotation marks; otherwise, you will be committing <u>plagiarism</u>.) When you write a summary, you condense the author's ideas into a few concise sentences. A summary is always much shorter than the original because it omits the examples, asides, analogies, and rhetorical strategies that writers use to add emphasis and interest. Your summary should accurately represent the author's ideas and should include only the ideas of your source, not your own interpretations or opinions. Finally, be sure to document all quoted words and paraphrases as well as the summary itself.

See Ch. 16

Close-up: Summaries

- **Summaries are original.** They should use your own language and phrasing, not the language and phrasing of your source.
- **Summaries are concise.** They should always be much shorter than the original.
- **Summaries are accurate.** They should precisely express the main idea of your source.
- **Summaries are objective.** They should not include your opinions.

Compare the following three passages. The first is an original source; the second, an acceptable summary; and the third, an unacceptable summary.

159

Original Source

Today, the First Amendment faces challenges from groups who seek to limit expressions of racism and bigotry. A growing number of legislatures have passed rules against "hate speech"—[speech] that is offensive on the basis of race, ethnicity, gender, or sexual orientation. The rules are intended to promote respect for all people and protect the targets of hurtful words, gestures, or actions.

Legal experts fear these rules may wind up diminishing the rights of all citizens. "The bedrock principle [of our society] is that government may never suppress free speech simply because it goes against what the community would like to hear," says Nadine Strossen, president of the American Civil Liberties Union and professor of constitutional law at New York University Law School. In recent years, for example, the courts have upheld the right of neo-Nazis to march in Jewish neighborhoods; protected cross-burning as a form of free expression; and allowed protesters to burn the American flag. The offensive, ugly, distasteful, or repugnant nature of expression is not reason enough to ban it, courts have said.

But advocates of limits on hate speech note that certain kinds of expression fall outside of First Amendment protection. Courts have ruled that "fighting words"—words intended to provoke immediate violence—or speech that creates a clear and present danger are not protected forms of expression. As the classic argument goes, freedom of speech does not give you the right to yell "Fire!" in a crowded theater. (Sudo, Phil. "Freedom of Hate Speech?" *Scholastic Update* 124.14 [1992]: 17–20)

Acceptable Summary: The right to freedom of speech, guaranteed by the First Amendment, is becoming more difficult to defend. Some people think that stronger laws against the use of "hate speech" weaken the First Amendment. But others argue that some kinds of speech remain exempt from this protection (Sudo 17).

This summary presents an accurate, objective overview of the original source without using its exact language or phrasing. (The one distinctive phrase borrowed from the source is placed within quotation marks.)

The following unacceptable summary uses words and phrases from the original without placing them in quotation marks. This use See Ch. 16 constitutes **plagiarism**. In addition, the unacceptable summary expresses the student writer's opinion ("Other people have the sense to realize...").

Unacceptable Summary: Today, the First Amendment faces challenges from lots of people. Some of these people are legal experts who want to let Nazis march in Jewish neighborhoods. Other people have the sense to realize that some kinds of speech fall outside of First Amendment protection because they create a clear and present danger (Sudo 17).

15b Writing a Paraphrase

A summary conveys just the main idea of a source; a **paraphrase** gives a *detailed* restatement of a source's important ideas in their entirety. It covers all the source's main points, and it also reflects its order, tone, and emphasis. Consequently, a paraphrase can sometimes be as long as the source itself.

When you paraphrase, make certain that you use your own words, except when you want to quote to give readers a sense of the original. If you include quotations, circle the quotation marks in your notes so that you will not forget to document them later. Try not to look at the source as you write, use language and syntax that come naturally to you, and avoid duplicating the wording or sentence structure of the original. Whenever possible, use synonyms that accurately convey the meaning of the original word or phrase. If you cannot think of a synonym for an important term, quote—but remember to document all direct quotations from your source as well as the entire paraphrase. Finally, be sure that your paraphrase reflects only the ideas of your source—not your analysis or interpretation of those ideas.

Close-up: Paraphrases

- **Paraphrases are original.** They should use your own original language and phrasing, not the language and phrasing of your source.
- **Paraphrases are accurate.** They should precisely reflect both the ideas and the emphasis of your source.
- **Paraphrases are objective.** They should not include your opinions.
- **Paraphrases are complete.** They should include all the important ideas in your source.

Following are an original passage, an acceptable paraphrase, and an unacceptable paraphrase.

Original Passage

When you play a video game, you enter into the world of the programmers who made it. You have to do more than identify with a character on a screen. You must act for it. Identification through action has a special kind of hold. Like playing a sport, it puts people into a highly focused and highly charged state of mind. For many people, what is being pursued in the video game is not just a score, but an altered state.

The pilot of a race car does not dare to take . . . attention off the road. The imperative of total concentration is part of the high. Video games demand the same level of attention. They can give people the feeling of being close to the edge because, as in a dangerous situation, there is no time for rest and the consequences of wandering attention [are] dire. With pinball, a false move can be recuperated. The machine can be shaken, the ball repositioned. In a video game, the program has no tolerance for error, no margin for safety. Players experience their every movement as instantly translated into game action. The game is relentless in its demand that all other time stop and in its demand that the player take full responsibility for every act, a point that players often sum up [with] the phrase "One false move and you're dead." (Turkle, Sherry. *The Second Self: Computers and the Human Spirit*. New York: Simon & Schuster, 1984. 83–84)

Acceptable Paraphrase: The programmer defines the reality of the video game. The game forces a player to merge with the character who is part of the game. The character becomes an extension of the player, who determines how he or she will think and act. According to Turkle, like sports, video games put a player into a very intense "altered state" of mind that is the most important part of the activity (83).

The total involvement they demand is what attracts many people to video games. These games can simulate the thrill of participating in a dangerous activity without any of the risks. There are no opportunities to correct errors of judgment. Unlike video games, pinball games are forgiving. A player can—within certain limits—manipulate a pinball game to correct minor mistakes. With video games, however, every move has immediate consequences. The game forces a player to adapt to its rules and to act carefully. One mistake can cause the death of the character on the screen and the end of the game (Turkle 83-84).

Although this paraphrase follows the order and emphasis of the original—and even quotes a key phrase—its wording and sentence structure are very different from those of the source. Still, it conveys the key ideas of the source and maintains an objective tone.

The following unacceptable paraphrase simply echoes the phrasing and syntax of the original, borrowing words and expressions without enclosing them in quotation marks. This constitutes

See Ch. 16 plagiarism. In addition, the paraphrase digresses into a discussion of the writer's own views about the relative merits of pinball and video games ("That is why I like ...").

Unacceptable Paraphrase: Playing a video game, you enter into a new world—one the programmer of the game made. You can't just play a video game; you have to identify with it. Your mind goes to a new level, and you are put into a highly focused state of mind.

> Just as you would if you were driving a race
> car or piloting a plane, you must not let your mind
> wander. Video games demand complete attention. But
> the sense that at any time you could make one false
> move and lose is their attraction—at least for me.
> That is why I like video games more than pinball.
> Pinball is just too easy. You can always recover.
> By shaking the machine or quickly operating the
> flippers, you can save the ball. Video games,
> however, are not so easy to control. Usually, one
> slip and you're dead (Turkle 83-84).

15c Quoting Sources

When you **quote,** you copy a writer's statements exactly as they appear in a source, word for word and punctuation mark for punctuation mark, enclosing the borrowed material in quotation marks. As a rule, you should not quote extensively in a research paper. Numerous quotations interrupt the flow of your discussion and give readers the impression that your paper is just a collection of other people's ideas.

Checklist: When to Quote

- ☐ Quote when a source's wording or phrasing is so distinctive that a summary or paraphrase would diminish its impact.
- ☐ Quote when a source's words—particularly those of a recognized expert on your subject—will lend authority to your presentation.
- ☐ Quote when an author's words are so concise that paraphrasing would create a long, clumsy, or incoherent phrase or would change the meaning of the original.
- ☐ Quote when you plan to disagree with a source. Using a source's exact words helps convince readers you are being fair.

NOTE: Remember to document all quotations that you use in your paper.

15d Integrating Source Material into Your Writing

Weave paraphrases, summaries, and quotations smoothly into your discussion, adding your own analysis or explanation to show the relevance of your source material to the points you are making.

(1) Integrating Quotations

Be sure to work quotations smoothly into your sentences. Quotations should never be awkwardly dropped into your paper, leaving the relationship between the quoted words and your point unclear. Instead, be careful to provide a context for the quotation, and quote only those words you need to make your point.

Acceptable: For the Amish, the public school system is a problem because it represents "the threat of absorption into mass society" (Hostetler 193).

Unacceptable: For the Amish, the public school system represents a problem. "A serious problem confronting Amish society from the viewpoint of the Amish themselves is the threat of absorption into mass society through the values promoted in the public school system" (Hostetler 193).

Whenever possible, use an **identifying tag** (a phrase that identifies the source) along with the quotation.

Identifying Tag: As John Hostetler points out, the Amish see the public school system as a problem because it represents "the threat of absorption into mass society" (193).

Close-up: Integrating Source Material into Your Writing

To make sure your sentences do not all sound the same, experiment with different methods of integrating source material into your paper.

- Vary the verbs you use to introduce a source's words or ideas (instead of repeating *says*).

acknowledges	discloses	observes
admits	explains	predicts
affirms	finds	proposes
believes	illustrates	reports
claims	implies	speculates
comments	indicates	suggests
concludes	insists	summarizes
concurs	notes	warns

- Vary the placement of the identifying tag, putting it in the middle or at the end of the quoted material instead of always at the beginning.

Quotation with Identifying Tag in Middle: "A serious problem confronting Amish society from the viewpoint of the Amish themselves," observes Hostetler, "is the threat of absorption into mass society through the values promoted in the public school system" (193).

Paraphrase with Identifying Tag at End: The Amish are also concerned about their children's exposure to the public school system's values, notes Hostetler (193).

Substitutions or Additions within Quotations When you make changes or additions to fit a quotation into your paper, indicate these changes by enclosing them in brackets.

Original Quotation: "Immediately after her wedding, she and her husband followed tradition and went to visit almost everyone who attended the wedding" (Hostetler 122).

Quotation Revised to Make Verb Tenses Consistent:
```
Nowhere is the Amish dedication to tradition more
obvious than in the events surrounding marriage.
Right after the wedding celebration, the Amish
bride and groom "visit almost everyone who [has]
attended the wedding" (Hostetler 122).
```

Quotation Revised to Supply an Antecedent for a Pronoun:
```
"Immediately after her wedding, [Sarah] and her
husband followed tradition and went to visit almost
everyone who attended the wedding" (Hostetler 122).
```

Quotation Revised to Change an Uppercase to a Lowercase Letter:
```
The strength of the Amish community is
illustrated by the fact that "[i]mmediately after
her wedding, she and her husband followed tradition
and went to visit almost everyone who attended the
wedding" (Hostetler 122).
```

Close-up: Punctuating Identifying Tags

Whether or not to use a comma with an identifying tag depends on where you place the tag in the sentence. If the identifying tag immediately precedes a quotation, use a comma. If the identifying tag does not immediately precede a quotation, do not use a comma.

```
As Hostetler points out, "The Amish are successful
in maintaining group identity" (56).
```

```
Hostetler points out that the Amish frequently "use
severe sanctions to preserve their values" (56).
```

NOTE: Never use a comma after *that*.

```
Hostetler says that, Amish society is "defined by
religion" (76).
```

Omissions within Quotations When you delete unnecessary or irrelevant words, substitute an <u>ellipsis</u> (three spaced periods) for the deleted words.

See
48f1

Original Quotation: "Not only have the Amish built and staffed their own elementary and vocational schools, but they have gradually organized on local, state, and national levels to cope with the task of educating their children" (Hostetler 206).

Quotation Revised to Eliminate Unnecessary Words: "Not only have the Amish built and staffed their own

elementary and vocational schools, but they have
gradually organized . . . to cope with the task of
educating their children" (Hostetler 206).

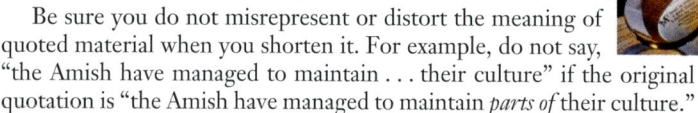

Close-up: Omissions within Quotations

Be sure you do not misrepresent or distort the meaning of
quoted material when you shorten it. For example, do not say,
"the Amish have managed to maintain . . . their culture" if the original
quotation is "the Amish have managed to maintain *parts of* their culture."

NOTE: If the passage you are quoting already contains ellipses, MLA
style requires that you place brackets around any ellipses you add.

See 47b

Long Quotations Set off a quotation of more than four typed lines
of **prose** (or more than three lines of **poetry**) by indenting it one inch
(ten spaces) from the left margin. Double-space, and do not use quotation marks. If you are quoting a single paragraph, do not indent the
first line. If you are quoting more than one paragraph, indent the first
line of each complete paragraph an additional one-quarter inch
(three spaces). Integrate the quotation into your paper by introducing
it with a complete sentence followed by a colon. Place parenthetical
documentation one space after the end punctuation.

> According to Hostetler, the Amish were not
> always hostile to public education:
>> The one-room rural elementary school
>> served the Amish community well in a
>> number of ways. As long as it was a public
>> school, it stood midway between the Amish
>> community and the world. Its influence was
>> tolerable, depending upon the degree of
>> influence the Amish were able to bring to
>> the situation. (196)

(2) Integrating Paraphrases and Summaries

FAQs

Introduce your paraphrases and summaries with identifying tags,
and end them with appropriate documentation. By doing so, you
make certain that your readers are able to differentiate your own
ideas from those of your sources.

**Correct (Identifying Tag Differentiates Ideas of Source from
Ideas of Writer):** Art can be used to uncover many
problems that children have at home, in school, or
with their friends. For this reason, many therapists
use art therapy extensively. According to William
Alschuler in *Art and Self-Image*, children's views
of themselves in society are often reflected by
their art style. For example, a cramped, crowded
art style using only a portion of the paper shows a
child's limited role (260).

Misleading (Ideas of Source Blend with Ideas of Writer):
```
Art can be used to uncover many problems that
children have at home, in school, or with their
friends. For this reason, many therapists use art
therapy extensively. Children's views of themselves
in society are often reflected by their art style.
For example, a cramped, crowded art style using
only a portion of the paper shows their limited
role (Alschuler 260).
```

(3) Synthesizing Sources

When you write a **synthesis,** you use paraphrase, summary, and quotation to combine material from two or more sources, along with your own ideas, in order to express an original viewpoint. (In this sense, an entire research paper is a synthesis.) You begin synthesizing material by comparing your sources and determining how they are alike and different, where they agree and disagree, and whether they reach the same conclusions. As you identify connections between one source and another or between a source and your own ideas, you develop your own perspective on your subject. It is this viewpoint, summarized in a thesis statement (in the case of an entire paper) or in a topic sentence (in the case of a paragraph), that becomes the focus of your synthesis.

As you write your synthesis, make your points one at a time, and use material from your sources to support these points. Be certain you use identifying tags as well as the transitional words and phrases that your readers will need to follow your discussion. Finally, remember that your own ideas, not the ideas of your sources, should be central to your discussion.

The following synthesis was written by a student as part of a research paper.

```
    Computers have already changed our lives.
They carry out (at incredible speed) many of the
everyday tasks that make our way of life possible.
For example, computer billing, with all its faults,
makes modern business possible, and without
computers we would not have access to the telephone
services or television reception that we take
for granted. But computers are more than fast
calculators. According to one computer expert,
they are well on their way to learning, creating,
and someday even thinking (Raphael 21). Another
computer expert, Douglas Hofstadter, agrees, saying
that someday a computer will have both "will . . .
and consciousness" (423). It seems likely, then,
that as a result of the computer, our culture will
change profoundly (Turkle 15).
```

CHAPTER 16

Avoiding Plagiarism

16a Defining Plagiarism

FAQs links

Plagiarism is presenting another person's ideas or words as if they were your own. Most plagiarism is unintentional—for example, inadvertently typing a quoted passage into a paper and forgetting to include the quotation marks and documentation. The availability on the Web of information that can be downloaded and pasted into a paper has increased the likelihood of accidental plagiarism. In fact, the freewheeling appropriation and circulation of information that routinely takes place on the Web may give the false impression that this material does not need to be documented. Whether they appear in print or in electronic form, however, the words, ideas, and images of others (including photographs, graphs, charts, and statistics) must be properly documented.

There is a difference, however, between an honest mistake and intentional plagiarism—for example, copying sentences from a journal article or submitting a paper that someone else has written. The penalties for unintentional plagiarism may sometimes be severe, but intentional plagiarism is almost always dealt with harshly: students who intentionally plagiarize can receive a failing grade for the paper (or the course) or even be expelled from school.

http://kirsznermandell.wadsworth.com

Computer Tip: Avoiding Plagiarism

The same technology that has made unintentional plagiarism more common has also made plagiarism easier to detect. By doing a *Google* search, an instructor can quickly find the source of a phrase that has been plagiarized from an online source. Some special software searches subscription databases and identifies plagiarized passages in student papers. *InSite* is a Web-based application that compares, word for word, the information contained on the Web and in *InfoTrac® College Edition* (a subscription database) with passages in student papers. This makes it possible for students to use *InSite* to search their own drafts for unintentionally plagiarized material before submitting final papers to their instructors. Below are the results of an *InSite* Originality Report indicating that certain parts of a paper have been plagiarized.

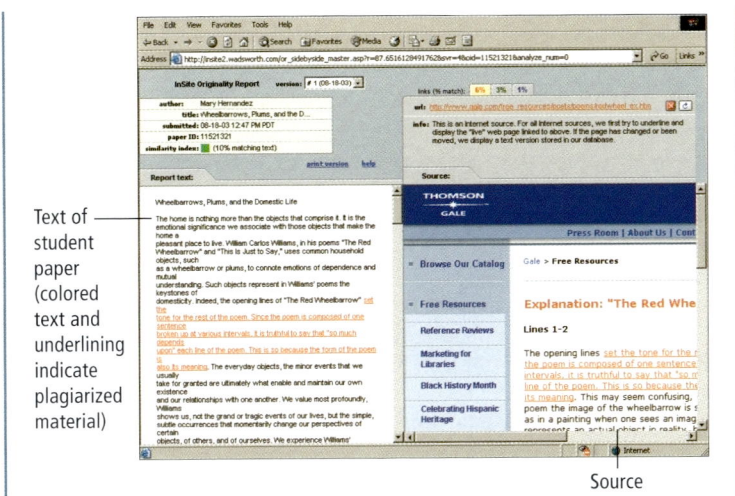

Text of student paper (colored text and underlining indicate plagiarized material)

Source

16b Avoiding Unintentional Plagiarism

The most common cause of unintentional plagiarism is sloppy research habits. To avoid this problem, start your research paper early. Do not cut and paste text from a Web site or full-text database directly into your paper. Never use sources that you have not actually read or invent sources that do not exist. If you paraphrase, do so correctly by following the advice in 15b; changing a few words here and there is not enough.

> ### ESL Tip
>
> Because writing in a second language can be difficult, you may be tempted to closely follow the syntax and word choice of your sources. Be aware, however, that this constitutes plagiarism.

In addition to taking careful notes and distinguishing between your ideas and those of your sources, you must also use proper documentation. In general, you must document any words, ideas, and images that you borrow from your sources (whether print or electronic). Of course, certain material need not be documented: **common knowledge** (information most readers probably know), facts available from a variety of reference sources, familiar sayings and well-known quotations, and your own original research (interviews and surveys, for example). Information that is another writer's

See Pts. 4–5

FAQs link

original contribution, however, must be acknowledged. So, although you do not have to document the fact that John F. Kennedy graduated from Harvard in 1940 or that he was elected president in 1960, you do have to document a historian's evaluation of his presidency.

Close-up: Avoiding Two Special Problems

In general, you should not submit a paper to one course that you have already received a grade for in another course. If you intend to substantially rework the paper, however, you may be able to use it—but be sure to get permission from both course instructors.

Collaborative work presents another problem. If you participate in a collaborative research project, make sure that you clearly identify the sections that each person worked on and that you get guidelines from your instructor for documenting collaborative work.

16c Revising to Eliminate Plagiarism

You can avoid plagiarism by using documentation wherever it is required and by following these guidelines.

(1) Enclose Borrowed Words in Quotation Marks

Original: Historically, only a handful of families have dominated the fireworks industry in the West. Details such as chemical recipes and mixing procedures were cloaked in secrecy and passed down from one generation to the next. . . . One effect of familial secretiveness is that, until recent decades, basic pyrotechnic research was rarely performed, and even when it was, the results were not generally reported in scientific journals. (Conkling, John A. "Pyrotechnics." *Scientific American* July 1990: 96)

Plagiarism: John A. Conkling points out that until recently, little scientific research was done on the chemical properties of fireworks, and when it was, the results were not generally reported in scientific journals (96).

Even though the writer documents the source of his information, he uses the source's exact words without placing them in quotation marks.

Correct (Borrowed Words in Quotation Marks): John A. Conkling points out that until recently, little scientific research was done on the chemical properties of fireworks, and when it was, "the results were generally not reported in scientific journals" (96).

Correct (Paraphrase): John A. Conkling points out that the little research conducted on the chemical composition of fireworks was seldom reported in the scientific literature (96).

http://kirsznermandell.wadsworth.com

Computer Tip: Plagiarism and Internet Sources

Any time you download text from the Internet, you run the risk of committing unintentional plagiarism. To avoid the possibility of plagiarism, follow these guidelines:

- Download information into individual files so that you can keep track of your sources.
- Do not simply cut and paste blocks of downloaded text into your paper; summarize or paraphrase this material first.
- If you record the exact words of your source, enclose them in quotation marks.
- Whether your information is from emails, online discussion groups, listservs, or Web sites, give proper credit by providing appropriate documentation.
- Always document figures, tables, charts, and graphs obtained from the Internet or from any other electronic source.

(2) Do Not Imitate a Source's Syntax and Phrasing

Original: Let's be clear: this wish for politically correct casting goes only one way, the way designed to redress the injuries of centuries. When Pat Carroll, who is a woman, plays Falstaff, who is not, casting is considered a stroke of brilliance. When Josette Simon, who is black, plays Maggie in *After the Fall*, a part Arthur Miller patterned after Marilyn Monroe and which has traditionally been played not by white women, but by blonde white women, it is hailed as a breakthrough.

But when the pendulum moves the other way, the actors' union balks. (Quindlen, Anna. "Error, Stage Left." *New York Times* 12 Aug. 1990, sec. 1: 21)

Plagiarism: Let us be honest. The desire for politically appropriate casting goes in only one direction, the direction intended to make up for the damage done over hundreds of years. When Pat Carroll, a female, is cast as Falstaff, a male, the decision is a brilliant one. When Josette Simon, a black woman, is cast as Maggie in *After the Fall*, a role that Arthur Miller based on Marilyn Monroe and that has usually been played by a woman who is not only white but also blonde, it is considered a major advance.

```
            But when the shoe is on the other foot, the actors'
      union resists (Quindlen 21).
```

Although this writer does not use the exact words of her source, she closely imitates the original's syntax and phrasing, simply substituting synonyms for the author's words.

> **Correct (Paraphrase; One Distinctive Phrase Placed in Quotation Marks):** According to Anna Quindlen, the actors' union supports "politically correct casting" (21) only when it means casting a woman or minority group member in a role created for a male or a Caucasian. Thus, it is acceptable for actress Pat Carroll to play Falstaff or for black actress Josette Simon to play Marilyn Monroe; in fact, casting decisions such as these are praised. But when it comes to casting a Caucasian in a role intended for an African American, Asian, or Hispanic, the union objects (21).

NOTE: Although the parenthetical documentation at the end identifies the passage's source, the quotation requires separate documentation.

(3) Document Statistics Obtained from a Source

Although many people assume that statistics are common knowledge, they are usually the result of original research and must therefore be documented. Moreover, providing the source of the statistics helps readers to assess their reliability.

> **Correct:** According to one study, male drivers between the ages of sixteen and twenty-four accounted for the majority of accidents. Of 303 accidents recorded almost one half took place before the drivers were legally allowed to drive at eighteen (Schuman et al. 1027).

(4) Differentiate Your Words and Ideas from Those of the Source

Original: At some colleges and universities traditional survey courses of world and English literature . . . have been scrapped or diluted. At others they are in peril. At still others they will be. What replaces them is sometimes a mere option of electives, sometimes "multicultural" courses introducing material from Third World cultures and thinning out an already thin sampling of Western writings, and sometimes courses geared especially to issues of class, race, and gender. Given the notorious lethargy of academic decision-making, there has probably been more clamor than change; but if there's enough clamor, there will be change. (Howe, Irving. "The Value of the Canon." *The New Republic* 2 Feb. 1991: 40–47)

> **Plagiarism:** Debates about expanding the literary canon take place at many colleges and universities across the United States. At many universities, the Western literature survey courses have been edged out by courses that emphasize minority concerns. These courses are "thinning out an already thin sampling of Western writings" in favor of courses geared especially to issues of "class, race, and gender" (Howe 40).

Because the writer does not differentiate his ideas from those of his source, it appears that only the quotations in the last sentence are borrowed when, in fact, the first sentence also owes a debt to the original. The writer should have clearly identified the boundaries of the borrowed material by introducing it with an identifying tag and ending with documentation. (Note that a quotation *always* requires its own documentation.)

> **Correct:** Debates about expanding the literary canon take place at many colleges and universities across the United States. According to critic Irving Howe, at many universities the Western literature survey courses have been edged out by courses that emphasize minority concerns (41). These courses, says Howe, are "thinning out an already thin sampling of Western writings" in favor of "courses geared especially to issues of class, race, and gender" (40).

Checklist: Avoiding Plagiarism

☐ **Take careful notes.** Be sure you have recorded information from your sources carefully and accurately.

☐ **In your notes, clearly identify borrowed material.** In handwritten notes, put all words borrowed from your sources inside circled quotation marks, and enclose your own comments within brackets. If you are taking notes on a computer, boldface all quotation marks.

☐ **In your paper, differentiate your ideas from those of your sources** by clearly introducing borrowed material with an identifying tag and by following it with documentation.

☐ **Enclose all direct quotations** used in your paper within quotation marks.

☐ **Review all paraphrases and summaries** in your paper to make certain they are in your own words and that any distinctive words and phrases from a source are quoted.

(continued)

Avoiding plagiarism (continued)

☐ **Document all quoted material and all paraphrases and summaries** of your sources.

☐ **Document all information** that is open to dispute or that is not common knowledge.

☐ **Document all opinions, conclusions, figures, tables, statistics, graphs, and charts** taken from a source.

☐ **Never submit the work of another person as your own.** Do not buy a paper from an online paper mill or use a paper written by a friend. In addition, never include in your paper passages that have been written by a friend, relative, or writing tutor.

PART 4

Documenting Sources: MLA Style

PART 4

Documenting Sources: MLA Style

FREQUENTLY ASKED QUESTIONS

DIRECTORY OF MLA PARENTHETICAL REFERENCES

DIRECTORY OF MLA WORKS-CITED LIST ENTRIES

Print Sources: Entries for Books

Authors

Editions, Multivolume Works, Forewords, Translations, Sacred Works

Parts of Books

Dissertations, Pamphlets, Government Publications, Legal Sources

Print Sources: Entries for Articles

Scholarly Journals

Magazines and Newspapers

Entries for Miscellaneous Print and Nonprint Sources

Lectures and Interviews

CHAPTER 17

MLA Documentation Style

Documentation is the formal acknowledgment of the sources you use in your paper. This chapter explains and illustrates the documentation style recommended by the Modern Language Association (MLA). Chapter 18 discusses the documentation style of the American Psychological Association (APA), Chapter 19 gives an overview of the format recommended by *The Chicago Manual of Style*, and Chapter 20 presents the formats recommended by the Council of Science Editors (CSE) and organizations in other disciplines.

17a Using MLA Style

MLA style* is required by instructors of English and other languages as well as by many instructors in other humanities disciplines. MLA documentation has three parts: *parenthetical references in the body of the paper (also known as in-text citations), a works-cited list, and content notes.*

(1) Parenthetical References

MLA documentation uses parenthetical references in the body of the paper keyed to a works-cited list at the end of the paper. A typical parenthetical reference consists of the author's last name and a page number.

> The colony appealed to many idealists in Europe (Kelley 132).

If you state the author's name or the title of the work in your discussion, do not include it in the parenthetical reference.

> Penn's political motivation is discussed by Joseph J. Kelley in <u>Pennsylvania, The Colonial Years, 1681-1776</u> (44).

To distinguish two or more sources by the same author, include the title after the author's name. If the title is long, use an abbreviated version. When you shorten a title, begin with the word by which the work is alphabetized in the list of works cited.

> Penn emphasized his religious motivation (Kelley, <u>Pennsylvania</u> 116).

---

*MLA documentation format follows the guidelines set in the *MLA Handbook for Writers of Research Papers*, 6th ed. New York, MLA, 2003.

Close-up: Punctuating with MLA Parenthetical References

Paraphrases and Summaries Parenthetical references are placed *before* the sentence's end punctuation.

```
Penn's writings epitomize seventeenth-century religious

thought (Dengler and Curtis 72).
```

Quotations Run In with the Text Parenthetical references are placed *after* the quotation but *before* the end punctuation.

```
As Ross says, "Penn followed his conscience in all

matters" (127).
```

```
According to Williams, "Penn's utopian vision was informed

by his Quaker beliefs . . ." (72).
```

Quotations Set Off from the Text When you quote more than four lines of **prose** or more than three lines of **poetry**, parenthetical references are placed one space *after* the end punctuation.

See 47b

```
According to Arthur Smith, William Penn envisioned a state

based on his religious principles:

          Pennsylvania would be a commonwealth in which

          all individuals would follow God's truth and

          develop according to God's law. For Penn, this

          concept of government was self-evident. It would

          be a mistake to see Pennsylvania as anything but

          an expression of Penn's religious beliefs. (314)
```

SAMPLE MLA PARENTHETICAL REFERENCES

1. A Work by a Single Author

```
Fairy tales reflect the emotions and fears of children

(Bettelheim 23).
```

2. A Work by Two or Three Authors

```
The historian's main job is to search for clues and solve

mysteries (Davidson and Lytle 6).
```

```
With the advent of behaviorism, psychology began a new phase

of inquiry (Cowen, Barbo, and Crum 31-34).
```

3. A Work by More Than Three Authors
List only the first author, followed by et al. ("and others").

> Helping each family reach its goals for healthy child
>
> development and overall family well-being was the primary
>
> approach of Project EAGLE (Bartle et al. 35).

Or, list the last names of all authors in the order in which they appear on the work's title page.

> Helping each family reach its goals for healthy child
>
> development and overall family well-being was the primary
>
> approach of Project EAGLE (Bartle, Couchonnal, Canda, and
>
> Staker 35).

4. A Work in Multiple Volumes
If you list more than one volume of a multivolume work in your works-cited list, include the appropriate volume and page number (separated by a colon followed by a space).

> Gurney is incorrect when he says that a twelve-hour limit is
>
> negotiable (6: 128).

5. A Work without a Listed Author
Use the full title (if brief) or a shortened version of the title (if long), beginning with the word by which it is alphabetized in the works-cited list.

> The group issued an apology a short time later ("Satire
>
> Lost" 22).

6. A Work That Is One Page Long
Do not include a page reference for a one-page article.

> Sixty percent of Arab Americans work in white-collar jobs
>
> (El-Badru).

7. An Indirect Source
If you use a statement by one author that is quoted in the work of another author, indicate that the material is from an indirect source with the abbreviation qtd. in ("quoted in").

> According to Valli and Lucas, "the form of the symbol is an
>
> icon or picture of some aspect of the thing or activity
>
> being symbolized" (qtd. in Wilcox 120).

8. More Than One Work

Cite each work as you normally would, separating one citation from the other with a semicolon.

```
The Brooklyn Bridge has been used as a subject by many

American artists (McCullough 144; Tashjian 58).
```

NOTE: Long parenthetical references can distract readers. Whenever possible, present them as **content notes**.

9. A Literary Work

When citing a work of **fiction,** it is often helpful to include more than the author's name and the page number in the parenthetical citation. Follow the page number with a semicolon, and then add any additional information that might be helpful.

```
In Moby-Dick, Melville refers to a whaling expedition funded

by Louis XIV of France (151; ch. 24).
```

Parenthetical references to **poetry** do not include page numbers. In parenthetical references to *long poems*, cite division and line numbers, separating them with a period.

```
In the Aeneid, Virgil describes the ships as cleaving the

"green woods reflected in the calm water" (8.124).
```

(In this citation, the reference is to book 8, line 124 of the *Aeneid.*)
When citing *short poems*, identify the poet and the poem in the text of the paper and use line numbers in the citation.

```
In "A Song in the Front Yard," Brooks's speaker says, "I've

stayed in the front yard all my life / I want a peek at the

back" (lines 1-2).
```

NOTE: When citing lines of a poem, include the word line (or lines) in the first parenthetical reference; use just the line numbers in subsequent references.

In citing a **play,** include the act, scene, and line numbers (in arabic numerals), separated by periods; titles of well-known literary works (such as Shakespeare's plays) are often abbreviated (Mac. 2.2.14-16).

10. The Bible

MLA style requires that a biblical citation include the version of the Bible (underlined) and the book (abbreviated if longer than four letters, but not underlined or enclosed in quotation marks), followed by the chapter and verse numbers (separated by a period).

```
The cynicism of the speaker is apparent when he says, "All

things are wearisome; no man can speak of them all" (New

English Bible, Eccles. 1.8).
```

NOTE: The first time you use a biblical citation, include the version in your parenthetical reference; after that, only include the book. If you are using more than one version of the Bible, however, include the version in each in-text citation.

11. An Entire Work
When citing an entire work, include the author's name and the work's title in the text of your paper rather than in a parenthetical reference.

```
Lois Lowry's Gathering Blue is set in a technologically

backward village.
```

12. Two or More Authors with the Same Last Name
To distinguish authors with the same last name, include their initials in your parenthetical references.

```
Recent increases in crime have caused thousands of urban

homeowners to install alarms (L. Cooper, 115). Some of these

alarms use sophisticated sensors that were developed by the

army (D. Cooper, 76).
```

13. A Government Document or a Corporate Author
Cite such works using the organization's name followed by the page number (American Automobile Association 34). You can avoid long parenthetical references by working the organization's name into your paper.

```
According to the President's Commission for the Study of

Ethical Problems in Medicine and Biomedical and Behavioral

Research, the issues relating to euthanasia are complicated

(76).
```

14. A Legal Source
Titles of acts or laws that appear in the text of your paper or in the works-cited list should not be underlined or enclosed in quotation marks. In the parenthetical reference, titles are usually abbreviated, and the act or law is referred to by sections. Include the USC (United States Code) and the year the act or law was passed (if relevant).

```
Such research should include investigations into the cause,
diagnosis, early detection, prevention, control, and
treatment of autism (42 USC 284q, 2000).
```

Names of legal cases are usually abbreviated (Roe v. Wade). They are underlined in the text of your paper but not in the works-cited list.

```
In Goodridge v. Department of Public Health, the court ruled
that the Commonwealth of Massachusetts had not adequately
provided a reasonable constitutional cause for barring
homosexual couples from civil marriages (2003).
```

15. An Electronic Source
If a reference to an electronic source includes paragraph numbers rather than page numbers, use the abbreviation par. or pars. followed by the paragraph number or numbers.

```
The earliest type of movie censorship came in the form of
licensing fees, and in Deer River, Minnesota, "a licensing
fee of $200 was deemed not excessive for a town of 1000"
(Ernst, par. 20).
```

If the electronic source has no page or paragraph numbers, try to cite the work in your discussion rather than in a parenthetical reference. By consulting your works-cited list, readers will be able to determine that the source is electronic and may therefore not have page numbers.

```
In her article "Limited Horizons," Lynne Cheney observes
that schools do best when students read literature not for
practical information but for its insights into the human
condition.
```

(2) Works-Cited List

 The **works-cited list,** which appears at the end of your paper, is an alphabetical listing of all the research materials you cite. Double-space within and between entries on the list, and indent the second and subsequent lines of each entry one-half inch (five spaces). (**See 17b** for full manuscript guidelines.)

MLA • Print Sources:
Entries for Books

Book citations include the author's name; book title (underlined); and publication information (place, publisher, date). Figures 17.1 and 17.2 show where you can find this information.

Figure 17.1 Title page from a book showing the location of the information needed for documentation.

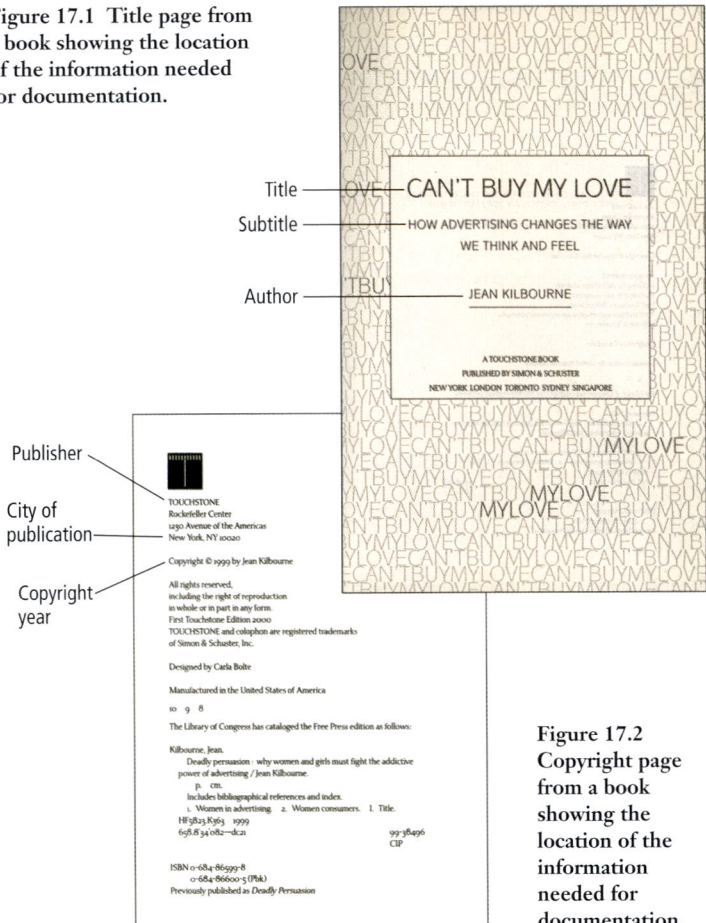

Title ——— CAN'T BUY MY LOVE

Subtitle ——— HOW ADVERTISING CHANGES THE WAY WE THINK AND FEEL

Author ——— JEAN KILBOURNE

A TOUCHSTONE BOOK
PUBLISHED BY SIMON & SCHUSTER
NEW YORK LONDON TORONTO SYDNEY SINGAPORE

Publisher

City of publication

Copyright year

TOUCHSTONE
Rockefeller Center
1230 Avenue of the Americas
New York, NY 10020

Copyright © 1999 by Jean Kilbourne

All rights reserved,
including the right of reproduction
in whole or in part in any form.
First Touchstone Edition 2000
TOUCHSTONE and colophon are registered trademarks
of Simon & Schuster, Inc.

Designed by Carla Bolte

Manufactured in the United States of America

10   9   8

The Library of Congress has cataloged the Free Press edition as follows:

Kilbourne, Jean.
Deadly persuasion : why women and girls must fight the addictive
power of advertising / Jean Kilbourne.
p.   cm.
Includes bibliographical references and index.
1. Women in advertising   2. Women consumers.   I. Title.
HF5823.K363   1999
658.8'34'082—dc21   99-38496
                                                         CIP

ISBN 0-684-86599-8
0-684-86600-5 (Pbk)
Previously published as Deadly Persuasion

Figure 17.2 Copyright page from a book showing the location of the information needed for documentation.

In your works-cited list citation, capitalize all major words of the book's title except articles, coordinating conjunctions, prepositions, and the *to* of an infinitive (unless such a word is the first or last word of the title or subtitle). Do not underline the period that follows a book's title.

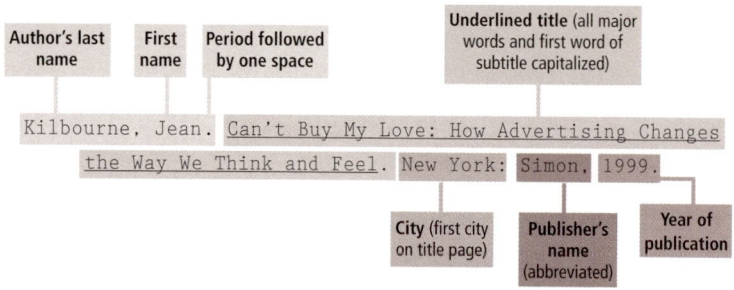

Author's last name | First name | Period followed by one space | Underlined title (all major words and first word of subtitle capitalized)

Kilbourne, Jean. Can't Buy My Love: How Advertising Changes the Way We Think and Feel. New York: Simon, 1999.

City (first city on title page) | Publisher's name (abbreviated) | Year of publication

---

Close-up: Publishers' Names

MLA requires that you use abbreviated forms of publishers' names in the list of works cited. In general, omit articles; abbreviations, such as *Inc.* and *Corp.*; and words such as *Publishers*, *Books*, and *Press*. If the publisher's name includes a person's name, use the last name only. Finally, use standard abbreviations whenever you can—*UP* for University Press and *P* for Press, for example.

Name	Abbreviation
Basic Books	Basic
Government Printing Office	GPO
The Modern Language Association of America	MLA
Oxford University Press	Oxford UP
Alfred A. Knopf, Inc.	Knopf
Random House, Inc.	Random
University of Chicago Press	U of Chicago P

Authors

1. A Book by One Author

Bettelheim, Bruno. The Uses of Enchantment: The Meaning and Importance of Fairy Tales. New York: Knopf, 1976.

2. A Book by Two or Three Authors

List the first author with last name first. List subsequent authors with first name first in the order in which they appear on the title page.

Peters, Michael A., and Nicholas C. Burbules. Poststructuralism and Educational Research. Lanham: Rowman, 2004.

3. A Book by More Than Three Authors

List the first author only, followed by et al. ("and others").

```
Badawi, El Said, et al. Modern Written Arabic. London:

    Routledge, 2004.
```

Or, include all the authors in the order in which they appear on the title page.

```
Badawi, El Said, Daud A. Abdu, Mike Carfter, and Adrian

    Gully. Modern Written Arabic. London: Routledge, 2004.
```

4. Two or More Books by the Same Author

List books by the same author in alphabetical order by title. After the first entry, use three unspaced hyphens followed by a period in place of the author's name.

```
Ede, Lisa. Situating Composition: Composition Studies and

    the Politics of Location. Carbondale: Southern Illinois

    UP, 2004.

---. Work in Progress. 6th ed. Boston: Bedford, 2004.
```

NOTE: If the author is the editor or translator of the second entry, place a comma and the appropriate abbreviation after the hyphens (---, ed.). See entry 6 for more on edited books and entry 13 for more on translated books.

5. A Book by a Corporate Author

A book is cited by its corporate author when individual members of the association, commission, or committee that produced it are not identified on the title page.

```
American Automobile Association. Western Canada and Alaska.

    Heathrow: AAA, 2004.
```

6. An Edited Book

An edited book is a work prepared for publication by a person other than the author. If your focus is on the *author's* work, begin your citation with the author's name. After the title, include the abbreviation Ed. ("Edited by"), followed by the editor or editors.

```
Twain, Mark. Adventures of Huckleberry Finn. Ed. Michael

    Patrick Hearn. New York: Norton, 2001.
```

If your focus is on the *editor's* work, begin your citation with the editor's name followed by the abbreviation ed. ("editor") if there is one editor or eds. ("editors") if there is more than one. After the title, give the author's name, preceded by the word By.

Hearn, Michael Patrick, ed. <u>Adventures of Huckleberry Finn</u>.

By Mark Twain. New York: Norton, 2001.

Editions, Multivolume Works, Forewords, Translations, Sacred Works

7. A Subsequent Edition of a Book

When citing an edition other than the first, include the edition number that appears on the work's title page.

Wilson, Charles Banks. <u>Search for the Native American</u>

<u>Purebloods</u>. 3rd ed. Norman: U of Oklahoma P, 2000.

8. A Republished Book

Include the original publication date after the title of a republished book—for example, a paperback version of a hardcover book.

Wharton, Edith. <u>The House of Mirth</u>. 1905. New York:

Scribner's, 1975.

9. A Book in a Series

If the title page indicates that the book is a part of a series, include the series name, neither underlined nor enclosed in quotation marks, and the series number, followed by a period, before the publication information.

Davis, Bertram H. <u>Thomas Percy</u>. Twayne's English Authors

Ser. 313. Boston: Twayne, 1981.

10. A Multivolume Work

When all volumes of a multivolume work have the same title, include the number of the volume you are using.

Fisch, Max H., ed. <u>Writings of Charles S. Peirce: A Chrono-</u>

<u>logical Edition</u>. Vol. 4. Bloomington: Indiana UP, 2000.

If you use two or more volumes that have the same title, cite the entire work.

Fisch, Max H., ed. <u>Writings of Charles S. Peirce: A Chrono-</u>

<u>logical Edition</u>. 6 vols. Bloomington: Indiana UP, 2000.

When the volume you are using has an individual title, you may cite the title without mentioning any other volumes.

Mares, Milan. <u>Fuzzy Cooperative Games: Cooperation with</u>

<u>Vague Expectations</u>. New York: Psysica-Verlag, 2001.

If you wish, however, you may include supplemental information, such as the number of the volume, the title of the entire work, the total number of volumes, or the inclusive publication dates.

11. The Foreword, Preface, or Afterword of a Book

    Campbell, Richard. Preface. <u>Media and Culture: An
        Introduction to Mass Communication</u>. By Bettina Fabos.
        Boston: Bedford, 2005. vi-xi.

12. A Book with a Title within Its Title

If the book you are citing contains a title that is normally underlined to indicate italics (a novel, play, or long poem, for example), do not underline the interior title.

    Fulton, Joe B. <u>Mark Twain in the Margins: The Quarry Farm
        Marginalia and</u> A Connecticut Yankee in King Arthur's
        Court. Tuscaloosa: U of Alabama P, 2000.

If the book you are citing contains a title that is normally enclosed in quotation marks, keep the quotation marks.

    Hawkins, Hunt, and Brian W. Shaffer, eds. <u>Approaches to
        Teaching Conrad's "Heart of Darkness" and "The Secret
        Sharer."</u> New York: MLA, 2002.

13. A Translation

    García Márquez, Gabriel. <u>One Hundred Years of Solitude</u>.
        Trans. Gregory Rabassa. New York: Avon, 1991.

14. The Bible

Underline the title, and give full publication information.

    <u>The New English Bible with the Apocrypha: Oxford Study
        Edition</u>. New York: Oxford UP, 1976.

Parts of Books

15. A Short Story, Play, or Poem in an Anthology

    Chopin, Kate. "The Storm." <u>Literature: Reading, Reacting,
        Writing</u>. Ed. Laurie G. Kirszner and Stephen R. Mandell.
        5th ed. Boston: Wadsworth, 2004. 176-79.

```
Shakespeare, William. Othello, The Moor of Venice.

     Shakespeare: Six Plays and the Sonnets. Ed. Thomas Marc

     Parrott and Edward Hubler. New York: Scribner's, 1956.

     145-91.
```

See entry 18 for information on how to cite more than one work from the same anthology.

16. A Short Story, Play, Poem, or Essay in a Collection of an Author's Work

```
Bukowski, Charles. "lonely hearts." The Flash of Lightning

     behind the Mountain: New Poems. New York: Ecco, 2004.

     115-16.
```

NOTE: The title of the poem is not capitalized because it appears in lowercase letters in the original.

17. An Essay in an Anthology
Even if you cite only one page of an essay in your paper, supply inclusive page numbers for the entire essay.

```
Crevel, Rene. "From Babylon." Surrealist Painters and Poets:

     An Anthology. Ed. Mary Ann Caws. Cambridge: MIT P,

     2001. 175-77.
```

18. More Than One Work from the Same Anthology
List each work from the same anthology separately, followed by a cross-reference to the entire anthology. Also list complete publication information for the anthology itself.

```
Agar, Eileen. "Am I a Surrealist?" Caws 3-7.

Caws, Mary Ann, ed. Surrealist Painters and Poets: An

     Anthology. Cambridge: MIT P, 2001.

Crevel, Rene. "From Babylon." Caws 175-77.
```

19. An Article in a Reference Book (Signed/Unsigned)
For a signed article, begin with the author's name. For unfamiliar reference books, include full publication information.

```
Drabble, Margaret. "Expressionism." The Oxford Companion to

     English Literature. 6th ed. New York: Oxford UP, 2000.
```

If the article is unsigned, begin with the title. For familiar reference books, do not include publication information.

```
"Cubism." The Encyclopedia Americana. 2004 ed.
```

NOTE: You may omit page numbers if the reference book lists entries alphabetically. If you are listing one definition among several from a dictionary, include the abbreviation `Def`. ("Definition") along with the letter or number that corresponds to the definition.

```
"Justice." Def. 2b. The Concise Oxford Dictionary. 10th ed.
    1999.
```

Dissertations, Pamphlets, Government Publications, Legal Sources

20. A Dissertation (Published/Unpublished)

Cite a published dissertation the same way you would cite a book, but add relevant dissertation information before the publication information. For dissertations published by University Microfilms International (UMI), include the order number at the end of the entry.

```
Rodriguez, Jason Anthony. Bureaucracy and Altruism: Managing
    the Contradictions of Teaching. Diss. U of Texas at
    Arlington, 2003. Arlington: UMI, 2004. ATT 1416857.
```

NOTE: University Microfilms, which publishes most of the dissertations in the United States, also publishes in CD-ROM. For the proper format for citing CD-ROMs, see entries 74 and 75.

Use quotation marks for the title of an unpublished dissertation.

```
Bon Tempo, Carl Joseph. "Americans at the Gate: The Politics
    of American Refugee Policy." Diss. U of Virginia, 2004.
```

21. A Pamphlet

Cite a pamphlet as you would a book. If no author is listed, begin with the title (underlined).

```
Choosing the Right Digital Camera. Rochester: Kodak, 2004.
```

22. A Government Publication

If the publication has no listed author, begin with the name of the government, followed by the name of the agency; you may use an abbreviation if its meaning is clear: `United States. Cong. Senate.`

```
United States. Office of Consumer Affairs. 2003 Consumer's
    Resource Handbook. Washington: GPO, 2003.
```

When citing two or more publications by the same government, use three unspaced hyphens in place of the name for the second and subsequent entries. If you also cite more than one work from the same agency of that government, use an additional set of unspaced hyphens in place of the agency name.

```
United States. FAA. Passenger Airline Safety in the Twenty-
     First Century. Washington: GPO, 2003.
---. ---. Recycled Air in Passenger Airline Cabins.
     Washington: GPO, 2002.
```

23. A Legal Source

In general, you do not need a works-cited entry for familiar historical documents or acts with USC (United States Code) numbers. Parenthetical references in the text are sufficient—(US Const., art. 3, sec. 2) or (15 USC 111g, 2003), for example. If you do cite an act in the works-cited list, include the name of the act, its Public Law (Pub. L.) number, its enactment date, and its Statutes at Large (Stat.) cataloging number.

```
Children's Health Act. Pub. L. 106-310. 17 Oct. 2000. Stat.
     114.1101.
```

In works-cited entries for legal cases, abbreviate names of cases, but spell out the first important word of each party's name. Include the case number, the name of the deciding court, and the decision date. Do not underline the case name in the works-cited list.

```
Goodridge v. Department of Public Health. No. SJC-08860.
     Supreme Ct. of Mass. 18 Nov. 2003.
```

MLA • Print Sources:
Entries for Articles

Article citations include the author's name; the title of the article (in quotation marks); the title of the periodical (underlined); the year or date of publication; and the pages on which the full article appears, without the abbreviations *p.* or *pp.* Figure 17.3 shows where you can find this information.

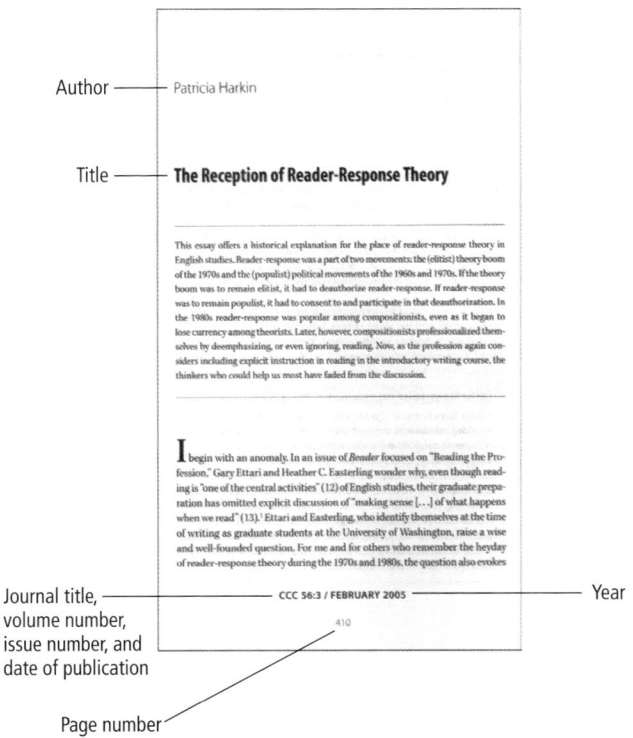

Author ——— Patricia Harkin

Title ——— **The Reception of Reader-Response Theory**

This essay offers a historical explanation for the place of reader-response theory in English studies. Reader-response was a part of two movements: the (elitist) theory boom of the 1970s and the (populist) political movements of the 1960s and 1970s. If the theory boom was to remain elitist, it had to deauthorize reader-response. If reader-response was to remain populist, it had to consent to and participate in that deauthorization. In the 1980s reader-response was popular among compositionists, even as it began to lose currency among theorists. Later, however, compositionists professionalized themselves by deemphasizing, or even ignoring, reading. Now, as the profession again considers including explicit instruction in reading in the introductory writing course, the thinkers who could help us most have faded from the discussion.

I begin with an anomaly. In an issue of *Reader* focused on "Reading the Profession," Gary Ettari and Heather C. Easterling wonder why, even though reading is "one of the central activities" (12) of English studies, their graduate preparation has omitted explicit discussion of "making sense […] of what happens when we read" (13).[1] Ettari and Easterling, who identify themselves at the time of writing as graduate students at the University of Washington, raise a wise and well-founded question. For me and for others who remember the heyday of reader-response theory during the 1970s and 1980s, the question also evokes

Journal title, ——— CCC 56:3 / FEBRUARY 2005 ——— Year
volume number,
issue number, and   410
date of publication

Page number ———

Figure 17.3 First page of an article showing the location of the information needed for documentation.

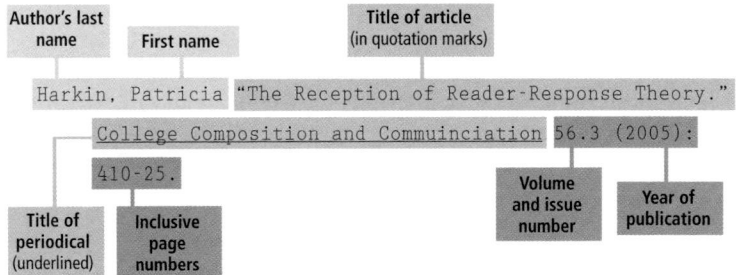

Author's last name — Harkin, Patricia
First name — Patricia
Title of article (in quotation marks) — "The Reception of Reader-Response Theory."
College Composition and Communinciation 56.3 (2005):
410-25.
Title of periodical (underlined)
Inclusive page numbers
Volume and issue number
Year of publication

Scholarly Journals

24. An Article in a Scholarly Journal with Continuous Pagination through an Annual Volume

For an article in a journal with continuous pagination—for example, one in which an issue ends on page 172 and the next issue begins with page 173—include the volume number, followed by the year of publication (in parentheses). Follow the year of publication with a colon, a space, and the inclusive page numbers.

```
Siderits, Mark. "Perceiving Particulars: A Buddhist

    Defense." Philosophy East and West 54 (2004): 367-83.
```

25. An Article in a Scholarly Journal with Separate Pagination in Each Issue

For a journal in which each issue begins with page 1, include the volume number, a period, and the issue number.

```
Hayes, B. Grant. "Group Counseling in Schools: Effective or

    Not?" The International Journal of Sociology and Social

    Policy 21.3 (2001): 12-21.
```

Magazines and Newspapers

26. An Article in a Weekly Magazine (Signed/Unsigned)

For signed articles, start with the author, last name first. In dates, the day precedes the month (abbreviated except for May, June, and July).

```
Corliss, Richard. "His Days in Hollywood." Time 14 June

    2004: 56-62.
```

For unsigned articles, start with the title of the article.

```
"Ronald Reagan." National Review 28 June 2004: 14-17.
```

27. An Article in a Monthly Magazine

```
Thomas, Evan. "John Paul Jones." American History Aug. 2003:

    22-25.
```

28. An Article That Does Not Appear on Consecutive Pages

When, for example, an article begins on page 120 and then skips to page 186, include only the first page number, followed by a plus sign.

```
Di Giovanni, Janine. "The Shiites of Iraq." National

    Geographic June 2004: 2+.
```

29. An Article in a Newspaper (Signed/Unsigned)

```
Krantz, Matt. "Stock Success Not Exactly Unparalleled." Wall

    Street Journal 11 June 2004: B1+.

"A Steadfast Friend on 9/11 Is Buried." New York Times 6

    June 2002: B8.
```

NOTE: Omit the article *the* from the title of a newspaper even if the newspaper's actual title includes the article.

30. An Editorial in a Newspaper

Brooks, David. "Living in the Age of Political Segregation."

    Editorial. <u>Dayton Daily News</u> 1 July 2004, final ed.:

    A12.

31. A Letter to the Editor of a Newspaper

Chang, Paula. Letter. <u>Philadelphia Inquirer</u> 10 Dec. 2003,

    suburban ed.: A17.

32. A Book Review in a Newspaper

Straw, Deborah. "Thinking about Tomorrow." Rev. of <u>Planning</u>

    <u>for the 21st Century: A Guide for Community Colleges</u>,

    by William A. Wojciechowski and Dedra Manes. <u>Community</u>

    <u>College Week</u> 7 June 2004: 15.

33. An Article with a Title within Its Title

If the article you are citing contains a title that is normally enclosed in quotation marks, use single quotation marks for the interior title.

Zimmerman, Brett. "Frantic Forensic Oratory: Poe's 'The

    Tell-Tale Heart.'" <u>Style</u> 35 (2001): 34-50.

If the article you are citing contains a title that is normally underlined to indicate italics, underline it in your works-cited entry.

Lingo, Marci. "Forbidden Fruit: The Banning of <u>The Grapes of</u>

    <u>Wrath</u> in the Kern County Free Library." <u>Libraries and</u>

    <u>Culture</u> 38 (2003): 351-78.

MLA • Entries for Miscellaneous Print and Nonprint Sources

Lectures and Interviews

34. A Lecture

Grimm, Mary. "An Afternoon with Mary Grimm." Visiting

    Writers Program, Dept. of English. Wright State U.

    16 Apr. 2004.

35. A Personal Interview

West, Cornel. Personal interview. 28 Dec. 2005.

Tannen, Deborah. Telephone interview. 8 June 2005.

36. A Published Interview

```
Huston, John. "The Outlook for Raising Money: An Investment
     Banker's Viewpoint." NJBIZ 30 Sept. 2002: 2-3.
```

Letters

37. A Personal Letter

```
Tan, Amy. Letter to the author. 7 Apr. 2001.
```

38. A Letter Published in a Collection

```
Joyce, James. "Letter to Louis Gillet." 20 Aug. 1931. James
     Joyce. By Richard Ellmann. New York: Oxford UP, 1965.
     631.
```

39. A Letter in a Library's Archives

```
Stieglitz, Alfred. Letter to Paul Rosenberg. 5 Sept. 1923.
     Stieglitz Archive. Yale U Arts Lib., New Haven.
```

Films, Videotapes, Radio and Television Programs, Recordings

40. A Film

Include the title of the film (underlined), the distributor, and the date, along with other information that may be useful to readers, such as the names of the performers, the director, and the writer.

```
Citizen Kane. Dir. Orson Welles. Perf. Welles, Joseph
     Cotten, Dorothy Comingore, and Agnes Moorehead. RKO,
     1941.
```

If you are focusing on the contribution of a particular person, begin with that person's name.

```
Welles, Orson, dir. Citizen Kane. Perf. Welles, Joseph
     Cotten, Dorothy Comingore, and Agnes Moorehead. RKO,
     1941.
```

41. A Videotape, DVD, or Laser Disc

Cite a videotape, DVD, or laser disc as you would cite a film, but include the medium before the name of the distributor.

```
Bowling for Columbine. Dir. Michael Moore. 2002. DVD. United
     Artists and Alliance Atlantis, 2003.
```

42. A Radio or Television Program

"War Feels Like War." P.O.V. Dir. Esteban Uyarra. PBS. WPTD,

   Dayton. 6 July 2004.

43. A Recording

List the composer, conductor, or performer (whichever you are focusing on), followed by the title (and, when citing jacket notes, a description of the material), manufacturer, and year of issue.

Boubill, Alain, and Claude-Michel Schönberg. Miss Saigon.

   Perf. Lea Salonga, Claire Moore, and Jonathan Pryce.

   Cond. Martin Koch. Geffen, 1989.

Marley, Bob. "Crisis." Lyrics. Bob Marley and the Wailers.

   Kava Island Records, 1978.

Paintings, Photographs, Cartoons, Advertisements

44. A Painting

Hopper, Edward. Railroad Sunset. 1929. Whitney Museum of

   American Art, New York.

45. A Photograph

Cite a photograph in a museum's collection in the same way you cite
a painting.

Stieglitz, Alfred. The Steerage. 1907. Los Angeles County

   Museum of Art.

To cite a personal photograph, begin with a descriptive title (neither underlined nor set in quotation marks), followed by the place
the photograph was taken, the photographer, and the date.

Rittenhouse Square, Philadelphia. Personal photograph by

   author. 6 May 2003.

46. A Cartoon or Comic Strip

Trudeau, Garry. "Doonesbury." Comic strip. Philadelphia

   Inquirer 15 Sept. 2003, late ed.: E13.

47. An Advertisement

Microsoft. Advertisement. National Review 8 June 2004: 17.

MLA • Electronic Sources:
Entries from Internet Sites

 MLA style* recognizes that full source information for Internet sources is not always available. Include in your citation whatever information you can reasonably obtain: the title of the Internet site (underlined); the editor of the site (if available); the version number of the source (if applicable); the date of electronic publication (or update); the number or range of pages, paragraphs, or sections (if available); the name of any institution or sponsor; the date of access to the source; and the URL. Figure 17.4 shows where you can find this information.

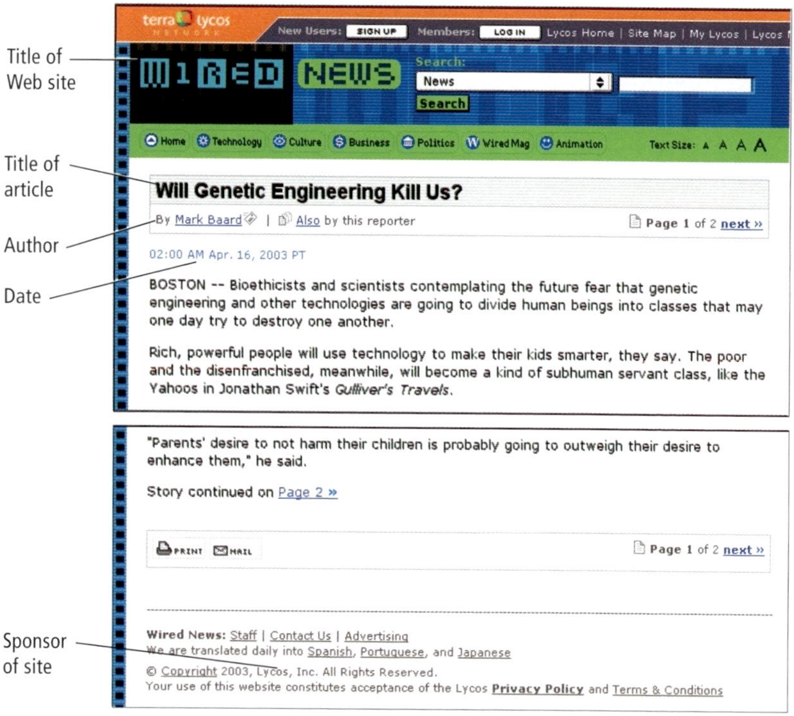

Title of Web site

Title of article

Author

Date

Sponsor of site

Figure 17.4 Part of an online article showing the location of the information needed for documentation.

---

*The documentation style for Internet sources presented here conforms to the most recent guidelines published in the *MLA Handbook for Writers of Research Papers* (6th ed.) and found online at <http://www.mla.org>.

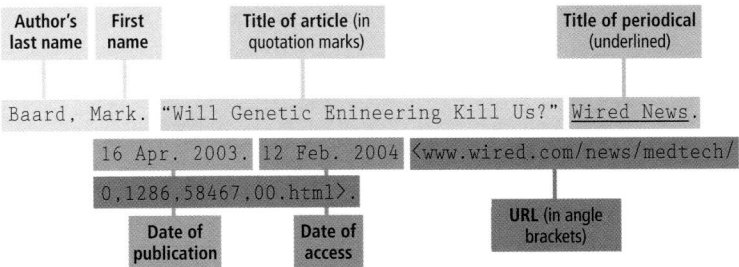

MLA requires that you enclose the electronic address (URL) within angle brackets to distinguish the address from the punctuation in the rest of the citation. If a URL will not fit on a line, the computer will carry the entire URL over to the next line. If you prefer to divide the URL, divide it after a slash. (Do not insert a hyphen.) If it is excessively long, give just the URL of the site's search page. Readers can then access the document by entering the author's name or the source's title.

Internet-Specific Sources

48. An Entire Web Site

Philadelphia Writers Project. Ed. Miriam Kotzen Green. May
    1998. Drexel U. 12 June 2001 <http://www.Drexel.edu/
    letrs/wwp>.

49. A Document within a Web Site

"D Day: June 7th, 1944." The History Channel Online. 1999.
    History Channel. 7 June 2002 <http://
    historychannel.com/thisday/today/997690.html>.

50. A Home Page for a Course

Mulry, David. Composition and Literature. Course home page.
    Jan. 2003-Apr. 2003. Dept. of English, Odessa College.
    6 Apr. 2003 <http://www.odessa.edu/dept/english/
    dmulryEnglish_1302.html>.

51. A Personal Home Page

Gainor, Charles. Home page. 22 July 2003. 10 Nov. 2003
    <http://www.chass.utoronto.ca:9094/~char>.

52. A Radio Program Accessed from an Internet Archive

```
Edwards, Bob. "Country Music's First Family." Morning
    Edition. 16 July 2002. NPR Archives. 2 Oct. 2002
    <http://www.npr.org/programs/ morning/index.html>.
```

53. An Email

```
Smith, Karen. Email to the author. 28 June 2004.
```

54. An Online Posting (Newsgroup or Online Forum)

```
Gilford, Mary. "Dog Heroes in Children's Literature." Online
    posting. 17 Mar. 1999. 12 Apr. 1999 <news:alt.animals.dogs>.
Schiller, Stephen. "Paper Cost and Publishing Costs." Online
    posting. 24 Apr. 2002. 11 May 2002. Book Forum. 17 May
    2002 <www.nytimes.com/webin/webx?13A^41356.ee765e/0>.
```

55. A Synchronous Communication (MOO or MUD)

MOOs (multiuser domain, object oriented) and MUDs (multiuser domain) are Internet programs that enable users to communicate in real time. To cite a communication posted in a MOO or a MUD, give the name (or names) of the writer(s), a description of the event, the date of the event, the forum (LinguaMOO, for example), the date of access, and the URL (starting with `telnet://`).

```
Guitar, Gwen. Online discussion of Cathy in Emily Brontë's
    Wuthering Heights. 17 Mar. 2002. LinguaMOO. 13 Sept.
    2004 <telnet://lingua.utdallas.edu:8888>.
```

Books, Articles, Reviews, Letters, and Reference Works on the Internet

56. A Book

```
Douglass, Frederick. My Bondage and My Freedom. Boston, 1855.
    8 June 2005 <gopher://gopher.vt.edu:10024/22/178/3>.
```

57. An Article in a Scholarly Journal

When you cite information from an electronic source that has a print version, include the publication information for the print source, the number of pages or paragraphs (if available), and the date you accessed it.

```
Dekoven, Marianne. "Utopias Limited: Post-Sixties and
     Postmodern American Fiction." Modern Fiction Studies
     41.1 (1995): 13 pp. 20 Jan. 2005 <http://muse.jhu.edu/
     journals/mfs.v041/ 41.1dwkovwn.html>.
```

58. An Article in a Magazine

```
Weiser, Jay. "The Tyranny of Informality." Time 26 Feb.
     1996. 1 Mar. 2002 <http://www.enews.com/magazines.tnr/
     current/022696.3.html>.
```

59. An Article in a Newspaper

```
Lohr, Steve. "Microsoft Goes to Court." New York Times on
     the Web 19 Oct. 1998. 29 Apr. 1999 <http://
     www.nytimes.com/web/docroot/library.ciber/week/
     1019business.html>.
```

60. An Article in a Newsletter

```
"Unprecedented Cutbacks in History of Science Funding." AIP
     Center for History of Physics 27.2 (Fall 1995). 26 Feb.
     1996 <http://www.aip.org/history/fall95.html>.
```

61. A Review

```
Ebert, Roger. Rev. of Star Wars: Episode I—The Phantom
     Menace, dir. George Lucas. Chicago Sun-Times Online
     8 June 2000. 22 June 2000 <http://www.suntimes.com/
     output/ebert1/08show.html>.
```

62. A Letter to the Editor

```
Chen-Cheng, Henry H. Letter. New York Times on the Web
     19 July 1999. 19 July 1999 <http://www.nytimes.com/
     hr/mo/day/letters/ichen-cheng.html>.
```

63. An Article in an Encyclopedia

Include the article's title, the title of the database (underlined), the version number (if available), the date of electronic publication, the sponsor, and the date of access as well as the URL.

```
"Hawthorne, Nathaniel." Encyclopaedia Britannica Online.
     2002. Encyclopaedia Britannica. 16 May 2002
     <http://www.search.eb.com>.
```

64. A Government Publication

Cite an online government publication as you would cite a print version; end with the information required for an electronic source.

United States. Dept. of Justice. Bureau of Justice
    Statistics. <u>Violence against Women: Estimates from the
    Redesigned National Crime Victimization Survey</u>. Jan.
    1995. 10 July 2003 <http://www.ojp.usdoj.gov/
    bjs/020131.pdf>.

Paintings, Photographs, Cartoons, and Maps on the Internet

65. A Painting

Seurat, Georges-Pierre. <u>Evening, Honfleur</u>. 1886. Museum of
    Mod. Art, New York. 8 Jan. 2004 <http://www.moma.org/
    collection/depts/paint_sculpt/blowups/
    paint_sculpt_002.html>.

66. A Photograph

Brady, Mathew. <u>Ulysses S. Grant 1822-1885</u>. <u>Mathew Brady's
    National Portrait Gallery</u>. 2 Oct. 2002 <http://
    www.npg.si.edu/exh/brady/gallery/56ga1.html>.

67. A Cartoon

Stossel, Sage. "Star Wars: The Next Generation." Cartoon.
    <u>Atlantic Unbound</u> 2 Oct. 2002. 14 Nov. 2002 <http://
    www.theatlantic.com/unbound/sage/ss990519.htm>.

68. A Map

"Philadelphia, Pennsylvania." Map. <u>U.S. Gazetteer</u>. US Census
    Bureau. 17 July 2000 <http://www.census.gov/cgi-bin/
    gazetteer>.

MLA • Electronic Sources:
Entries from Subscription Services

Subscription services can be divided into those to which you sub-scribe (**personal subscription services**), such as America Online, and those to which your library subscribes (**library subscription services**), such as Gale Group Databases, LexisNexis, and ProQuest Direct.

To cite information from a **personal subscription service,** in-clude the name of the database (underlined) as well as the name of the subscription service. If the personal subscription service provides a URL for a specific document, follow the examples in entries 48–55. Personal subscription services usually supply information without a URL, however. If the subscription service enables you to use a **keyword** to access material, type Keyword followed by a colon and the keyword (after the date of access).

> "Kafka, Franz." Compton's Encyclopedia Online. Vers. 3.1.
>
>   2000. America Online. 8 June 2003. Keyword: Compton's.

If instead of using a keyword you follow a series of **topic labels,** type the word Path followed by a colon and then the sequence of topics (separated by semicolons) you followed to get to the material.

> "Elizabeth Adams." History Resources. 28 Apr. 2002. America
>
>   Online. 11 Nov. 2002. Path: Research; Biography; Women
>
>   in Science; Biographies.

To cite information from a **library subscription service,** supply the publication information (including page numbers, if available) followed by the name of the database (underlined), the name of the subscription service, the library at which you accessed the database, the date of access, and the URL of the service's home page.

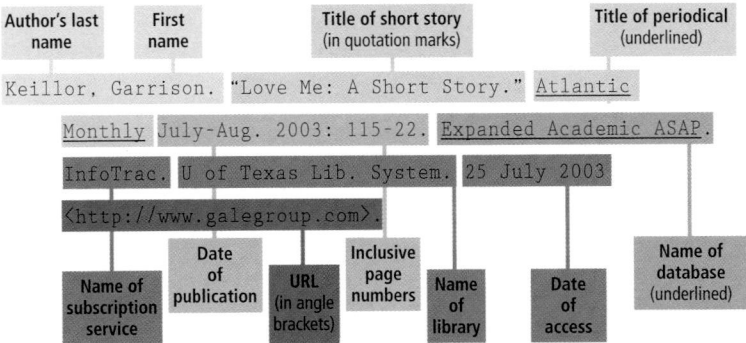

Journal Articles, Magazine Articles, and News Services from Subscription Services

69. A Scholarly Journal Article with Separate Pagination in Each Issue

```
Schaefer, Richard J. "Editing Strategies in Television News
        Documentaries." Journal of Communication 47.4 (1997):
        69-89. InfoTrac OneFile Plus. Gale Group Databases.
        Augusta R. Kolwyck Lib., Chattanooga, TN. 2 Oct. 2002
        <http://www.galegroup.com>.
```

NOTE: Along with the name of the library, you may include the city and state if you think they would be helpful.

70. A Scholarly Journal Article with Continuous Pagination throughout an Annual Volume

```
Hudson, Nicholas. "Samuel Johnson, Urban Culture, and the
        Geography of Postfire London." Studies in English
        Literature 42 (2002): 557-80. MasterFILE Premier.
        EBSCOhost. Augusta R. Kolwyck Lib., Chattanooga, TN.
        15 Sept. 2003 <http://www.epnet.com>.
```

71. A Monthly Magazine Article

```
Livermore, Beth. "Meteorites on Ice." Astronomy July 1993:
        54-58. Expanded Academic ASAP Plus. Gale Group
        Databases. Augusta R. Kolwyck Lib., Chattanooga, TN.
        12 Nov. 2003 <http://www.galegroup.com>.
Wright, Karen. "The Clot Thickens." Discover Dec. 1999.
        MasterFILE Premier. EBSCOhost. Augusta R. Kolwyck Lib.,
        Chattanooga, TN. 10 Oct. 2003 <http://www.epnet.com>.
```

72. A News Service

```
Ryan, Desmond. "Some Background on the Battle of
        Gettysburg." Knight Ridder/Tribune News Service 7 Oct.
        1993. InfoTrac OneFile Plus. Gale Group Databases.
        Augusta R. Kolwyck Lib., Chattanooga, TN. 16 Nov. 2003
        <http://www.galegroup.com>.
```

73. A Newspaper Article

```
Meyer, Greg. "Answering Questions about the West Nile
     Virus." Dayton Daily News 11 July 2002: Z3-7. Academic
     Universe News. LexisNexis. Augusta R. Kolwyck
     Lib., Chattanooga, TN. 17 Feb. 2003 <http://
     web.lexis-nexis.com>.
```

MLA • Other Electronic Sources

DVDs and CD-ROMs

74. A Nonperiodical Publication on DVD, CD-ROM, or Diskette Database

Cite a nonperiodical publication on DVD, CD-ROM, or diskette the same way you would cite a book, but also include a description of the medium of publication.

```
"Windhover." The Oxford English Dictionary. 2nd ed. DVD.
     Oxford: Oxford UP, 2001.
"Whitman, Walt." DiskLit: American Authors. CD-ROM. Boston:
     Hall, 2000.
```

75. A Periodical Publication on a DVD or CD-ROM Database

```
Zurbach, Kate. "The Linguistic Roots of Three Terms."
     Linguistic Quarterly 37 (1994): 12-47. InfoTrac:
     Magazine Index Plus. CD-ROM. Information Access. Jan.
     2001.
```

(3) Content Notes

Content notes—multiple bibliographical citations or other material that does not fit smoothly into your paper—are indicated by a **superscript** (raised numeral) in the text. Notes can appear either as footnotes at the bottom of the page or as endnotes on a separate sheet entitled Notes, placed after the last page of the paper and before the works-cited list. Content notes are double-spaced within and between entries. The first line is indented one-half inch (five spaces), and subsequent lines are typed flush left.

For Multiple Citations

In the Paper

> Many researchers emphasize the necessity of having
> dying patients share their experiences.[1]

In the Note

> [1]Kübler-Ross 27; Stinnette 43; Poston 70; Cohen
> and Cohen 31-34; Burke 1:91-95.

For Other Material

In the Paper

> The massacre during World War I is an event the
> survivors could not easily forget.[2]

In the Note

> [2]For a firsthand account of these events, see
> Bedoukian 178-81.

17b MLA-Style Manuscript Guidelines

Although MLA papers do not usually include abstracts, internal headings, tables, or graphs, this situation is changing. Be sure you know what your instructor expects.

The following guidelines are based on the latest version of the *MLA Handbook for Writers of Research Papers.*

FAQs
links

Checklist: Typing Your Paper

Checklist
☑ Write an essay
☐ Do research sourc
☐ Document discipline
☐ Learn doc strate
☐ Devise stra
process
☐ Integrate sen
☐ Improve comm

When typing your paper, use the student paper in **17c** as your model.

☐ Type your paper with a one-inch margin at the top and bottom and on both sides. Double-space your paper throughout.

☐ Type your name, your instructor's name, the course title, and the date on separate lines flush with the upper-left margin. Double-space, center, and type the title. Double-space again, and begin typing the text of the paper.

☐ Capitalize all important words in your title, but not prepositions, articles, coordinating conjunctions, or the *to* in infinitives (unless they begin or end the title or subtitle). Do not underline your title or enclose it in quotation marks. Never put a period after the title, even if it is a sentence.

☐ Set off quotations of more than four lines of prose or more than three lines of poetry by indenting the whole quotation one inch (or ten spaces). If you quote a single paragraph or part of a paragraph, do not indent the first line beyond one inch. If you quote two or more paragraphs, however, indent the first line of each paragraph an additional quarter inch. (If the first sentence does not begin a paragraph, do not indent it. Indent the first line only in successive paragraphs.)

☐ Number all pages of your paper consecutively—including the first—in the upper right-hand corner, one-half inch from the top, flush right. Type your name followed by a space before the page number on every page.

☐ If you use source material in your paper, follow **MLA documentation style**.

See 17a

Checklist: Using Visuals

See 24d

☐ Insert **visuals** into the text as close as possible to where they are discussed.

☐ Label each table with the word `Table` followed by an arabic numeral (for instance, `Table 1`). Double-space, and type a descriptive caption, with the first line flush with the left-hand margin; indent subsequent lines one-quarter inch. Capitalize the caption as if it were a title. (Both the table number and the descriptive caption should appear above the table.) Below the table, type the word `Source`, followed by a colon and all source information. Type the first line of the source information flush with the left-hand margin; indent subsequent lines one-quarter inch.

☐ Label other types of visual material—graphs, charts, photographs, clip art, drawings, and so on—`Fig.` (Figure) followed by an arabic numeral (for example, `Fig. 2`). Type each label and a title or caption on the same line, followed by source information, directly below the visual. Type all lines flush with the left-hand margin.

☐ Do not include the source of the visual in the works-cited list unless you use other material from that source elsewhere in the paper.

Checklist: Preparing the MLA Works-Cited List

FAQs links

See 17a3

☐ Begin the works-cited list on a new page after the last page of text or **content notes**, numbered as the next page of the paper.

☐ Center the title `Works Cited` one inch from the top of the page. Double-space between the title and the first entry.

(continued)

Preparing the MLA works-cited list (continued)

☐ Each entry on the works-cited list has three divisions: author, title, and publication information. Separate divisions with a period and one space.

☐ List entries alphabetically, with last name first. Use the author's full name as it appears on the title page. If a source has no listed author, alphabetize it by the first word of the title (not counting the article).

☐ Type the first line of each entry flush with the left-hand margin; indent subsequent lines one-half inch (or five spaces).

☐ Double-space within and between entries.

☐ Enclose URLs in angle brackets. If a URL carries over to the next line, break the URL after a slash; do not insert a hyphen. If your word-processing program automatically converts URLs to hotlinks, turn off this feature. (You can do this with *Microsoft Word* by opening the AutoCorrect function under the Tools menu, and then selecting AutoFormat.)

17c Sample MLA-Style Research Paper

 The following student paper, "The Great Digital Divide," uses MLA documentation style. It includes MLA-style in-text citations, a bar graph, a notes page, and a works-cited list.

Romney 1

Kimberly Romney

Professor Smith

English 102

8 March 2005

                    The Great Digital Divide

     Today, a basic understanding of computers and
how to use them is necessary for success. For this
reason, those who are unfamiliar with modern digital
technology find themselves at a great disadvantage
when it comes to education and employment. One of the
most exciting digital technologies available is the
information superhighway, better known as the
Internet. The Internet, with its accompanying software
and services, is rapidly changing the way we access
and see information. Clearly, the Internet offers
great promise, but some argue that it is creating many
problems as well. Although the Internet has changed
our lives for the better, it threatens to leave many
people behind, creating two distinct classes—those
who have access and those who do not.

     In the late 1990s, many argued that the Internet
had ushered in a new age, one in which instant
communication would bring people closer together and
eventually eliminate national boundaries. In
"Building a Global Community," former Vice President
Al Gore took this optimistic view, seeing the Internet
as a means "to deepen and extend our oldest and most
cherished global values: rising standards of living
and literacy, an ever-widening circle of freedom, and
individual empowerment." Gore went on to say that he
could envision the day when we would "extend our

Romney 2

knowledge and our prosperity to our most isolated
inner cities, to the barrios, the favelas, the
colonias, and our most remote rural villages."

Others, however, argued that for many people,
the benefits of the Internet were not nearly this
obvious or far-reaching. They maintained that the
Internet was creating what many have called a
"digital divide," which excludes a large percentage
of the poor, elderly, disabled, and members of many
minority groups from current technological
advancements (Digital Divide Network).

A survey conducted by the US Department of
Commerce in 2002 showed that white people and those
with higher annual incomes were more likely to own
computers than minorities and people from low-income
households. In households where the average income
was $75,000 and over, 89% had access to a computer.
In households earning $10,000-$14,999, only 25% had
access to a computer. Moreover, although 61% of white
households had access to a computer, only 37.1% of
African-American and 40% of Hispanic households had
home computers.

While the Department of Commerce study suggested
that financial circumstances were largely responsible
for the "digital divide," the gap in computer
ownership across incomes indicated that other factors
might also be contributing to the disparity. For
example, in a 1999 New York Times op-ed article,
Henry Louis Gates Jr. argued that bridging the
digital divide would "require more than cheap PC's";
it would "involve content" (500).[1] African Americans

Parenthetical documentation refers to material accessed from a Web site

Paragraph synthesizes information from a Commerce Department study and a newspaper article

Superscript number identifies content note

Romney 3

were not interested in the Internet, Gates wrote,
because the content rarely appealed to them. Gates
compared the lack of interest in the Internet with
the history of African Americans' relationship to the
recording industry. According to Gates, blacks began
to buy records "only when mainstream companies . . .
introduced so-called race records, blues and jazz
discs aimed at a nascent African American market"
(501). Gates suggested that Web sites that address
the needs of African Americans could play the same
role that race records did for the music industry.
Ignoring the race problem, Gates warned, would lead
to a form of "cybersegregation" that would devastate
the African-American community (501).

Ellipsis indicates that the student has deleted words from the quotation

   It was clear to many that people without
Internet access had difficulty at school, trouble
obtaining jobs, and fewer opportunities to save
money and time as consumers. They also lacked a
ccess to educational materials and to jobs posted on
the Internet. With access to only a portion of
available goods and services, people who were offline
did not have the advantages that people who were
online could routinely get. The Internet was clearly
widening the economic and social divide that already
separated people in this country.

Student's original conclusions; no documentation necessary

   In response, the government, corporations,
nonprofit organizations, and public libraries made
efforts to bridge the gap between the "haves" and
"have-nots." For example, the Education Department's
Community Technology Centers Program helped finance
computer activity centers for students and adults.

Romney 4

Parenthetical documentation includes abbreviated title when two or more works by the same author are cited in the paper

Also, the Department of Commerce's Technology Opportunities Program (TOP) provided money and services to organizations that needed more technology to operate efficiently. One recipient was America's Second Harvest, which used the funds to track donations to its national network of food banks (Schwartz, "Report").

Nonprofit organizations also worked to bridge the digital divide. The Bill and Melinda Gates Foundation, for example, has provided libraries across the country with funding that allows them to purchase computers and connect to the Internet (Egan). Nonprofit organizations also sponsor Web sites, such as <u>The Digital Divide Network</u>, a site that posts stories about the digital divide from a variety of perspectives. By posting information, the site's sponsor hopes to raise awareness of the problems that the digital divide causes.

Recently, however, some people have begun to question the need for many of these initiatives. In fact, as illustrated in fig. 1, computer use by young people between the ages of three and twenty-four rose dramatically between 1998 and 2001.

Several recent studies seem to support this view. For example, a 2004 study by the Pew Research Center found that nearly 66% of whites and Hispanics and 61% of African Americans use the Internet (Nelson). Another study conducted by the University of Texas at Dallas also found that the digital divide seems to be closing. According to Professor Donald Hicks, research shows that "broadband

Romney 5

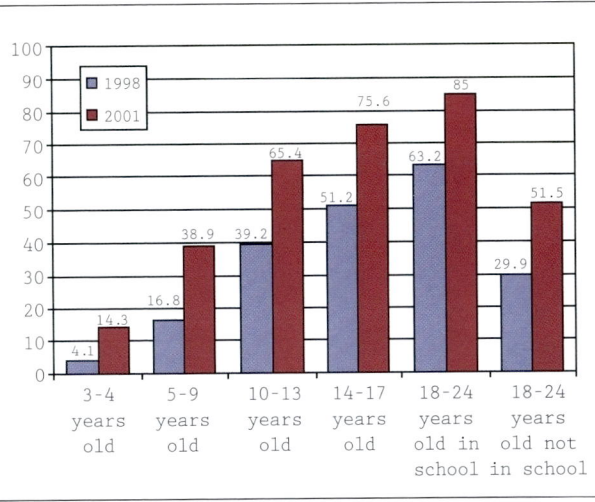

Graph summarizes relevant data. Source information is typed directly below the figure.

Fig. 1. United States, Dept. of Commerce, Economics and Statistics Admin., Natl. Telecommunications and Information Admin., <u>A Nation Online: How Americans Are Expanding Their Use of the Internet</u> (Washington: GPO, 2002) 43, 20 Jan. 2005 <http://www.ntia.doc.gov/ntiahome/dn/nation_online.pdf>.

Internet is more readily available in minority neighborhoods than in areas that are home to more whites" (Nelson). Even earlier, a 2002 report by the US Department of Commerce, using the most recent census data then available, concluded that Internet access in homes had increased significantly between 1999 and 2001, even among minorities.

Arguing that significant strides have been made to bridge the digital divide, the Bush administration believes that programs like the Community Technology Centers Program and the Technology Opportunities

Romney 6

Program are no longer needed ("Digital Divide
Debated"). At the same time, as the result of the
.com bust, private industry has withdrawn some
support for efforts to bridge the digital divide. One
organization, called PowerUp, worked with
corporations to create community-based technology
centers. In places like Austin, Texas, PowerUp worked
to establish a computer center in the city's
impoverished neighborhoods by collaborating with AOL
Time Warner and the Austin Urban League (Doggett).
Despite its initial success, the organization was
hard hit by the economic downturn. According to a
PowerUp spokesperson, "The model that was launched in
late 1999 . . . was a model that had its bloodlines
in different economic times. The model isn't
necessarily the best one for these economic times"
(Schwartz, "Lack"). In 2002, PowerUp closed its
offices, leaving the community centers they created
to find funding on their own.

In other cases, the groups targeted by digital
divide programs argue that such programs might do
more harm than good. A 2001 article in the Chronicle
of Higher Education observes that many African-
American and other minority groups argue that digital
divide rhetoric might actually stereotype
minorities. The article says that digital divide
rhetoric "could discourage businesses or academics
from creating content or services tailored for
minority communities—ultimately making the digital
divide a self-fulfilling prophecy" (Young). Many
scholars and leaders in the African-American

Romney 7

community fear that a focus on the digital divide
will lead to its being seen as a fact to be accepted
rather than as a problem to be solved. Tara L.
McPherson agrees, arguing that "the idea of
challenging the digital divide is not about denying
its existence. But it is to ensure that the focus on
the digital divide doesn't naturalize a kind of
exclusion of investment" (qtd. in Young).

Qtd. in indicates that McPherson's comments were quoted in Young's article

However, despite the appearance that the digital
divide is closing and the claims that digital divide
rhetoric may actually be harmful, many public
officials and private interest groups continue to
voice their concerns that gaps in technological
literacy and availability remain a problem among
many populations and communities. In fact, a 2002
report published by the Benton Foundation disagrees
with the US Department of Commerce's findings. This
report contends that federal funding is key in
continuing to bring more people into the digital age.

While the Department of Commerce report
maintains that most people have access to computers in
their homes, the Benton Foundation's report uses the
same statistics to argue that many people continue to
have difficulty accessing the Internet. The Benton
report found that 75% of people with household incomes
of less than $15,000 and 66% with incomes between
$15,000 and $35,000 were not yet using the Internet.
Wealthier Americans, however, had significantly
greater access to the Internet. Of the Americans with
incomes of $50,000-$75,000 a year, 67.3% used the
Internet. As a result, the Benton Foundation

Romney 8

strongly disagreed with the Bush administration's
recommendation to cut programs like the Department of
Commerce's Technology Opportunities Program (TOP) and
the Community Technology Centers Program (CTC):

Quotation of more than four lines is typed as a block, indented 1" (or ten spaces) and double-spaced, with no quotation marks

> TOP and CTC are important engines of digital
> opportunity. They are emblematic of the
> importance of federal leadership in the
> effort to bridge the digital divide. Federal
> leadership brings the power of information
> to underserved communities. A federal
> retreat from that leadership role would
> undermine innovative efforts to bring
> digital opportunity to underserved
> communities and jeopardize many successful
> community programs. Rather than walking
> away from the investment, the federal

Parenthetical documentation is placed one space after end punctuation

> government should build upon the success of
> these programs to bring digital opportunity
> to the entire nation. (Benton Foundation)

The success of programs offered by the public
library system also challenges the wisdom of the
federal government's desire to cut funding for
programs that increase computer literacy. According
to a recent article published in the Knight
Ridder/Tribune Business News, the New York public
library system's computer literacy courses drew over
eighteen thousand people in 2003. The demand for
these classes is so high that many classes fill up,
leaving people frustrated and disappointed (Dalton).
The clear conclusion is that although the gap between
the haves and have-nots may be closing, continued

success depends on continued financial support of successful programs.[2]

Superscript number identifies content note

It is not only minorities and the impoverished who are affected by the digital divide. Many people know that children in inner-city schools lack access to computer technology and to the Internet, but few know that children attending schools in rural areas are also at risk. Vicky Wellborn, a high school English teacher in a small town, reports that her school only recently instituted a computer literacy program. As they ordered computers, the instructors realized that one of their biggest challenges would be training themselves. Certainly the computer literacy program has been helpful to many students, but the difficulties of teaching an unfamiliar subject continue to challenge teachers at the school (Wellborn).

Although many strides have been made in closing the gap between those who have access to the Internet and those who do not, problems and new challenges remain. Steps must be taken to solve these problems. First, we must continue efforts to make the Internet available to the widest possible audience. We must also ensure that the rhetoric surrounding the term digital divide is used to close this gap, not to create a new one by establishing or reinforcing stereotypes about minorities. A broader definition of what the digital divide is might help us to see that it has the potential to marginalize many groups of people—the poor, the elderly, the disabled, and rural schoolchildren, for example—not just members

Conclusion recommends solutions for problem of "digital divide"

Romney 10

Because concluding paragraph introduces no new material (it summarizes material already discussed and presents student's original conclusions), no documentation is necessary

of minority groups. On a practical level, the federal
government should continue to fund programs that
increase access to computer technology in general,
and to the Internet in particular. Unless we take
steps to make these resources available to all, we
will quickly become two separate and unequal
societies: one "plugged-in" and privileged and one
"unplugged" and marginalized.

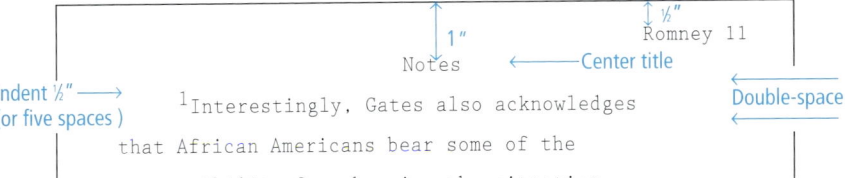

Romney 11

Notes   ←——Center title

Indent ½" ——→
(or five spaces)

Double-space

1" ↑

¹Interestingly, Gates also acknowledges that African Americans bear some of the responsibility for changing the situation.

²Other evidence suggests that the digital divide is a problem not only of Internet access, but also of access to technology in general. For example, in areas where punch-card voting machines were used, voters were seven times more likely to have their ballots discarded than in areas that used other types of ballots. When minority voters had access to better technology, however, their votes were more likely to register (Kennard).

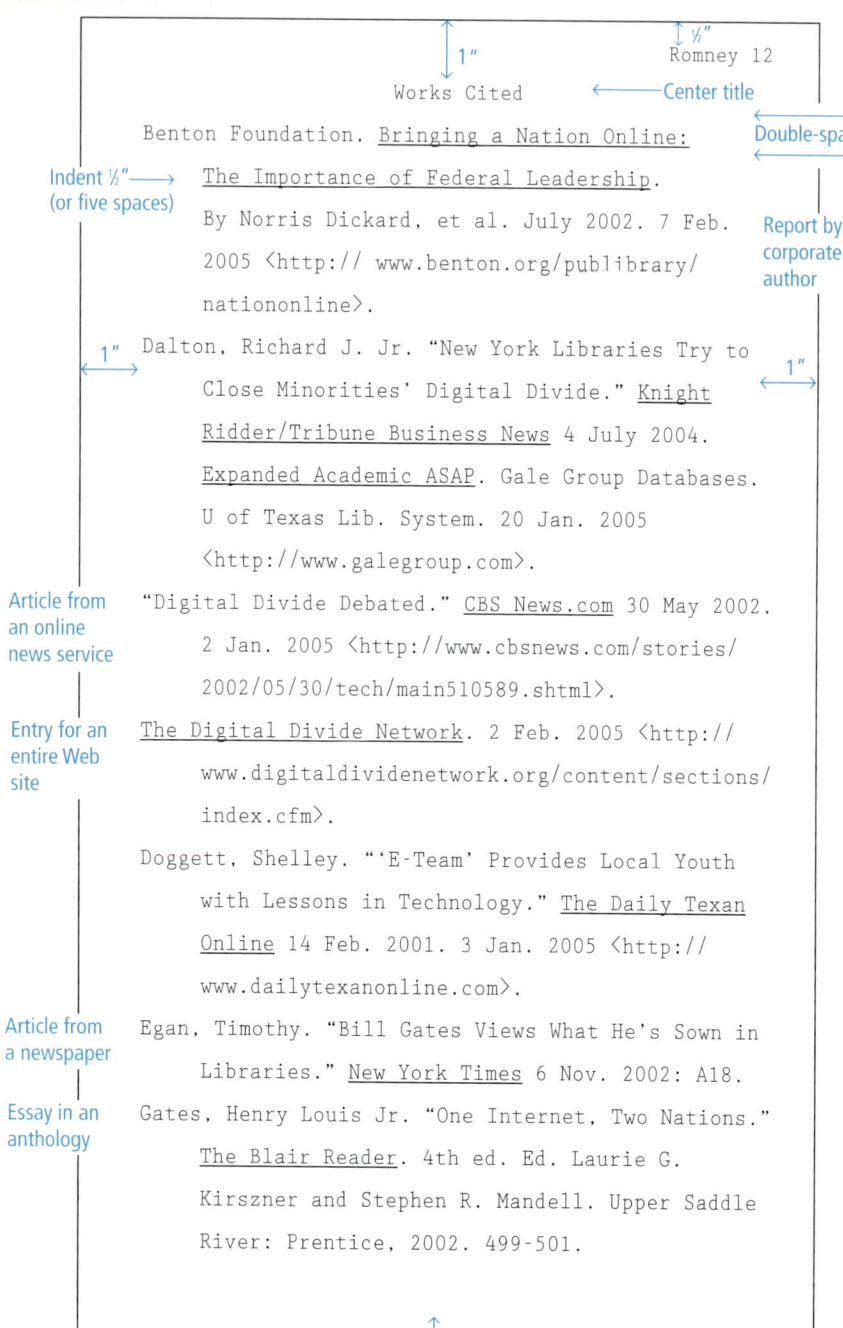

½"
1"   Romney 12

Works Cited   ← Center title

Indent ½" →
(or five spaces)

Benton Foundation. <u>Bringing a Nation Online:</u>   Double-space
        <u>The Importance of Federal Leadership</u>.
        By Norris Dickard, et al. July 2002. 7 Feb.   Report by a
        2005 <http:// www.benton.org/publibrary/   corporate
                                                             author
        nationonline>.

Dalton, Richard J. Jr. "New York Libraries Try to
        Close Minorities' Digital Divide." <u>Knight</u>
        <u>Ridder/Tribune Business News</u> 4 July 2004.
        <u>Expanded Academic ASAP</u>. Gale Group Databases.
        U of Texas Lib. System. 20 Jan. 2005
        <http://www.galegroup.com>.

Article from   "Digital Divide Debated." <u>CBS News.com</u> 30 May 2002.
an online   2 Jan. 2005 <http:/www.cbsnews.com/stories/
news service
                         2002/05/30/tech/main510589.shtml>.

Entry for an   <u>The Digital Divide Network</u>. 2 Feb. 2005 <http://
entire Web   www.digitaldividenetwork.org/content/sections/
site
                         index.cfm>.

Doggett, Shelley. "'E-Team' Provides Local Youth
        with Lessons in Technology." <u>The Daily Texan</u>
        <u>Online</u> 14 Feb. 2001. 3 Jan. 2005 <http://
        www.dailytexanonline.com>.

Article from   Egan, Timothy. "Bill Gates Views What He's Sown in
a newspaper   Libraries." <u>New York Times</u> 6 Nov. 2002: A18.

Essay in an   Gates, Henry Louis Jr. "One Internet, Two Nations."
anthology   <u>The Blair Reader</u>. 4th ed. Ed. Laurie G.
                         Kirszner and Stephen R. Mandell. Upper Saddle
                         River: Prentice, 2002. 499-501.

1"

Romney 13

Gore, Al. "Building a Global Community." <u>Remarks</u>
    <u>Prepared for the 15th International ITU</u>
    <u>Conference</u>. 12 Oct. 1998. 12 Jan. 2005
    <http://clinton3.nara.gov/WH/EOP/OVP/speeches/
    itu.html>.

Kennard, William E. "Democracy's Digital Divide."
    <u>Christian Science Monitor</u> 7 Mar. 2002.
    <u>Academic Universe: News</u>. LexisNexis. U of
    Texas Lib. System. 17 Jan. 2005 <http://
    web.lexis-nexis.com>.

Nelson, Colleen McCain. "Ethnic Gap on Internet
    Narrowing, Study Says." <u>Knight Ridder/Tribune</u>
    <u>Business News</u> 10 June 2004. <u>Expanded Academic</u>
    <u>ASAP</u>. Gale Group Databases. U of Texas Lib.
    System. 20 Jan. 2005 <http://www.galegroup.com>.

Schwartz, John. "A Lack of Money Forces Computer
    Initiative to Close." <u>New York Times</u> 30 Oct.
    2002. <u>Expanded Academic ASAP</u>. Gale Group
    Databases. U of Texas Lib. System. 20 Jan. 2005
    <http://www.galegroup.com>.

---. "Report Disputes Bush Approach to Bridging
    'Digital Divide.'" <u>New York Times</u> 11 July 2002.
    <u>Expanded Academic ASAP</u>. Gale Group Databases.
    U of Texas Lib. System. 19 Jan. 2005 <http://
    www.galegroup.com>.

United States. Dept. of Commerce. Economics and
    Statistics Admin., Natl. Telecommunications
    and Information Admin. <u>A Nation Online: How</u>
    <u>Americans Are Expanding Their Use of the</u>

Speech accessed from an Internet site

Newspaper article accessed from a library subscription database

Three unspaced hyphens used instead of repeating author's name

Government document accessed from the Internet

Romney 14

<u>Internet</u>. Washington: GPO, 2002. 20 Jan. 2005
    ⟨http://www.ntia.doc.gov/ntiahome/dn/
    Nation_Online.pdf⟩.

Wellborn, Vicky. "Re: Computer Literacy." Email to
    the author. 23 Jan. 2005.

Young, Jeffrey R. "Does 'Digital Divide' Rhetoric
    Do More Harm Than Good?" <u>Chronicle of Higher
    Education</u> 9 Nov. 2001. 10 Jan. 2005 ⟨http://
    chronicle.com⟩.

PART 5

Documenting Sources: APA and Other Styles

PART 5

Documenting Sources: APA and Other Styles

FREQUENTLY ASKED QUESTIONS

DIRECTORY OF APA IN-TEXT CITATIONS

DIRECTORY OF APA REFERENCE LIST ENTRIES

Print Sources: Entries for Books

Authors

Editions, Multivolume Works, Forewords

Parts of Books

Government Reports

Print Sources: Entries for Articles

Scholarly Journals

12. An article in a scholarly journal with separate pagination in each issue (p. 236)

Magazines and Newspapers

13. A magazine article (p. 236)
14. A newspaper article (p. 236)
15. A letter to the editor of a newspaper (p. 236)

Entries for Miscellaneous Print Sources

Letters

16. A personal letter (p. 236)
17. A published letter (p. 237)

Entries for Other Sources

Television Broadcasts, Films, CDs, Audiocassette Recordings, Computer Software

18. A television broadcast (p. 237)
19. A television series (p. 237)
20. A film (p. 237)
21. A CD recording (p. 237)
22. An audiocassette recording (p. 237)
23. Computer software (p. 237)

Electronic Sources: Entries from Internet Sites

Internet-Specific Sources

24. An Internet article based on a print source (p. 238)
25. An article in an Internet-only journal (p. 239)
26. A document from a university Web site (p. 239)
27. A Web document (no author identified, no date) (p. 239)
28. An email (p. 239)
29. A message posted to a newsgroup (p. 239)
30. A searchable database (p. 239)

Abstracts, Newspaper Articles

31. An abstract (p. 240)
32. An article in a daily newspaper (p. 240)

CHAPTER 18

APA Documentation Style

18a Using APA Style

APA style* is used extensively in the social sciences. APA documen- tation has three parts: *parenthetical references in the body of the paper,* a *reference list,* and optional *content footnotes.*

(1) Parenthetical References

APA documentation uses short parenthetical references in the body of the paper keyed to an alphabetical list of references that follows the paper. A typical parenthetical reference consists of the author's last name (followed by a comma) and the year of publication.

    Many people exhibit symptoms of depression after the death
    of a pet (Russo, 2000).

If the author's name appears in an introductory phrase, include the year of publication there as well.

    According to Russo (2000), many people exhibit symptoms of
    depression after the death of a pet.

Note that you may include the author's name and the date either in the introductory phrase or in parentheses at the end of the borrowed material.

When quoting directly, include the page number in parentheses after the quotation.

    According to Weston (1996), children from one-parent homes
    read at "a significantly lower level than those from two-
    parent homes" (p. 58).

NOTE: A long quotation (forty words or more) is not set in quotation marks. It is set as a block, and the entire quotation is double-spaced and indented one-half inch (or five to seven spaces) from the left margin. Parenthetical documentation is placed one space after the final punctuation.

---

*APA documentation format follows the guidelines set in the *Publication Manual of the American Psychological Association,* 5th ed. Washington, DC: APA, 2001.

SAMPLE APA IN-TEXT CITATIONS

1. A Work by a Single Author

```
Many college students suffer from sleep deprivation (Anton,
1999).
```

2. A Work by Two Authors

```
There is growing concern over the use of psychological
testing in elementary schools (Albright & Glennon,
1982).
```

3. A Work by Three to Five Authors

FAQs

If a work has more than two but fewer than six authors, mention all names in the first reference; in subsequent references in the same paragraph, cite only the first author followed by et al. ("and others"). When the reference appears in later paragraphs, include the year.

First Reference

```
(Sparks, Wilson, & Hewitt, 2001)
```

Subsequent References in the Same Paragraph

```
(Sparks et al.)
```

Reference in Later Paragraphs

```
(Sparks et al., 2001)
```

4. A Work by Six or More Authors

When a work has six or more authors, cite the name of the first author followed by et al. and the year in all references.

```
(Miller et al., 1995)
```

Close-up: Citing Works by Multiple Authors

When referring to multiple authors in the text of your paper, join the last two names with and.

```
According to Rosen, Wolfe, and Ziff (1988). . . .
```

In-text citations (as well as reference list entries) require an **ampersand** (&).

```
(Rosen, Wolfe, & Ziff, 1988)
```

5. Works by Authors with the Same Last Name

If your reference list includes works by two or more authors with the same last name, use each author's initials in all in-text citations.

> F. Bor (2001) and S. D. Bor (2000) concluded that no further
> study was needed.

6. A Work by a Corporate Author

If the name of a corporate author is long, abbreviate it after the first citation.

First Reference

> (National Institute of Mental Health [NIMH], 2001)

Subsequent Reference

> (NIMH, 2001)

7. A Work with No Listed Author

If a work has no listed author, cite the first two or three words of the title (followed by a comma) and the year. Use quotation marks around titles of periodical articles and chapters of books; use italics for titles of books, periodicals, brochures, reports, and the like.

> ("New Immigration," 2000)

8. A Personal Communication

Cite letters, memos, telephone conversations, personal interviews, emails, messages from electronic bulletin boards, and so on only in the text—*not* in the reference list.

> (R. Takaki, personal communication, October 17, 2001)

9. An Indirect Source

> Cogan and Howe offer very different interpretations of the
> problem (cited in Swenson, 2000).

10. A Specific Part of a Source

Use abbreviations for the words *page* (p.), *pages* (pp.), *chapter* (chap.), and *section* (sec.).

> These theories have an interesting history (Lee, 1966,
> chap. 2).

11. An Electronic Source

For an electronic source that does not show page numbers, use the paragraph number preceded by a ¶ symbol or the abbreviation para.

```
Conversation at the dinner table is an example of a family

ritual (Kulp, 2001,¶ 3).
```

In the case of an electronic source that has neither page nor paragraph numbers, cite the heading in the source and the number of the paragraph following the heading in which the material is located.

```
Healthy eating is a never-ending series of free choices

(Shapiro, 2001, Introduction section, para. 2).
```

If the source has no headings, you may not be able to specify an exact location.

12. Two or More Works within the Same Parenthetical Reference

List works by different authors in alphabetical order, separated by semicolons.

```
This theory is supported by several studies (Barson & Roth,

1995; Rose, 2001; Tedesco, 2002).
```

List two or more works by the same author or authors in order of date of publication (separated by commas), with the earliest date first.

```
This theory is supported by several studies (Rhodes &

Dollek, 2000, 2002, 2003).
```

For two or more works by the same author published in the same year, designate the work whose title comes first alphabetically *a*, the one whose title comes next *b*, and so on; repeat the year in each citation.

```
This theory is supported by several studies (Shapiro, 2003a,

2003b).
```

13. A Table

If you use a table from a source, give credit to the author in a note at the bottom of the table. Do not include this information in the reference list.

```
Note. From "Predictors of Employment and Earnings Among JOBS

Participants," by P. A. Neenan and D. K. Orthner, 1996,

Social Work Research, 20(4), p. 233.
```

(2) Reference List

The **reference list** gives the publication information for all the sources you cite. It should appear at the end of your paper on a new numbered page titled `References`. Entries in the reference list should be arranged alphabetically. Double-space within and between reference list entries, and indent the second and subsequent lines of each entry one-half inch (five spaces). (**See 18b** for full manuscript guidelines.)

APA • Print Sources:
Entries for Books

Book citations include the author's name (last name first); the year of publication (in parentheses); the book title (italicized); and publication information. Capitalize only the first word of the title and subtitle and any proper nouns. Include any additional necessary information—edition, report number, or volume number, for example—in parentheses after the title.

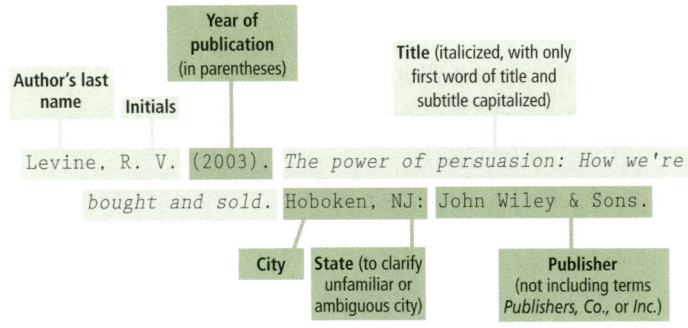

Author's last name   Initials   Year of publication (in parentheses)   Title (italicized, with only first word of title and subtitle capitalized)

Levine, R. V. (2003). *The power of persuasion: How we're bought and sold.* Hoboken, NJ: John Wiley & Sons.

City   State (to clarify unfamiliar or ambiguous city)   Publisher (not including terms *Publishers, Co.,* or *Inc.*)

Authors

1. A Book with One Author
Use a short form of the publisher's name. Write out in full the names of associations, corporations, and university presses. Include the words `Book` and `Press`, but do not include terms such as `Publishers, Co.,` or `Inc.`

> Maslow, A. H. (1974). *Toward a psychology of being.*
>   Princeton: Van Nostrand.

2. A Book with More Than One Author
List up to six authors by last name and initials, using an **ampersand** (&) to connect the last two names. For more than six authors, add `et al.` after the sixth name.

```
Wolfinger, D., Knable, P., Richards, H. L., & Silberger, R.
       (1990). The chronically unemployed. New York: Berman
       Press.
```

3. A Book with No Listed Author or Editor

```
Writing with a computer. (2000). Philadelphia: Drexel
       Press.
```

4. A Book with a Corporate Author

When the author and the publisher are the same, include the word `Author` at the end of the citation instead of repeating the publisher's name.

```
League of Women Voters of the United States. (2001). Local
       league handbook. Washington, DC: Author.
```

5. An Edited Book

```
Lewin, K., Lippitt, R., & White, R. K. (Eds.). (1985).
       Social learning and imitation. New York: Basic Books.
```

Editions, Multivolume Works, Forewords

6. A Work in Several Volumes

```
Jones, P. R., & Williams, T. C. (Eds.). (1990–1993).
       Handbook of therapy (Vols. 1–2). Princeton: Princeton
       University Press.
```

7. The Foreword, Preface, or Afterword of a Book

```
Taylor, T. (1979). Preface. In B. B. Ferencz, Less than
       slaves (pp. ii–ix). Cambridge: Harvard University Press.
```

Parts of Books

8. A Selection from an Anthology

Give inclusive page numbers preceded by `pp.` (in parentheses) after the title of the anthology. The title of the selection is not enclosed in quotation marks.

```
Lorde, A. (1984). Age, race, and class. In P. S. Rothenberg
       (Ed.), Racism and sexism: An integrated study
       (pp. 352–360). New York: St. Martin's Press.
```

NOTE: If you cite two or more selections from the same anthology, give the full citation for the anthology in each entry.

9. An Article in a Reference Book

```
Edwards, P. (Ed.). (1987). Determinism. In The encyclopedia
    of philosophy (Vol. 2, pp. 359-373). New York:
    Macmillan.
```

Government Reports

10. A Government Report

```
National Institute of Mental Health. (1987). Motion pictures
    and violence: A summary report of research (DHHS
    Publication No. ADM 91-22187). Washington, DC: U.S.
    Government Printing Office.
```

APA • Print Sources: Entries for Articles

Article citations include the author's name (last name first); the date of publication (in parentheses); the title of the article; the title of the periodical (italicized); the volume number (italicized); the issue number, if any (in parentheses); and the inclusive page numbers (including all digits). Capitalize only the first word of the article's title and subtitle. Do not underline or italicize the title of the article or enclose it in quotation marks. Give the periodical title in full, and capitalize all words except articles, prepositions, and conjunctions of fewer than four letters. Use p. or pp. when referring to page numbers in newspapers, but omit this abbreviation when referring to page numbers in journals and popular magazines.

Initial

Author's last name

Year of publication (in parentheses)

Title of article (only first word capitalized)

Italicized title of periodical (capitalize all major words)

Italicized volume number

Inclusive page numbers (include all digits)

```
Wax, M. (1995). Knowledge and ethics in qualitative social
    research. The American Sociologist, 26, 122-135.
```

Scholarly Journals

11. An Article in a Scholarly Journal with Continuous Pagination through an Annual Volume

```
Miller, W. (1969). Violent crimes in city gangs. Journal of
      Social Issues, 27, 581–593.
```

12. An Article in a Scholarly Journal with Separate Pagination in Each Issue

```
Williams, S., & Cohen, L. R. (1984). Child stress in early
      learning situations. American Psychologist, 21(10),
      1–28.
```

NOTE: Do not leave a space between the volume and issue numbers.

Magazines and Newspapers

13. A Magazine Article

```
McCurdy, H. G. (1983, June). Brain mechanisms and
      intelligence. Psychology Today, 46, 61–63.
```

14. A Newspaper Article

If an article appears on nonconsecutive pages, give all page numbers, separated by commas (for example, A1, A14). If the article appears on consecutive pages, indicate the full range of pages (for example, A7–A9).

```
James, W. R. (1993, November 16). The uninsured and health
      care. Wall Street Journal, pp. A1, A14.
```

15. A Letter to the Editor of a Newspaper

```
Williams, P. (2000, July 19). Self-fulfilling stereotypes
      [Letter to the editor]. Los Angeles Times, p. A22.
```

APA • Entries for Miscellaneous Print Sources

Letters

16. A Personal Letter

References to unpublished personal letters, like references to all other personal communications, should be included only in the text of the paper, not in the reference list.

17. A Published Letter

Joyce, J. (1931). Letter to Louis Gillet. In Richard
        Ellmann, *James Joyce* (p. 631). New York: Oxford
        University Press.

APA • Entries for Other Sources

Television Broadcasts, Films, CDs, Audiocassette Recordings, Computer Software

18. A Television Broadcast

Murphy J. (Executive Producer). (2002, March 4). *The CBS
        evening news* [Television broadcast]. New York: Columbia
        Broadcasting Service.

19. A Television Series

Sorkin, A., Schlamme, T., & Wells, J. (Executive Producers).
        (2002). *The west wing* [Television series]. Los Angeles:
        Warner Bros. Television.

20. A Film

Spielberg, S. (Director). (1994). *Schindler's list* [Motion
        picture]. United States: Universal.

21. A CD Recording

Marley, B. (1977). Waiting in vain. On *Exodus* [CD]. New
        York: Island Records.

22. An Audiocassette Recording

Skinner, B. F. (Speaker). (1972). *Skinner on Skinnerism*
        [Cassette recording]. Hollywood, CA: Center for
        Cassette Studies.

23. Computer Software

Sharp, S. (1995). *Career Selection Tests* (Version 5.0)
        [Computer software]. Chico, CA: Avocation Software.

APA • Electronic Sources:
Entries from Internet Sites

 APA guidelines for documenting electronic sources focus on Web sources, which often do not include all the bibliographic information that print sources do. For example, Web sources may not include page numbers or a place of publication. At a minimum, a Web citation should have a title, a date (the date of publication, update, or retrieval), and an electronic address (URL). If possible, also include the author(s) of a source. When you need to divide a URL at the end of a line, break it after a slash or before a period (do not add a hyphen). Do not add a period at the end of the URL. (Current guidelines for citing electronic sources can be found on the APA Web site at <www.apa.org>.)

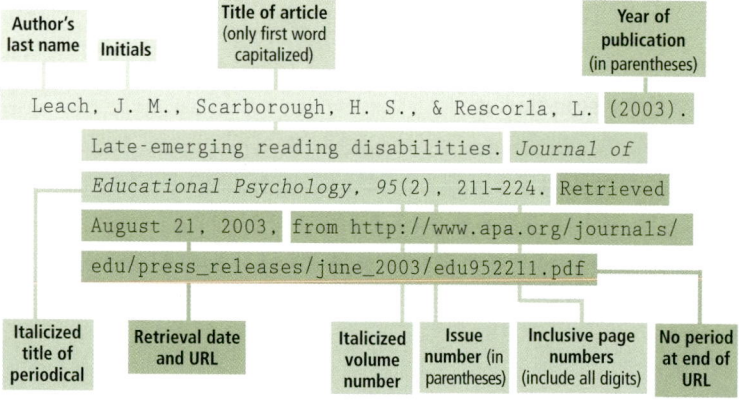

Internet-Specific Sources

24. An Internet Article Based on a Print Source
If you have seen the article only in electronic format, include the phrase `Electronic version` in brackets after the title.

> Winston, E. L. (2000). The role of art therapy in treating
>
>   chronically depressed patients [Electronic version].
>
>   *Journal of Bibliographic Research, 5*, 54-72.

NOTE: If you think the article you retrieved may be different from the print version, add the date you retrieved it and the URL.

25. An Article in an Internet-Only Journal

Hornaday, J., & Bunker, C. (2001). The nature of the

entrepreneur. *Personal Psychology, 23*, Article 2353b.

Retrieved November 21, 2001, from http://journals.apa

.org/volume23/pre002353b.html

26. A Document from a University Web Site

Beck, E. (1997, July). *The good, the bad & the ugly: Or, why*

it's a good idea to evaluate web sources. Retrieved

January 7, 2002, from New Mexico State University

Library Web site: http://lib.nmsu.edu/instruction/

evalcrit.html

27. A Web Document (No Author Identified, No Date)

The stratocaster appreciation page. (n.d.). Retrieved July

27, 2002, from http://members.tripod.com/~AFH/

NOTE: The abbreviation n.d. stands for "no date."

28. An Email

As with all other personal communication, references to personal email should be included only in the text of your paper, not in the reference list.

29. A Message Posted to a Newsgroup

List the author's full name—or, if that is not available, the screen name. In brackets after the title, provide information that will help readers access the message.

Shapiro, R. (2001, April 4). Chat rooms and interpersonal

communication [Msg 7]. Message posted to news://sci

.psychology.communication

30. A Searchable Database

Nowroozi, C. (1992). What you lose when you miss sleep.

Nation's Business, 80(9), 73–77. Retrieved April 22,

2001, from Expanded Academic ASAP database.

Abstracts, Newspaper Articles

31. An Abstract

Guinot, A., & Peterson, B. R. (1995). *Forgetfulness and partial cognition* (Drexel University Cognitive Research Report No. 21). Abstract retrieved December 4, 2001, from http://www.Drexel.edu/~guinot/deltarule-abstract .html

32. An Article in a Daily Newspaper

Farrell, P. D. (1997, March 23). New high-tech stresses hit traders and investors on the information superhighway. *Wall Street Journal*. Retrieved April 4, 1999, from http://wall-street.news.com/forecasts/stress/stress.html

(3) Content Footnotes

APA format permits content notes, indicated by superscripts (raised numerals) in the text. The notes are listed on a separate numbered page, titled Footnotes, following the appendixes (or after the reference list if there are no appendixes). Double-space all notes, indenting the first line of each note one-half inch (or five to seven spaces) and beginning subsequent lines flush left. Number the notes with superscripts that correspond to the numbers in your text.

18b   APA-Style Manuscript Guidelines

Social science papers have internal headings (internal sections may include an untitled introduction and the headings Method, Results, and Discussion). Each section of a social science paper is a complete unit with a beginning and an end so that it can be read separately and still make sense out of context. The body of the paper may include charts, graphs, maps, photographs, flowcharts, or tables.

The following guidelines are based on the latest version of the *Publication Manual of the American Psychological Association*.

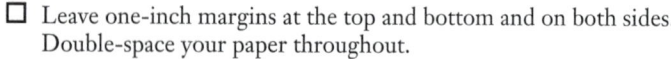

Checklist: Typing Your Paper

When typing your paper, use the student paper in **18c** as your model.

☐ Leave one-inch margins at the top and bottom and on both sides. Double-space your paper throughout.

☐ Indent the first line of every paragraph and the first line of every content footnote one-half inch (or five to seven spaces) from the left-hand margin.

☐ Set off a **long quotation** (more than forty words) in a block format by indenting the entire quotation five to seven spaces (or one-half inch) from the left-hand margin.

☐ Number all pages consecutively. Each page should include a **page header** (an abbreviated title) and a page number typed one-half inch from the top and one inch from the right-hand edge of the page. Leave five spaces (or one-half inch) between the page header and the page number.

☐ Center and type major <u>headings</u> with uppercase and lowercase letters. Place minor headings flush left, typed with uppercase and lowercase letters and italicized.

☐ Format items in a series as a numbered <u>list</u>.

☐ Arrange the pages of the paper in the following order:

- Title page (page 1) with a page header, running head, title, and byline (your name)
- Abstract (page 2)
- Text of paper (beginning on page 3)
- Reference list (new page)
- Appendixes (start each on a new page)
- Content footnotes (new page)

☐ If you use source material in your paper, citations should be consistent with **APA documentation style**.

See 24b

See 24c

See 18a

http://kirsznermandell.wadsworth.com

Computer Tip: Document Formatting

Several document formatting options in your word-processing program can help you format your research paper according to APA style. For example, you can use the Header/Footer option (see below) to place the appropriate words consistently at the top right of your paper. To use this tool, select the View menu and scroll down to Header/Footer.

Checklist: Using Visuals

APA style distinguishes between two types of visuals: **tables** and **figures** (charts, graphs, photographs, and diagrams). In

(continued)

Using visuals (continued)

manuscripts not intended for publication, tables and figures are included in the text. A short table or figure should appear on the page where it is discussed; a long table or figure should be placed on a separate page just after the page where it is discussed.

Tables

Number all **tables** consecutively. Each table should have a *label* and a *title*.

☐ The **label** consists of the word `Table` (not in italics), along with an arabic numeral, typed flush left above the table.
☐ Double-space and type a brief explanatory **title** for each table (in italics) flush left below the label. Capitalize the first letters of principal words of the title.

`Table 7`

Frequency of Negative Responses of Dorm Students to Questions Concerning Alcohol Consumption

Figures

Number all **figures** consecutively. Each figure should have a *label* and a *caption*.

☐ The **label** consists of the word `Figure` (typed flush left below the figure) followed by the figure number (both in italics).
☐ The **caption** explains the figure and serves as a title. Double-space the caption, but do not italicize it. Capitalize only the first word, and end the caption with a period. The caption follows the label (on the same line).

Figure 1. Duration of responses measured in seconds.

NOTE: If you use a table or figure from an outside source, include full source information in a note at the bottom of the table or figure. This information does not appear in your reference list.

Checklist: Preparing the APA Reference List

☐ Begin the reference list on a new page after the last page of text, numbered as the next page of the paper.
☐ Center the title `References` at the top of the page.
☐ List the items in the reference list alphabetically (with author's last name first).
☐ Type the first line of each entry at the left-hand margin. Indent subsequent lines one-half inch (or five to seven spaces).
☐ Separate the major divisions of each entry with a period and one space.
☐ Double-space the reference list within and between entries.

Checklist: Arranging Entries in the APA Reference List

☐ Single-author entries precede multiple-author entries that begin with the same name.

    Field, S. (1987)

    Field, S., & Levitt, M. P. (1984)

☐ Entries by the same author or authors are arranged according to date of publication, starting with the earliest date.

    Ruthenberg, H., & Rubin, R. (1985)

    Ruthenberg, H., & Rubin, R. (1987)

☐ Entries with the same author or authors and date of publication are arranged alphabetically according to title. Lowercase letters (*a*, *b*, *c*, and so on) that indicate the order of publication are placed within parentheses.

    Wolk, E. M. (1996a). Analysis . . .

    Wolk, E. M. (1996b). Hormonal . . .

18c Sample APA-Style Research Paper

The following student paper, "Sleep Deprivation in College Students," uses APA documentation style. It includes a title page, an abstract, a reference list, a table, and a bar graph.

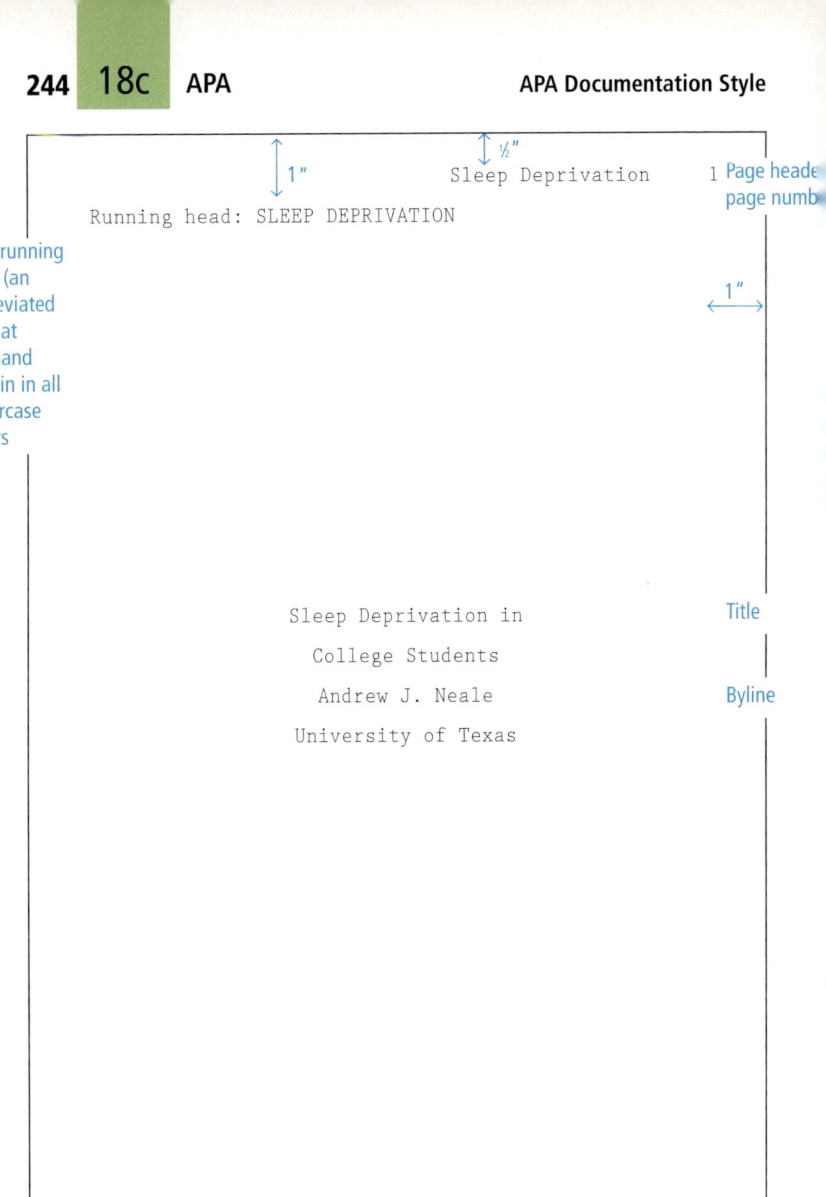

1"   ½"
              Sleep Deprivation   1 Page header
                                          page number
Running head: SLEEP DEPRIVATION

Type running
head (an   1"
abbreviated
title) at
left-hand
margin in all
uppercase
letters

                Sleep Deprivation in   Title
                 College Students
                 Andrew J. Neale   Byline
               University of Texas

             Psychology 215, Section 4   Course
                    Dr. Reiss   Instructor's name
                  May 6, 2005   Date

Center heading

1"   Sleep Deprivation   2

Abstract typed as a single paragraph in block format

Abstract

A survey of 50 first-year college students in an introductory biology class was conducted. The survey consisted of 5 questions regarding the causes and results of sleep deprivation and specifically addressed the students' study methods and the grades they received on the fall midterm. The study's hypothesis was that although students believe that forgoing sleep to study will yield better grades, sleep deprivation actually causes a decrease in performance. In support of this hypothesis, 43% of the students who received either an A or a B on the fall midterm deprived themselves of sleep in order to cram for the test, whereas 90% of those who received a C or a D were sleep deprived.

Full title
(centered)

Sleep Deprivation   3

Sleep Deprivation in College Students

Indent ½"———▶
(or five spaces)

For many college students, sleep is a luxury   Double-space
they feel they cannot afford. Bombarded with tests
and assignments and limited by a 24-hour day,

Introduction

students often attempt to make up time by doing
without sleep. Ironically, however, students may
actually hurt their academic performance by failing
to get enough sleep. According to several

Thesis
statement

psychological and medical studies, sleep deprivation
can lead to memory loss and health problems, both
of which are more likely to harm a student's academic
performance than to help it.

Sleep is often overlooked as an essential part

1"
◀——▶

"of a healthy lifestyle. Millions of Americans wake   1"
◀——▶
up daily to alarm clocks because their bodies have

Literature
review
(¶s 2–7)

not gotten enough sleep. This indicates that for many
people, sleep is viewed as a luxury rather than a
necessity. As National Sleep Foundation Executive
Director Richard L. Gelula observes, "Some of the

Quotation
requires its
own docu-
mentation
and a page
number.
A paragraph
number
is included
for Internet
sources

problems we face as a society—from road rage to
obesity—may be linked to lack of sleep or poor sleep"
(National Sleep Foundation, 2002, ¶ 3). In fact,
according to the National Sleep Foundation, "excessive
sleepiness is associated with reduced short-term
memory and learning ability, negative mood,
inconsistent performance, poor productivity and loss
of some forms of behavioral control" (2000, ¶ 2).

Sleep deprivation is particularly common among
college students, many of whom have busy lifestyles
and are required to memorize a great deal of material
before their exams. It is common for college students

1"

Sleep Deprivation   4

to take a quick nap between classes or fall asleep
while studying in the library because they are sleep
deprived. Approximately 44% of young adults
experience daytime sleepiness at least a few days a
month (National Sleep Foundation, 2002, ¶6). Many
students face daytime sleepiness on the day of an
exam because they stayed up all night studying. These
students believe that if they read and review
immediately before taking a test—even though this
usually means losing sleep—they will remember more
information and thus get better grades. However, this
is not the case.

A study conducted by professors Mary Carskadon
at Brown University in Providence, Rhode Island, and
Amy Wolfson at the College of the Holy Cross in
Worcester, Massachusetts, showed that high school
students who got adequate sleep were more likely to
do well in their classes (Carpenter, 2001).
According to their study of the correlation between
grades and sleep, students who went to bed earlier
on both weeknights and weekends earned mainly A's
and B's. The students who received D's and F's
averaged about 35 minutes less sleep per day than
the high achievers (cited in Carpenter). Apparently,
then, sleep is essential to high academic
achievement.

Once students reach college and have the freedom
to set their own schedules, however, many believe
that sleep is a luxury they can do without. For
example, students believe that if they use the time
they would normally sleep to study, they will do

Student uses past tense when discussing other researchers' studies

Cited in indicates an indirect source

better on exams. A recent survey of 144 undergraduate
students in introductory psychology classes
contradicted this assumption. According to this
study, "long sleepers," those individuals who slept 9
or more hours out of a 24-hour day, had significantly
higher grade point averages (GPAs) than "short
sleepers," individuals who slept less than 7 hours
out of a 24-hour day. Therefore, contrary to the
belief of many college students, more sleep is often
required to achieve a high GPA (Kelly, Kelly, &
Clanton, 2001).

Many students believe that sleep deprivation
is not the cause of their poor performance,
but rather that a host of other factors might be to
blame. A study in the *Journal of American College
Health* tested the effect that several factors have on
a student's performance in school, as measured by
students' GPAs. Some of the factors considered
included exercise, sleep, nutritional habits, social
support, time management techniques, stress
management techniques, and spiritual health (Trockel,
Barnes, & Egget, 2000). The most significant
correlation discovered in the study was between GPA
and the sleep habits of students. Sleep deprivation
had a more negative impact on GPAs than any other
factor did (Trockel et al.).

Despite these findings, many students continue
to believe that they will be able to remember more
material if they do not sleep at all before an exam.
They fear that sleeping will interfere with their
ability to retain information. Pilcher & Walters

First reference includes all three authors; *et al.* replaces second and third authors in subsequent reference in same paragraph

Sleep Deprivation   6

(1997), however, showed that sleep deprivation actually impaired learning skills. In this study, one group of students was sleep-deprived, while the other got 8 hours of sleep before the exam. Each group estimated how well they had performed on the exam. The students who were sleep-deprived believed their performance on the test was better than did those who were not sleep-deprived, but actually the performance of the sleep-deprived students was significantly worse than that of those who got 8 hours of sleep prior to the test (Pilcher & Walters, 1997, cited in Bubolz, Brown, & Soper, 2001). This study confirms that sleep deprivation harms cognitive performance and reveals that many students believe that the less sleep they get, the better they will do.

    A survey of students in an introductory biology class at the University of Texas demonstrated the effects of sleep deprivation on academic performance and supported the hypothesis that despite students' beliefs, forgoing sleep does not lead to better test scores.

Student uses past tense when discussing his own research study

Method

    To determine the causes and results of sleep deprivation, a study of the relationship between sleep and test performance was conducted. A survey of 50 first-year college students in an introductory biology class was completed, and their performance on the fall midterm was analyzed.

    Each student was asked to complete a survey consisting of the following five questions about their sleep patterns and their performance on the

fall midterm:

1. Do you regularly deprive yourself of sleep
   when studying for an exam?

2. Did you deprive yourself of sleep when
   studying for the fall midterm?

3. What was your grade on the exam?

4. Do you feel your performance was helped or
   harmed by the amount of sleep you had?

5. Will you deprive yourself of sleep when you
   study for the final exam?

To maintain confidentiality, the students were

not asked to put their names on the survey. Also, to

determine whether the students answered question 3

truthfully, the group grade distribution from the

surveys was compared to the number of A's, B's, C's,

and D's shown in the instructor's record of the test

results. The two frequency distributions were

identical.

Results

Analysis of the survey data indicated a

significant difference between the grades of students

who were sleep-deprived and the grades of those who

were not. The results of the survey are presented in

Table 1.

The grades in the class were curved so that

out of 50 students, 10 received A's, 20 received B's,

10 received C's, and 10 received D's. For the

purposes of this survey, an A or B on the exam

indicates that the student performed well. A grade

of C or D on the exam is considered a poor grade.

List is indented ½" (or five to seven spaces) and treated as long block quotation

Table 1 introduced

Sleep Deprivation   8

Table 1

Results of Survey of Students in University
of Texas Introduction to Biology Class
Examining the Relationship between Sleep
Deprivation and Academic Performance

Table placed on page where it is discussed

Grade Totals	Sleep-Deprived	Not Sleep-Deprived	Usually Sleep-Deprived	Improved	Harmed	Continue Sleep Deprivation?
A = 10	4	6	1	4	0	4
B = 20	9	11	8	8	1	8
C = 10	10	0	6	5	4	7
D = 10	8	2	2	1	3	2
Total	31	19	17	18	8	21

Of the 50 students in the class, 31 (or 62%) said they deprived themselves of sleep when studying for the fall midterm. Of these students, 17 (or 34% of the class) answered yes to the second question, reporting they regularly deprive themselves of sleep before an exam.

Statistical findings in table reported

Of the 31 students who said they deprived themselves of sleep when studying for the fall midterm, only 4 earned A's, and the majority of the A's in the class were received by those students who were not sleep-deprived. Even more significant was the fact that of the 4 students who were sleep-deprived and got A's, only one student claimed usually to be sleep-deprived on the day of an exam. Thus, assuming the students who earn A's in a class do well in general, it is possible that sleep deprivation did not help or harm these students'

Sleep Deprivation   9

grades. Not surprisingly, of the 4 students who
received A's and were sleep-deprived, all said they
would continue to use sleep deprivation to enable
them to study for longer hours.

The majority of those who used sleep deprivation
in an effort to obtain a higher grade received B's
and C's on the exam. A total of 20 students earned a
grade of B on the exam. Of those students, only 9, or
18% of the class, said they were deprived of sleep
when they took the test.

Students who said they were sleep-deprived when
they took the exam received the majority of the poor
grades. Ten students got C's on the midterm, and of
these 10 students, 100% said they were sleep-deprived
when they took the test. Of the 10 students (20% of
the class) who got D's, 8 said they were sleep-
deprived. Figure 1 shows the significant relationship
that was found between poor grades on the exam and
sleep deprivation.

Discussion

For many students, sleep is viewed as a luxury
rather than as a necessity. Particularly during the
exam period, students use the hours in which they
would normally sleep to study. However, this method
does not seem to be effective. The survey discussed
here reveals a clear correlation between sleep
deprivation and lower exam scores. In fact, the
majority of students who performed well on the exam,
earning either an A or a B, were not deprived of
sleep. Therefore, students who choose studying
oversleep should rethink their approach and consider

Figure 1
introduced

Sleep Deprivation   10

that sleep deprivation may actually lead to impaired

academic performance.

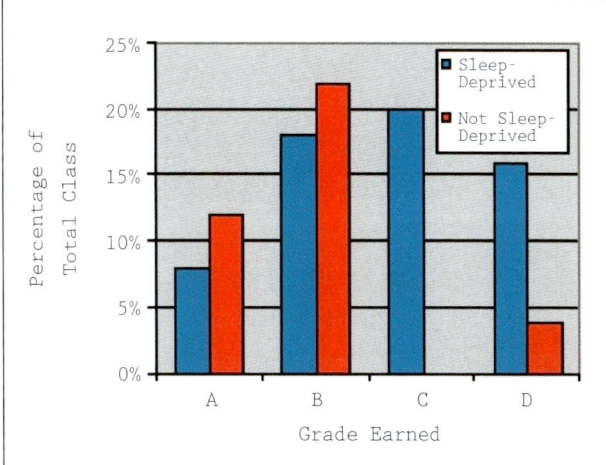

Figure 1. Results of survey of students in University

of Texas introduction to biology class examining the

relationship between sleep deprivation and academic

performance.

Figure placed
as close as
possible to
discussion in
paper

Label

Caption

(No source
information
needed for
graph based
on student's
original
data)

1″   Sleep Deprivation   11

References ← ——— Center title

Bubolz, W., Brown, F., & Soper, B. (2001). Sleep
    habits and patterns of college students:
    A preliminary study. *Journal of American
    College Health, 50,* 131-135.

Carpenter, S. (2001). Sleep deprivation may be
    undermining teen health. *Monitor on Psychology,
    32*(9). Retrieved March 9, 2005, from http://www
    .apa.org/monitor/oct01/sleepteen.html

Kelly, W. E., Kelly, K. E., & Clanton, R. C. (2001).
    The relationship between sleep length and
    grade-point average among college students.
    College Student Journal, 35(1), 84-90.

National Sleep Foundation. (2000). *Adolescent sleep
    needs and patterns: Research report and
    resource guide.* Retrieved March 16, 2005, from
    http://www.sleepfoundation.org/publications/
    sleep_and_teens_report1.pdf

National Sleep Foundation. (2002, April). *Epidemic
    of daytime sleepiness linked to increased
    feelings of anger, stress, and pessimism.*
    Retrieved March 14, 2005, from
    http://www.sleepfoundation.org/nsaw/
    pk_pollresultsmood.html

Trockel, M., Barnes, M., & Egget, D. (2000). Health-
    related variables and academic performance
    among first-year college students: Implications
    for sleep and other behaviors. *Journal of
    American College Health, 49,* 125-131.

Indent ½″ ——→
(or five spaces)

Double-space

Entries listed
in alphabetical
order

DIRECTORY OF CHICAGO-STYLE ENDNOTES AND BIBLIOGRAPHY ENTRIES

Print Sources: Entries for Books

Print Sources: Entries for Articles

Entries for Miscellaneous Print and Nonprint Sources

Videotapes, DVDs, and Recordings

Electronic Sources: Entries from Internet Sites

Internet-Specific Sources

Electronic Sources: Entries from Subscription Services

Documents from a Database

CHAPTER 19

Chicago Documentation Style

19a Using Chicago Style

The Chicago Manual of Style is used in history and in some social science and humanities disciplines. **Chicago style*** has two parts: *notes at the end of the paper* (**endnotes**) and *a list of bibliographic citations.* (Chicago style encourages the use of endnotes, but it allows the use of footnotes at the bottom of the page.)

(1) Endnotes and Footnotes

The notes format calls for a **superscript** (raised numeral) in the text after source material you have either quoted or referred to. This numeral, placed after all punctuation marks except dashes, corresponds to the numeral that accompanies the note.

Endnote and Footnote Format: Chicago Style

In the Text

> By November of 1942, the Allies had proof that the Nazis
> were engaged in the systematic killing of Jews.[1]

In the Note

> 1. David S. Wyman, *The Abandonment of the Jews: America
> and the Holocaust 1941–1945* (New York: Pantheon Books,
> 1984), 65.

---

*Chicago-style documentation follows the guidelines set in *The Chicago Manual of Style*, 15th ed. Chicago: University of Chicago Press, 2003. The manuscript guidelines and sample research paper at the end of this chapter follow guidelines set in Kate L. Turabian's *A Manual for Writers of Term Papers, Theses, and Dissertations*, 6th ed. Chicago: University of Chicago Press, 1993. Turabian style, which is based on Chicago style, addresses formatting concerns specific to college writers.

> ### Close-up: Subsequent References to the Same Work
>
> In the first reference to a work, use the full citation; in subsequent references to the same work, list only the author's last name, followed by a comma, an abbreviated title, a comma, and a page number.
>
> **First Note on Espinoza**
>
>   1. J. M. Espinoza, *The First Expedition of Vargas in
>   New Mexico, 1692* (Albuquerque: University of New Mexico
>   Press, 1949), 10-12.
>
> **Subsequent Note**
>
>   5. Espinoza, *First Expedition,* 29.
>
> **NOTE:** *The Chicago Manual of Style* allows the use of the abbreviation *ibid.* ("in the same place") for subsequent references to the same work as long as there are no intervening references. *Ibid.* takes the place of the author's name and the work's title—but not the page number.
>
> **First Note on Espinoza**
>
>   1. J. M. Espinoza, *The First Expedition of Vargas in
>   New Mexico, 1692* (Albuquerque: University of New Mexico
>   Press, 1949), 10-12.
>
> **Subsequent Note**
>
>   2. Ibid., 23.

(2) Bibliography

In addition to the heading `Bibliography,` Chicago style allows `Selected Bibliography,` `Works Cited,` and `References.` Bibliography entries are arranged alphabetically. Double-space within and between entries.

Chicago • Print Sources:
Entries for Books

Capitalize the first, last, and all major words of titles and subtitles. Chicago style recommends the use of italics for titles, but underlining to indicate italics is also acceptable.

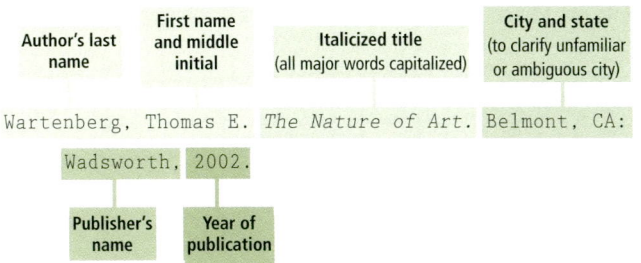

Wartenberg, Thomas E. *The Nature of Art.* Belmont, CA: Wadsworth, 2002.

- Author's last name
- First name and middle initial
- Italicized title (all major words capitalized)
- City and state (to clarify unfamiliar or ambiguous city)
- Publisher's name
- Year of publication

Authors

1. A Book by One Author
Endnote

>   1. Robert Dallek, *An Unfinished Life: John F. Kennedy 1917–1963* (New York: Little Brown, 2003), 213.

Bibliography

> Dallek, Robert. *An Unfinished Life: John F. Kennedy 1917–1963.* New York: Little Brown, 2003.

2. A Book by Two or Three Authors
Endnote
Two Authors

>   2. Jack Watson and Grant McKerney, *A Cultural History of the Theater* (New York: Longman, 1993), 137.

Three Authors

>   2. Nathan Caplan, John K. Whitmore, and Marcella H. Choy, *The Boat People and Achievement in America: A Study of Economic and Educational Success* (Ann Arbor: University of Michigan Press, 1990), 51.

Bibliography
Two Authors

> Watson, Jack, and Grant McKerney. *A Cultural History of the Theater.* New York: Longman, 1993.

Three Authors

> Caplan, Nathan, John K. Whitmore, and Marcella H. Choy. *The Boat People and Achievement in America: A Study of Economic and Educational Success.* Ann Arbor: University of Michigan Press, 1990.

3. A Book by More Than Three Authors
Endnote
Chicago style favors `and others` rather than `et al.` in endnotes.

> 3. Robert E. Spiller and others, eds., *Literary History of the United States* (New York: Macmillan, 1953), 24.

Bibliography
All authors' names are listed in the bibliography.

> Spiller, Robert E., Willard Thorp, Thomas H. Johnson, and Henry Seidel Canby, eds. *Literary History of the United States*. New York: Macmillan, 1953.

4. A Book by a Corporate Author
If the title page of a publication issued by an organization does not identify a person as the author, the organization is listed as the author, even if its name is repeated in the title, in the series title, or as the publisher.

Endnote

> 4. National Geographic Society, *National Parks of the United States*, 3rd ed. (Washington, DC: National Geographic Society, 1997), 77.

Bibliography

> National Geographic Society. *National Parks of the United States*. 3rd ed. Washington, DC: National Geographic Society, 1997.

5. An Edited Book
Endnote

> 5. William Bartram, *The Travels of William Bartram*, ed. Mark Van Doren (New York: Dover Press, 1955), 85.

Bibliography

> Bartram, William. *The Travels of William Bartram*. Edited by Mark Van Doren. New York: Dover Press, 1955.

Editions, Multivolume Works
6. A Subsequent Edition of a Book
Endnote

> 6. Laurie G. Kirszner and Stephen R. Mandell, *The Wadsworth Handbook*, 7th ed. (Boston: Wadsworth, 2005), 52.

Bibliography

> Kirszner, Laurie G., and Stephen R. Mandell. *The Wadsworth Handbook*. 7th ed. Boston: Wadsworth, 2005.

7. A Multivolume Work

Endnote

> 7. Kathleen Raine, *Blake and Tradition* (Princeton, NJ: Princeton University Press, 1968), 1:143.

Bibliography

> Raine, Kathleen. *Blake and Tradition*. Vol. 1. Princeton, NJ: Princeton University Press, 1968.

Parts of Books

8. A Chapter in a Book

Endnote

> 8. Roy Porter, "Health, Disease, and Cure," in *Quacks: Fakers and Charlatans in Medicine*.(Gloucestershire, UK: Tempus Publishing, 2003), 182–205.

Bibliography

> Porter, Roy. "Health, Disease, and Cure." Chap. 5 in *Quacks: Fakers and Charlatans in Medicine* Gloucestershire, UK: Tempus Publishing, 2003.

9. An Essay in an Anthology

Endnote

> 9. G. E. R. Lloyd, "Science and Mathematics," in *The Legacy of Greece*, ed. Moses Finley (New York: Oxford University Press, 1981), 270.

Bibliography

> Lloyd, G. E. R. "Science and Mathematics." In *The Legacy of Greece*, edited by Moses Finley, 256–300. New York: Oxford University Press, 1981.

Religious Works

10. A Religious Work

References to religious works (such as the Bible) are usually confined to the text or notes and not listed in the bibliography. In citing the Bible, include the book (abbreviated), the chapter (followed by a colon), and the verse numbers. Identify the version, but do not include a page number.

Endnote

      10. Phil. 1:9–11 (King James Version).

Chicago • Print Sources: Entries for Articles

Scholarly Journals

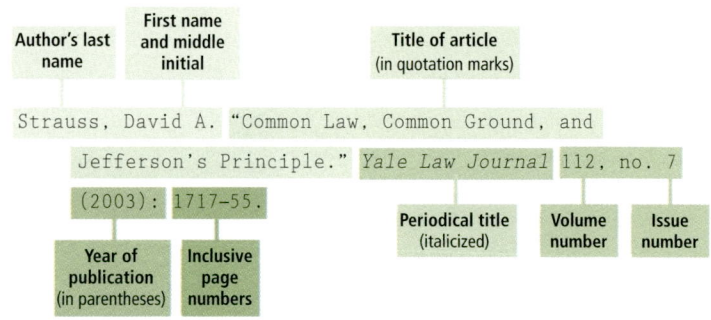

Author's last name | First name and middle initial | Title of article (in quotation marks)

Strauss, David A. "Common Law, Common Ground, and Jefferson's Principle." *Yale Law Journal* 112, no. 7 (2003): 1717–55.

Periodical title (italicized) | Volume number | Issue number

Year of publication (in parentheses) | Inclusive page numbers

11. An Article in a Scholarly Journal with Continuous Pagination through an Annual Volume

Endnote

      11. John Huntington, "Science Fiction and the Future," *College English* 37 (Fall 1975): 341.

Bibliography

      Huntington, John. "Science Fiction and the Future." *College English* 37 (Fall 1975): 340–58.

12. An Article in a Scholarly Journal with Separate Pagination in Each Issue

Endnote

      12. R. G. Sipes, "War, Sports, and Aggression: An Empirical Test of Two Rival Theories," *American Anthropologist* 4, no. 2 (1973): 80.

Bibliography

Sipes, R. G. "War, Sports, and Aggression: An Empirical Test
of Two Rival Theories." *American Anthropologist* 4, no.
2 (1973): 65–84.

Magazines and Newspapers

Although endnotes for magazines specify page numbers, the bibliography entries include page numbers only when the pages are consecutive.

13. An Article in a Weekly Magazine (Signed/Unsigned)
Endnote
Signed

13. Pico Iyer, "A Mum for All Seasons," *Time*, April 8,
2002, 51.

Unsigned

13. "Burst Bubble," *NewScientist*, July 27, 2002, 24.

Bibliography
Signed

Iyer, Pico. "A Mum for All Seasons." *Time*, April 8, 2002.

Unsigned

"Burst Bubble." *NewScientist*, July 27, 2002, 24–25.

14. An Article in a Monthly Magazine (Signed/Unsigned)
Endnote
Signed

14. Tad Suzuki, "Reflecting Light on Photo Realism,"
American Artist, March 2002, 47.

Unsigned

14. "Repowering the U.S. with Clean Energy
Development." *BioCycle*, July 2002, 14.

Bibliography
Signed

Suzuki, Tad. "Reflecting Light on Photo Realism." *American
Artist*, March 2002, 46–51.

Unsigned

> "Repowering the U.S. with Clean Energy Development."
>
>   *BioCycle*, July 2002, 14.

15. An Article in a Newspaper (Signed/Unsigned)
Endnote

Because the pagination of newspapers can change from edition to edition, Chicago style recommends not supplying page numbers for newspaper articles.

Signed

>   15. Francis X. Clines, "Civil War Relics Draw Visitors, and Con Artists," *New York Times*, August 4, 2002, national edition, sec. A.

Unsigned

>   15. "Feds Lead Way in Long-Term Care," *Atlanta Journal-Constitution*, July 21, 2002, sec. E.

Bibliography
Signed

> Clines, Francis X. "Civil War Relics Draw Visitors, and Con Artists." *New York Times*, August 4, 2002, national edition, sec. A.

Unsigned

> "Feds Lead Way in Long-Term Care." *Atlanta Journal-Constitution*, July 21, 2002, sec. E.

NOTE: Omit the article *the* from the newspaper's title, but include a city name in the title, even if it is not part of the actual title.

Chicago • Entries for Miscellaneous Print and Nonprint Sources

Interviews

16. A Personal Interview
Endnote

>   16. Cornel West, interview by author, tape recording, June 8, 2003.

Bibliography
Personal interviews are not listed in the bibliography.

17. A Published Interview
Endnote

> 17. Gwendolyn Brooks, interview by George Stavros, *Contemporary Literature* 11, no. 1 (Winter 1970): 12.

Bibliography

> Brooks, Gwendolyn. Interview by George Stavros. *Contemporary Literature* 11, no. 1 (Winter 1970): 1–20.

Letters, Government Documents

18. A Personal Letter
Endnote

> 18. Julia Alvarez, letter to the author, April 10, 2002.

Bibliography
Personal letters are not listed in the bibliography.

19. A Government Document
Endnote

> 19. U.S. Department of Transportation, *The Future of High-Speed Trains in the United States: Special Study, 2001* (Washington, DC: GPO, 2002), 203.

Bibliography

> U.S. Department of Transportation. *The Future of High-Speed Trains in the United States: Special Study, 2001.* Washington, DC: GPO, 2002.

Videotapes, DVDs, and Recordings

20. A Videotape or DVD
Endnote

> 20. *Interview with Arthur Miller*, dir. William Schiff, 17 min., The Mosaic Group, 1987, videocassette.

Bibliography

> *Interview with Arthur Miller*. Directed by William Schiff. 17 min. The Mosaic Group, 1987. Videocassette.

21. A Recording
Endnote

> 21. Bob Marley, "Crisis," *Bob Marley and the Wailers*, Kava Island Records 423 095-3, compact disc.

Bibliography

> Marley, Bob. "Crisis." *Bob Marley and the Wailers*. Kava Island Records 423 095-3. Compact disc.

Chicago • Electronic Sources: Entries from Internet Sites

Internet citations for electronic sources include the author's name; the title of the document (enclosed in quotation marks); the title of the Internet site (italicized); the publication date (or, if no date is available, the abbreviation n.d.); the URL; and the date of access (in parentheses).

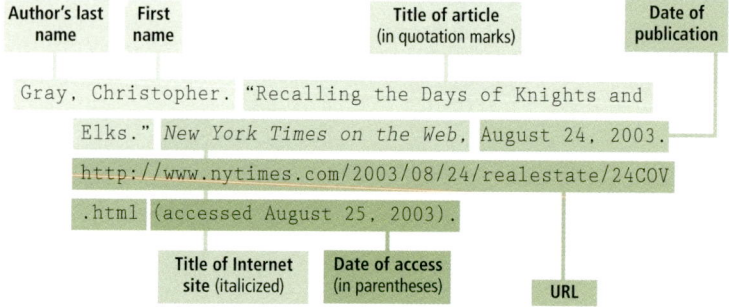

Internet-Specific Sources

22. An Article in an Online Journal
Endnote

> 22. Robert F. Brooks, "Communication as the Foundation of Distance Education," *Kairos: A Journal of Rhetoric, Technology, and Pedagogy* 7, no. 2 (2002), http://english .ttu.edu/kairos/index.html (accessed March 20, 2002).

Bibliography

> Brooks, Robert F. "Communication as the Foundation of Distance Education." *Kairos: A Journal of Rhetoric,*

Technology, and Pedagogy 7, no. 2 (2002). http://english
.ttu.edu/kairos/index.html (accessed March 20, 2002).

23. An Article in an Online Magazine
Endnote

23. Steven Levy, "I Was a Wi-Fi Freeloader," *Newsweek*,
October 9, 2002, http://www.msnbc.com/news/816606.asp
(accessed January 9, 2004).

Bibliography

Levy, Steven. "I Was a Wi-Fi Freeloader." *Newsweek*, October
9, 2002. http://www.msnbc.com/news/816606.asp (accessed
January 9, 2004).

24. An Article in an Online Newspaper
Endnote

24. William J. Broad, "Piece by Piece, the Civil War
Monitor Is Pulled from the Atlantic's Depths," *New York Times
on the Web*, July 18, 2002, http://query.nytimes.com/search/
advanced (accessed June 15, 2004).

Bibliography

Broad, William J. "Piece by Piece, the Civil War *Monitor* Is
Pulled from the Atlantic's Depths." *New York Times on
the Web*, July 18, 2002. http://query.nytimes.com/
search/advanced (accessed June 15, 2004).

25. A Web Site or Home Page
Endnote

25. David Perdue, "Dickens's Journalistic Career," *David
Perdue's Charles Dickens Page*, September 24, 2002, http://www
.fidnet.com/~dap1955/dickens (accessed September 10, 2003).

Bibliography

Perdue, David. "Dickens's Journalistic Career." *David
Perdue's Charles Dickens Page*. September 24, 2002.
http://www.fidnet.com/~dap1955/dickens (accessed
September 10, 2003).

26. An Email Message
Do not include the author's email address after his or her name.

Endnote

> 26. Meg Halverson, "Scuba Report," email message to author, April 2, 2004.

Bibliography

Email messages are not listed in the bibliography.

27. A Listserv Message

Include the name of the list and the date of the individual posting. Include the listserv address after the date of publication.

Endnote

> 27. Dave Shirlaw, email to Underwater Archeology discussion list, September 6, 2002, http://lists.asu.edu/ archives/sub-arch.html (accessed May 12, 2002).

Bibliography

Listserv messages are not listed in the bibliography.

Chicago • Electronic Sources:
Entries from Subscription Services

Documents from a Database

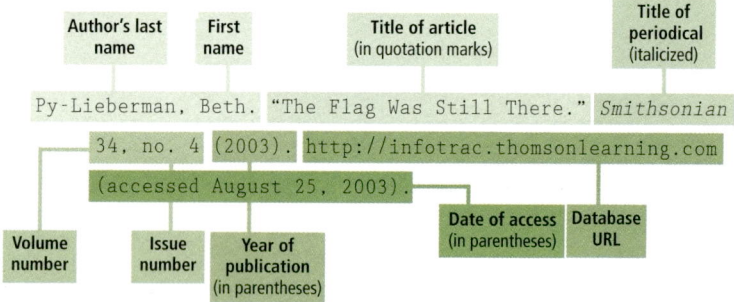

Author's last name | First name | Title of article (in quotation marks) | Title of periodical (italicized)

Py-Lieberman, Beth. "The Flag Was Still There." *Smithsonian* 34, no. 4 (2003). http://infotrac.thomsonlearning.com (accessed August 25, 2003).

Volume number | Issue number | Year of publication (in parentheses) | Date of access (in parentheses) | Database URL

28. A Scholarly Journal Article from a Database

Include as much publication information as you can. Always give the URL of the subscription service's main page; the date of access (in parentheses) is optional.

Endnote

> 28. Richard J. Schaefer, "Editing Strategies in
> Television Documentaries," *Journal of Communication* 47, no.
> 4 (1997): 80, http://www.galegroup.com/onefile (accessed
> October 2, 2003).

Bibliography

> Schaefer, Richard J. "Editing Strategies in Television
>   Documentaries." *Journal of Communication* 47, no. 4
>   (1997): 80. http://www.galegroup.com/onefile (accessed
>   October 2, 2003).

19b Chicago-Style Manuscript Guidelines

Checklist: Typing Your Paper

When you type your paper, use the student paper in **19c** as your model.

☐ On the title page, include the full title of your paper as well as your name. Also include the course title, the instructor's name, and the date. Each element on the title page is considered a major heading and should appear entirely in capitals.

☐ Type your paper with a one-inch margin at the top, at the bottom, and on both sides.

☐ Double-space your paper throughout.

☐ Indent the first line of each paragraph one-half inch. Set off a long prose quotation (ten or more typed lines or more than one paragraph) from the text by indenting the entire quotation one-half inch from the left-hand margin. Do not use quotation marks. If the quotation is a full paragraph, include the paragraph indentation.

☐ Number all pages consecutively at the top of the page, with the number either centered or flush right. Page numbers should appear at a consistent distance (at least one-half inch) from the top edge. The title page is not numbered; the first full page of the paper is numbered page 1.

☐ Use superscript numbers to indicate in-text citations. Type superscript numbers at the end of cited material (quotations, paraphrases, or summaries). Leave no space between the superscript number and the preceding letter or punctuation mark. The number follows any punctuation mark except for a dash, which it precedes. The note number should be placed at the end of a sentence (or at the end of a clause).

☐ When you cite source material in your paper, use **Chicago documentation style**.

See
19a

Checklist: Using Visuals

According to *The Chicago Manual of Style*, there are two types of visuals: **tables** and **figures** (or **illustrations**), including charts, graphs, photographs, maps, and diagrams.

Tables

☐ Give each **table** a label and an arabic number (TABLE 1, TABLE 2, and so on).
☐ Give each table a descriptive title in the form of a sentence. Place the title after the table number.
☐ Place both the label and the title above the table.
☐ Place source information below the table, introduced by the word Source. (If there is more than one source, begin with Sources.)

> Source: David E. Fisher and Marshall Jon Fisher, *Tube:*
>
> *The Invention of Television* (Washington, DC:
>
> Counterpoint Press, 1996), 185.

If the sources are listed in the bibliography, use a shortened form below the table.

> Source: Fisher and Fisher 1996.

Figures

☐ Give each **figure** a label, an arabic number, and a caption. The label Figure may be abbreviated Fig. (Figure 1, Fig. 1).
☐ Place both the label and caption below the figure, on the same line.
☐ Place source information in parentheses at the end of the title or caption.

> Fig. 1. Television and its influence on young children.
>
> (Photograph from ABC Photos.)

Checklist: Preparing Chicago-Style Endnotes

☐ Begin the endnotes on a new page (after the last page of the paper and before the bibliography).
☐ Type the title NOTES entirely in capitals, and center it two inches from the top of the page.
☐ Number the page on which the endnotes appear as the next page of the paper.
☐ Type and number notes in the order in which they appear in the paper, beginning with number 1.
☐ Type the note number on (not above) the line, followed by a period and one space.
☐ Indent the first line of each note one-half inch (or five spaces); type subsequent lines flush with the left-hand margin.
☐ Double-space within and between entries.
☐ Break URLs after slashes, before punctuation marks, or before or after the symbols = and &.

19c Sample Chicago-Style Research Paper (Excerpts)

The following pages are from a student paper, "The Flu of 1918 and the Potential for Future Pandemics," written for a history course. The paper uses Chicago-style documentation and includes a title page, a notes page, and a bibliography.

Title page is
not numbered

THE FLU OF 1918 AND THE POTENTIAL FOR

FUTURE PANDEMICS

Title is centered
and followed by
name

BY

RITA LIN

Course title

AMERICAN HISTORY 301

Instructor's name

DR. WALTER HIGH

Date

MAY 3, 2005

1"

↕ ½"
1

The Flu of 1918 and the Potential for

tle (centered) ———→   Future Pandemics

dent ½" ———→   In November 2002, a mysterious new illness
r five spaces)   surfaced in China. By May 2003, what became known as

SARS (Severe Acute Respiratory Syndrome) had been

troduction   transported by air travelers to Europe, South

America, South Africa, Australia, and North America,

uperscript   and the worldwide death toll had grown to 250.[1] By
umbers refer
endnotes   June 2003, there were more than 8,200 suspected cases

of SARS in 30 countries and 750 deaths related to the

outbreak, including 30 in Toronto. Just when SARS

appeared to be waning in Asia, a second outbreak in

Toronto, the hardest hit of all cities outside of

Asia, reminded everyone that SARS remained a deadly

1"   threat.[2] As SARS continued to claim more victims and   1"

expand its reach, fears of a new pandemic spread

throughout the world.

The belief that a pandemic could occur in the

future is not a far-fetched idea. During the

twentieth century, there were three, and the most

deadly one, in 1918, has several significant

similarities to the SARS outbreak. As David Brown

points out, in many ways, the 1918 influenza pandemic

is a mirror reflecting the causes and symptoms, as

well as the future potential, of SARS. Both are

caused by a virus, result in respiratory illness, and

spread through casual contact and coughing. Outbreaks

for both are often traced to one individual,

quarantine is the major weapon against the spread of

both, and both likely arose from mutated animal

viruses. Moreover, as Brown observes, the greatest

Double-space

1"

2

fear regarding SARS is that it will become so
widespread that transmission chains will be
undetectable, and health officials will be helpless
to restrain outbreaks. Such was the case with the
1918 influenza, which also began mysteriously in
China and was transported around the globe (at that
time by World War I military ships). By the time the
flu lost its power in the spring of 1919, in a year's
time it had killed more than 50 million people
worldwide,[3] more than twice as many as those who died
during the four and a half years of World War I.
Thus, if SARS is a reflection of the potential for a
future flu pandemic—and experts believe it is—the
international community needs to acknowledge the
danger, accelerate its research, and develop an
extensive virus-surveillance system.

Thesis
statement

    The 1918 flu was different from anything
previously known to Americans. Among the
peculiarities of the pandemic was its origin and
cause. In the spring of 1918, the virus, in

History of 1918
pandemic

10

2″

centered

NOTES

indent ½″
(or five
spaces)

Double-space

1. Nancy Shute, "SARS Hits Home," *U.S. News & World Report*, May 5, 2003, 42.

Endnotes
listed in
order in
which they
appear in
the paper

2. "Canada Waits for SARS News as Asia Under Control," *Sydney Morning Herald on the Web*, June 2, 2003, http://www.smh.com.au/text/articles/ 2003/06/01/1054406076596.htm (accessed April 2, 2005).

3. David Brown, "A Grim Reminder in SARS Fight: In 1918, Spanish Flu Swept the Globe, Killing Millions," *MSNBC News Online*, June 4, 2003, http://www.msnbc.com/news/921901.asp (accessed April 2, 2005).

4. Doug Rekenthaler, "The Flu Pandemic of 1918: Is a Repeat Performance Likely?— Part 1 of 2," *Disaster Relief: New Stories*, February 22, 1999, http://www.disasterrelief.org/Disasters/990219Flu/ (accessed March 9, 2005).

5. Lynette Iezzoni, *Influenza 1918: The Worst Epidemic in American History* (New York: TV Books, 1999), 40.

Subsequent
references
to the same
source
include
author's last
name,
shortened
title, and
page
number(s)

6. "1918 Influenza Timeline," *Influenza 1918*, 1999, http://www.pbs.org/wgbh/amex/influenza/ timeline/index.html (accessed March 9, 2005).

7. Iezonni, *Influenza 1918*, 131–132.

8. Brown, "Grim Reminder."

9. Iezonni, *Influenza 1918*, 88–89.

10. Ibid, 204.

Ibid. is used
for a subse-
quent refer-
ence to the
same source
when there
are no
intervening
references

13

2″

BIBLIOGRAPHY ← Center

"1918 Influenza Timeline." *Influenza 1918*, 1999.
http://www.pbs.org/wgbh/amex/influenza/timeline/
index.html (accessed March 9, 2005).

Billings, Molly. "The Influenza Pandemic of 1918."
*Human Virology at Stanford: Interesting Viral
Web Pages*, June 1997. http://www.stanford.edu/
group/virus/uda/index.html (accessed March 17,
2005).

Brown, David. "A Grim Reminder in SARS Fight: In
1918, Spanish Flu Swept the Globe, Killing
Millions." *MSNBC News Online*, June 4, 2003.
http://www.msnbc .com/news/921901.asp (accessed
April 2, 2005).

"Canada Waits for SARS News as Asia Under Control."
Sydney Morning Herald on the Web, June 2, 2003.
http://www.smh.com.au/text/articles/2003/06/01/
1054406076596.htm (accessed April 2, 2005).

Cooke, Robert. "Drugs vs. the Bug of 1918: Virus'
Deadly Code Is Unlocked to Test Strategies to
Fight It." *Newsday*, October 1, 2002.

Double-space

First line of each entry is flush with the left-hand margin; subsequent lines are indented 5 spaces

Entries are listed alphabetically according to the author's last name

DIRECTORY OF CSE REFERENCE LIST ENTRIES

Print Sources: Entries for Books

Authors

1. A book with one author (p. 280)
2. A book with more than one author (p. 280)
3. An edited book (p. 280)

Parts of Books

4. A chapter or other part of a book with a separate title but with the same author (p. 280)
5. A chapter or other part of a book with a different author (p. 280)

Religious Works, Classical Literature

6. A religious work (p. 281)
7. Classical literature (p. 281)

Print Sources: Entries for Articles

Scholarly Journals

8. An article in a journal paginated by issue (p. 282)
9. An article in a journal with continuous pagination (p. 282)

Magazines and Newspapers

10. A magazine article (signed/unsigned) (p. 282)
11. A newspaper article (signed/unsigned) (p. 282)

Entries for Miscellaneous Print and Nonprint Sources

Films, Videotapes, Recordings, Maps

12. An audiocassette (p. 282)
13. A film, videotape, or DVD (p. 283)
14. A map (p. 283)

Electronic Sources: Entries from Internet Sites

Internet-Specific Sources

15. An online book (p. 283)
16. An online journal (p. 284)

CHAPTER 20

CSE and Other Documentation Styles

20a Using CSE Style

 CSE style,* recommended by the Council of Science Editors (CSE), is used in biology, zoology, physiology, anatomy, and genetics. CSE style has two parts—*documentation in the text* and a *reference list.*

(1) Documentation in the Text

CSE style permits either of two documentation formats: *citation-sequence format* and *name-year format.*

Citation-Sequence Format The **citation-sequence format** calls for either **superscripts** (raised numbers) in the text of the paper (the preferred form) or numbers inserted parenthetically in the text of the paper.

```
One study[1] has demonstrated the effect of low dissolved

oxygen.
```

These numbers correspond to a list of references at the end of the paper. When the writer refers to more than one source in a single note, the numbers are separated by a hyphen if they are in sequence and by a comma if they are not.

```
Some studies[2-3] dispute this claim.

Other studies[3,6] support these findings.
```

Name-Year Format The **name-year format** calls for the author's name and the year of publication to be inserted parenthetically in the text. If the author's name is used to introduce the source material, only the date of publication is needed in the parenthetical citation.

---

*CSE style follows the guidelines set in the style manual of the Council of Biology Editors: *Scientific Style and Format: The CBE Manual for Authors, Editors, and Publishers,* 6th ed. New York: Cambridge UP, 1994. The Council of Biology Editors has changed its name to the Council of Science Editors.

```
A great deal of heat is often generated during this process

(McGinness 1999).

According to McGinness (1999), a great deal of heat is often

generated during this process.
```

When two or more works are cited in the same parentheses, the sources are arranged chronologically (from earliest to latest) and separated by semicolons.

```
Epidemics can be avoided by taking tissue cultures (Domb

1998) and by intervention with antibiotics (Baldwin and

Rigby 1984; Martin and others 1992; Cording 1998).
```

NOTE: The citation `Baldwin and Rigby 1984` refers to a work by two authors; the citation `Martin and others 1992` refers to a work by three or more authors.

(2) Reference List

The format of the reference list depends on the documentation format you use. If you use the **name-year** documentation format, your reference list will resemble the reference list for an <u>APA</u> paper. If you use the **citation-sequence** documentation style (as in the paper in 20c), your sources will be listed by number, in the order in which they appear in your paper, on a `References` page. Double-space within and between entries. Type the number flush left, followed by a period and one space. Align the second and subsequent lines with the first letter of the author's last name.

See Ch. 18

CSE • Print Sources:
Entries for Books

List the author or authors by last name; after one space, list the initial or initials (unspaced) of the first and middle names (followed by a period); the title (not underlined, and with only the first word capitalized); the place of publication; the full name of the publisher (followed by a semicolon); the year (followed by a period); and the total number of pages (including back matter, such as the index).

Authors

1. A Book with One Author

> 1. Hawking SW. Brief history of time: from the big bang to black holes. New York: Bantam; 1995. 198 p.

NOTE: No comma follows the author's last name, and no period separates the initials of the first and middle names.

2. A Book with More Than One Author

> 2. Horner JR, Gorman J. Digging dinosaurs. New York: Workman; 1988. 210 p.

3. An Edited Book

> 3. Goldfarb TD, editor. Taking sides: clashing views on controversial environmental issues. 2nd ed. Guilford (CT): Dushkin; 1987. 323 p.

NOTE: The name of the publisher's state, province, or country can be added within parentheses to clarify the location. The two-letter postal service abbreviation can be used for the state or province.

Parts of Books

4. A Chapter or Other Part of a Book with a Separate Title but with the Same Author

> 4. Asimov I. Exploring the earth and cosmos: the growth and future of human knowledge. New York: Crown; 1984. Part III, The horizons of matter; p 245–94.

NOTE: No period follows the p when it precedes a page number.

5. A Chapter or Other Part of a Book with a Different Author

> 5. Gingerich O. Hints for beginning observers. In: Mallas JH, Kreimer E, editors. The Messier album: an observer's handbook. Cambridge: Cambridge Univ Pr; 1978: p 194–5.

NOTE: When giving inclusive page numbers, give only the nonrepeated digits—for example, 197–8 (*not* 197–198).

Religious Works, Classical Literature

6. A Religious Work

6. The New Jerusalem Bible. Garden City (NY): Doubleday;
   1985. Luke 15:11-32. p 1715-6.

7. Classical Literature

7. Homer. Odyssey; Book 17:319-32. In: Lombardo S,
   translator and editor. The essential Homer: selections
   from the Iliad and the Odyssey. Indianapolis: Hackett;
   2000. p 391-2.

CSE • Print Sources:
Entries for Articles

List the author or authors (last name first); the title of the article (not in quotation marks, and with only the first word capitalized); the abbreviated name of the journal (with all major words capitalized, but not italicized or underlined); the year (followed by a semicolon); the volume number (followed by a colon); and inclusive page numbers. No spaces separate the year, the volume number, and the page numbers. Month names longer than three letters are abbreviated to their first three letters.

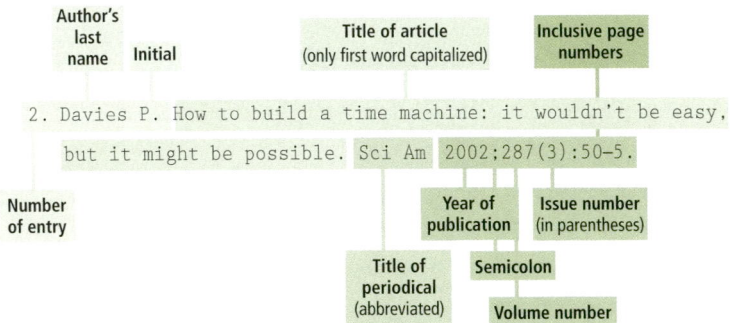

Scholarly Journals

8. An Article in a Journal Paginated by Issue

```
8. Sarmiento JL, Gruber N. Sinks for anthropogenic carbon.
   Phy Today 2002;55(8):30-6.
```

9. An Article in a Journal with Continuous Pagination

```
9. Brazil K, Krueger P. Patterns of family adaptation to
   childhood asthma. J Pediatr Nurs 2002;17:167-73.
```

NOTE: Omit the month (and day for weeklies) and issue number for journals with continuous pagination in volumes.

Magazines and Newspapers

10. A Magazine Article (Signed/Unsigned)
Signed

```
10. Nadis S. Using lasers to detect E.T. Astronomy 2002
    Sep:44-9.
```

Unsigned

```
10. [Anonymous]. Brown dwarf glows with radio waves.
    Astronomy 2001 Jun:28.
```

11. A Newspaper Article (Signed/Unsigned)
Signed

```
11. Husted B. Don't wiggle out of untangling computer wires.
    Atlanta Journal-Constitution 2002 Jul 21;Sect Q1(col 1).
```

Unsigned

```
11. [Anonymous]. Scientists find gene tied to cancer risk.
    New York Times 2002 Apr 22;Sect A:18(col 6).
```

CSE • Entries for Miscellaneous Print and Nonprint Sources

Films, Videotapes, Recordings, Maps

12. An Audiocassette

```
12. Ascent of man [audiocassette]. Bronowski J. New York:
    Jeffrey Norton Pub; 1974. 1 audiocassette: 2-track,
    55 min.
```

13. A Film, Videotape, or DVD

13. Women in science [videocassette]. Stoneberger B, Clark
    R, editor, American Society for Microbiology, producer.
    Madison (WI): Hawkhill; 1998. 1 videocassette: 42 min,
    sound, color, 1/2 in. Accompanied by: 1 guide.

14. A Map
A Sheet Map

14. Amazonia: a world resource at risk [ecological map].
    Washington: Nat Geographic Soc; 1992. 1 sheet.

A Map in an Atlas

14. Central Africa [political map]. In: Hammond citation
    world atlas. Maplewood (NJ): Hammond; 1996. p 114–5.
    Color, scale 1:13,800,000.

CSE • Electronic Sources:
Entries from Internet Sites

Internet-Specific Sources

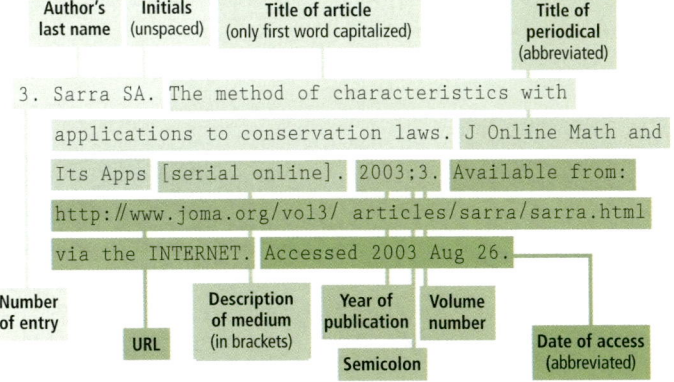

15. An Online Book

15. Bohm D. Causality and chance in modern physics [monograph
    online]. Philadelphia: Univ of Pennsylvania Pr; 1999.

```
Available from: http://www.netlibrary.com/ebook_info
.asp?product_id517169 via the INTERNET. Accessed 2002
Aug 17.
```

16. An Online Journal

```
16. Lasko P. The Drosophila melanogaster genome: translation
    factors and RNA binding proteins. J Cell Biol [serial
    online]. 2000;150(2):F51-6. Available from: http://www
    .jcb.org/search.dtl via the INTERNET. Accessed 2002
    Aug 15.
```

20b CSE-Style Manuscript Guidelines

Checklist: Typing Your Paper

When you type your paper, use the student paper in **20c** as your model.

☐ Type your name, the course, and the date flush left one inch from the top of the first page.

☐ If required, include an **abstract** (a 250-word summary of the paper) on a separate numbered page following the title page.

☐ Double-space throughout.

☐ Insert tables and figures in the body of the paper. Number tables and figures in separate sequences (`Table 1`, `Table 2`; `Figure 1`, `Figure 2`; and so on).

☐ Number pages consecutively in the upper right-hand corner; include a shortened title before the number.

See 20a ☐ When you cite source material in your paper, follow <u>CSE documentation style</u>.

Checklist: Preparing the CSE Reference List

☐ Begin the reference list on a new page after the last page of the paper, numbered as the next page.

☐ Center the title `References`, `Literature Cited`, or `References Cited` about one inch from the top of the page.

☐ List the entries in the order in which they first appear in the paper, *not alphabetically.*

☐ Number the entries consecutively; type the note numbers flush left on (not above) the line, followed by a period.

☐ Leave one space between the period and the first letter of the entry; align subsequent lines directly beneath the first letter of the author's last name.

☐ Double-space within and between entries.

20c Sample CSE-Style Research Paper (Excerpts)

The following pages are from a student paper that explores the dangers of global warming for humans and wildlife. The paper, which cites seven sources and includes a graph, illustrates the CSE citation-sequence format.

Abbreviated
                                                         title and
                                                         page number

Sara Castillo

Ecology 4223.01

April 10, 2005

Polar Ice Caps Could Melt by the   ← Center title
End of This Century

Indent ½" →   The Arctic and Antarctica are homes to the   Double-space
(or five spaces)
arth's polar ice caps, and globalwarming appears to

be melting them. When polar temperatures increase,

parts of floating ice sheets and glaciers break off

Introduction   and melt. This process could eventually cause the

ocean levels to rise and have disastrous effects on

plants, animals, and human beings. There are ways to

prevent this disaster,but they will only be effective

Thesis   if governments have the will to implement them
statement
immediately.

The polar ice caps are melting at a rapid rate,

and much of the scientific community agrees that

global warming is one of the causes. The greenhouse

effect, the mechanism that causes global warming,

occurs when molecules of greenhouse gases in the

atmosphere reflect the rays of the sun back to the

earth. This mechanism enables our planet to maintain

Superscript   a temperature adequate for life. However, as the
numbers
correspond   concentration of greenhouse gases in the atmosphere
to sources in
the reference   increases, more heat from the sun is retained, and
list
the temperature of the earth rises.[1]

Greenhouse gases include carbon dioxide (CO_2),

methane, and nitrous oxide.[2] Since the beginning of

the industrial revolution in the late 1800s, people

have been burning fossil fuels that create CO_2.[3] This

CO_2 has led to an increase in the greenhouse effect

Polar Ice Caps 2

and has contributed to the global warming that is
melting the polar ice caps. As Figure 1 shows, the
surface temperature of the earth has increased by
about 1 degree Celsius (1.8 degrees Fahrenheit) since
the 1850s. Some scientists have predicted that
temperatures will increase even further.

It is easy to see the effects of global warming.
For example, the Pine Island Glacier in Antarctica was
depleted at a rate of 1.6 meters per year between 1992
and 1999. This type of melting is very likely to
increase the freshwater that drains into the oceans

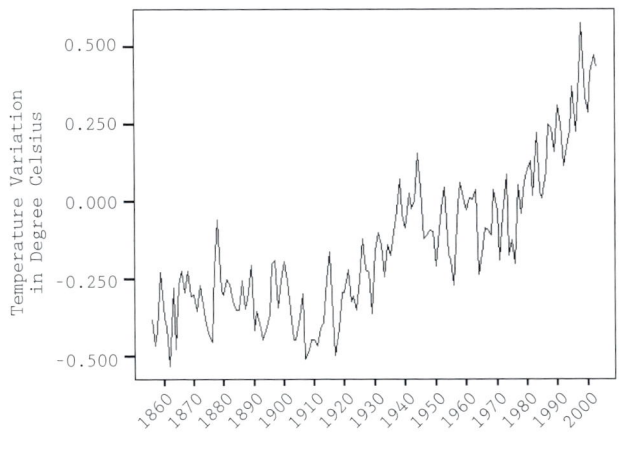

Figure 1   Global temperature variation from the
average during the base period 1961–1990
(adapted from Climatic research unit: data:
temperature 2003). Available from:
http://www.cru.uea.ac.uk/cru/data/
temperature via the INTERNET. Accessed 2005
Mar 11.

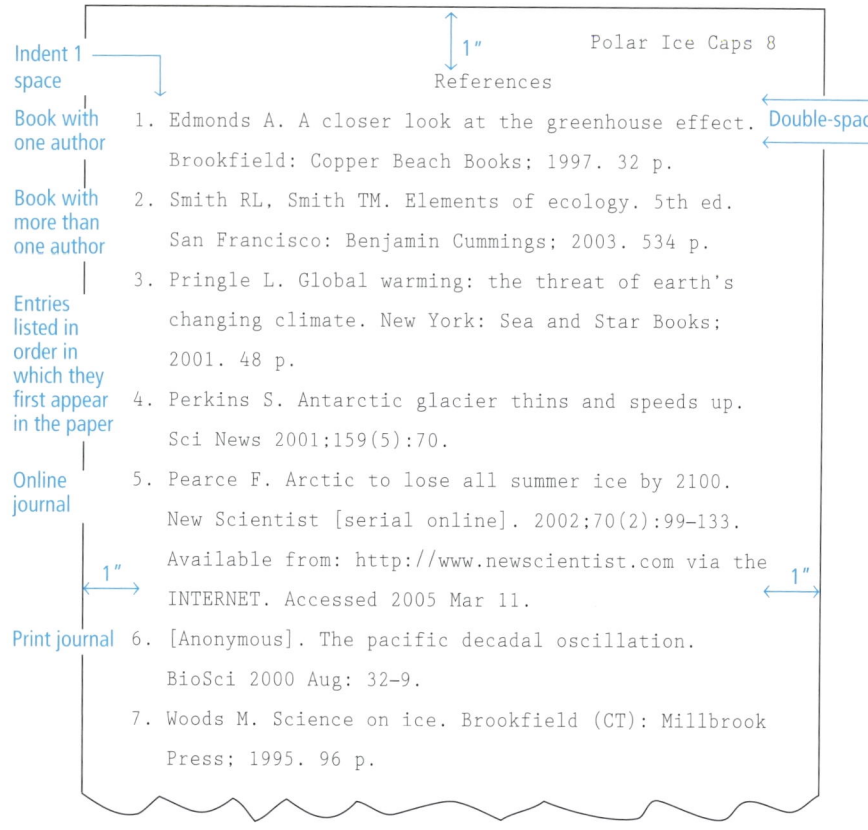

Indent 1 space

Book with one author

Book with more than one author

Entries listed in order in which they first appear in the paper

Online journal

Print journal

1"

Double-space

Polar Ice Caps 8

References

1. Edmonds A. A closer look at the greenhouse effect. Brookfield: Copper Beach Books; 1997. 32 p.

2. Smith RL, Smith TM. Elements of ecology. 5th ed. San Francisco: Benjamin Cummings; 2003. 534 p.

3. Pringle L. Global warming: the threat of earth's changing climate. New York: Sea and Star Books; 2001. 48 p.

4. Perkins S. Antarctic glacier thins and speeds up. Sci News 2001;159(5):70.

5. Pearce F. Arctic to lose all summer ice by 2100. New Scientist [serial online]. 2002;70(2):99–133. Available from: http://www.newscientist.com via the INTERNET. Accessed 2005 Mar 11.

6. [Anonymous]. The pacific decadal oscillation. BioSci 2000 Aug: 32–9.

7. Woods M. Science on ice. Brookfield (CT): Millbrook Press; 1995. 96 p.

20d Using Other Documentation Styles

FAQs links The following style manuals describe documentation formats and manuscript guidelines used in various fields.

Chemistry

Dodd, Janet S. American Chemical Society. *The ACS Guide: A Manual for Authors and Editors.* 2nd ed. Washington: Amer. Chemical Soc., 1997.

Geology

United States Geological Survey. *Suggestions to Authors of the Reports of the United States Geological Survey.* 7th ed. Washington: GPO, 1991.

Government Documents

Garner, Diane L. *The Complete Guide to Citing Government Information Resources: A Manual for Writers and Librarians.* Rev. ed. Bethesda: Congressional Information Service, 1993.

United States Government Printing Office. *Style Manual.* Washington: GPO, 2000.

Journalism

Goldstein, Norm, ed. *Associated Press Stylebook and Briefing on Media Law.* 35th ed. New York: Associated P, 2000.

Law

The Bluebook: A Uniform System of Citation. Comp. Editors of *Columbia Law Review* et al. 16th ed. Cambridge: Harvard Law Rev. Assn., 1996.

Mathematics

American Mathematical Society. *AMS Author Handbook.* Providence: Amer. Mathematical Soc., 1998.

Medicine

Iverson, Cheryl. *Manual of Style: A Guide for Authors and Editors.* 9th ed. Chicago: Amer. Medical Assn., 1997.

Music

Holman, D. Kirn, ed. *Writing about Music: A Style Sheet from the Editors of 19th-Century Music.* Berkeley: U California P, 1988.

Physics

American Institute of Physics. *AIP Style Manual.* 5th ed. New York: Am. Inst. of Physics, 1995.

Scientific and Technical Writing

Rubens, Philip, ed. *Science and Technical Writing: A Manual of Style.* 2nd ed. New York: Routledge, 2001.

PART 6

Developing Strategies for Academic Success

Strategies for Academic Success 293–368

PART 6

Developing Strategies for Academic Success

CHAPTER 21

Ten Habits of Successful Students

As you have probably already observed, the students who are most successful in college are not always the ones who enter with the best grades. In fact, successful students have *learned* to be successful: they have developed specific strategies for success, and they apply those strategies to their education. If you take the time, you can learn the habits of successful students and apply them to your own college education—and, later on, to your career.

21a Learn to Manage Your Time Effectively

One of the most difficult things about college is the demands it makes on your time. It is hard, especially at first, to balance studying, coursework, family life, friendships, and a job. But if you do not take control of your schedule, it will take control of you; if you do not learn to manage your time, you will always be struggling to catch up.

Fortunately, there are two tools you can use to help you manage your time: a **personal organizer** and a **monthly calendar.** (Of course, simply buying an organizer and a calendar will not solve your time-management problems—you have to *use* them. Moreover, you have to use them effectively and regularly.)

Carry your organizer with you at all times, and post your calendar in a prominent place (perhaps above your desk or next to your phone). Remember to record *in both places* not only school-related deadlines, appointments, and reminders (every assignment due date, study group meeting, conference appointment, and exam) but also outside responsibilities like work hours and dental appointments. Record tasks and dates as soon as you learn of them; if you do not write something down immediately, you are likely to forget it. (If you make an entry in your organizer while you are in class, be sure to copy it onto your calendar when you get home.)

You can also use your organizer to help you plan a study schedule, as illustrated in Figure 21.1 on page 294. You do this by blocking out times to study or to complete assignment-related tasks—such as a library database search for a research paper—in addition to appointments and deadlines. (It is a good idea to make these entries in pencil so you can adjust your schedule as new responsibilities arise.)

293

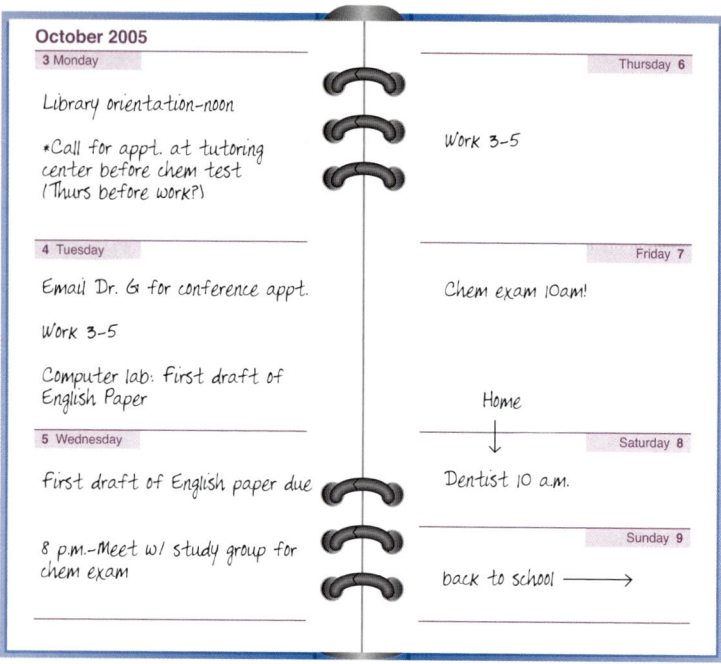

Figure 21.1 **Sample organizer pages for one week.**

http://kirsznermandell.wadsworth.com

Computer Tip: Using Electronic Organizers

If you prefer, you can keep your schedule on your computer (or on a handheld electronic organizer). For example, *Microsoft Outlook* enables you to set up a calendar/organizer in day-, week-, or month-at-a-glance formats. Once you have set up your calendar and organizer pages, you can easily add and delete entries, move appointments and reminders from one day to another, and print out pages.

The bottom line is this: your college years can be a very stressful time, but although some degree of stress is inevitable, it can be kept in check. If you are organized, you will be better able to handle the pressures of a college workload.

21b Put Studying First

To be a successful student, you need to understand that studying is something you do *regularly*, not just right before an exam. You also need to know that studying does not mean simply memorizing facts; it also means reading, rereading, and discussing ideas until you understand them.

To make studying a regular part of your day, set up a study space that includes everything you need (supplies, good light, a comfortable chair) and does not include anything you do not need (clutter, distractions). Then, set up a tentative study schedule that reflects your priorities. Try to designate at least two hours each day to complete assignments due right away, to work on those due later on, and to reread class notes. When you have exams and papers to do, you can adjust your schedule accordingly.

Successful students often form **study groups,** and this is a strategy you should use whenever you can—particularly in courses you find challenging. A study group of four or five students who meet regularly (not just the night before an exam) can make studying more focused and effective as well as more enjoyable and less stressful. By discussing concepts with your classmates, you can try out your ideas and get feedback, clarify complex concepts, and formulate questions for your instructor.

Checklist: Working in a Study Group

Working collaboratively in a **study group** requires some degree of organization. To get the most out of your study group, you need to set some ground rules.

- ☐ Meet regularly.
- ☐ Decide in advance who will be responsible for particular tasks.
- ☐ Set deadlines.
- ☐ Listen when someone else is speaking.
- ☐ Don't reject other people's ideas and suggestions without considering them very carefully.
- ☐ Take stock of problems and progress at regular intervals.
- ☐ Be mindful of other students' learning styles and special needs.

21c Be Sure You Understand School and Course Requirements

To succeed in school, you need to know what is expected of you; if you are not sure, ask.

When you first arrived at school, you probably received various orientation materials—a student handbook, library handouts, and so on—that set forth the rules and policies of your school. Read these documents carefully (if you have not already done so), and be sure you understand what they ask of you. If you do not, ask your peer counselor or your adviser for clarification.

You also need to understand the specific requirements of each course you take. Education is a series of contracts between you and your instructors, and each course syllabus explains the terms of a particular contract. In a syllabus, you learn each instructor's policies about attendance and lateness, assignments and deadlines, plagiarism, and classroom etiquette. In addition, a syllabus may explain penalties for late assignments or missed quizzes, tell how much each assignment is worth, or note additional requirements, such as fieldwork or group projects. Requirements vary significantly from course to course, so read each syllabus carefully—and pay close attention to any supplementary handouts your instructors distribute.

As the semester progresses, your instructors will give you additional information about their expectations. For example, before an exam you will be told what material will be covered, how much time you will have to complete the test, and whether you will be expected to write an essay or fill in an answer sheet that will be graded electronically. When a paper is assigned, you may be given specific information not only about its content, length, and due date but also about its format (font size, line spacing, and margin width, for example). If your instructor does not give you this information, it is your responsibility to find out what is expected of you.

ESL Tip

If you did not attend high school in the United States, some of your instructors' class policies and procedures may seem strange to you. To learn more about the way US college classes are run, read the syllabus for each of your courses, and talk to your instructors about your concerns. You may also find it helpful to talk to older students with cultural backgrounds similar to your own.

21d Be an Active Learner in the Classroom

Education is not about sitting passively in class and waiting for information and ideas to be given to you. It is up to you to be an active participant in your own education.

First, take as many small classes as you can. These classes give you the opportunity to interact with other students and with your instructor. If a large course has recitation sections, be sure to attend these regularly even if they are not required. Also be sure to take as many classes as possible that require writing. Good writing skills are essential to your success as a student, and you need all the practice you can get.

Take responsibility for your education by attending class regularly and arriving on time. Listen attentively, and take careful, complete notes. (Try to review these notes later with other students to make sure you have not missed anything important.) Do your homework on time, and keep up with the reading. When you read an assignment, apply the techniques of **active reading**, interacting with the text instead of just looking passively at what is on the page. If you have time, read beyond the assignment, looking on the Internet and in books, magazines, and newspapers for related information that interests you.

See Ch. 2

As important as it is to listen and take notes in class, it is just as important (particularly in small classes and recitations) to participate in class discussions: to ask and answer questions, volunteer opinions, and give helpful feedback to other students. By participating in such discussions, you learn more about the subject matter being discussed, and you also learn to listen to other points of view, to test your ideas, and to respect the ideas of others.

ESL Tip

Especially in small classes, US instructors usually expect students to participate in class discussion. If you feel nervous about speaking up in class, you might start by expressing your support of a classmate's opinion.

21e Be an Active Learner Outside the Classroom

Taking an active role in your education is also important outside the classroom. Don't be afraid to approach your instructors; take advantage of their office hours, and keep in touch with them by email. Get to know your major adviser well, and be sure he or she knows who you are and where your academic interests lie. Make appointments, ask questions, discuss possible solutions to problems: this is how you learn.

It is also important to participate in the life of your school. Read your school newspaper, check the college Web site regularly, join clubs, and apply for internships. This participation in life outside the classroom can help you develop new interests and friendships as well as enhance your education.

Close-up: Finding Internships

Many businesses, nonprofit organizations, and government agencies offer **internships** (paid or unpaid) to qualified students. These internships, which can last for a summer, a single term, or an entire academic year, give students the opportunity to learn about a particular career or field of study while earning college credit. Internships may also offer the chance to experience life in another part of the country—or in another part of the world. If your school does not have an office that coordinates internships, ask your academic adviser, a reference librarian, or your career services personnel for help.

Finally, participate in the life of your community. Take service-learning courses, if they are offered at your school, or volunteer at a local school or social agency. As successful students know, education is more than just attending classes.

21f   Take Advantage of College Services

Colleges and universities offer students a wide variety of support services. Most students will need help of one kind or another at some point during their college careers; if help is available, it makes sense to use it.

For example, if you are struggling with a particular course, you can go to the tutoring service offered by your school's academic support center or by an individual department. Often, the tutors are students who have done well in the course, and their perspective will be very helpful. If you need help with writing or revising a paper, you can make an appointment with the writing lab, where tutors will give you advice (but will *not* rewrite or edit your paper for you). If you are having trouble deciding what courses to take or what to major in, see your academic adviser. If you are having trouble adjusting to college life, your peer counselor or (if you live in a dorm) your resident adviser may be able to help you. If you have a personal or family problem you would rather not discuss with another student, make an appointment at your school's counseling center, where you can get advice from professionals who understand student problems.

Of course, other services are available—for example, at your school's computer center, job placement service, and financial aid office. Your academic adviser or instructors can tell you where to find the help you need, but it is up to you to make the appointment.

ESL Tip

Many ESL students find using their school's writing lab (sometimes called a writing center) very helpful. In fact, many writing labs have tutors who specialize in working with ESL students. Most writing labs provide assistance with assignments for any course, and they often assist with writing job application letters and résumés.

21g Use the Library

As more and more material becomes available on the Internet, you may begin to think of your college library as outdated or even obsolete. But learning to use the **library** is an important part of your education.

See 13a–c

The library has a lot to offer. For one thing, it can provide a quiet place to study—something you may need if you have a large family or noisy roommates. The library also houses materials that cannot be found online—rare books, special collections, audiovisual materials—as well as electronic databases that contain articles you will not find on the Internet.

Finally, the library is the place where you have access to the experience and expert knowledge of your school's reference librarians. These professionals can answer questions, guide your research, and point you to sources that you might never have found on your own.

21h Use Technology

Technological competence is essential for success in college. For this reason, it makes sense to develop good word-processing skills and to become comfortable with the **Internet**. You should also know how to send and receive email from your university account as well as how to attach files to your email. Beyond the basics, you should learn how to manage the files you download, how to evaluate Web sites, and how to use the electronic resources of your library. You might also find it helpful to know how to scan documents (containing images as well as text) and how to paste text and images into your documents.

See Ch. 14

If you do not have these skills, you need to locate campus services that will help you get them. Workshops and online tutorials may be available through your school library, and individual assistance with software and hardware is available in computer labs.

> **Computer Tip: Emailing Your Instructor**
>
> If you use **email** to contact your instructor, be aware that the same etiquette you would use in a face-to-face setting applies online. You can enhance your credibility by including a specific request or question in the subject line, by addressing your instructor in the same way he or she prefers to be addressed in the classroom, and by including your name at the end of the email, particularly when your email address does not clearly indicate your identity. Finally, be sure to check your message for grammatical and mechanical errors.

Part of being technologically savvy in college involves being aware of the online services your campus has to offer. For example, many campuses rely on customizable information-management systems called **portals.** Not unlike commercial services, such as Yahoo! or America Online, a portal requires you to log in with a user ID and password to access services, such as locating and contacting your academic adviser and viewing your class schedule or your grades.

Finally, you need to know not only how to use technology to enhance a project—for example, how to use *PowerPoint* for an oral presentation or *Excel* to make a table—but also when to use technology (and when *not* to).

See 24d1

21i Make Contacts—and Use Them

One of the most important things you can do for yourself, both for the short term and for the long term, is to make contacts while you are in school and to use them both during college and after you graduate.

Your first contacts are your fellow students. Be sure you have the names, phone numbers, and email addresses of at least two students in each of your classes. These contacts will be useful to you if you miss class, if you need help understanding your notes, or if you want to find someone to study with.

You should also build relationships with students with whom you participate in college activities, such as the college newspaper or the tutoring center. These people are likely to share your goals and interests, so you may want to get feedback from them as you move on to choose a major, consider further education, and make career choices.

Finally, develop relationships with your instructors, particularly those in your major area of study. One of the factors cited most often in studies of successful students is the importance of **mentors,** experienced individuals whose advice they trust. Long after you leave college, you will find these contacts useful.

Close-up: Finding Mentors

The most obvious way to locate a **mentor** is to develop a relationship with an instructor you admire, perhaps taking several courses with him or her. Alternatively, you can develop a close professional relationship with a supervisor at work or in an internship. You should also consider the advantages of working for one of your professors—as a research assistant, in a work-study job, or even as a babysitter or petsitter. A professor who knows you well will be likely to take a special interest in your education and in your career.

21j Be a Lifelong Learner

Your education should not stop when you graduate from college, and this is something you should be aware of from the first day you set foot on campus. To be a successful student, you need to see yourself as a lifelong learner.

Get in the habit of reading newspapers; know what is happening in the world outside school. Talk to people outside the college community, so you don't forget there are issues that have nothing to do with courses and grades. Never miss an opportunity to learn: try to get in the habit of attending plays and concerts sponsored by your school or community and lectures offered at your local library or bookstore.

And think about your future, the life you will lead after college. Think about who you want to be and what you have to do to get there. This is what successful students do.

Checklist: Becoming a Successful Student

☐ Do you have a personal organizer? a calendar? Do you use them regularly?
☐ Have you set up a comfortable study space?
☐ Have you planned a study schedule?
☐ Have you joined a study group?
☐ Have you read your course syllabi and orientation materials carefully?
☐ Are you attending classes regularly and keeping up with your assignments?
☐ Do you take advantage of your instructors' office hours?
☐ Do you participate in class?
☐ Do you participate in college life?
☐ Do you know where to get help if you need it?
☐ Do you know how to use your college library? Do you use it?

(continued)

Becoming a successful student (continued)

☐ Are you satisfied with your level of technological expertise?
   Do you know where to get additional instruction?
☐ Are you trying to make contacts and find mentors?
☐ Do you see yourself as a lifelong learner?

CHAPTER 22

Writing in the Disciplines

When you write in college, your <u>audience</u> is usually your instructor. All instructors, regardless of academic **discipline,** have certain expectations when they read a paper. They expect to see standard English usage, correct grammar and spelling, logical thinking, and clear documentation of sources. In addition, they expect to see sensible organization, convincing support, and careful editing. Despite these similarities, however, instructors in various academic disciplines in the humanities, the social sciences, and the sciences have different expectations about a paper—for example, they expect different documentation styles and different specialized vocabularies. To a large extent, then, learning to write in a particular discipline involves learning the conventions that scholars in that field have agreed to follow, as summarized in the chart on pages 304–05.

See 1b2

22a Understanding Purpose and Audience

In the many courses you will take throughout your college career— and even after graduation, when you are writing for professional or personal purposes—you will find that each field has its own way of communicating in speech and writing. This means that each field will not only have different formats and technical vocabularies, but also different conventions regarding the <u>style</u> and level of writing. In addition, different disciplines have different expectations about purpose and audience.

See 22c1

In many of your classes, the <u>purpose</u> of writing will be for you to show your instructor that you have learned certain course concepts and terms. Your writing will demonstrate that you have thought about why the course material matters and that you have learned how to <u>think critically</u> about the content of the course. In a sense, your instructors are asking you to demonstrate that you know how to think like an entomologist, a philosopher, a sociologist, an accountant, or a software designer, and the way you write needs to mirror as closely as possible the way professionals communicate with one another in that field.

See 1a

See Ch. 8

While the <u>audience</u> for much of your college writing will be your classmates or your instructor, you may also be asked (especially in upper-division courses) to write for an expert audience. For an expert

See 1b

audience, you should use a more specialized vocabulary and terminology than you would for a **general audience,** readers who do not
have as much specialized technical knowledge in the area; for these
readers, you need to provide more background information and to
define your terms. It is important to know for whom you are writing;
if you are unsure about who your audience is, ask your instructor for
clarification.

Humanities

Disciplines	Assignments	Style and Format
Languages	Response essay	*Style*
Literature	Summary essay	Specialized vocabulary
Philosophy	Annotated bibliography	Direct quotations from
History	Bibliographic essay	sources
Linguistics	Analysis essay	*Format*
Religion		Little use of internal
Art history		headings or visuals
Music		

Social Sciences

Disciplines	Assignments	Style and Format
Anthropology	Personal experience	*Style*
Psychology	essay	Specialized vocabulary,
Economics	Book review	including statistical
Business	Case study	terminology
Education	Annotated bibliography	*Format*
Sociology	Review of research essay	Internal headings
Political science	Proposal	Visuals (graphs, maps,
Social work		flowcharts, photographs)
Criminal justice		Numerical data (in tabular
		form)

Natural and Applied Sciences

Disciplines	Assignments	Style and Format
Natural Sciences	Laboratory report	*Style*
Biology	Observation/essay	Frequent use of
Chemistry	Literature survey	passive voice
Physics	Abstract	Few direct quotations
Astronomy	Biographical essay	*Format*
Geology		Internal headings
Mathematics		Tables, graphs, and
		illustrations (exact
Applied Sciences		formats vary)
Engineering		
Computer science		
Nursing		
Pharmacy		

22b Understanding Writing Assignments

Because each discipline has a different set of concerns, writing assignments vary from course to course. A sociology course, for example, may require a statistical analysis; a literature course may
require a literary analysis. Therefore, it is not enough simply to
know the material about which you are asked to write; you must also

Documentation	Research Methods and Sources
English, languages, philosophy: MLA	Library sources (print and electronic)
History, art history: Chicago	Interviews
	Observations (museums, concerts)
	Oral history
	Internet

Documentation	Research Methods and Sources
APA	Library sources (print and electronic)
	Surveys
	Observations (behavior of groups and individuals)
	Internet

Documentation	Research Methods and Sources
Biology: CSE	Library sources (print and electronic)
Other scientific disciplines use a variety of different documentation styles; **see 20d**	Observations
	Experiments
	Surveys
	Internet

be aware of what the instructor in a particular discipline expects of you. For example, when your art history instructor asks you to write a paper on the Brooklyn Bridge, she does not expect you to write an analysis of Hart Crane's long poem *The Bridge* (a topic suitable for a literature class), nor does she want a detailed discussion of the steel cables used in bridge building (a topic suitable for a materials engineering class). What she might expect is for you to discuss the use of the bridge as an artistic subject—as it is in the paintings of Joseph Stella and the photographs of Alfred Stieglitz, for example.

When approaching a writing assignment, you should also be sure you understand your purpose:

- For your writing in the **humanities,** it is often important to **persuade** your readers of something even if that does not appear to be the explicit purpose of the assignment. For example, a critical analysis essay for a Spanish literature class might have an argumentative thesis—one with which your audience could agree or disagree—that relies on your analysis of literary texts for support. When writing a response essay about a work of art, you might set out to convince your audience how effective the work of art is. Whether you are analyzing, evaluating, or comparing, it is important to consider exactly what it is you want your readers to believe after they read your essay.

- In the **social sciences,** on the other hand, the purpose of your writing assignments will probably be to **inform.** A book review, a case study, and a bibliographic essay all share a similar goal: to convey information to your audience in an objective manner. Your task of persuading in the social sciences will involve maintaining your own credibility as a researcher and writer by choosing appropriate sources and by using disciplinary conventions correctly. Still, whether you are writing a formal report, a summary, or an informal personal experience essay, your purpose is primarily informative.

- In the **natural and applied sciences,** most of your formal writing—laboratory reports, reviews of published sources in the discipline, records of your field observations—will be produced in order to **inform** your readers of new findings. In these cases, it is particularly important that you follow the discourse guidelines provided by the discipline—not only so that your professional colleagues can understand your purpose for writing, but also so that you can establish for them that you are a professional who is carrying out credible research.

When you get any assignment, be sure you understand exactly what you are being asked to do; if you are not sure, ask your instructor for clarification. Then, acquaint yourself with the ideas that are of interest to those who publish on your topic. Take the time to surf the Internet, look through your textbook and class notes, or do some <u>exploratory library research</u> to get a sense of the theories, concerns, and controversies pertinent to your topic.

See 13a

22c Understanding Conventions of Style, Format, and Documentation

(1) Style

Specialized Vocabulary When you write a paper for a particular course, you use the specialized vocabulary of those who publish in the discipline. For example, when you write a paper for a literature course, you use the literary terms you hear in class and read in your textbook—*point of view*, *persona*, *imagery*, and so on.

Close-up: Using Specialized Vocabulary

Although technical terms facilitate communication within a discipline, outside that discipline they become <u>jargon</u> and do exactly the opposite. Moreover, in many disciplines, scholars are often so narrowly specialized that even those in the same field may have difficulty understanding their colleagues' technical vocabulary. Therefore, when you write for a general audience, some basic definitions may be helpful.

See 40d

ESL Tip

If English is your second language, it may be difficult to determine which vocabulary words are commonly used and which ones are too technical for a general audience. If you are writing for a general audience, ask a friend in a different major to read your work and tell you if you are using any jargon or terms that lay readers are not likely to understand.

Level of Diction Within any field, particular assignments call for different <u>levels of diction</u>. Regardless of discipline, research papers tend to be formal: they use learned words, are grammatically correct, avoid contractions and colloquialisms, and use third-person rather than first-person pronouns. Proposals—whether they are in the humanities, social sciences, or natural sciences—are also relatively formal.

See 40a

Other assignments, by their very nature, are less formal than proposals and research papers. For example, because its purpose is to present an individual's personal reactions, a response essay may use subjective language, first person, and active voice. A lab report may also be informal, but because its purpose is to report the observations themselves—not the observer's reactions—it frequently uses objective language and passive voice ("The acid was poured" rather than "I poured the acid"). For the most part, then, it is an assignment's purpose and audience, not its discipline, that determines its level of diction.

Tone The **tone** of your writing—the way you convey your attitude—is another important consideration in each of the disciplines. For example, in the natural and applied sciences, you will almost without exception be required to use an impersonal tone, often writing in the passive voice. This tone would not be appropriate for a personal self-reflection essay assignment in the humanities, which would lose much of its power and effectiveness if you used an objective tone. Similarly, if you were to write a mechanical engineering report that relied on vivid and poetic visual description of the lab equipment, that report would not be acceptable to other mechanical engineers.

To become familiar with the tone used by a particular discipline, read work written by professionals in that field. If you have questions about the level of formality or about other stylistic conventions used in a particular discipline, ask your instructor or visit your campus writing center.

ESL Tip

You may have memorized various English-language idioms in your ESL classes. However, when you are striving for a formal tone in your writing, it is usually better to avoid these colloquial phrases, which are more commonly used in conversation and in very informal writing.

FAQs
See
24a
See
24b

(2) Format

Each discipline has certain formatting conventions that govern the way written information is presented on the page. A **format** is an accepted way of displaying material in a document. A format may govern the arrangement of an entire document (such as a lab report, which has certain prescribed sections) or determine whether writers use internal **headings** in their papers. Formatting conventions also determine how certain kinds of information are presented or displayed *within* a document. For example, social scientists expect statistical data to be presented in **tables or graphs**. Specific mechanical concerns, such as whether to spell out **numbers** or use numerals, also differ from discipline to discipline.

Professional organizations, such as the Modern Language Association, define the guidelines that govern document formats and citation conventions within their disciplines. Typically, a professional organization will issue or recommend a handbook or style sheet that defines the standards for spelling, mechanics, punctuation, and capitalization. This style sheet also gives guidelines for the use and placement of information in diagrams, graphs, tables, and photographs within a paper as well as guidelines for typing conventions, such as the placement of page numbers and the arrangement of information on a title page, and for **documentation.** Because significant differences in format exist among disciplines, you should consult the appropriate style sheet before you begin your paper.

(3) Documentation

Different disciplines use different styles of **documentation**. Four of the most widely used styles are those recommended by the Modern Language Association (MLA), the American Psychological Association (APA), *The Chicago Manual of Style* (Chicago), and the Council of Science Editors (CSE).

Instructors in the humanities usually prefer **MLA style,** which uses parenthetical references within the text to refer to a works-cited list at the end of the paper, or **Chicago style,** which uses footnotes or endnotes keyed to citations listed in a bibliography at the end of the paper. Instructors in some of the social sciences, such as psychology and education, prefer **APA style,** which uses parenthetical references that differ from MLA references and a reference list at the end of the paper. Other disciplines—the physical and biological sciences, for example—prefer a number-reference format, such as **CSE style,** which uses raised numbers that refer to a numbered list of works at the end of the paper.

While a works-cited list, a bibliography, and a reference list have similar purposes—to inform readers where the writer found his or her sources—their different formats reflect the different concerns of the fields: APA and CSE styles position the date early in the citation because social scientists and scientists generally place greater importance on researching the most current sources than do many writers in the humanities.

Because of the lack of uniformity among the disciplines, it is important that you consult your instructor to see which documentation style is required. If your instructor does not require a particular documentation style, it is your responsibility to determine which style to use—for example, by looking at an important journal in the field and following its documentation style.

Checklist: Documentation

☐ Make sure you understand what information must be documented.

☐ Do not assume the documentation style you use in one class is appropriate for another class.

☐ Use one documentation style consistently throughout your paper, and follow its guidelines.

☐ Make sure you have a copy of the appropriate style sheet so that you can consult it as you write.

☐ When you proofread the final draft of your paper, make certain that you have documented all information that needs documentation and that you have punctuated all entries correctly.

22d Avoiding Plagiarism

See Ch. 16
Although research methods and sources, citation styles, and formats may differ from discipline to discipline, all academic fields respect the intellectual property of others. Therefore, plagiarism is treated as a serious offense. The general rule that applies to all disciplines is that you must acknowledge *any words or ideas that are not your own*, whether quoted directly or paraphrased, and regardless of where you found them, except for information that is considered to be **common knowledge**.

Close-up: Common Knowledge

What is "common knowledge" will differ according to discipline. Common knowledge to a biology student will not be the same as common knowledge to a history or literature student. If you are not sure whether something is common knowledge in your discipline, ask your instructor—or follow the "when in doubt, cite" rule.

Many students think that plagiarism applies only to published work, but in fact you may not use (without proper acknowledgment) information taken from unpublished works, lecture notes, email discussions, laboratory reports, computer codes, musical scores, photographs or other types of visuals, interviews, or Web sites.

NOTE: One ethical issue is specific to the sciences and the social sciences. In these disciplines, the deliberate falsification of data in order to deceive—or the deliberate omission of information or data that might disprove a theory or alter research results—is a serious offense. There are no acceptable reasons for dishonesty of this kind, and the penalties are severe.

22e Using Visuals

As you take courses across the disciplines, you will see that the role of **visuals** and the technology used to produce or access them differs significantly. Different disciplines use visuals differently to communicate information, and they also differ in how such visual representations present information or serve as evidence. Depending on what types of visuals are common to the discipline (images, video clips, or statistical charts, for example), many technology options are available for producing and accessing these images.

See
Ch. 3,
Ch. 10

Many images are available through the Internet or in printed texts. To access these visuals, you will need to know how to download images from the World Wide Web or scan images from a print source, how to save images in appropriate formats for both electronic and print use, and how to insert these images into your documents. You will also need to document the source of each visual you use, just as you would for any other source.

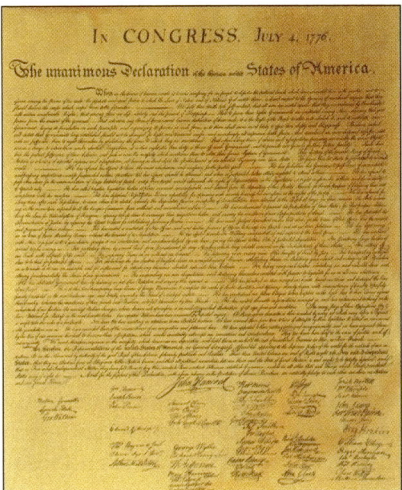

Figure 22.1 The Declaration of Independence.

Humanities disciplines such as theater, film, literature, or art might use photographs, such as an image of a famous painting. Other disciplines, such as history, may rely on archival photographs in libraries or in special collections in historical museums as well as digitized versions of important historical documents (see Figure 22.1). The use of such visuals in your written work provides specific support for your interpretations of the significance of works of literature and art or of historical documents.

Disciplines in the **social sciences** (such as psychology and sociology) and the **physical sciences** (such as biology, chemistry, and geology) frequently rely on charts, tables, and graphs—such as the line graph shown in Figure 22.2—to represent complex statistics, conceptual models or design prototypes, and results of scientific experiments. In the physical sciences, technical photographs (such as the one shown in Figure 22.3) may also be used. Because of the need to communicate technical information clearly and accurately, these disciplines use technologies that manage, analyze, and display data—for example, *Microsoft Excel*—and, in some instances, a range of computer-aided drawing programs (such as *CAD*).

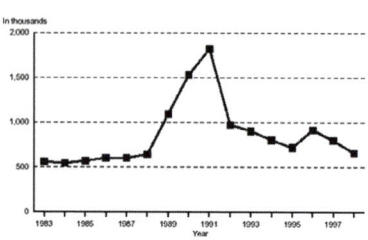

Figure 22.2 Line graph from statistical analysis report.

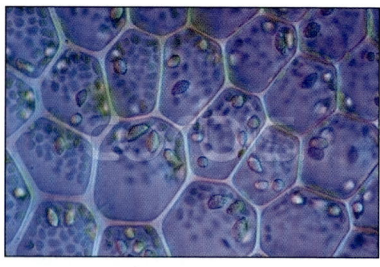

Figure 22.3 Plant cells.

See
Ch. 24

Regardless of your discipline, it is important to become familiar with the types of visuals, methods of <u>document design</u>, and technology options (including discipline-specific software) that are available. These tools can help you to become an effective communicator in your field.

22f Research Methods and Sources

Gathering information is basic to all disciplines, but the methods used to gather that information and the kinds of sources used vary from discipline to discipline. For example, in the humanities (especially literature and history), the currency of information is not usually vital. It may be important to know the latest interpretation of Shakespeare's *Hamlet* or the causes of World War I, but the best and most insightful analyses may have been published many years ago. Print sources, whether found on shelves in the library or accessed from a database, are central to research in the humanities, but digitized collections of primary source documents and electronic books are becoming increasingly available and important to humanities scholars.

Those who work in the natural sciences and social sciences also spend a lot of time examining the literature of a particular topic, but in these disciplines, it is much more important to use the most up-to-date information. A research paper on genetic modification of foods, for example, should be based on the latest findings regardless of whether the paper's focus is on scientific, ethical, moral, or economic issues. Therefore, scientists and social scientists rely less on information found in books (which may be out of date) and more on information found in conference proceedings, preprints, technical reports, and current journal articles (because these are the places where new theories, discoveries, ideas, and research results are first presented).

Social scientists also rely heavily on observation of behavior, interviews, and surveys. Because of the kinds of data they generate, social scientists typically use statistical methodology and record their results in charts, graphs, and tables. Those who work in the natural sciences (such as biology, chemistry, and physics) and the applied sciences (engineering and computer science, for example) rely almost exclusively on **empirical data**—information obtained through controlled laboratory experiments or from mathematical models. They use the data they collect to help them formulate theories that explain their observations.

The information you gather from print and electronic resources in the library, in the field, on the Internet, or in the laboratory will help you support the points you make when you write. Whether you want to make a point about the color gray in a short story by Herman Melville or about the effect of a particular amino acid on the respiratory system, your intent is the same: to find the support you need to convince readers that what you are saying is reasonable.

The kind of support that is acceptable and persuasive, however, varies from discipline to discipline. For example, students of literature often use quotations from fiction or poetry to support their statements, whereas historians are likely to refer to original documents, such as court or church records. Social scientists frequently rely on statistics to support their conclusions; those in the natural sciences use the empirical data they derive from controlled experiments.

Because each discipline has its own sources and methodology and its own conventions of style, format, and documentation, the way you conduct research will vary according to the discipline in which you are writing. Whatever the discipline, however, the same standards of accuracy, grammatical and mechanical correctness, and academic honesty apply.

CHAPTER 23

Writing a Literary Analysis

Learning to read, respond to, and write about literature are important skills that can scrve you while you are a college student, as well as later, in your life beyond the classroom.

23a Reading Literature

When you read a literary work you plan to write about, you use the same critical thinking skills and **active reading** strategies you apply to other works you read: preview the work, and highlight it to identify key ideas and cues to meaning; then, annotate it carefully.

As you read and take notes, focus on the special concerns of literary analysis, considering elements like a short story's plot, a poem's rhyme or meter, or a play's staging. Look for *patterns*, related groups of words, images, or ideas that run through a work. Look for *anomalies*, unusual forms, unique uses of language, unexpected actions by characters, or original treatments of topics. Finally, look for *connections*, links with other literary works, with historical events, or with biographical information.

FAQs

> ### Close-up: Reading Literature
>
> When you read a work of literature, keep in mind that you do not read to discover the one correct meaning the writer has hidden between the lines. The "meaning" of a literary work is created by the interaction between a text and its readers. Do not assume, however, that a work can mean whatever you want it to mean; ultimately, your interpretation must be consistent with the stylistic signals, thematic suggestions, and patterns of imagery in the text.

23b Writing about Literature

When you have finished your reading and annotating, you decide on a topic, and then you **brainstorm** to find ideas to write about; then, you decide on a **thesis** and use it to help you organize your material. As you arrange related material into categories, you will begin to see a structure for your paper. At this point, you are ready to start drafting your essay.

When you write about literature, your goal is to make a point and support it with appropriate references to the work under discussion or to related works or secondary sources. In this sense, an essay on a literary topic is often a kind of **argumentative essay** in which you use sources and your own insights to support a thesis statement. As you write, you observe the conventions of literary criticism, which has its own specialized vocabulary and formats. You also respond to certain discipline-specific assignments. For instance, you may be asked to **analyze** a work, to take it apart and consider one or more of its elements—perhaps the plot or characters in a story or the use of language in a poem. Or, you may be asked to **interpret** a work, to try to discover its possible meanings. Finally, you may be called on to **evaluate** a work, to judge its strengths and weaknesses.

See
Ch. 9

More specifically, you may be asked to trace the critical or popular reception to a work, to compare two works by a single writer (or by two different writers), or to consider the relationship between a work of literature and a literary movement or historical period. You may be asked to analyze a character's motives or the relationship between two characters or to comment on a story's setting or tone. Whatever the case, understanding exactly what you are expected to do will make your writing task easier.

Checklist: Writing about Literature

☐ Use present-tense verbs when discussing works of literature (`The character of Mrs. Mallard's husband is not developed`).

☐ Use past-tense verbs only when discussing historical events (`Owen's poem conveys the destructiveness of World War I, which at the time the poem was written was considered to be. . . .`); when presenting historical or biographical data (`Her first novel, published in 1811 when Austen was thirty-six,. . . .`); or when identifying events that occurred prior to the time of the story's main action (`Miss Emily is a recluse; since her father died she has lived alone except for a servant`).

☐ Support all points with specific, concrete examples from the work you are discussing, briefly summarizing key events, quoting dialogue or description, describing characters or setting, or paraphrasing ideas.

☐ Combine paraphrase, summary, and quotation with your own interpretations, weaving quotations smoothly into your paper (**see Ch. 15**).

☐ Be careful to acknowledge all the sources you use, including the literary work or works under discussion. Introduce the words or ideas of others with a reference to the source, and follow borrowed material with appropriate parenthetical documentation (**see 17a1**). Be sure you have quoted accurately and enclosed the words of others in quotation marks.

(continued)

Writing about literature (continued)

- ☐ Include a works-cited list (**see 17a2**) in accordance with MLA documentation style.
- ☐ When citing a part of a short story or novel, supply the page number (168). For a poem, give the line numbers (2-4). For a classic verse play, include act, scene, and line numbers (1.4.29-31). For other plays, supply act and/or scene numbers. (When quoting more than four lines of prose or more than three lines of poetry, follow the guidelines outlined in 47b.)
- ☐ Avoid subjective expressions like *I feel, I believe, it seems to me,* and *in my opinion.* These weaken your paper by suggesting that its ideas are "only" your opinion and have no validity in themselves.
- ☐ Avoid unnecessary plot summary. Your goal is to draw a conclusion about one or more works and to support that conclusion with pertinent details. If a plot development supports a point you wish to make, a *brief* summary is acceptable, but plot summary is no substitute for analysis.
- ☐ Use literary terms accurately. For example, be careful not to confuse *narrator* or *speaker* with *writer.* Feelings or opinions expressed by a narrator or character do not necessarily represent those of the writer. You should not say, "In the poem's last stanza, *Frost* expresses his indecision," when you mean the poem's *speaker* is indecisive.
  NOTE: For a glossary of literary terms, go to http://kirsznermandell.wadsworth.com ▶ *The Brief Wadsworth Handbook* ▶ Chapter 23 ▶ Literary Terms, or *The Brief Wadsworth Handbook* Animated CD-ROM ▶ Resources ▶ Chapter 23 ▶ Literary Terms.
- ☐ Underline titles of books and plays (**see 51a**); enclose titles of short stories and poems in quotation marks (**see 47c**). Book-length poems are treated as long works, and their titles should be underlined.

FAQs link

23c Sample Literary Analysis (without Sources)

Daniel Johanssen, a student in an introductory literature course, wrote an essay about Delmore Schwartz's 1959 poem "The True-Blue American," which appears below. Daniel's essay, which begins on page 318, includes annotations that highlight some conventions of writing about poetry. (Note that because all students in the class selected poems from the same text, Daniel's instructor did not require a works-cited list.)

The True-Blue American

Jeremiah Dickson was a true-blue American,

For he was a little boy who understood America, for he felt that he must

Think about *everything*; because that's all there is to think about,

Knowing immediately the intimacy of truth and comedy,
Knowing intuitively how a sense of humor was a necessity   5
For one and for all who live in America. Thus, natively, and
Naturally when on an April Sunday in an ice cream parlor
    Jeremiah
Was requested to choose between a chocolate sundae and a
    banana split
He answered unhesitatingly, having no need to think of it
Being a true-blue American, determined to continue as he began: 10
Rejecting the either-or of Kierkegaard,[1] and many another
    European;
Refusing to accept alternatives, refusing to believe the choice
    of between;
Rejecting selection; denying dilemma; electing absolute
    affirmation:
knowing
    in his breast   15
        The infinite and the gold
        Of the endless frontier, the deathless West.
"Both: I will have them both!" declared this true-blue American
In Cambridge, Massachusetts, on an April Sunday, instructed
        By the great department stores, by the Five-and-Ten,   20
Taught by Christmas, by the circus, by the vulgarity and
    grandeur of Niagara Falls and the Grand Canyon,
Tutored by the grandeur, vulgarity, and infinite appetite
    gratified and
    Shining in the darkness, of the light
On Saturdays at the double bills of the moon pictures,
The consummation of the advertisements of the imagination   25
    of the light
Which is as it was—the infinite belief in infinite hope—
    of Columbus, Barnum, Edison, and Jeremiah Dickson.

---

[1]Søren Kierkegaard (1813–1855)—Danish philosopher who greatly
influenced twentieth-century existentialism. *Either-Or* (1841) is one of his
best-known works.

Daniel Johanssen

Professor Stang

English 1001

8 April 2005

Irony in "The True-Blue American"

The poem "The True-Blue American," by Delmore
Schwartz, is not as simple and direct as its title
suggests. In fact, the title is extremely ironic. At
first, the poem seems patriotic, but actually the
flag-waving strengthens the speaker's criticism.
Even though the poem seems to support and celebrate
America, it is actually a bitter critique of the
negative aspects of American culture.

According to the speaker, the primary problem
with America is that its citizens falsely believe
themselves to be authorities on everything. The
following lines introduce the theme of the "know-it-
all" American: "For he was a little boy who
understood America, for he felt that he must / Think
about <u>everything</u>; because that's <u>all</u> there is to
think about" (lines 2-3). This theme is developed
later in a series of parallel phrases that seem to
celebrate the value of immediate intuitive knowledge
and a refusal to accept or to believe anything other
than what is American (4-6).

Americans are ambitious and determined, but
these qualities are not seen in the poem as virtues.
According to the speaker, Americans reject
sophisticated "European" concepts like doubt and
choices and alternatives and instead insist on

FAQs
links

Title of
poem is in
quotation
marks

Thesis
statement

Slash
separates
lines of
poetry
(space
before and
after slash)

Parenthetical
documenta-
tion indicates
line numbers
(the word
line or *lines*
is included
only in the
first refer-
ence)

Johanssen 2

"absolute affirmation" (13)—simple solutions to complex problems. This unwillingness to compromise translates into stubbornness and materialistic greed. This tendency is illustrated by the boy's asking for <u>both</u> a chocolate sundae <u>and</u> a banana split at the ice cream parlor—not "either-or" (11). Americans are characterized as pioneers who want it all, who will stop at nothing to achieve "The infinite and the gold / Of the endless frontier, the deathless West" (16-17). For the speaker, the pioneers and their "endless frontier" are not noble or self-sacrificing; they are like greedy little boys at an ice cream parlor.

According to the speaker, the greed and materialism of America began as grandeur but ultimately became mere vulgarity. Similarly, the "true-blue American" is not born a vulgar parody of grandeur; he learns from his true-blue fellow Americans, who in turn were taught by experts:

> By the great department stores, by the
> Five-and-Ten,
> Taught by Christmas, by the circus, by the
> vulgarity and grandeur of Niagara
> Falls and the Grand Canyon,
> Tutored by the grandeur, vulgarity,
> and infinite appetite
> gratified. . . . (20-22)

Among the "tutors" the speaker lists are such American institutions as department stores and national monuments. Within these institutions, grandeur and vulgarity coexist; in a sense, they are one and the same.

More than 3 lines of poetry are set off from text. Quotation is indented 1 " (or ten spaces) from left margin; no quotation marks are used. Documentation is placed one space after final punctuation.

Johanssen 3

The speaker's negativity climaxes in the phrase
"Shining in the darkness, of the light" (23). This
paradoxical statement suggests that negative truths
are hidden beneath America's glamorous surface. All
the grand and illustrious things of which Americans
are so proud are personified by Jeremiah Dickson, the
spoiled brat in the ice cream parlor.

Conclusion reinforces thesis

Like America, Jeremiah has unlimited potential.
He has native intuition, curiosity, courage, and a
pioneer spirit. Unfortunately, however, both America
and Jeremiah Dickson are limited by their willingness
to be led by others, by their greed and impatience,
and by their preference for quick, easy, unambiguous
answers rather than careful philosophical analysis.
Regardless of his—and America's—potential, Jeremiah
Dickson is doomed to be hypnotized and seduced by
glittering superficialities, light without substance,
and to settle for the "double bills of the moon
pictures" (24) rather than the enduring truths of a
philosopher such as Kierkegaard.

23d   Sample Literary Analysis (with Sources)

See
17a

Margaret Chase, a student in an introductory literature course, wrote
the following analysis of Alice Walker's short story "Everyday Use."
The paper uses **MLA documentation style** and cites three outside
sources.

Margaret Chase

Professor Sierra

English 1001

6 May 2005

The Politics of "Everyday Use"

Alice Walker's "Everyday Use" focuses on a   *Introduction*
mother, Mrs. Johnson, and her two daughters, Maggie and
Dee, and how they look at their heritage. The story's
climax comes when Mrs. Johnson rejects Dee's request to
take a hand-stitched quilt away with her so that she
can hang it on her wall. Knowing that Maggie will put
the quilt to "everyday use," Dee is horrified, and she
tells her mother and Maggie that they do not understand
their heritage. Although many literary critics read   *Thesis*
Dee's character as materialistic and shallow, a closer   *statement*
examination of the social and historical circumstances
in which Walker wrote this 1973 story encourages a more
generous interpretation of Dee's behavior.

At several points in the story, Walker clearly   *Dee con-*
establishes that Dee is quite different from Mrs.   *trasted with*
Johnson and Maggie. As the story opens, the reader   *Maggie*
learns that Dee, the college-educated daughter, is
coming home to visit her mother and sister after an
absence of several years. Maggie, Dee's younger, less
ambitious sister, has remained at home with her
mother. Unlike Dee, Maggie is shy and introverted.
She is described as looking like a lame animal that
has been run over by a car. According to the
narrator, "She has been like this, chin in on chest,
eyes on ground, feet in shuffle" (355) ever since she
was burned in a fire.

Dee con-
trasted with
Mrs. Johnson

As Mrs. Johnson waits for Dee to arrive, she
thinks about a dream she had about how Dee's
homecoming might look on a television talk show. In
her dream, Mrs. Johnson is slim and attractive,
talking to the host with a "quick and witty tongue"
(355). In reality, she acknowledges, she would never
look "a strange white man in the eye" (355), but
"Dee . . . would always look anyone in the eye.
Hesitation was no part of her nature" (355). In
addition to highlighting the fact that the Johnson
women are African Americans who live in a racist
society, Mrs. Johnson's dream also begins to
establish the difference between her and Dee. For
Mrs. Johnson, looking a white man in the eye is
dangerous; for Dee, it is an act of defiance and
courage.

Contrast
between Dee
and others,
continued

Later in the story, Mrs. Johnson says that
unlike Dee, she never received an education. After
second grade, she explains, the school closed down.
She says, "Don't ask me why: in 1927 colored asked
fewer questions than they do now" (356). Mrs. Johnson
concedes that she accepts the status quo even though
she knows that it is unjust. This admission further
establishes the difference between Mrs. Johnson and
Dee. Mrs. Johnson has accepted her circumstances,
while Dee has worked to change hers. Their
differences are illustrated in the film version of
the story by their contrasting dress. As shown in
fig. 1, Dee and her boyfriend, Hakim, dress in the
Afro-American style of the late 1960s, embracing
their African heritage; Mrs. Johnson and Maggie dress
in plain, conservative clothing.

Chase 3

Fig. 1. Dee and Hakim arrive at the family home.
"Everyday Use," <u>The Wadsworth Original Film Series
in Literature: "Everyday Use,"</u> dir. Bruce R. Schwartz,
DVD, Wadsworth, 2005.

Although Mrs. Johnson makes several statements
that hint at her admiration of Dee's defiant
character, she also points to incidents that highlight
Dee's materialism and selfish ambition. When their
first house burned down, Dee watched it burn while she
stood under a tree with "a look of concentration"
(356) rather than remorse. Mrs. Johnson knows how much
Dee hated their small, dingy house, and she knows too
that Dee must have been glad it was destroyed. In
fact, as Walker acknowledges in an interview with her
biographer, Evelyn C. White ("Stitches in Time"), Dee
might even have set the fire that destroyed the house
and scarred her sister. Even now, Dee is ashamed of
the tin-roofed house her family lives in, and she has
said that she would never bring her friends there.

Dee's
character
(past)

Chase 4

Mrs. Johnson has always known that Dee wanted "nice
things" (356); even at sixteen, "she had a style of
her own: and knew what style was" (356). With these
observations by Mrs. Johnson, Walker establishes that
Dee has always been materialistic and self-serving as
well as strong willed.

Dee's character (present)

When Dee arrives home with her new boyfriend, it
is clear that her essential character is, for the most
part, unchanged. As she eyes her mother's belongings
and asks Mrs. Johnson if she can take the top of the
butter churn home with her, it is clear that she is
still materialistic. Moreover, her years away from
home have also politicized her. Dee now wants to be
called "Wangero" because she believes (although
mistakenly) that her given name comes from whites who
owned her ancestors. She now wears African clothing
and talks about how it is a new day for African
Americans. Still selfish, she is determined to
maintain her own independent identity even if doing so
will estrange her from her mother and her sister.

Social and political context for Dee's behavior

The meaning and political importance of Dee's
decision to adopt an African name and wear African
clothing cannot be fully understood without a
knowledge of the social and political context in
which Walker wrote this story. Walker's own
comments about this time period explain Dee's
behavior and add meaning to it. In her interview with
White, Walker explains that the late 1960s were a
time of awakening for African Americans. Many turned
ideologically and culturally to Africa, adopting the
dress, hairstyles, and even the names of their

Chase 5

African ancestors. Walker admits that as a young
woman she too became interested in discovering her
African heritage. (In fact, she herself was given the
name <u>Wangero</u> during a visit to Kenya in the late
1960s.) Walker tells White that she considered
keeping this new name, but eventually realized that
to do so would be to "dismiss" her family and her
American heritage. When she researched her American
family, she found that her great-great grandmother
had walked from Virginia to Georgia carrying two
children. "If that's not a Walker," she says, "I
don't know what is." Thus, Walker realized that, over
time, African Americans actually transformed the
names they had originally taken from their enslavers.
To respect the ancestors she knew, Walker says, she
decided it was important to retain her name.

Along with adopting symbols of their African
heritage, many African Americans also worked to elevate
these symbols in their own families, such as the quilt
shown in fig. 2, to the status of high art (Salaam 42).
One way of doing this was to put these objects in
museums; another was to hang them on the walls of their
homes (Salaam 42). Such acts were aimed at convincing
racist whites that African Americans were indeed
cultured and civilized and consequently deserved not
only basic civil rights, but also respect (Salaam 43).
These gestures were also meant to improve self-esteem
and pride within black communities (Salaam 42).

According to literary critics Houston Baker and
Charlotte Pierce-Baker, when Mrs. Johnson chooses at
the end of the story to give the quilt to Maggie, she

Social and political context, continued

Critics' analysis of Mrs. Johnson's decision

Chase 6

Fig. 2. Traditional hand-stitched quilt. Evelyn
C. White, "Alice Walker: Stitches in Time,"
interview, <u>The Wadsworth Original Film Series
in Literature: "Everyday Use,"</u> dir. Bruce
R. Schwartz, DVD, Wadsworth, 2005.

is challenging Dee's simplistic understanding of
heritage by recognizing that quilts signify "sacred
generations of women who have made their own special
kind of beauty separate from the traditional artistic
world" (qtd. in Piedmont-Marton 45). According to
Baker and Peirce-Baker, Mrs. Johnson's epiphany is
that her daughter Maggie, whom she has long dismissed
because of her quiet nature and shyness, understands
the true meaning of the quilt in a way that Dee never
will (Piedmont-Marton 45). Readers can tell that
Maggie, unlike Dee, has paid close attention to the
traditions and skills of her mother and grandmother:
she has actually learned to quilt. More important, by
staying with her mother instead of going away to
school, she has gotten to know her family, as she

Student's
analysis of
Maggie's
final
gesture

Chase 7

clearly shows when she tells her mother that Dee can
have the quilt because she does not need it to
remember her grandmother.

Although Maggie's and Mrs. Johnson's   Conclusion
understandings of heritage may be more emotionally
profound than Dee's, it is important not to dismiss
the significance of Dee's desire to elevate the quilt
to the level of high art. The political stakes of
defining such an object as art in the late 1960s and
early 1970s were high, and the fight for equality
went beyond basic civil rights. Clearly, Dee is a
materialistic woman who does not understand the
emotional meanings of her heritage. Still, her desire
to hang the quilt should not be dismissed as a
completely selfish act. At the time the story was   Defense
written, displaying the quilt would have been not   of Dee's
                                                         actions
only a personal act, but a political act as well.

Works Cited

Piedmont-Marton, Elisabeth. "An Overview of 'Everyday
    Use.'" <u>Short Stories for Students</u> 2 (1997):
    42-45. <u>Literature Resource Center</u>. Gale Group
    Databases. U of Texas Lib. System, TX. 20 Apr.
    2005 <http://www.galegroup.com>.

Salaam, Kalamu Ya. "A Primer of the Black Arts
    Movement: Excerpts from <u>The Magic of Juju: An
    Appreciation of the Black Arts Movement.</u>" <u>Black
    Renaissance/Renaissance Noire</u> 2002: 40-59.
    <u>Expanded Academic ASAP</u>. Gale Group Databases. U
    of Texas Lib. System, TX. 21 Apr. 2005 <http://
    www.galegroup.com>.

Walker, Alice. "Alice Walker: Stitches in Time."
    Interview with Evelyn C. White. <u>The Wadsworth
    Original Film Series in Literature: "Everyday
    Use."</u> Dir. Bruce R. Schwartz. DVD. Wadsworth,
    2005.

---. "Everyday Use." <u>Literature: Reading, Reacting,
    Writing</u>. Ed. Laurie G. Kirszner and Stephen R.
    Mandell. 5th ed. Boston: Wadsworth, 2004.
    354-60.

CHAPTER 24

Designing Effective Documents

Document design refers to the principles that help you determine how to design a piece of written work—a research paper, report, or Web page, for example—so that it communicates your ideas clearly and effectively. Although formatting requirements—for example, how tables and charts are constructed and how information is presented on a title page—may differ from discipline to discipline, all well-designed documents share the same general characteristics: an *effective format, clear headings, useful lists,* and *helpful visuals.*

24a Creating an Effective Visual Format

An effective document includes visual elements that help readers find, read, and interpret information on a page. For example, wide margins can give a page a balanced, uncluttered appearance; white space can break up a long discussion; and a distinctive type size or typeface can make a word or phrase stand out on a page.

(1) Margins

Margins frame a page and keep it from looking overcrowded. Because long lines of text can overwhelm readers and make a document difficult to read, a page should have margins of at least one inch all around. If the material you are writing about is highly technical or unusually difficult, use wider margins (one and a half inches).

In most cases, you should **justify** (uniformly align, except for paragraph indentations) the left-hand margin of your pages. You can either leave a ragged edge on the right or justify your text so all the words are aligned evenly along the right margin of your page. (A ragged edge is often preferable because it varies the visual landscape of your text, making it easier to read.)

(2) White Space

White space denotes the areas of a page that are intentionally left blank: the spaces between lines of text, the space between text and visuals, and, of course, the margins. Used effectively, white space can isolate material and thereby focus a reader's attention on it. You can use white space around a block of text—a paragraph or a section, for example—or around visuals such as charts, graphs, and photographs. White space can eliminate clutter, break a discussion into manageable components, and focus readers' attention on a particular element on a page.

> **Computer Tip: Borders, Horizontal Rules, and Shading**
>
> Most word-processing programs enable you to create borders, horizontal rules, and shaded areas of text. Border and shading options are usually found under the Format menu of your word-processing program. With these features, you can select line style, thickness, and color and adjust white space, boxed text, and the degree of shading.

(3) Color

Like white space, **color** (when used in moderation) can help to emphasize and clarify information while making it visually appealing. In addition to using color to emphasize information, you can use it to distinguish certain types of information—for example, titles can be one color and subheadings can be another, complementary color. You can also use color to differentiate the segments of a chart or the bars on a graph. Many software applications, including *Microsoft Word* and *PowerPoint*, contain design templates (such as the one in Figure 24.1) that make it easy for you to choose a color scheme or to create your own. Remember, however, that too many colors can distract readers and obscure your visual emphasis.

(4) Typeface and Type Size

Your computer gives you a wide variety of typefaces and type sizes (measured in **points**) from which to choose. **Typefaces** are distinctively designed sets of letters, numbers, and punctuation marks. The typeface you choose should be suitable for your purpose and audience. In your academic writing, avoid fancy or elaborate typefaces—*script* or 𝔬𝔩𝔡 𝔈𝔫𝔤𝔩𝔦𝔰𝔥, for example—that call attention to themselves and distract readers. Instead, select a typeface that is simple and direct—Courier, Times New Roman, or Arial, for example. In nonacademic documents—such as Web pages and flyers—decorative typefaces may be used to emphasize a point or attract a reader's attention.

You also have a wide variety of **type sizes** available to you. For most of your academic papers, you will use a 10- or 12-point type (headings will sometimes be larger). Documents such as advertisements, brochures, and Web pages, however, may use a variety of type sizes. (Keep in mind that point size alone is not a reliable guide for size. For instance, 12-point type in **Chicago** is much larger than 12-point type in Courier or Arial Condensed Light.)

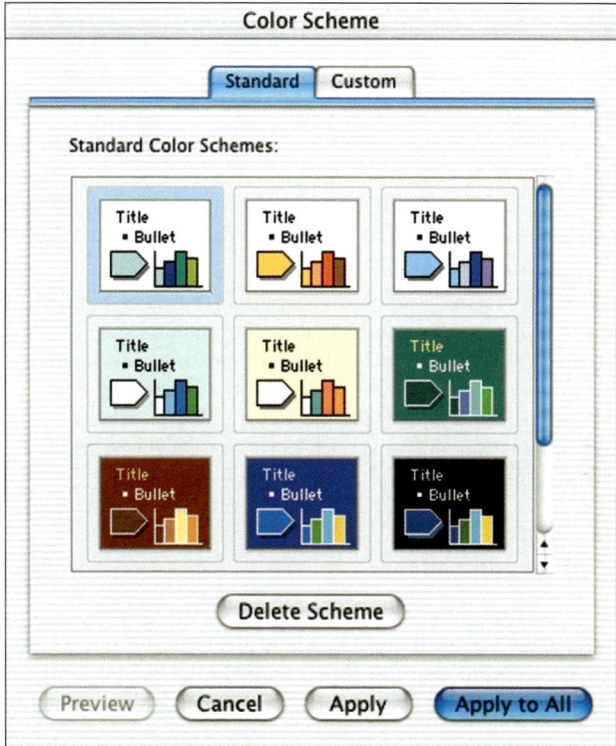

Figure 24.1 *Microsoft PowerPoint* Color Scheme menu.

(5) Line Spacing

Line spacing refers to the amount of space between the lines of a document. If the lines are too far apart, the text will seem to lack cohesion; if the lines are too close together, the text will appear crowded and be difficult to read. The type of writing you do may determine line spacing: the paragraphs of business letters, memos, and some reports are usually single-spaced and separated by a double space, but the paragraphs of academic papers are usually double-spaced.

24b Using Headings

Used effectively, headings help readers understand information, and they also break up a text, making it inviting and easy to read. Different academic disciplines have different requirements concerning headings. For this reason, you should consult the appropriate style manual before inserting headings in a paper.

Close-up: Using Headings

Headings perform several functions in a document:

- *Headings tell readers that a new idea is being introduced.* In this way, headings tell readers what to expect in a section before they actually read it.

- *Headings emphasize key ideas.* By summarizing an idea and isolating it from the text around it, headings help readers identify importantinformation.

- *Headings indicate how information is organized in a text.* Headings use various typefaces and type sizes (as well as indentation) to indicate the relative importance of ideas. For example, the most important information in a text will be set off as first-level headings and have the same typeface and type size. The next most important information will be set off as second-level headings, also with the same typeface and type size.

---

(1) Number of Headings

The number of headings you need depends on the document. A long, complicated document will need more headings than a shorter, less complicated one. Keep in mind that too few headings may not be of much use, but too many headings will make your document look like an outline.

(2) Phrasing

Headings should be brief, descriptive, and to the point. They can be single words—*Summary* or *Introduction*, for example—or they can be phrases (always stated in <u>parallel</u> terms): *Traditional Family Patterns, Alternate Family Patterns, Modern Family Patterns.* Finally, headings can be questions (*How Do You Choose a Major?*) or statements (*Choose Your Major Carefully*).

See
Ch. 39

(3) Indentation

Indenting is one way of distinguishing one level of heading from another. In general, the more important a heading is, the closer it is to the left-hand margin: first-level headings are justified left, second-level headings are indented five spaces, and third-level headings are indented further. Alternatively, headings may be centered, with different levels of subheadings placed flush left or run into the text.

(4) Typographical Emphasis

You can emphasize important words in headings by using **boldface,** *italics,* or ALL CAPITAL LETTERS. Used in moderation, these distinctive typefaces make a text easier to read. Used excessively, however, they slow readers down.

(5) Consistency

Headings at the same level should have the same format—the same typeface, type size, and degree of indentation—as well as parallel phrasing. If one first-level heading is boldfaced and centered, all other first-level headings must be boldfaced and centered. Using consistent patterns reinforces the connection between content and ideas and makes a document easier to understand.

NOTE: Never separate a heading from the text that goes with it: if a heading is at the bottom of one page and the text that goes with it is on the next page, move the heading onto the next page so readers can see the heading and the text together.

Close-up: Sample Heading Formats

Flush Left, Boldfaced, Uppercase and Lowercase
   Indented, Boldfaced, Uppercase and Lowercase
      Indented, italicized, lowercase; run into the text at the beginning of a paragraph; ends with a period.

Or

Centered, Boldfaced, Uppercase and Lowercase
Flush Left, Underlined, Uppercase and Lowercase
   Indented, underlined, lowercase; run into the text at the beginning of a paragraph; ends with a period.

Or

ALL CAPITAL LETTERS, CENTERED

24c Constructing Lists

By breaking long discussions into a series of key ideas, a list makes information easier to understand. By isolating individual pieces of information this way and by providing visual cues (such as bullets or numbers), a list directs readers to important information on a page.

Checklist: Constructing Effective Lists

When constructing lists, follow these guidelines:

☐ **Indent each item.** Each item on a list should be indented so that it stands out from the text around it.

(continued)

Constructing effective lists (continued)

☐ **Set off items with numbers or bullets.** Use **bullets** when items are not organized according to any particular sequence or priority (the members of a club, for example). Use **numbers** when you want to indicate that items are organized according to a sequence (the steps in a process, for example) or priority (the things a company should do to decrease spending, for example).

☐ **Introduce a list with a complete sentence.** Do not simply drop a list into a document; introduce it with a complete sentence (followed by a colon) that tells readers what kind of information the list contains and why you are including it in your discussion.

☐ **Use parallel structure.** Lists are easiest to read when all items are parallel and about the same length.

> A number of factors can cause high unemployment:
> - a decrease in consumer spending
> - a decrease in factory orders
> - a decrease in factory output

☐ **Punctuate correctly.** If the items on a list are fragments (as in the previous example), begin each item with a lowercase letter, and do not end it with a period. However, if the items on a list are complete sentences (as in the example below), begin each item with a capital letter and end it with a period.

> Here are the three steps we must take to reduce our spending:
> 1. We must cut our workforce by 10 percent.
> 2. We must use less expensive vendors.
> 3. We must decrease overtime payments.

☐ **Don't overuse lists.** Too many lists will undercut a document's effectiveness by making it seem cluttered. In addition, a document that contains one list after another will give readers the impression that you are simply listing points instead of discussing them.

NOTE: Figure 24.2 shows a page from a student's report that incorporates some of the effective design elements discussed in 24a–c.

24d   Using Visuals

Visuals—such as *tables, graphs, diagrams,* and *photographs*—can help you convey complex ideas that are difficult to communicate with words, and they can also help you attract readers' attention.

You can create your own tables and graphs by using applications in software packages like *Excel, Lotus,* or *Word*. In addition, many

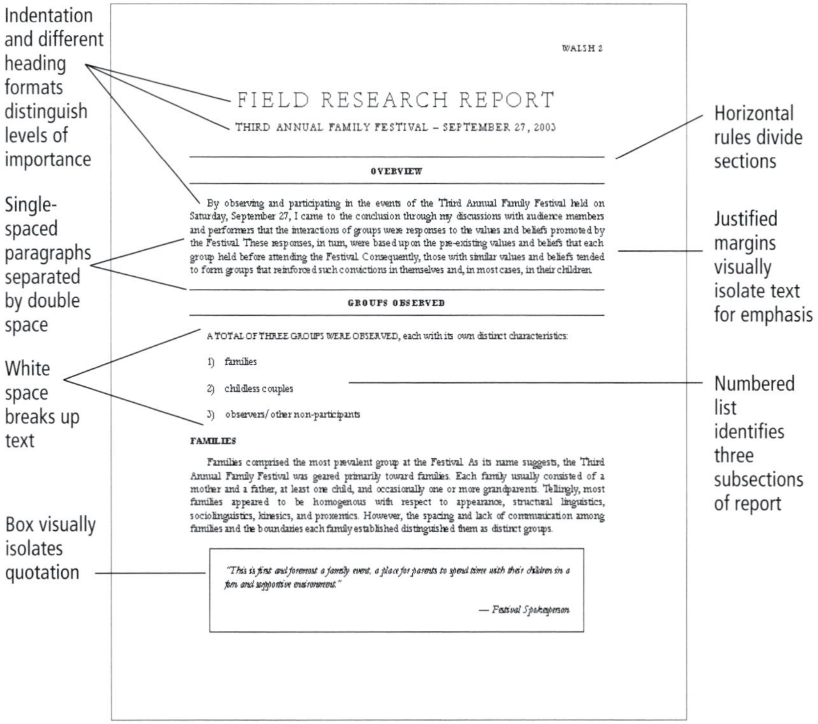

Indentation and different heading formats distinguish levels of importance

Single-spaced paragraphs separated by double space

White space breaks up text

Box visually isolates quotation

Horizontal rules divide sections

Justified margins visually isolate text for emphasis

Numbered list identifies three subsections of report

WALSH 2

FIELD RESEARCH REPORT
THIRD ANNUAL FAMILY FESTIVAL – SEPTEMBER 27, 2003

OVERVIEW

By observing and participating in the events of the Third Annual Family Festival held on Saturday, September 27, I came to the conclusion through my discussions with audience members and performers that the interactions of groups were responses to the values and beliefs promoted by the Festival. These responses, in turn, were based upon the pre-existing values and beliefs that each group held before attending the Festival. Consequently, those with similar values and beliefs tended to form groups that reinforced such convictions in themselves and, in most cases, in their children.

GROUPS OBSERVED

A TOTAL OF THREE GROUPS WERE OBSERVED, each with its own distinct characteristics:

1) families

2) childless couples

3) observers/other non-participants

FAMILIES

Families comprised the most prevalent group at the Festival. As its name suggests, the Third Annual Family Festival was geared primarily toward families. Each family usually consisted of a mother and a father, at least one child, and occasionally one or more grandparents. Tellingly, most families appeared to be homogenous with respect to appearance, structural linguistics, sociolinguistics, kinesics, and proxemics. However, the spacing and lack of communication among families and the boundaries each family established distinguished them as distinct groups.

> "This is first and foremost a family event, a place for parents to spend time with their children in a fun and supportive environment."
>
> — Festival Spokesperson

Figure 24.2 A well-designed page from a student's report.

---

stand-alone graphics software packages enable you to create complex charts, tables, and graphs that contain three-dimensional effects. You can also photocopy or scan diagrams and photographs from a print source or download them from the Internet or from CD-ROMs or DVDs. Remember, however, that if you use a visual from a source, you must use appropriate **documentation**.

See
Pts. 4–5

(1) Tables

Tables present data in a condensed, visual format—arranged in rows and columns. Tables may contain numerical data, text, or a combination of the two. When you plan your table, make sure you include only the data that you will need; discard information that is too detailed or difficult to understand. Keep in mind that tables can distract readers, so include only those necessary to support your discussion. (The table in Figure 24.3 on page 336 reports the student writer's original research and therefore needs no documentation.)

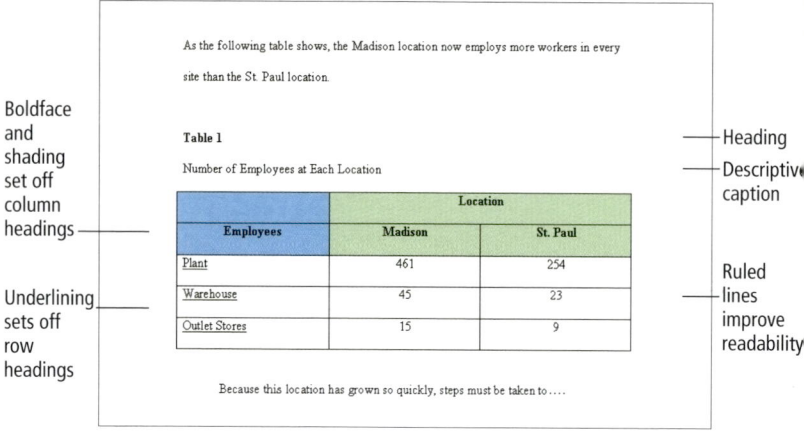

Figure 24.3 Table from a student paper.

(2) Graphs

Like tables, graphs present data in visual form. Whereas tables may present specific numerical data, graphs show the general pattern or

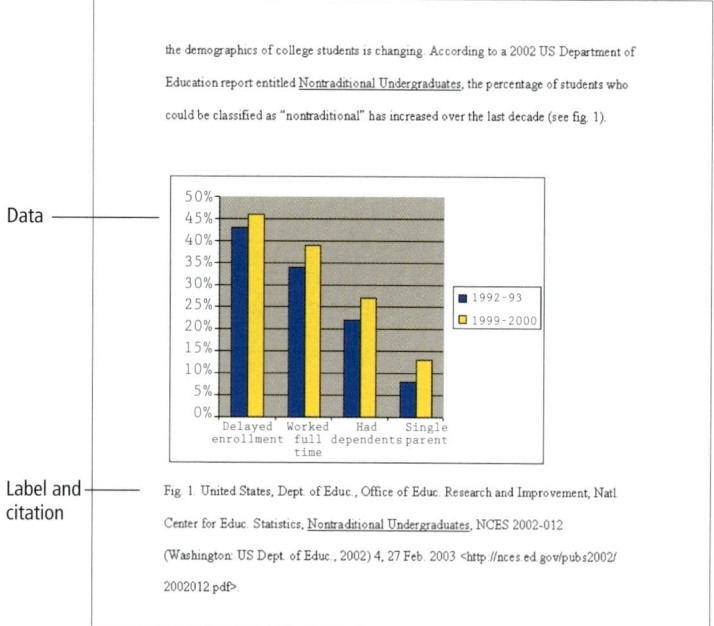

Figure 24.4 Graph from a student paper.

trend that the data suggest. Because graphs tend to be more general (and therefore less accurate) than tables, they are frequently accompanied by tables. Figure 24.4 on page 336 is an example of a bar graph showing data from a source.

(3) Diagrams

A diagram calls readers' attention to specific details of a mechanism or object. Diagrams are often used in scientific and technical writing to clarify concepts that are difficult to explain in words. Figure 24.5, which illustrates the sections of an orchestra, serves a similar purpose in a music education paper.

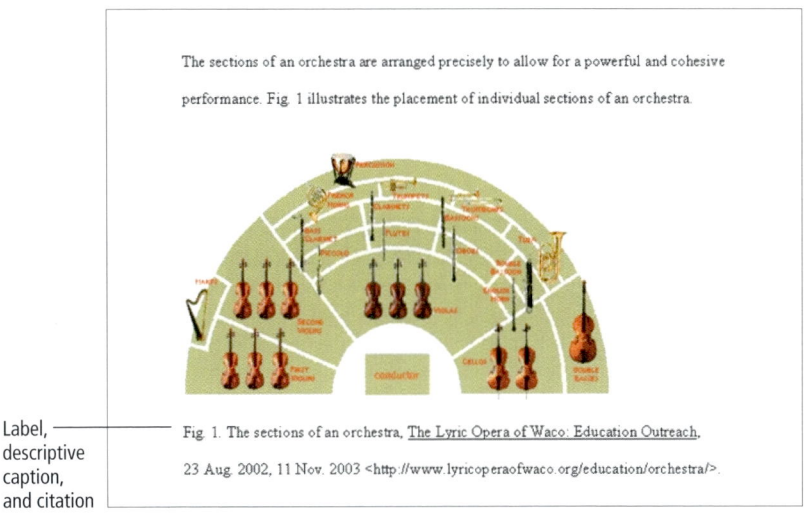

The sections of an orchestra are arranged precisely to allow for a powerful and cohesive performance. Fig. 1 illustrates the placement of individual sections of an orchestra.

Label, descriptive caption, and citation

Fig. 1. The sections of an orchestra, *The Lyric Opera of Waco: Education Outreach.*
23 Aug. 2002, 11 Nov. 2003 <http://www.lyricoperaofwaco.org/education/orchestra/>.

Figure 24.5 Diagram from a student paper.

(4) Photographs

Photographs enable you to show exactly what something or someone looks like—an animal in its natural habitat, a work of fine art, or an actor in costume, for example. Although computer technology that enables you to paste photographs directly into a text is widely available, you should use it with restraint. Not every photograph will support or enhance your written text; in fact, an irrelevant photograph will distract readers. The photograph of a wooded trail in Figure 24.6 on page 338 illustrates the student writer's description of a local recreational area.

Photo sized and placed appropriately within text with consistent white space above and below

travelers are well advised to be prepared, to always carry water and dress for the

conditions. Loose fitting, lightweight wicking material covering all exposed skin is

necessary in summer, and layers of warm clothing are needed for cold weather outings.

Hats and sunscreen are always a good idea no matter what the temperature, although

most of the trails are quite shady with huge oak trees. Figure 1 shows a shady portion of

the trail.

Reference to photo provides context

Figure 1   Greenbelt Trail in springtime (author photo)

Label and descriptive caption

Figure 24.6 Photograph from a student paper.

Close-up: Visuals and Copyright

Copyright gives an author the legal right to control the copying of his or her work—visuals as well as text. The law makes a clear distinction between visuals used in documents prepared for school assignments and visuals used in documents that will be published. In general, you may use graphics from a source—print or electronic—as long as your instructor gives you permission to do so and as long as you document the source, just as you would any other source.

If you use visuals in documents that will be published, however, you must obtain permission in writing from the person or organization that holds the copyright. Sometimes the copyright holder will grant permission without charge, but often there will be a fee. (Some software packages, especially those that contain "clip art," include permission fees in the cost of the software package.) Remember, it is your responsibility to determine whether or not permission is required.

Checklist: Using Visuals

☐ Use a visual only when it contributes something important to the discussion, not simply for embellishment.
☐ Place the visual in the text only if you plan to refer to it in your paper (otherwise, place the visual in an appendix).
☐ Introduce each visual with a complete sentence.

- ☐ Follow each visual with a discussion of its significance.
- ☐ Leave wide margins around each visual.
- ☐ Place the visual as close as possible to the section of your document in which it is discussed.
- ☐ Label each visual appropriately.
- ☐ Document each visual borrowed from a source.

CHAPTER 25

Designing a Web Site

See
Ch. 24

At some point in your college career, you may be asked to create a Web page or even a full Web site—for example, as a course assignment or as a way of marketing your job skills. Like other documents, Web pages follow the conventions of <u>document design</u>. Because so much of the content is meant to be read online, your choices of text, color, and navigation strategy are especially important.

FAQs
links

> **Close-up: Components of a Web Page**
>
>
>
> A **personal home page** usually contains information about how to contact the author, along with a brief biography. A home page can also be the first page of a **Web site,** a group of related **Web pages** focusing on a personal, professional, or academic topic. In this case, the home page contains **links**—highlighted words, images, or URLs—that allow users to move from one page to another or to another Web site.

25a Planning Your Web Site

See
Ch. 1

When you plan your Web site, you should consider your <u>purpose</u>, <u>audience</u>, and tone, just as you would when planning a print document. You should also consider what content to include. Finally, just as an essay or research paper may have a set page limit, your own Web site may have size and file-type limitations.

See
5d

Begin planning your Web site by sketching a basic plan or <u>story-board</u> of your site's content (both text and visuals). Then, consider how your Web pages will be connected and what links you will provide to other Web sites. Because users will start with your home page and navigate from one part of your site to another, the home page should provide an overview of your site and give readers a clear sense of what material the site will contain. As you lay out the pages of your Web site, place related items together, and use text sparingly. Keep in mind that too many graphics and elaborate type styles will distract or confuse users.

As you plan your Web site, consider how your pages will be organized. If your site will have relatively few pages, you can arrange them so that one page leads sequentially to the next. If your site will include numerous pages, however, you will have to group pages under headings or categories in order of importance. For example, the home page of the student's Web site shown in Figure 25.1 indicates that information is grouped under the headings *About me*, *Résumé*, *Portfolio*, *Services*, and *Contact*.

Figure 25.1 Home page of student's Web site.

25b Creating Your Web Site

Once you have planned your Web site, you will need to select a method for actually creating the site. Essentially, there are three ways to do this: you can use Web authoring software packages; you can use Web tools within your word-processing program; or you can create a page from scratch by using **HTML** (hypertext markup language), the programming language used to convert standard documents into World Wide Web hypertext documents.

- **Web Authoring Packages** Many Web authoring packages—for example, *Macromedia Dreamweaver* and *Microsoft FrontPage*—will automatically translate your pages into HTML. The advantage of an authoring package is that you do not have to have a working knowledge of HTML in order to develop your site. Some of these packages even make certain interactive functions—such as navigation bars, forms, or media effects—easier to implement.
- **Web Tools within Your Word-Processing Program** Most word processors have an option under the File menu or the Save menu that automatically saves word-processed documents as HTML documents suitable for Web delivery. Although this option is appropriate for a single document, such as your résumé, it does

not have the features you will need to create an entire Web site. For example, you cannot insert navigation buttons or include columns and tables that will transfer to the Web.

- **Text Editors that Allow Coding "By Hand"** If you have advanced knowledge of HTML, this is a good option. Text editors, including *Simple Text* for the Mac and *Notepad* for the PC, enable you to control all elements of your Web site design. The major drawback of using a text editor is that HTML coding can be confusing, and some special effects require complicated codes.

25c Selecting and Inserting Visuals

You can find visuals for your Web site by looking for sites on the Web that make visuals available for others to use. *Google*, for example, has an image directory at <http://images.google.com> that you can search. You can also create and upload visuals yourself by using either a digital camera or a scanner. Once a visual has been created and saved electronically, you can use a graphics package such as *Adobe Photoshop* to adjust the visual's size, contrast, or color scheme; to crop the image; or to add text. Other visual options include creating your own banners and backgrounds with special colors and textures. Figure 25.2 shows a Web page that includes a visual.

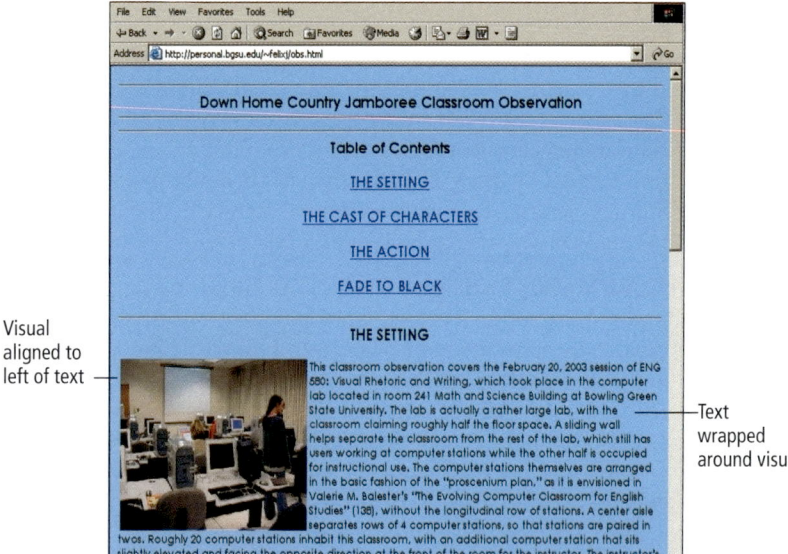

Figure 25.2 Web page with visual.

Once you have edited a visual, you will need to save it in one of two standard formats for the Web: JPG (for photographic images containing a wide range of colors) or GIF (for graphic files with fewer colors, line art, and text).

25d Planning Navigation

Web sites use a number of design features to make navigation easier. As you create the pages of your Web site, consider the following options for helping readers navigate your site:

- **Splash Pages** Many Web designers include a splash page on their Web sites. A splash page, such as the one shown in Figure 25.3, is more visual than textual, usually containing only limited background information and navigation features, such as links to the site's content. The purpose of a splash page is to create interest and draw users into the site; a more detailed overview of the site appears on another page that serves as the true home page.

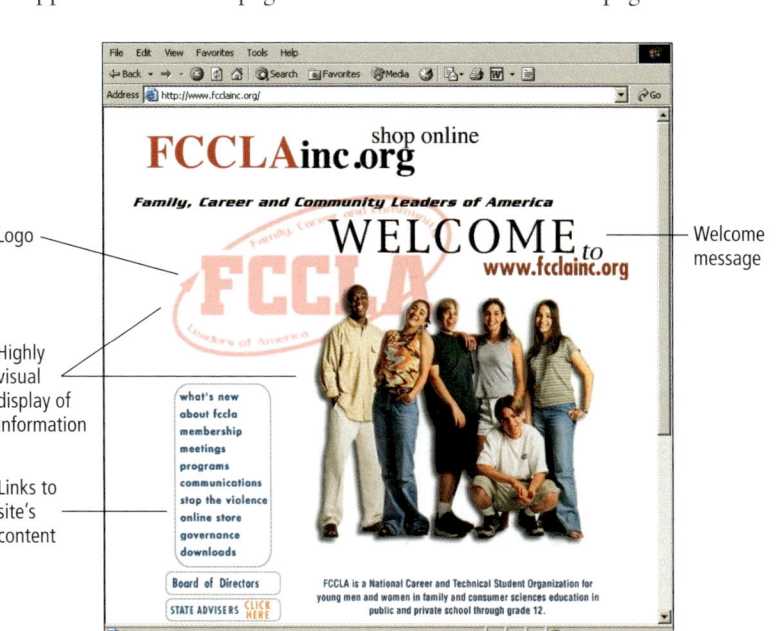

Figure 25.3 Splash page.

- **Navigation Text, Buttons, and Bars** Navigation text, buttons, bars, or other graphic icons, such as arrows or pictures, enable readers to move from one page of a Web site to another (see Figure 25.4 on page 344).

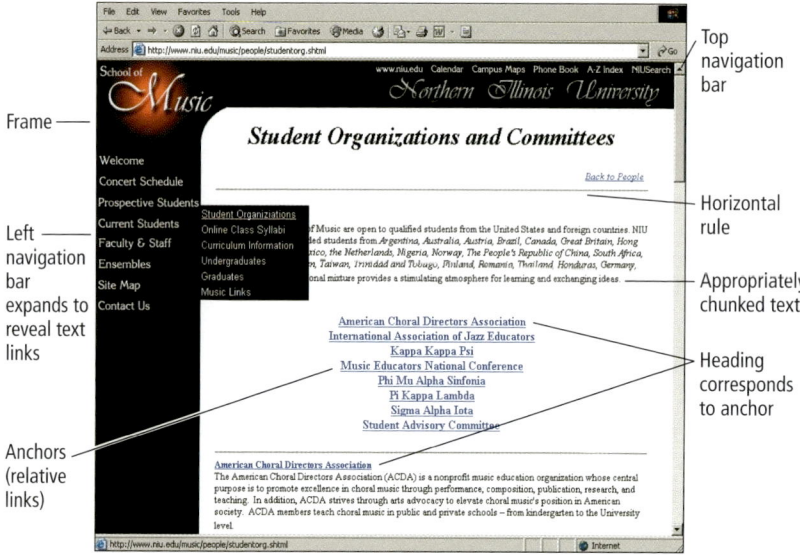

Frame

Left navigation bar expands to reveal text links

Anchors (relative links)

Top navigation bar

Horizontal rule

Appropriately chunked text

Heading corresponds to anchor

Figure 25.4 Web page with navigation links, anchors, and frames.

- **Anchors** Anchors (or **relative links**) enable readers to jump from one part of a Web page to another (see Figure 25.4).
- **Horizontal Rules** Horizontal rules divide sections and parts of a page (see Figure 25.4). You can use colored or patterned rules that coordinate with the color scheme of the Web site.
- **Chunking or Clustering** Chunking or clustering means placing related items of text close to one another (see Figure 25.4). This technique cuts down on scrolling and helps users read content easily on the screen. By surrounding clusters of information with white space, you can create distinct areas of content.
- **Frames** Like tables, frames organize text and graphics. Unlike tables, however, frames enable you to divide a single Web page into multiple windows (see Figure 25.4).
- **Text Formatting Features** Like printed texts, Web texts follow the principles of **document design**, using design elements such as single-spaced text, headings, subheadings, and bulleted lists, as well as boldface and italics to emphasize points. (Underlining is usually not used in Web texts because readers might mistake underlined text for a hyperlink.)

See
Ch. 24

25e Linking Your Content

Links (short for **hyperlinks**) are obviously a very important part of Web design. When you provide a link, you are directing people to a particular Web site. For this reason, you should make sure that the site you link to is up and running and that the information appearing there is both accurate and reliable.

It is important to select a visible color for your text-based links to indicate that they are in fact links and not just highlighted text. You will need three colors to indicate the status of a link: one for the link before it is clicked; one for the active link (or the change in color as the link itself is being clicked); and one for the visited link (the color after the link has been successfully accessed).

Finally, make certain that you have the exact URL for the sites to which you are linking. The Web relies on exact URLs to deliver information; if even one letter or punctuation mark is incorrect, the page will not load.

Close-up: Web Sites and Copyright

As a rule, assume that any material on a Web site is **copyrighted** unless the author makes an explicit statement to the contrary. This means you must obtain written permission if you are going to reproduce this material on your Web site. (You are, however, allowed to provide a link to a Web site without permission.) The only exception to this rule is the **fair use doctrine,** which allows the use of copyrighted material for the purpose of commentary, parody, or research and education.

NOTE: Material you quote in a research paper for one of your classes falls under the fair use doctrine and does not require permission.

25f Editing and Proofreading Your Web Site

Before you post your Web site, you should <u>edit and proofread</u> it just as you would any other document. (Even if you run a spell check and a grammar check, you must still proofread carefully.)

See 6d

Checklist: Style Conventions of Writing for the Web

☐ Avoid long, wordy sentences. Using active verbs will help keep your sentences short and concise.

☐ Avoid long paragraphs. Chunk content into small sections that are easy to read and access online.

☐ Speak directly to your audience, using the first person (*I*) and the second person (*you*) to establish a connection with readers.

☐ Avoid technical terminology that only a certain segment of your audience will understand.

(continued)

Style conventions of writing for the Web (continued)

☐ Choose your external links wisely. Do not provide so many that your audience is drawn away from your site.
☐ Use headings and bulleted lists to organize information visually and textually.
☐ Provide a title in the browser window for each page within your site to help users keep track of where they are.
☐ Proofread carefully offline before loading your content online.

25g Posting Your Web Site

Once you have designed a Web site, you will need to upload (**post**) it so you can view it on the Web. Most commonly, Web pages are posted with FTP (File Transfer Protocol) software.

To get your site up on the Web, you transfer your files to an **Internet server,** a computer that is connected at all times to the Internet. Your Internet service provider will instruct you on how to use FTP to transfer your files. Once your site is up and running, any mistakes you have made will be apparent as soon as you view your pages on the Web.

Checklist: Designing a Web Site

☐ Identify the audience and purpose of your Web site.
☐ Plan the content of your site.
☐ Consider how you want your site to be organized.
☐ Draw a basic plan of your site.
☐ Compose text and choose visuals.
☐ Lay out text and graphics so that they present your ideas clearly and logically.
☐ Choose design features that facilitate navigation.
☐ Provide clear and informative links, and make sure they are active.
☐ Proofread your text.
☐ Make sure you have acknowledged all material that you have borrowed from a source.
☐ Post your site to an Internet server.

CHAPTER 26

Writing for the Workplace

Work is often a part of the college experience, with many students holding part-time jobs, internships, work-study positions, or cooperative education experiences. The skills that you develop in these positions are frequently transferable to the employment that you will have after you graduate. For this reason, it is important that you learn how to write for the workplace.

26a Writing Business Letters

Business letters should be brief and to the point, with important information placed early in the letter. Be concise, avoid digressions, and try to sound as natural as possible.

The first paragraph of your letter should introduce your subject and mention any pertinent previous correspondence. The body of your letter should present the information readers need to understand your points. (If your ideas are complicated, present your points in a bulleted or numbered list.) Your conclusion should reinforce your message.

See 24c

Single-space within paragraphs, and double-space between paragraphs. (Note that paragraphs in business letters are not indented.) Proofread carefully to make sure there are no errors in spelling or punctuation. Most often, business letters use **block format,** with all parts of the letter aligned with the left-hand margin.

26b Writing Letters of Application

A **letter of application** summarizes your qualifications for a specific position. Letters of application should be short and focused. When you apply for employment, your primary objective is to obtain an interview.

FAQs

Begin your letter of application by identifying the job you are applying for and stating where you heard about it—in a newspaper, in a professional journal, on a Web site, or from your school's job placement service, for example. Be sure to include the date of the advertisement and the exact title of the position. End your introduction with a statement that expresses your ability to do the job.

Sample Letter of Application: Block Format

Heading

246 Hillside Drive
Urbana, IL 61801
Kr237@metropolis.105.com

October 20, 2005

Inside address

Mr. Maurice Snyder, Personnel Director
Guilford, Fox, and Morris
22 Hamilton Street
Urbana, IL 61822

Salutation (followed by a colon)

Dear Mr. Snyder:

My college advisor, Dr. Raymond Walsh, has told me that you are interested in hiring a part-time accounting assistant. I believe that my academic background and my work experience qualify me for this position.

Body

I am presently a junior accounting major at the University of Illinois. During the past year, I have taken courses in taxation, trusts, and business law. I am also proficient in <u>Lotus</u> and <u>ClarisWorks</u>. Last spring, I gained practical accounting experience by working in our department's tax clinic.

Double-space ⟶

After I graduate, I hope to get a master's degree in taxation and then return to the Urbana area. I believe that my experience in taxation as well as my familiarity with the local business community would enable me to contribute to your firm.

Single-space ⟶

I have enclosed a résumé for your examination. I will be available for an interview any time after midterm examinations, which end October 25. I look forward to hearing from you.

Complimentary close

Sincerely yours,

Written signature

Sandra Kraft

Typed signature

Sandra Kraft
Enc: Résumé

Additional data

In the body of your letter, provide the information that will convince your reader of your qualifications—for example, relevant courses you have taken and pertinent job experience. Be sure to address any specific points mentioned in the advertisement. Above all, emphasize your strengths, and explain how they relate to the specific job for which you are applying.

Conclude by saying that you have enclosed your résumé and stating that you are available for an interview, noting any dates on which you will not be available. (Be sure to include your phone number and your email address.)

http://kirsznermandell.wadsworth.com

Computer Tip: Letter Templates

The templates found within your word-processing program can help you structure your letters (as well as résumés, memos, faxes, and brochures).

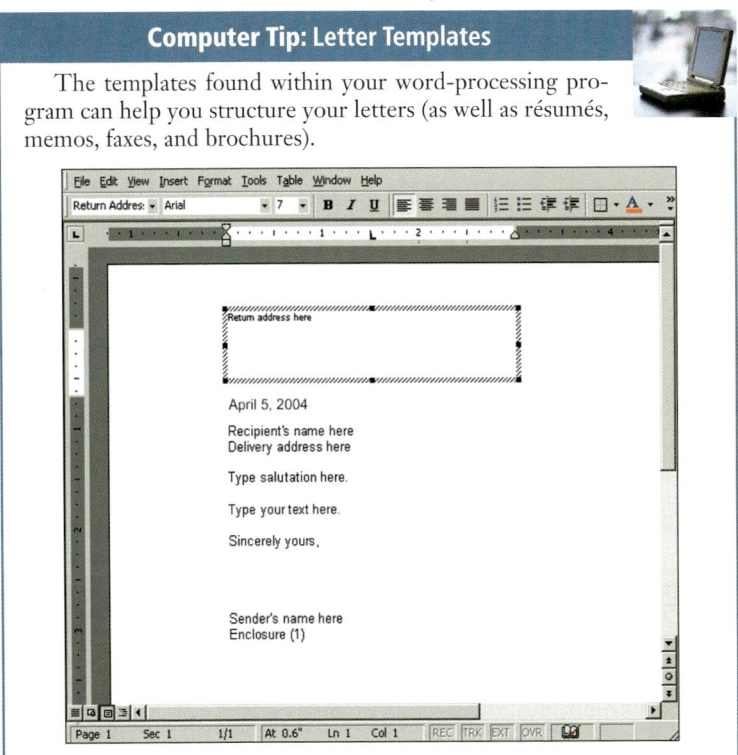

Close-up: Writing Follow-Up Letters

After you have been interviewed, you should send a **follow-up** letter to the person (or persons) who interviewed you. First, thank your interviewer for taking the time to see you. Then, briefly summarize your qualifications and your interest in the position.

(continued)

Writing follow-up letters (continued)

Because so few applicants write follow-up letters, such letters make a very positive impression.

Dear Mr. Snyder:

Thank you for interviewing me last week for the internship positon and for showing me your offices. Your computer department was very impressive, and the information I obtained there has helped me focus my career goals.

I especially enjoyed seeing how you use computers to track your clients' tax liabilities. The conversation I had with the employees in the computer department confirmed my belief that Guillford, Fox, and Morris would be an excellent place to work. I hope to see all of you again this summer.

Sincerely yours,

Sandra Kraft

Sandra Kraft

26c   Designing Print Résumés

A résumé lists relevant information about your education, your job experience, your goals, and your personal interests.

There is no single correct format for a résumé. You may decide to arrange your résumé in **chronological order** (see page 351), listing your education and work experience in sequence (beginning with the most recent) or in **emphatic order** (see page 352) beginning with the material that will be of most interest to an employer (for example, important skills). Whatever a résumé's arrangement, it should be brief—one page is usually sufficient for an undergraduate—easy to read, clear and emphatic, logically organized, and completely free of errors.

Sample Résumé: Chronological Order

KAREN L. OLSON

SCHOOL
3812 Hamilton St. Apt. 18
Philadelphia, PA 19104
215-382-0831
olsont@dunm.ocs.drexel.edu

HOME
110 Ascot Ct.
Harmony, PA 16037
412-452-2944

EDUCATION

DREXEL UNIVERSITY, Philadelphia, PA 19104
Bachelor of Science in Graphic Design
Anticipated Graduation: June 2006
Cumulative Grade Point Average: 3.2 on a 4.0 scale

COMPUTER SKILLS AND COURSEWORK

HARDWARE
Familiar with both Macintosh and PC systems
SOFTWARE
Adobe Illustrator, Photoshop, and *Type Align; QuarkXPress; CorelDRAW; Micrografx Designer*
COURSES
Corporate Identity, Environmental Graphics, Typography, Photography, Painting
and Printmaking, Sculpture, Computer Imaging, Art History

EMPLOYMENT EXPERIENCE

THE TRIANGLE, Drexel University, Philadelphia, PA 19104
January 2003–present
Graphics Editor. Design all display advertisements submitted to Drexel's student
newspaper.

UNISYS CORPORATION, Blue Bell, PA 19124
June–September 2003, Cooperative Education
Graphic Designer. Designed interior pages as well as covers for target marketing brochures. Created various logos and spot art designed for use on interoffice memos and
departmental publications.

CHARMING SHOPPES, INC, Bensalem, PA 19020
June–December 2002, Cooperative Education
Graphic Designer/Fashion Illustrator, Created graphics for future placement on garments. Did some textile designing. Drew flat illustrations of garments to scale in computer. Prepared presentation boards.

DESIGN AND IMAGING STUDIO, Drexel University, Philadelphia, PA 19104
October 2001–June 2003
Monitor. Supervised computer activity in studio. Answered telephone. Assisted other
graphic design students in using computer programs.

ACTIVITIES AND AWARDS

The Triangle, Graphics Editor: 2003–present
Kappa Omicron Nu Honor Society, vice president: 2001–present
Dean's List: spring 2000, fall and winter 2001
Graphics Group, vice president: 2001–present

REFERENCES AND PORTFOLIO

Available upon request.

Sample Résumé: Emphatic Order

Michael D. Fuller

SCHOOL
27 College Avenue
University of Maryland
College Park, MD 20742
(301) 357-0732
mful532@aol.com

HOME
1203 Hampton Road
Joppa, MD 21085
(301) 877-1437

Restaurant Experience

McDonald's Restaurant, Pikesville, MD. Cook.
Prepared hamburgers. Acted as assistant manager for two weeks while manager was on vacation. Supervised employees, helped prepare payroll and work schedules. Was named employee of the month. Summer 2002.

University of Maryland, College Park, MD. Cafeteria busboy.
Cleaned tables, set up cafeteria, and prepared hot trays. September 2003–May 2004.

Other Work Experience

University of Maryland Library, College Park, MD. Reference assistant. Filed, sorted, typed, shelved, and catalogued. Earnings offset college expenses. September 2002–May 2003.

Education

University of Maryland, College Park, MD (sophomore).
Biology major. Expected date of graduation: June 2006.
Forest Park High School, Baltimore, MD.

Interests

Member of University Debating Society.
Tutor in University's Academic Enrichment Program.

References

Mr. Arthur Sanducci, Manager
McDonald's Restaurant
5712 Avery Road
Pikesville, MD 22513

Mr. William Czernick, Manager
Cafeteria
University of Maryland
College Park, MD 20742

Ms. Stephanie Young, Librarian
Library
University of Maryland
College Park, MD 20742

Checklist: Components of a Résumé

☐ The **heading** includes your name, school address, home address, telephone number, and email address.

☐ A statement of your **career objective** (optional), placed at the top of the page, identifies your professional goals.

☐ The **education section** includes the schools you have attended, starting with the most recent one and moving back in time. (After graduation from college, do not list your high school unless you have a compelling reason to do so—for instance, if it is nationally recognized for its academic standards or it has an active alumni network in your field.)

☐ The **summary of work experience** generally starts with your most recent job and moves backward in time.

☐ The **background** or **interests section** lists your most important (or most relevant) special interest and community activities.

☐ The **honors section** lists academic achievements and awards.

☐ The **references section** lists the full names and addresses of at least three references. If your résumé is already one full page long, a line saying that your references will be sent upon request is sufficient.

ESL Tip

When describing honors received in another country that may not be familiar to potential employers, it is wise to provide explanatory information. For example, you might indicate what percentage of graduates receive the honor you have been awarded. You may also wish to indicate your visa status and your language skills on your résumé.

NOTE: In some countries, job applicants list information about their age and marital status in their job application materials. However, in the United States, this is usually not done because employers are not legally allowed to discriminate on the basis of such factors.

Close-up: Résumé Style

Use strong action verbs to describe your duties, responsibilities, and accomplishments.

accomplished	achieved	supervised
communicated	collaborated	instructed
completed	implemented	proposed
performed	organized	trained

NOTE: Use past tense for past positions and present tense for current positions.

Computer Tip: Résumé Templates

Just as they can help you format professional letters, the various templates found within your word-processing program can help you design your résumé. Although templates make the task of formatting easier, you must provide the details that will lead a prospective employer to conclude that you are a strong candidate for a job.

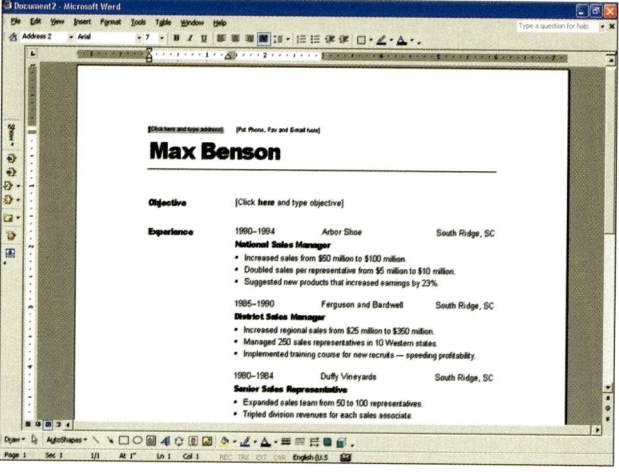

26d Designing Electronic Résumés

Most résumés are still submitted on paper, but electronic résumés—scannable and Web-based—are quickly gaining in popularity. Many believe the paper résumé will soon be a thing of the past.

(1) Scannable Résumés

Many employers request scannable résumés that they can download into a database for future reference. If you have to prepare such a résumé, keep in mind that scanners will not pick up columns, bullets, or italics and that shaded or colored paper will make your résumé difficult to scan.

Whereas in a print résumé you use specific action verbs (*edited*) to describe your accomplishments, in a scannable résumé you use key nouns (*editor*) that can be entered into a company database. These words will help employers find your résumé when they carry out a keyword search for applicants with certain skills. To facilitate keyword

Sample Résumé: Scannable

Constantine G. Doukakis
2000 Clover Lane
Fort Worth, TX 76107

Phone: (817) 735-9120
Email: Douk@aol.com

Employment Objective: Entry-level position in an organization that will enable me to use my academic knowledge and the skills that I learned in my work experience.

Education:

University of Texas at Arlington, Bachelor of Science in Civil Engineering, June 2004. Major: Structural Engineering. Graduated Magna Cum Laude. Overall GPA: 3.754 on a 4.0 base.

Scholastic Honors and Awards:

Member of Phi Eta Sigma First-Year Academic Honor Society, Chi Epsilon Civil Engineering Academic Society, Tau Beta Pi Engineering Academic Society, Golden Key National Honor Society.

Jack Woolf Memorial Scholarship for Outstanding Academic Performance.

Cooperative Employment Experience:

Dallas-Fort Worth International Airport, Tarrant County, TX, Dec. 2002 to June 2003. Assistant Engineer. Supervised and inspected airfield paving, drainage, and utility projects as well as terminal building renovations. Performed on-site and laboratory soil tests. Prepared concrete samples for load testing.

Dallas-Fort Worth International Airport, Tarrant County, TX, Jan. 2003 to June 2003. Draftsperson in Design Office. Prepared contract drawings and updated base plans as well as designed and estimated costs for small construction projects.

Johnson County Electric Cooperative, Clebume, TX, Jan. 2002 to June 2002. Junior Engineer in Plant Dept. of Maintenance and Construction Division. Inspected and supervised in-plant construction. Devised solutions to construction problems. Estimated costs of materials for small construction projects. Presented historical data relating to the function of the department.

Key Words:

Organizational and leadership skills. Written and oral communication skills, C++, IBM, Macintosh, DOS, Windows XP, and Mac OS 10.3, Word, Excel, FileMakerPro, PowerPoint, WordPerfect, Internet client software. Computer model development. Technical editor.

searches, applicants often include Keyword sections on their résumés. For example, if you wanted to emphasize your computer skills, you would include keywords such as *WordPerfect*, *FileMaker Pro*, and *Power-Point*.

(2) Web-Based Résumés

See
Ch. 25

It is becoming common to have a version of your résumé posted on a personal **Web site**. Usually, a Web-based résumé is an alternative to a print résumé that you have mailed or a scannable version that you have submitted to a database or as an email attachment. Figure 26.1 shows a Web-based version of a student's résumé. The student has also included on her Web site a PDF (portable document format) version of her résumé that is available for downloading and printing (see Figure 26.2).

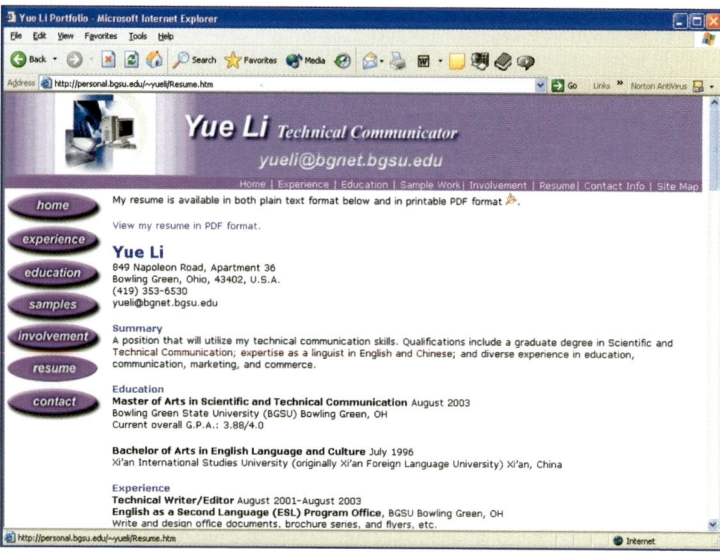

Figure 26.1 Student Web-based résumé.

http://kirsznermandell.wadsworth.com

Computer Tip: PDF Résumés

    A PDF résumé allows you to maintain the original design of your word-processed résumé file, including the use of boldface and italic type, bullets, and horizontal rules. Another advantage of this type of résumé is that anyone can view and print a PDF file with the free, downloadable *Adobe Acrobat Reader* <http://www.adobe.com/products/acrobat/readermain.html>.

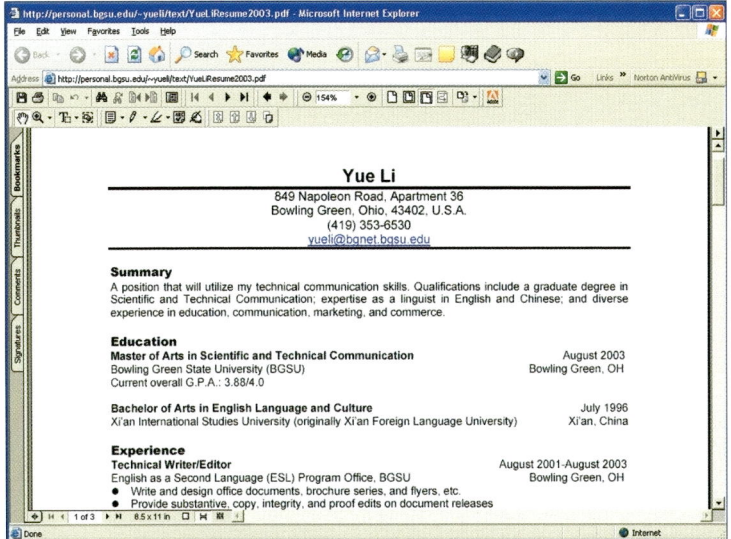

Figure 26.2 Student PDF résumé.

26e Writing Memos

Memos (see page 358) communicate information within an organization. A memo can be short or long, depending on its purpose.

Begin your memo with a purpose statement that presents your reason for writing it. Follow this statement with a background section that gives readers the information they will need to understand the current situation. Then, in the body of your memo, present the detailed information that constitutes your support. If your document is short, use bulleted or numbered lists to emphasize information. If it is long—more than two or three paragraphs—use headings to designate the various sections of the memo (*Summary, Background, Benefits*, and so on). End your memo with a statement of your conclusions and recommendations.

Sample Memo

<table>
<tr><td>Opening
component</td><td>TO:
FROM:
SUBJECT:
DATE:</td><td>Ina Ellen, Senior Counselor
Kim Williams, Student Tutor Supervisor
Construction of a Tutoring Center
November 10, 2005</td></tr>
</table>

Purpose
statement

This memo proposes the establishment of a tutoring center in the Office of Student Affairs.

BACKGROUND
Under the present system, tutors must work with students at a number of facilities scattered across the university campus. As a result, tutors waste a lot of time running from one facility to another and are often late for appointments.

Body

NEW FACILITY
I propose that we establish a tutoring facility adjacent to the Office of Student Affairs. The two empty classrooms next to the office, presently used for storage of office furniture, would be ideal for this use. We could furnish these offices with the desks and file cabinets already stored in these rooms.

BENEFITS
The benefits of this facility would be the centralizing of the tutoring services and the proximity of the facility to the Office of Student Affairs. The tutoring facility could also use the secretarial services of the Office of Student Affairs.

Conclusion RECOMMENDATIONS
To implement this project we would need to do the following:
1. Clean up and paint rooms 331 and 333
2. Use folding partitions to divide each room into five single-desk offices
3. Use stored office equipment to furnish the center

I am certain these changes would do much to improve the tutoring service. I look forward to discussing this matter with you in more detail.

26f Writing Emails and Sending Faxes

(1) Writing Emails

In many workplaces, virtually all internal (and some external) communications are transmitted as email. Although personal email tends to be quite informal, business email should observe the conventions of standard written communication.

Checklist: Writing Emails

The following guidelines can help you communicate effectively in an electronic business environment:

- ☐ Write in complete sentences. Avoid the slang, imprecise diction, and abbreviations that are commonplace in personal email.
- ☐ Use an appropriate tone. Address readers with respect, just as you would in a standard business letter.
- ☐ Include a subject line that clearly identifies your content. If your subject line is vague, your email may be deleted without being read.
- ☐ Make your message as short as possible. Because most emails are read on the screen, long discussions are difficult to follow.
- ☐ Use short paragraphs, and leave an extra space between paragraphs.
- ☐ Use lists and internal headings to make your message easy to read and understand. (Keep in mind, however, that your recipient may not be able to view certain formatting elements, such as boldface, italics, and indentation.)
- ☐ Take the time to edit your email and delete excess words and phrases.
- ☐ Proofread carefully before sending your email. Look for errors in grammar, spelling, and punctuation.
- ☐ Make sure that your list of recipients is accurate and that you do not send your email to unintended recipients.
- ☐ Do not send your email until you are absolutely certain your message says exactly what you want it to say.
- ☐ Do not forward an email unless you have the permission of the sender.
- ☐ Watch what you write. Always remember that email written at work is the property of the employer, who has the legal right to access it, even without your permission.

---

(2) Sending Faxes

In spite of the prevalence of email, businesses still routinely send and receive many faxes. Forms that need signatures, papers that cannot easily be digitized, copies of printed documents, and printed communications that must be sent immediately all are transmitted by fax.

Close-up: Sending Messages by Fax

Faxes are often received not by an individual but at a central location, so include a cover sheet that contains the recipient's name and title, the date, the company and department, the fax and telephone numbers, and the total number of pages faxed. In addition, supply your own name and telephone and fax numbers. (It is also a good idea to call ahead to alert the addressee that a fax is coming.)

Close-up: Using Voice Mail

Like email, voice mail can present challenges. The following tips will help you deliver a voice-mail message clearly and effectively:

- **Organize your message before you deliver it.** Long, meandering, or repetitive messages will frustrate listeners.

- **Begin your message with your name and affiliation as well as the date and time of your call.**

- **State the subject of your message first.** Then, fill in the details.

- **Speak slowly.** Many experts advise people to speak much more slowly than they would in normal conversation.

- **Speak clearly.** Enunciate your words precisely so a listener will understand your message the first time. Be sure to spell your name.

- **Give your phone number twice—once at the beginning and again at the end of your message.** No one wants to replay a long voice-mail message just to get a phone number.

CHAPTER 27

Making Oral Presentations

At school and on the job, you may be called on to make **oral presentations.** Although many people are uncomfortable about giving oral presentations, the guidelines that follow can make the experience easier and less stressful.

27a Getting Started

Just as with writing an essay, the preparation stage of an oral presentation is as important as the speech itself. The time you spend on this stage of the process will make your task easier later on.

Identify Your Topic The first thing you should do is to identify the topic of your speech. Sometimes you are given a topic; at other times, you have the option of choosing your own. Once you have a topic, you will be able to decide how much information, as well as what kind of information, you will need.

Consider Your Audience The easiest way to determine what kind of information you will need is to consider the nature of your audience. Is your audience made up of experts or of people who know little about your topic? How much background information will you have to provide? Can you use technical terms, or should you avoid them? Do you think your audience will be interested in your topic, or will you have to create interest? What opinions about your topic will the members of your audience bring with them?

ESL Tip

When making oral presentations, some ESL students choose topics related to their cultural backgrounds or home countries. This is a good idea because they are often able to provide insightful information on these topics that is new to their instructor and classmates. If you choose such a topic, try to determine beforehand how much background your audience has by speaking with your instructor and classmates.

Consider Your Purpose Your speech should have a specific purpose that you can sum up concisely. To help you zero in on your purpose, ask yourself what you are trying to accomplish with your presentation. It is a good idea to write out this purpose and to keep it in front of you as you plan your speech.

```
Purpose: to suggest ways to make registration easier for
students
```

Consider Your Constraints How much time do you have for your presentation? (Obviously, a ten-minute presentation requires more information and preparation than a three-minute presentation.) Do you already know enough about your topic, or will you have to do research?

Close-up: Group Presentations

Whether you are participating in a panel discussion or delivering one part of a long speech, you should be aware that group presentations require a lot of coordination. Before you begin planning, you should understand your role as well as everyone else's. Who is in charge? Who is responsible for each part of the presentation? Who will prepare and display the visuals? In addition, all group members should understand that they must stick to a schedule for both research and rehearsal.

27b Planning Your Speech

In the planning phase, you focus on your ideas about your topic and develop a thesis; then, you decide what specific points you will discuss and divide your speech into a few manageable sections.

Develop a Thesis Statement Before you actually plan your speech, you need to develop a **thesis statement** that clearly and concisely presents your main idea—the key idea you want to communicate to your audience. If you know a lot about your topic, you can develop a thesis on your own. If you do not know a lot, you will have to gather information and review it before you can decide on a thesis.

Decide on Your Points Once you have developed a thesis, you can decide what points you will discuss. Unlike readers, who can read a passage again and again until they understand it, listeners must understand information the first time they hear it. For this reason, effective speeches usually focus on points that are clear and easy to follow. Your thesis statement should state (or at least strongly imply) these points.

Gather Support You cannot expect your listeners to automatically accept what you say. You must supply details, facts, and examples that will convince them that what you are saying is both accurate and reasonable. You can gather this supporting material in the library, on the Web, or from your own experience.

Outline the Individual Parts of Your Speech Every speech has a beginning, a middle, and an end. Your **introduction** should introduce your subject, engage your audience's interest, and state your thesis—but it should *not* present an in-depth discussion or summary of your topic. The **body,** or middle section, of your speech should present the points that support your thesis. It should also include the facts, examples, and other information that will clarify your points and help convince listeners your thesis is reasonable. Your **conclusion** should bring your speech to a definite end and reinforce your thesis.

27c Preparing Your Notes

Most people use notes of some form when they give a speech. Each system of notes has advantages and disadvantages.

Full Text Some people like to write out the full text of their speech and refer to it during their presentation. If the type is large enough, and if you triple-space, this strategy can be useful. One disadvantage of using the full text of your speech is that it is easy to lose your place and become disoriented; another is that you may find yourself simply reading your speech.

3" × 5" Cards Some people write important parts of their speech—for example, a list of key points or definitions—on 3″ × 5″ note cards. Cards are portable, so they can be flipped through easily. They are also small, so they can be placed inconspicuously on a podium or a table. With some practice, you can learn to use note cards effectively. You have to be careful, however, not to become so dependent on the cards that you lose eye contact with your audience or begin fidgeting with the cards as you speak.

Outlines Some people like to refer to an outline when they give a speech. As they speak, they can glance down at the outline to get their bearings or to remind themselves of a point they have to make. Because an outline does not contain the full text of a speech, the temptation to read is eliminated. However, if for some reason you draw a blank, an outline gives you very little to fall back on.

27d Preparing Visual Aids

Visual aids, such as overhead transparencies or posters, can reinforce important information and make your speech easier to understand.

For a simple speech, a visual aid may be no more than a definition or a few key terms, names, or dates written on the board or distributed in a handout. A more complicated presentation might require charts, graphs, diagrams, or photographs—or even objects. The major consideration for including a visual aid is whether it actually adds something to your speech.

If you are using equipment such as a slide projector or a laptop, make sure you know how to operate it—and have a contingency plan just in case the equipment does not work the way it should. If possible, visit the room in which you will be giving your speech ahead of time, and see whether it has the equipment you need (and whether the equipment works). Finally, make sure that whatever visual aid you use is large enough for everyone in your audience to see. Printing or typing should be neat and free of errors, and graphics should be clearly labeled and easy to see.

Microsoft PowerPoint, the most commonly used **presentation software package,** enables you to organize an oral presentation and prepare attractive, professional slides (see Figure 27.1).

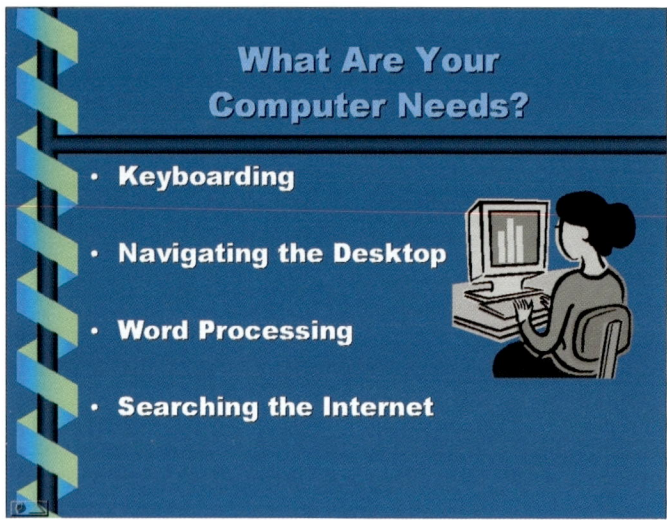

Figure 27.1 *PowerPoint* slide.

PowerPoint's more advanced features enable you to create multimedia presentations that combine images, video, audio, and animation. You can also use the Insert menu to insert various items—for example, clip art, word art, and image files you have created with a digital cam-

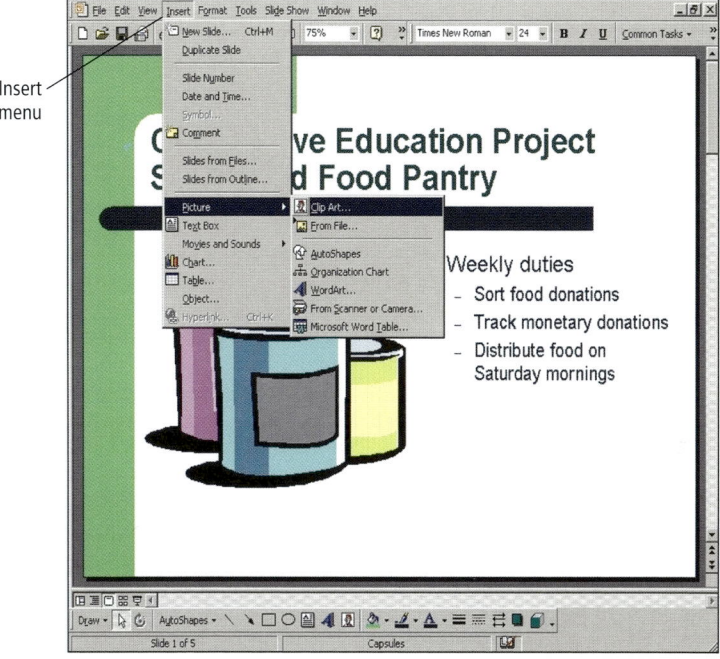

Insert menu

Figure 27.2 *Microsoft PowerPoint* **Insert menu.**

era or scanner—into your slide templates (see Figure 27.2). You can even import charts and tables from *Microsoft Word* and *Excel* and download images from Internet sites directly into your slide templates.

Checklist: Designing Visual Aids

☐ Do not put more than three or four major points on a single visual.

☐ Use single words or short phrases, not sentences or paragraphs.

☐ Limit the number of visuals. For a three- to five-minute presentation, five or six visuals are usually enough.

☐ Use type that is large enough for your audience to see (44- to 50-point type for major headings and 30- to 34-point type for text).

☐ Do not use elaborate graphics or special effects just because your computer software enables you to do so (this is especially relevant for users of *PowerPoint*).

☐ Check your visuals carefully for typos, inaccurate captions or labels, or other errors.

Using Visual Aids in Your Presentations

Visual Aid	Advantages	Disadvantages
Computer presentations	Clear Easy to read Professional Graphics, video, sound, and animated effects Portable (disk or CD-ROM)	Special equipment needed Expertise needed Special software needed Software might not be compatible with all computer systems
Overhead projectors	Transparencies are inexpensive Transparencies are easily prepared with computer or copier Transparencies are portable Transparencies can be written on during presentation Projector is easy to operate	Transparencies can stick together Transparencies can be placed upside down Transparencies must be placed on projector by hand Some projectors are noisy Speaker must avoid power cord to projector during presentation
Slide projector	Colorful Professional Projector is easy to use Order of slides can be reversed during presentation Portable (slide carousel)	Slides are expensive to produce Special equipment needed for lettering and graphics Dark room needed for presentation Slides can jam in projector
Posters or flip charts	Low-tech and personal Good for small-group presentations Portable	May not be large enough to be seen in some rooms Artistic ability needed May be expensive if prepared professionally Must be secured to an easel
Chalkboards or whiteboards	Available in most rooms Easy to use Easy to erase or change information during presentation	Difficult to draw complicated graphics Handwriting must be legible Must catch errors while writing Cannot face audience when writing or drawing Very informal

27e Rehearsing Your Speech

You should practice your speech often—at least five times—and make sure you practice delivering your speech with your visuals. Do not try to memorize your entire speech, but be sure you know it well enough so you can move from point to point without constantly looking at your notes. If possible, rehearse your speech in the actual room you will be using, and try standing at the back of the room to make sure your visuals can be seen clearly. Finally, time yourself. Make certain your three-minute speech actually takes three minutes to deliver.

27f Delivering Your Speech

The most important part of your speech is your delivery. Keep in mind that a certain amount of nervousness is normal, so try not to focus on it too much. Channel the nervous energy into your speech, and let it work for you. While you are waiting to begin, take some deep breaths. Once you get to the front of the room, don't start right away. Make sure everything you will need is there and all your equipment is positioned properly.

Before you speak, make sure both feet are flat on the floor and that you are facing the audience. As you speak, pace yourself. Speak slowly and clearly, and look at the entire audience, one person at a time. Make sure you speak *to* your audience, not *at* them. Even though your speech is planned, your delivery should sound natural and conversational. Speak loudly enough for everyone in the room to hear you, and remember to vary your pitch and your volume so that you do not speak in a monotone. Try using pauses to emphasize important points and to give listeners time to consider what you have said. Finally, sound enthusiastic about your subject. If you appear to be bored or distracted, your audience will be too.

Your movements should be purposeful and natural. Don't pace or lean against a desk or the wall. Move around only when the need arises—for example, to change a visual, to point to a chart, or to distribute a handout. Never turn your back to your audience; if you have to write on the board, make sure you are angled toward the audience. Use hand movements to emphasize points. Don't play with pens or note cards as you speak or put your hands in your pockets.

Finally, dress for the occasion. How you look will be the first thing that listeners notice. (Although shorts and a T-shirt may be appropriate for an afternoon in the park, they are not suitable for a presentation.) Dressing appropriately demonstrates your respect for your audience and shows that you are someone who deserves to be taken seriously.

ESL Tip

Some ESL students are nervous about delivering a speech, especially if they have noticeable accents. However, even students who have difficulties with English can deliver effective speeches by following the tips in this section on body language, eye contact, and pacing.

Checklist: Delivering Your Speech

- ☐ Take your time before you begin.
- ☐ Make sure your visuals are positioned properly.
- ☐ Make sure your equipment is operating properly.
- ☐ Position yourself effectively.
- ☐ Stand straight.
- ☐ Speak slowly and clearly.
- ☐ Maintain eye contact with the audience.
- ☐ Use natural gestures.
- ☐ Face the audience at all times.
- ☐ Do not block your visuals.
- ☐ Try to relax.
- ☐ Don't get flustered if something unexpected happens.
- ☐ If you forget something, don't let your audience know. Work the information in later.
- ☐ Don't sit down immediately after your speech. Leave time for questions.
- ☐ Distribute any handouts before or after the speech, not during it.

PART 7

Revising Common Sentence Errors

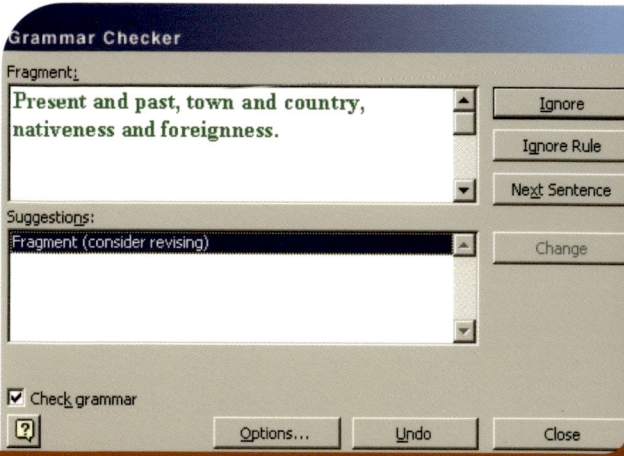

Grammar Checker

Fragment:

Present and past, town and country, nativeness and foreignness.

Suggestions:
Fragment (consider revising)

Ignore
Ignore Rule
Next Sentence
Change

☑ Check grammar

Options...   Undo   Close

FREQUENTLY ASKED QUESTIONS

CHAPTER 28

Revising Sentence Fragments

28a Recognizing Sentence Fragments

A **sentence fragment** is an incomplete sentence—a clause or a phrase—that is incorrectly punctuated as though it were a sentence. A sentence may be incomplete for any of the following reasons:

- It lacks a subject.

  Many astrophysicists now believe that galaxies are distributed in clusters. And even form supercluster complexes.

- It lacks a verb.

  Every generation has its defining events. Usually the events with the most news coverage.

- It lacks both a subject and a verb.

  Researchers are engaged in a variety of studies. Suggesting a link between alcoholism and heredity. (*Suggesting* is a **verbal**, which cannot serve as a sentence's main verb.)

  See A3

- It is a **dependent clause**, a clause that begins with a subordinating conjunction or relative pronoun.

  See B3.2

  Bishop Desmond Tutu was awarded the 1984 Nobel Peace Prize. Because he struggled to end apartheid.

  The pH meter and the spectrophotometer are two scientific instruments. That changed the chemistry laboratory dramatically.

Close-up: Maintaining Sentence Boundaries

When readers cannot see where sentences begin and end, they have difficulty understanding what you have written. For instance, in the following sequence, it is impossible to tell to which sentence the fragment belongs.

The course requirements were changed last year. Because a new professor was hired at the very end of the spring semester. I was unable to find out about this change until after preregistration.

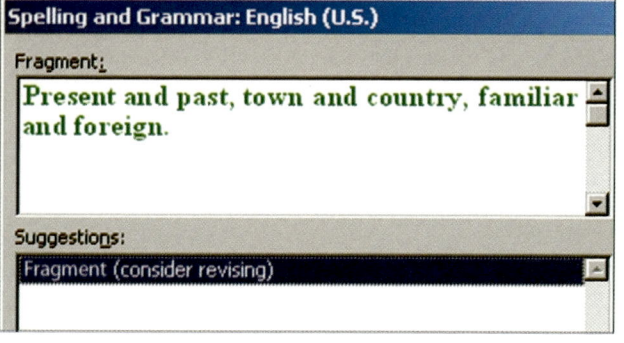

28b Correcting Sentence Fragments

FAQs To correct a sentence fragment, use one or more of the following strategies:

- Attach the fragment to an adjacent independent clause that contains the missing words.
- Delete the subordinating conjunction or relative pronoun.
- Supply the missing subject or verb (or both).

(1) Attaching the Fragment to an Independent Clause

See
B3.2

In most cases, the simplest way to correct a fragment is by attaching it to an adjacent **independent clause** that contains the missing words.

See
B3.1

President Johnson did not seek reelection. ^for^ For a number of reasons. (**prepositional phrase** fragment)

See
B3.1

Students sometimes take a leave of absence. ^to^ To decide on definite career goals. (**verbal phrase** fragment)

, *realizing*
The pilot changed course, ~~Realizing~~ that the weather was worsening. (verbal phrase fragment)

, *the*
Brian was the star forward of the Blue Devils, ~~The~~ team with the most wins. (**appositive** fragment)

See 34b3

, *such*
Fairy tales are full of damsels in distress, ~~Such~~ as Rapunzel. (appositive fragment)

and
People with dyslexia have trouble reading, ~~And~~ may also find it difficult to write. (part of compound predicate)

and
They took only a compass and a canteen, ~~And~~ some trail mix. (part of compound object)

although
Property taxes rose sharply, ~~Although~~ city services declined. (**dependent clause** fragment)

See B3.2

, *which*
The battery is dead, ~~Which~~ means the car won't start. (dependent clause fragment)

Close-up: Lists

See 48a1

When a fragment takes the form of a **list**, add a colon to connect the list to the independent clause that introduces it.

:
Tourists often outnumber residents in four European cities, Venice, Florence, Canterbury, and Bath.

---

(2) Deleting the Subordinating Conjunction or Relative Pronoun

When a fragment consists of a dependent clause punctuated as though it were a complete sentence, you can correct it by attaching it to an adjacent independent clause, as illustrated in **28b1.** Alternatively, you can simply delete the subordinating conjunction or relative pronoun.

City
Property taxes rose sharply. ~~Although city~~ services declined. (subordinating conjunction *although* deleted)

This
The battery is dead. ~~Which~~ means the car won't start. (relative pronoun *which* replaced by *this,* a word that can serve as the sentence's subject)

However, (as in the two examples on the previous page) simply deleting the subordinating conjunction or relative pronoun is usually the least desirable way to revise a sentence fragment because it is likely to create two choppy sentences and obscure the connection between them.

(3) Supplying the Missing Subject or Verb

Another way to correct a fragment is to add the missing words (a subject or a verb or both) that are needed to make the fragment a sentence.

In 1948, India became independent. ₍It was divided₎ ~~Divided~~ into the nations of India and Pakistan. (verbal phrase fragment)

A familiar trademark can increase a product's sales. ₍It reminds₎ ~~Reminding~~ shoppers that the product has a longstanding reputation. (verbal phrase fragment)

Close-up: Fragments Introduced by Transitions

See 7b

Many fragments are word groups introduced by **transitional words and phrases**, such as *also*, *finally*, *in addition*, and *now*, but are missing subjects and verbs. To correct such a fragment, add the missing subject and verb.

Finally, ₍he found₎ a new home for the family.

In addition, ₍we need₎ three new keyboards for the computer lab.

28c Using Fragments Intentionally

In professional and academic writing, sentence fragments are generally not acceptable except in certain special situations.

Checklist: Using Fragments Intentionally

☐ In lists
☐ In captions that accompany visuals
☐ In topic outlines
☐ In quoted dialogue
☐ In *PowerPoint* presentations
☐ In titles and subtitles of papers and reports
☐ In personal email and other informal communication

Figure 28.1 Magazine ad for Orange Glo polishing cloths.

Fragments are, however, often used in speech and in personal email and other informal writing—as well as in journalism, political slogans, bumper stickers, creative writing, and advertising. Magazine advertisements, such as the one for Orange Glo polishing cloths shown in Figure 28.1, often rely heavily on fragments to isolate (and thereby emphasize) key concepts about the product. Sometimes these fragments are formatted as bulleted lists of the product's key features; sometimes, as in the Orange Glo ad, the fragments are used in a central message or tag line (*Leaves other wipes in the dust*).

CHAPTER 29

Revising Comma Splices and Fused Sentences

29a Recognizing Comma Splices and Fused Sentences

A **run-on sentence** is an error created when two **independent clauses** are joined incorrectly.

A **comma splice** is a run-on that occurs when two independent clauses are joined by just a comma. A **fused sentence** is a run-on that occurs when two independent clauses are joined with no punctuation.

> **Comma Splice:** Charles Dickens created the character of Mr. Micawber, he also created Uriah Heep.

> **Fused Sentence:** Charles Dickens created the character of Mr. Micawber he also created Uriah Heep.

Grammar Checker: Revising Comma Splices

Your word processor's grammar checker will highlight comma splices and prompt you to revise them.

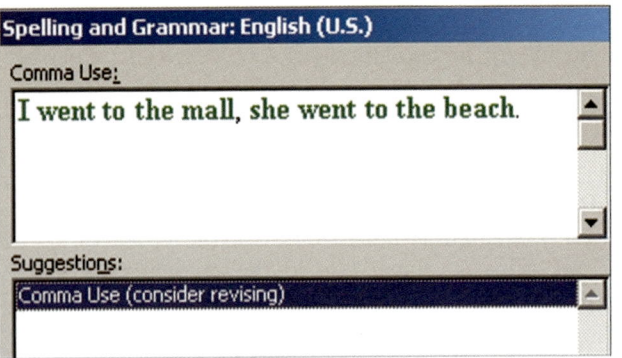

Your grammar checker may also highlight fused sentences, but it may identify them as long sentences that need revision. Moreover, it will not offer suggestions for revising fused sentences.

29b   Correcting Comma Splices and Fused Sentences

To correct a comma splice or fused sentence, use one of the follow- ing strategies:

- Add a period between the clauses.
- Add a semicolon between the clauses.
- Add an appropriate coordinating conjunction.
- Subordinate one clause to the other, creating a complex sentence.

(1) Adding a Period

You can correct a comma splice or fused sentence by adding a period between the independent clauses, creating two separate sentences. This is a good strategy to use when the clauses are long or when they are not closely related.

> In 1894 Frenchman Alfred Dreyfus was falsely convicted of
> treason, his struggle for justice pitted the army against the civil
> libertarians.

Close-up: Comma Splices and Fused Sentences

Using a comma to punctuate an interrupted quotation that consists of two complete sentences creates a comma splice. Instead, use a period.

> "This is a good course," Eric said, "in fact, I wish I'd taken it sooner."

---

(2) Adding a Semicolon

You can correct a comma splice or fused sentence by adding a semicolon between two closely related clauses that convey parallel or contrasting information.

> See 45a

> Chippendale chairs have straight legs, however, Queen Anne
> chairs have curved legs.

NOTE: When you use a **transitional word or phrase** (such as *however, therefore,* or *for example*) to connect two independent clauses, the transitional element must be preceded by a semicolon and followed by a comma. If you use a comma alone, you create a comma splice. If you omit punctuation entirely, you create a fused sentence.

> See 7b2

(3) Adding a Coordinating Conjunction

You can use a coordinating conjunction (*and, or, but, nor, for, so, yet*) to join two closely related clauses of equal importance into one **compound sentence**. The coordinating conjunction you choose indicates the relationship between the clauses: addition (*and*), contrast (*but, yet*), causality (*for, so*), or a choice of alternatives (*or, nor*). Be sure to add a comma before the coordinating conjunction.

See 36a1

> Elias Howe invented the sewing machine, ^*and*^ Julia Ward Howe was a poet and social reformer.

(4) Creating a Complex Sentence

When the ideas in two independent clauses are not of equal importance, you can use an appropriate subordinating conjunction or a relative pronoun to join the clauses into one **complex sentence**, placing the less important idea in the dependent clause.

See 36a2

> Stravinsky's ballet *The Rite of Spring* shocked Parisians in 1913,/^*because*^ its rhythms seemed erotic.

> Lady Mary Wortley Montagu^*, who*^ had suffered from smallpox herself,^ ~~she~~ helped spread the practice of inoculation.

CHAPTER 30

Revising Agreement Errors

Agreement is the correspondence between words in number, gender, and person. Subjects and verbs agree in **number** (singular or plural) and **person** (first, second, or third); pronouns and their antecedents agree in number, person, and **gender** (masculine, feminine, or neuter).

ESL
55a

30a Making Subjects and Verbs Agree

Singular subjects take singular verbs, and plural subjects take plural verbs. **Present tense** verbs, except *be* and *have*, add *-s* or *-es* when the subject is third-person singular. (Third-person singular subjects include nouns; the personal pronouns *he*, *she*, *it*, and *one*; and many **indefinite pronouns**.)

ESL
55a2

See
30a4

> The <u>president</u> <u>has</u> the power to veto congressional legislation.

> <u>She</u> frequently <u>cites</u> statistics to support her points.

> In every group <u>somebody</u> <u>emerges</u> as a natural leader.

Present tense verbs do not add *-s* or *-es* when the subject is a plural noun, a first-person or second-person pronoun (*I*, *we*, *you*), or a third-person plural pronoun (*they*).

> <u>Experts</u> <u>recommend</u> that dieters avoid processed meat.

> At this stratum, <u>we</u> <u>see</u> rocks dating back ten million years.

> <u>They</u> <u>say</u> that some wealthy people default on their student loans.

In the special situations discussed below, subject-verb agreement can cause problems for writers.

(1) When Words Come between Subject and Verb

If a modifying phrase comes between subject and verb, the verb should agree with the subject, not with a word in the modifying phrase.

> The <u>sound</u> of the drumbeats <u>builds</u> in intensity in Eugene O'Neill's play *The Emperor Jones*.

> The <u>games</u> won by the intramural team <u>are</u> few and far between.

379

NOTE: When phrases introduced by *along with, as well as, in addition to, including,* and *together with* come between subject and verb, these phrases do not change the subject's number: Heavy <u>rain</u>, along with high winds, <u>causes</u> hazardous driving conditions.

(2) When Compound Subjects Are Joined by *And*

Compound subjects joined by *and* usually take plural verbs.

<u>Air bags and antilock brakes</u> <u>are</u> standard on all new models.

There are, however, two exceptions to this rule. First, compound subjects joined by *and* that stand for a single idea or person are treated as a unit and take singular verbs.

<u>Rhythm and blues</u> <u>is</u> a forerunner of rock and roll.

Second, when *each* or *every* precedes a compound subject joined by *and*, the subject takes a singular verb.

<u>Every desk and file cabinet</u> <u>was</u> searched before the letter was found.

(3) When Compound Subjects Are Joined by *Or*

Compound subjects joined by *or* (or by *either . . . or* or *neither . . . nor*) may take singular or plural verbs.

If both subjects are singular, use a singular verb; if both subjects are plural, use a plural verb.

<u>Either radiation or chemotherapy</u> <u>is</u> combined with surgery for effective results. (Both *radiation* and *chemotherapy* are singular, so the verb is singular.)

<u>Either radiation treatments or chemotherapy sessions</u> <u>are</u> combined with surgery for effective results. (Both *treatments* and *sessions* are plural, so the verb is plural.)

If one subject is singular and the other is plural, the verb agrees with the subject that is nearer to it.

<u>Either radiation treatments or chemotherapy</u> <u>is</u> combined with surgery for effective results. (Singular verb agrees with *chemotherapy*.)

<u>Either chemotherapy or radiation treatments</u> <u>are</u> combined with surgery for effective results. (Plural verb agrees with *treatments*.)

(4) When Indefinite Pronouns Serve as Subjects

Most <u>indefinite pronouns</u>—*another, anyone, everyone, one, each, either, neither, anything, everything, something, nothing, nobody,* and *somebody* —are singular and take singular verbs.

<u>Anyone</u> <u>is</u> welcome to apply for this grant.

Some indefinite pronouns—*both, many, few, several, others*—are always plural and take plural verbs.

<u>Several</u> of the articles <u>are</u> useful.

A few indefinite pronouns—*some, all, any, more, most,* and *none*—can be singular or plural, depending on the noun they refer to.

<u>Some</u> of this trouble <u>is</u> to be expected. *(Some* refers to *trouble.)*

<u>Some</u> of the spectators <u>are</u> getting restless. *(Some* refers to *spectators.)*

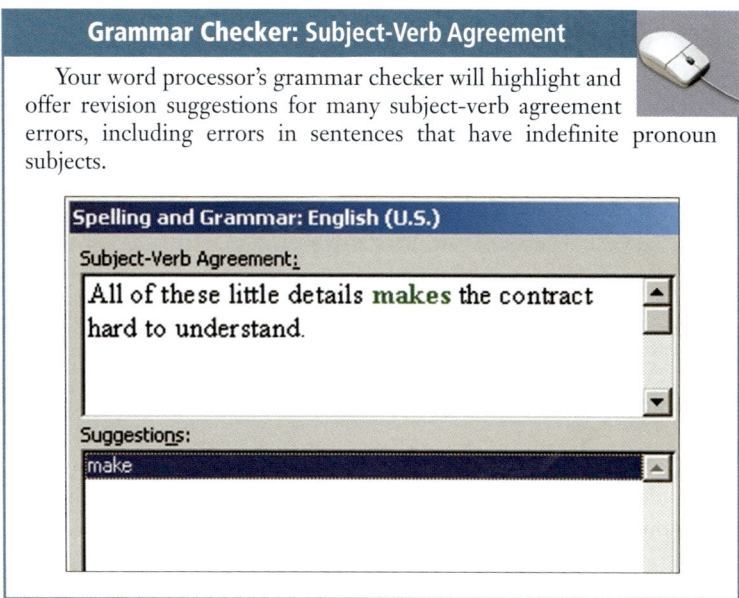

Grammar Checker: Subject-Verb Agreement

Your word processor's grammar checker will highlight and offer revision suggestions for many subject-verb agreement errors, including errors in sentences that have indefinite pronoun subjects.

Spelling and Grammar: English (U.S.)

Subject-Verb Agreement:

All of these little details **makes** the contract hard to understand.

Suggestions:

make

(5) When Collective Nouns Serve as Subjects

A **collective noun** names a group of persons or things—for instance, *navy, union, association, band.* When it refers to the group as a unit (as it usually does), a collective noun takes a singular verb; when it refers to the individuals or items that make up the group, it takes a plural verb.

To many people, the royal <u>family</u> <u>symbolizes</u> Great Britain. (The family, as a unit, is the symbol.)

The <u>family</u> all <u>eat</u> at different times. (Each family member eats separately.)

NOTE: If a plural verb sounds awkward with a collective noun, re-word the sentence: <u>Family members</u> all <u>eat</u> at different times.

ESL Tip

In British English, which you may have learned if you took ESL classes outside the United States, collective nouns tend to take plural verbs more often than they do in American English:

Management <u>are</u> considering giving workers a bonus.

Phrases that name fixed amounts—*three-quarters, twenty dollars, the majority*—are treated like collective nouns. When the amount denotes a unit, it takes a singular verb; when it denotes part of the whole, it takes a plural verb.

<u>Three-quarters</u> of his usual salary <u>is</u> not enough to live on.

<u>Three-quarters</u> of the patients <u>improve</u> after treatment.

Close-up: Subject-Verb Agreement with Collective Nouns

The number is always singular, and *a number* is always plural.

<u>The number</u> of voters <u>has</u> declined.

<u>A number</u> of students <u>have</u> missed preregistration.

---

(6) When Singular Subjects Have Plural Forms

A singular subject takes a singular verb, even if the form of the subject is plural.

<u>Statistics</u> <u>deals</u> with the collection and analysis of data.

When such a word has a plural meaning, however, use a plural verb.

The <u>statistics</u> <u>prove</u> him wrong.

NOTE: Some nouns retain their Latin plural forms, which do not look like English plural forms. Be particularly careful to use the correct verbs with such words: *criterion is, criteria are; medium is, media are; bacterium is, bacteria are.*

(7) When Subject-Verb Order Is Inverted

ESL
55f Even when **word order** is inverted and the verb comes before the subject (as it does in questions and in sentences beginning with *there is* or *there are*), the subject and verb must agree.

Is either answer correct?

There are currently thirteen circuit courts of appeals in the federal system.

(8) With Linking Verbs

A linking verb should agree with its subject, not with the subject complement.

> See 35a

The problem was termites.

Termites were the problem.

(9) With Relative Pronouns

When you use a relative pronoun (*who, which, that,* and so on) to introduce a dependent clause, the verb in that clause agrees with the pronoun's **antecedent,** the word to which the pronoun refers.

> See A2

The farmer is among the ones who suffer during a grain embargo.

The farmer is the only one who suffers during a grain embargo.

30b Making Pronouns and Antecedents Agree

Singular pronouns—such as *he, him, she, her, it, me, myself,* and *one-self*—should refer to singular antecedents. Plural pronouns—such as *we, us, they, them,* and *their*—should refer to plural antecedents.

(1) With Compound Antecedents

In most cases, use a plural pronoun to refer to a **compound antecedent** (two or more antecedents connected by *and* or *or*).

Mormonism and Christian Science were similar in their beginnings.

However, this general rule has several exceptions:

- If a compound antecedent denotes a single unit—one person or thing or idea—use a singular pronoun to refer to the compound antecedent.

  In 1904, the husband and father brought his family to America.

- Use a singular pronoun when a compound antecedent is preceded by *each* or *every.*

  Every programming language and software package has its limitations.

- Use a singular pronoun to refer to two or more singular antecedents linked by *or* or *nor*:

  <u>Neither Thoreau nor Whitman</u> lived to see <u>his</u> work read widely.

- When one part of a compound antecedent joined by *or* or *nor* is singular and one part is plural, the pronoun agrees in person and number with the antecedent that is nearer to it.

  <u>Neither the boy nor his parents</u> had <u>their</u> seatbelts fastened.

(2) With Collective Noun Antecedents

If the meaning of a collective noun antecedent is singular (as it will be in most cases), use a singular pronoun. If the meaning is plural, use a plural pronoun.

  The teachers' <u>union</u> announced <u>its</u> plan to strike. (The members act as a unit.)

  The <u>team</u> ran on to the field and took <u>their</u> positions. (Each member acts individually.)

(3) With Indefinite Pronoun Antecedents

Most **indefinite pronouns**—*each, either, neither, one, anyone,* and the like—are singular and are used with singular pronouns.

  <u>Neither</u> of the men had <u>his</u> proposal ready by the deadline.

  <u>Each</u> of these neighborhoods has <u>its</u> own traditions and values.

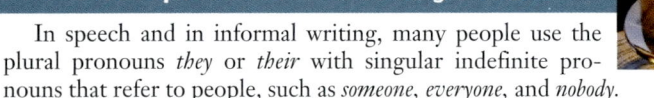

Close-up: Pronoun-Antecedent Agreement

In speech and in informal writing, many people use the plural pronouns *they* or *their* with singular indefinite pronouns that refer to people, such as *someone, everyone,* and *nobody.*

  <u>Everyone</u> can present <u>their</u> own viewpoint.

In college writing, however, you should not use a plural pronoun to refer to a singular subject. Instead, you can use both masculine and feminine pronouns.

  <u>Everyone</u> can present <u>his or her</u> own viewpoint.

Or, you can make the sentence's subject plural.

  <u>All participants</u> can present <u>their</u> own viewpoints.

The use of *his* alone to refer to a singular indefinite pronoun (Everyone can present *his* own viewpoint) is considered **sexist language**.

See
40e2

Grammar Checker: Pronoun-Antecedent Agreement

Your word processor's grammar checker will highlight and offer revision suggestions for many pronoun-antecedent agreement errors.

Spelling and Grammar: English (U.S.)

Pronoun Use:

Someone should take responsibility for **their** actions.

Suggestions:

his or her

CHAPTER 31

Revising Awkward or Confusing Sentences

The most common causes of awkward or confusing sentences are *unwarranted shifts, mixed constructions, faulty predication,* and *illogical comparisons.*

31a Revising Unwarranted Shifts

(1) Shifts in Tense

See 33b

ESL 55a2

Verb <u>tense</u> in a sentence or in a related group of sentences should not shift without good reason—to indicate changes of time, for example. Unwarranted shifts in tense can be confusing.

> I registered for the advanced philosophy seminar because I wanted a challenge. However, by the first week I ~~start~~ *started* having trouble understanding the reading. (unwarranted shift from past to present)

> Jack Kerouac's novel *On the Road* follows a group of friends who ~~drove~~ *drive* across the United States in the 1950s. (unwarranted shift from present to past)

NOTE: The present tense is used in discussions of literary works.

(2) Shifts in Voice

See 33d

ESL 55a6

Unwarranted shifts from active to passive <u>voice</u> (or from passive to active) can be confusing. In the following sentence, for instance, the shift from active (*wrote*) to passive (*was written*) makes it unclear who wrote *The Great Gatsby.*

> F. Scott Fitzgerald wrote *This Side of Paradise,* and later *The Great Gatsby* ~~was written.~~ *wrote*

NOTE: Sometimes a shift from active to passive voice within a sentence may be necessary to give the sentence proper emphasis: Even though consumers <u>protested</u>, the sales tax <u>was increased</u>. (To say *the legislature increased the sales tax* would draw the sentence's emphasis away from *consumers*.)

(3) Shifts in Mood

Unwarranted shifts in **mood** can also create awkward sentences.

>   *be*
> Next, heat the mixture in a test tube, and ~~you should make~~ sure it does not boil. (unwarranted shift from imperative to indicative)

(4) Shifts in Person and Number

Person indicates who is speaking (first person—*I, we*), who is spoken to (second person—*you*), and who is spoken about (third person—*he, she, it, one,* and *they*). Unwarranted shifts between the second and the third person are most often responsible for awkward sentences.

>   *you look*
> When ~~one looks~~ for a car loan, you compare the interest rates of several banks. (unwarranted shift from third to second person)

Number indicates one (singular—*novel, it*) or more than one (plural—*novels, they, them*). Singular pronouns should refer to singular **antecedents** and plural pronouns to plural antecedents.

>   *he or she*
> If a person does not study regularly, ~~they~~ will have a difficult time passing Spanish. (unwarranted shift from singular to plural)

(5) Shifts from Direct to Indirect Discourse

Direct discourse reports the exact words of a speaker or writer. It is always enclosed in quotation marks and is often accompanied by an identifying tag (*he says, she said*). **Indirect discourse** summarizes the words of a speaker or writer. No quotation marks are used, and the reported words are often introduced with the word *that* or, in the case of questions, with *who, what, why, whether, how,* or *if*.

> **Direct Discourse:** My instructor said, "I want your paper by this Friday."

> **Indirect Discourse:** My instructor said that he wanted my paper by this Friday.

Unwarranted shifts between indirect and direct discourse are often confusing.

>   *he was*
> During the trial, John Brown repeatedly defended his actions and said that ~~I am~~ not guilty. (shift from indirect to direct discourse)

"Are you ?"
My mother asked, ~~was I~~ ever going to get a job, (neither indirect nor direct discourse)

31b Revising Mixed Constructions

A **mixed construction** is an error created when a dependent clause, prepositional phrase, or independent clause is incorrectly used as the subject of a sentence.

Because she studies every day, ~~explains why~~ she gets good grades. (dependent clause used as subject)

, you can
By calling for information, ~~is the way to~~ learn more about the benefits of ROTC. (prepositional phrase used as subject)

Being
~~He was~~ late ~~was what~~ made him miss Act 1. (independent clause used as subject)

31c Revising Faulty Predication

Faulty predication occurs when a sentence's predicate does not logically complete its subject.

(1) Incorrect Use of *Be*

Faulty predication is especially common in sentences that contain a **linking verb**—a form of the verb *be*, for example—and a subject complement.

caused
Mounting costs and decreasing revenues, ~~were~~ the downfall of the hospital.

This sentence incorrectly states that mounting costs and decreasing revenues *were* the downfall of the hospital when, in fact, they were the *reasons* for its downfall.

(2) *Is When* or *Is Where*

Faulty predication also occurs in one-sentence definitions that contain a construction like *is where* or *is when*.

the construction of
Taxidermy is, ~~where you construct~~ a lifelike representation of an animal from its preserved skin. (In a definition, *is* must be preceded and followed by nouns or noun phrases.)

(3) *The Reason . . . Is Because*

Finally, faulty predication occurs when the phrase *the reason is* precedes *because*. In this situation, *because* (which means "for the reason that") is redundant and should be deleted.

>   *that*
> The reason we drive is ~~because~~ we are afraid to fly.

Grammar Checker: Revising Faulty Predication

Your word processor's grammar checker will highlight certain instances of faulty predication and offer suggestions for revision. Your grammar checker will also highlight some other causes of awkward or confusing sentences, including shifts in voice, person, and number, and will frequently offer revision suggestions. However, the grammar checker will miss many unwarranted shifts, mixed constructions, and incomplete or illogical constructions, so you will need to proofread carefully for these errors.

31d   Revising Incomplete or Illogical Comparisons

A comparison tells how two things are alike or unlike. When you make a comparison, be sure it is **complete** (that readers can tell which two items are being compared) and **logical** (that it equates two comparable items).

>   *than Nina's*
> My chemistry course is harder. (What two things are being compared?)

>   *dog's*
> A pig's intelligence is greater than a ~~dog~~. (illogically compares "a pig's intelligence" to "a dog")

CHAPTER 32

Revising Misplaced and Dangling Modifiers

A **modifier** is a word, phrase, or clause that describes, limits, or qualifies another word or word group in a sentence. A modifier should be placed close to the word it modifies. **Faulty modification** is the confusing placement of modifiers or the modification of nonexistent words.

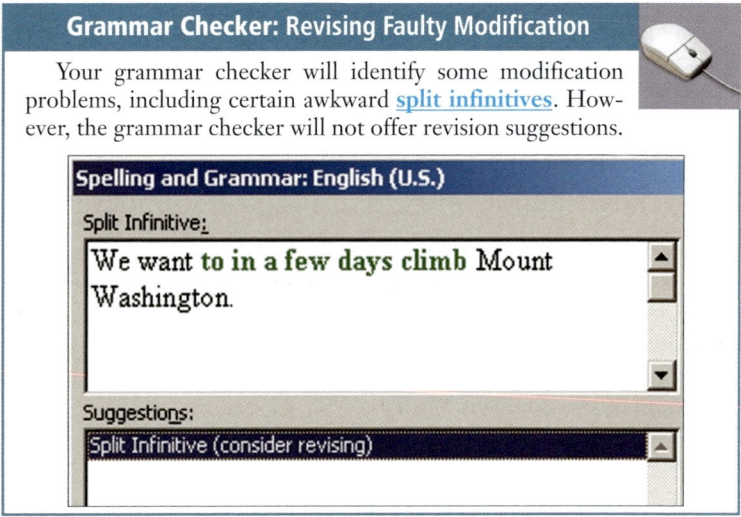

See
32b

Grammar Checker: Revising Faulty Modification

Your grammar checker will identify some modification problems, including certain awkward <u>split infinitives</u>. However, the grammar checker will not offer revision suggestions.

Spelling and Grammar: English (U.S.)

Split Infinitive:

We want **to in a few days climb** Mount Washington.

Suggestions:

Split Infinitive (consider revising)

32a Revising Misplaced Modifiers

A **misplaced modifier** is a word or word group whose placement suggests that it modifies one word (or phrase or clause) when it is intended to modify another.

> *Wendy watched the storm, fierce*
> ˄F̶i̶e̶r̶c̶e̶ and threatening,/ W̶e̶n̶d̶y̶ w̶a̶t̶c̶h̶e̶d̶ t̶h̶e̶ s̶t̶o̶r̶m̶,/ (The storm, not Wendy, was fierce and threatening.)

> *The lawyer argued that the defendant, with*
> ˄W̶i̶t̶h̶ an IQ of just 52, t̶h̶e̶ l̶a̶w̶y̶e̶r̶ a̶r̶g̶u̶e̶d̶ t̶h̶a̶t̶ t̶h̶e̶ d̶e̶f̶e̶n̶d̶a̶n̶t̶ should not get the death penalty. (The defendant, not the lawyer, had an IQ of 52.)

(1) Placing Modifying Words Precisely

Limiting modifiers—such as *almost, only, even, hardly, merely, nearly, exactly, scarcely, simply,* and *just*—should always immediately precede the words they modify. A different placement will change the meaning of the sentence.

Nick *just* set up camp at the edge of town. (He did it just now.)

Just Nick set up camp at the edge of town. (He did it alone.)

Nick set up camp *just* at the edge of town. (His camp was precisely at the edge.)

When a limiting modifier is placed so that it is not clear whether it modifies a word before it or one after it, it is called a **squinting modifier.**

The life that everyone thought would fulfill her <u>totally</u> bored her.

To correct a squinting modifier, place the modifier so that it is clear which word it modifies.

The life that everyone thought would <u>totally</u> fulfill her bored her. (Everyone expected her to be totally fulfilled.)

The life that everyone thought would fulfill her bored her <u>totally</u>. (She was totally bored.)

(2) Relocating Misplaced Phrases

Placing a modifying phrase incorrectly can change the meaning of a sentence or create an unclear or confusing (or even unintentionally humorous) construction.

To avoid ambiguity, place **verbal phrase** modifiers directly before or directly after the words or word groups they modify.

Roller-skating along the shore,
Jane watched the boats. ~~roller skating along the shore.~~

Place **prepositional phrase** modifiers immediately after the words they modify.

with no arms
Venus de Milo is a statue created by a famous artist ~~with no arms.~~

(3) Relocating Misplaced Dependent Clauses

A dependent clause that serves as a modifier must be clearly related to the word it modifies.

An **adjective clause** appears immediately *after* the word it modifies.

During the Civil War, Lincoln was the president <u>who governed the United States.</u>

An **adverb clause** can appear in any of several positions, as long as its relationship to the word or word group it modifies is clear.

When Lincoln was president, the Civil War raged.

The Civil War raged when Lincoln was president.

32b Revising Intrusive Modifiers

An **intrusive modifier** awkwardly interrupts a sentence, making it difficult to understand.

Revise when a long modifying phrase comes between an auxiliary verb and a main verb.

> *Without*
> She had, without giving it a second thought or considering the
> *she had*
> consequences, planned to reenlist.

Revise when a modifier creates an awkward **split infinitive**—that is, when a modifier comes between the word *to* and the base form of the verb.

> *defeat his opponent*
> He hoped to quickly and easily defeat his opponent.

NOTE: A split infinitive is acceptable when the intervening modifier is short, especially if the alternative would be awkward or ambiguous: She expected to almost beat her previous record.

32c Revising Dangling Modifiers

A **dangling modifier** is a word or phrase that cannot logically modify any word in the sentence.

> **Dangling:** Using this drug, many undesirable side effects are experienced. (Who is using this drug?)

One way to correct this dangling modifier is to **create a new subject** by adding a word or word group that *using this drug* can logically modify.

> **Revised:** Using this drug, patients experience many undesirable side effects.

Another way to correct the dangling modifier is to **create a dependent clause.**

> **Revised:** Many undesirable side effects are experienced when this drug is used.

These two options for correcting dangling modifiers are further illustrated below.

(1) Creating a New Subject

the technician lifted
Using a pair of forceps, ^the skin of the rat's abdomen ~~was lifted~~. (Modifier cannot logically modify *skin*.)

Meg found
With fifty more pages to read, ^*War and Peace* ~~was~~ absorbing. (Modifier cannot logically modify *War and Peace*.)

Close-up: Dangling Modifiers and the Passive Voice

   Most sentences that include dangling modifiers are in the passive voice. Changing the **passive voice** to **active voice** corrects the dangling modifier by changing the subject of the sentence's main clause to a word that the dangling modifier can logically modify.

See
33d

ESL
55a6

---

(2) Creating a Dependent Clause

Before   *was implemented,*
^~~To implement~~ a plus/minus grading system, ^all students were polled. (Modifier cannot logically modify *students*.)

Because the magazine had been on
^~~On~~ the newsstands only an hour, its sales surprised everyone. (Modifier cannot logically modify *sales*.)

PART 8

Writing Grammatical Sentences

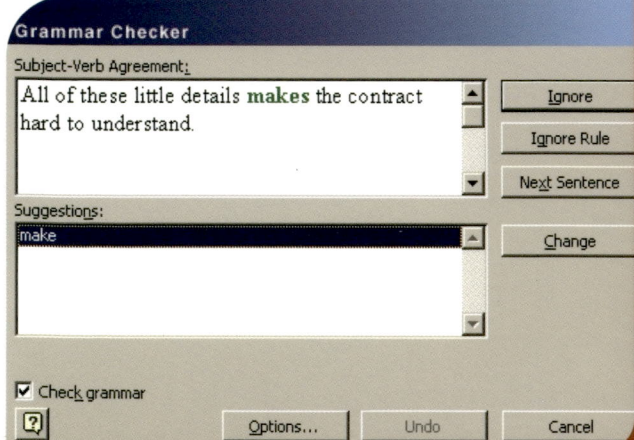

PART 8

Writing Grammatical Sentences

FREQUENTLY ASKED QUESTIONS

CHAPTER 33

Using Verbs: Form, Tense, Mood, and Voice

33a Understanding Verb Forms

Every verb has four **principal parts:** a **base form** (the form of the verb used with *I, we, you,* and *they* in the present tense), a **present participle** (the *-ing* form of the verb), a **past tense form,** and a **past participle.**

NOTE: The verb *be* is so irregular that it is the one exception to this definition; its base form is *be.*

(1) Regular Verbs

A **regular verb** forms both its past tense and its past participle by adding *-d* or *-ed* to the base form of the verb.

Principal Parts of Regular Verbs		
Base Form	**Past Tense Form**	**Past Participle**
smile	smiled	smiled
talk	talked	talked
jump	jumped	jumped

(2) Irregular Verbs

Irregular verbs do not follow the pattern discussed above. The chart that follows lists the principal parts of the most frequently used irregular verbs.

Frequently Used Irregular Verbs		
Base Form	**Past Tense Form**	**Past Participle**
arise	arose	arisen
awake	awoke, awaked	awoke, awaked
be	was/were	been
beat	beat	beaten
begin	began	begun

(continued)

Frequently used irregular verbs (continued)

Base Form	Past Tense Form	Past Participle
bend	bent	bent
bet	bet, betted	bet
bite	bit	bitten
blow	blew	blown
break	broke	broken
bring	brought	brought
build	built	built
burst	burst	burst
buy	bought	bought
catch	caught	caught
choose	chose	chosen
cling	clung	clung
come	came	come
cost	cost	cost
deal	dealt	dealt
dig	dug	dug
dive	dived, dove	dived
do	did	done
drag	dragged	dragged
draw	drew	drawn
drink	drank	drunk
drive	drove	driven
eat	ate	eaten
fall	fell	fallen
fight	fought	fought
find	found	found
fly	flew	flown
forget	forgot	forgotten, forgot
freeze	froze	frozen
get	got	gotten
give	gave	given
go	went	gone
grow	grew	grown
hang (execute)	hanged	hanged
hang (suspend)	hung	hung
have	had	had
hear	heard	heard
keep	kept	kept
know	knew	known
lay	laid	laid
lead	led	led
lend	lent	lent
let	let	let
lie (recline)	lay	lain
lie (tell an untruth)	lied	lied
make	made	made
prove	proved	proved, proven
read	read	read
ride	rode	ridden

Base Form	Past Tense Form	Past Participle
ring	rang	rung
rise	rose	risen
run	ran	run
say	said	said
see	saw	seen
set (place)	set	set
shake	shook	shaken
shrink	shrank, shrunk,	shrunk, shrunken
sing	sang	sung
sink	sank	sunk
sit	sat	sat
sneak	sneaked	sneaked
speak	spoke	spoken
speed	sped, speeded	sped, speeded
spin	spun	spun
spring	sprang	sprung
stand	stood	stood
steal	stole	stolen
strike	struck	struck, stricken
swear	swore	sworn
swim	swam	swum
swing	swung	swung
take	took	taken
teach	taught	taught
throw	threw	thrown
wake	woke, waked	waked, woken
wear	wore	worn
wring	wrung	wrung
write	wrote	written

Grammar Checker: Using Correct Verb Forms

Your word processor's grammar checker will highlight incorrect verb forms in your writing and offer revision suggestions.

Spelling and Grammar: English (U.S.)

Verb Form:

My father had already drove my sister home by the time the party began.

Suggestions:

driven

Close-up: *Lie/Lay* and *Sit/Set*		

Lie means "to recline" and does not take an object ("He likes to *lie* on the floor"); *lay* means "to place" or "to put" and does take an object ("He wants to *lay* a rug on the floor").

Base Form	**Past Tense Form**	**Past Participle**
lie	lay	lain
lay	laid	laid

Sit means "to assume a seated position" and does not take an object ("She wants to *sit* on the table"); *set* means "to place" or "to put" and usually takes an object ("She wants to *set* a vase on the table").

Base Form	**Past Tense Form**	**Past Participle**
sit	sat	sat
set	set	set

33b Understanding Tense

ESL
55a2

Tense is the form a verb takes to indicate when an action occurred or when a condition existed.

English Verb Tenses

Simple Tenses
Present (I *finish*, she or he *finishes*)
Past (I *finished*)
Future (I *will finish*)

Perfect Tenses
Present perfect (I *have finished*, she or he *has finished*)
Past perfect (I *had finished*)
Future perfect (I *will have finished*)

Progressive Tenses
Present progressive (I *am finishing*, she or he *is finishing*)
Past progressive (I *was finishing*)
Future progressive (I *will be finishing*)
Present perfect progressive (I *have been finishing*)
Past perfect progressive (I *had been finishing*)
Future perfect progressive (I *will have been finishing*)

(1) Using the Simple Tenses

The **simple tenses** include *present*, *past*, and *future*.

The **present tense** usually indicates an action that is taking place at the time it is expressed in speech or writing. It can also indicate an action that occurs regularly.

I <u>see</u> your point. (an action taking place when it is expressed)

We <u>wear</u> wool in the winter. (an action that occurs regularly)

Close-up: Special Uses of the Present Tense

The present tense has four special uses:

1. **To Indicate Future Time:** The grades <u>arrive</u> next Thursday.
2. **To State a Generally Held Belief:** Studying <u>pays</u> off.
3. **To State a Scientific Truth:** An object at rest <u>tends</u> to stay at rest.
4. **To Discuss a Literary Work:** *Family Installments* <u>tells</u> the story of a Puerto Rican family.

The **past tense** indicates that an action has already taken place.

John Glenn <u>orbited</u> the earth three times on February 20, 1962. (an action completed in the past)

As a young man, Mark Twain <u>traveled</u> through the Southwest. (an action that occurred once or many times in the past but did not extend into the present)

The **future tense** indicates that an action will or is likely to take place.

Halley's Comet <u>will reappear</u> in 2061. (a future action that will definitely occur)

The land boom in Nevada <u>will</u> probably <u>continue</u>. (a future action that is likely to occur)

(2) Using the Perfect Tenses

The <u>**perfect tenses**</u> designate actions that were or will be completed before other actions or conditions. The perfect tenses are formed with the appropriate tense form of the auxiliary verb *have* plus the past participle.

ESL 55a2

The **present perfect** tense can indicate either of two kinds of continuing action beginning in the past.

Dr. Kim <u>has finished</u> studying the effects of BHA on rats. (an action that began in the past and is finished at the present time)

My mother <u>has invested</u> her money wisely. (an action that began in the past and extends into the present)

The **past perfect** tense indicates an action occurring before a certain time in the past.

By 1946, engineers <u>had built</u> the first electronic digital computer.

The **future perfect** tense indicates that an action will be finished by a certain future time.

By Tuesday, the transit authority <u>will have run</u> out of money.

Close-up: *Could Have, Should Have,* and *Would Have*

Do not use the preposition *of* after *would, should, could,* and *might*. Use the auxiliary verb *have* after these words.

> *have*
> I should ⌃of left for class earlier.

---

(3) Using the Progressive Tenses

ESL
55a2
The <u>progressive tenses</u> express continuing action. They are formed with the appropriate tense of the verb *be* plus the present participle.

The **present progressive** tense indicates that something is happening at the time it is expressed in speech or writing.

The volcano <u>is erupting</u>, and lava <u>is flowing</u> toward the town.

The **past progressive** tense can indicate either of two kinds of past action.

Roderick Usher's actions <u>were becoming</u> increasingly bizarre. (a continuing action in the past)

The French revolutionary Marat was stabbed to death while he <u>was bathing</u>. (an action occurring at the same time in the past as another action)

The **future progressive** tense indicates a continuing action in the future.

The treasury secretary <u>will be monitoring</u> the money supply regularly.

The **present perfect progressive** tense indicates action continuing from the past into the present and possibly into the future.

Rescuers <u>have been working</u> around the clock.

The **past perfect progressive** tense indicates that a past action went on until another one occurred.

Before President Kennedy was assassinated, he <u>had been working</u> on civil rights legislation.

The **future perfect progressive** tense indicates that an action will continue until a certain future time.

By eleven o'clock we <u>will have been driving</u> for seven hours.

(4) Using Verb Tenses in a Sentence

You use different tenses in a sentence to indicate that actions are taking place at different times. By choosing tenses that accurately express these times, you enable readers to follow the sequence of actions. The following situations require special attention:

- **When a verb appears in a dependent clause,** *its tense depends on the tense of the main verb in the independent clause.* When the main verb in the independent clause is in the past tense, the verb in the dependent clause is usually in the past or past perfect tense. When the main verb in the independent clause is in the past perfect tense, the verb in the dependent clause is usually in the past tense. (When the main verb in the independent clause is in any tense except the past or past perfect, the verb in the dependent clause may be in any tense needed for meaning.)

Main Verb	Verb in Dependent Clause
George Hepplewhite <u>was</u> (past) an English cabinetmaker	who <u>designed</u> (past) distinctive chair backs.
The battle <u>had ended</u> (past perfect)	by the time reinforcements <u>arrived</u>. (past)

- **When an infinitive appears in a verbal phrase,** *the tense it expresses depends on the tense of the sentence's main verb.* The *present infinitive* (the *to* form of the verb) indicates an action happening at the same time as or later than the main verb. The *perfect infinitive* (*to have* plus the past participle) indicates action happening earlier than the main verb.

Main Verb	Infinitive
I <u>went</u>	<u>to see</u> the Rangers play last week. (The going and seeing occurred at the same time.)
I <u>want</u>	<u>to see</u> the Rangers play tomorrow. (Wanting occurs in the present, and seeing will occur in the future.)
I would <u>like</u>	<u>to have seen</u> the Rangers play. (Liking occurs in the present, and seeing would have occurred in the past.)

- **When a participle appears in a verbal phrase,** *its tense depends on the tense of the sentence's main verb.* The *present participle* indicates action happening at the same time as the action of the main verb. The *past participle* or the *present perfect participle* indicates action occurring before the action of the main verb.

Participle	Main Verb
<u>Addressing</u> the 1896 Democratic Convention,	William Jennings Bryan <u>delivered</u> his Cross of Gold speech. (The addressing and the delivery occurred at the same time.)
<u>Having written</u> her term paper,	Camille <u>studied</u> for her history final. (The writing occurred before the studying.)

33c Understanding Mood

Mood is the form a verb takes to indicate whether a writer is making a statement or asking a question (*indicative mood*), giving a command (*imperative mood*), or expressing a wish or a contrary-to-fact statement (*subjunctive mood*).

- The **indicative** mood expresses an opinion, states a fact, or asks a question: Jackie Robinson had a great impact on professional baseball. (The indicative is the mood used in most English sentences.)
- The **imperative** mood is used in commands and direct requests. Usually, the imperative includes only the base form of the verb without a subject: Use a dictionary.
- The **subjunctive** mood was common in the past, but it now is used less and less often, and usually only in formal contexts.

(1) Forming the Subjunctive Mood

The **present subjunctive** uses the base form of the verb, regardless of the subject. The **past subjunctive** has the same form as the past tense of the verb. (However, when *be* is used as an auxiliary verb, it takes the form *were* regardless of the number or person of the subject.)

> Dr. Gorman suggested that he study the Cambrian Period. (present subjunctive)

> The sign recommended that we be careful

> I wish I were going to Europe. (past subjunctive)

(2) Using the Subjunctive Mood

The present subjunctive is used in *that* clauses after words such as *ask, suggest, require, recommend*, and *demand*.

> The report recommended that juveniles be given mandatory counseling.

> Captain Ahab insisted that his crew hunt the white whale.

The past subjunctive is used in **conditional statements** (statements beginning with *if* that are contrary to fact, including statements that express a wish).

> If John were here, he could see Marsha. (John is not here.)

> The father acted as if he were having the baby. (The father couldn't be having the baby.)

> I wish I were more organized. (expresses a wish)

NOTE: In many situations, the subjunctive mood sounds stiff or formal. Alternative expressions can eliminate the need for subjunctive constructions.

The group asked ~~that~~ the mayor ^to^ ban smoking in public places.

33d Understanding Voice

Voice is the form a verb takes to indicate whether its subject acts or is acted upon. When the subject of a verb does something—that is, acts—the verb is in the **active voice.** When the subject of a verb is the recipient of the action—that is, is acted upon—the verb is in the **passive voice.**

Active Voice: Hart Crane <u>wrote</u> *The Bridge.*

Passive Voice: *The Bridge* <u>was written</u> by Hart Crane.

Close-up: Voice

The active voice places emphasis on the person or thing performing an action, and it is usually briefer, clearer, and more emphatic than the passive voice.

For this reason, you should generally use active constructions in your college writing. Some situations, however, require use of the passive voice. For example, you should use passive constructions when the actor is unknown or unimportant or when the recipient of an action should logically receive the emphasis.

Grits <u>are eaten</u> throughout the South. (Passive voice emphasizes the fact that grits are eaten, not who eats them.)

DDT <u>was found</u> in soil samples. (Passive voice emphasizes the discovery of DDT; who found it is not important.)

A study <u>was conducted</u> by the Department of Health and Human Services to determine the seriousness of the problem. (Passive voice emphasizes the study; the government agency is less important than the study it conducted.)

---

(1) Changing Verbs from Passive to Active Voice

You can change a verb from passive to active voice by making the subject of the passive verb the object of the active verb. The person or thing performing the action then becomes the subject of the new sentence.

Passive: The novel *Frankenstein* <u>was written</u> by Mary Shelley.

Active: Mary Shelley <u>wrote</u> the novel *Frankenstein.*

If a passive verb has no object, you must supply one that will become the subject of the active verb.

Passive: Baby elephants are taught to avoid humans. (By whom are baby elephants taught?)

Active: <u>Adult elephants</u> teach baby elephants to avoid humans.

(2) Changing Verbs from Active to Passive Voice

You can change a verb from active to passive voice by making the object of the active verb the subject of the passive verb. The person or thing performing the action then becomes the object of the passive verb.

Active: Sir James Murray <u>compiled</u> *The Oxford English Dictionary.*

Passive: *The Oxford English Dictionary* <u>was compiled</u> by Sir James Murray.

If an active verb has no object, you must supply one. This object will become the subject of the passive sentence.

Active: Jacques Cousteau invented.
         Cousteau invented ____?____ .

Passive: ___?___ was invented by Jacques Cousteau.

         The scuba was invented by Jacques Cousteau.

CHAPTER 34

Using Nouns and Pronouns

34a Understanding Case

Case is the form a noun or pronoun takes to indicate its function in a sentence. Nouns change form only in the possessive case: the *cat's* eyes, *Molly's* book. Pronouns, however, have three cases: *subjective*, *objective*, and *possessive*.

			Pronoun Case Forms			
Subjective						
I	he, she	it	we	you	they	who
						whoever
Objective						
me	him, her	it	us	you	them	whom
						whomever
Possessive						
my	his, her	its	our	your	their	whose
mine	hers		ours	yours	theirs	

(1) Subjective Case

A pronoun takes the **subjective case** in the following situations.

> **Subject of a Verb:** <u>I</u> bought a new mountain bike.

> **Subject Complement:** It was <u>he</u> who volunteered to drive.

(2) Objective Case

A pronoun takes the **objective case** in the following situations.

> **Direct Object:** Our supervisor asked Adam and <u>me</u> to work on the project.

> **Indirect Object:** The plumber's bill gave <u>him</u> quite a shock.

> **Object of a Preposition:** Between <u>us</u>, we own ten shares of stock.

Close-up: Pronoun Case in Compound Constructions   FAQs links

I is not necessarily more appropriate than *me*. In compound constructions such as the following, *me* is correct.

Just between you and <u>me</u> [not *I*], I think we're going to have a quiz. (*Me* is the object of the preposition *between*.)

---

(3) Possessive Case

See
A3

A pronoun takes the **possessive case** when it indicates ownership (*our* car, *your* book). The possessive case is also used before a **gerund**.

> Napoleon gave <u>his</u> approval to <u>their</u> ruling Naples. (*His* indicates ownership; *ruling* is a gerund.)

34b Determining Pronoun Case in Special Situations

(1) Comparisons with *Than* or *As*

When a comparison ends with a pronoun, the pronoun's function in the sentence determines your choice of pronoun case. If the pronoun functions as a subject, use the subjective case; if it functions as an object, use the objective case. You can determine the function of the pronoun by completing the comparison.

> Darcy likes John more than <u>I</u>. (*I* is the subject: *more than I like John.*)

> Darcy likes John more than <u>me</u>. (*Me* is the object: *more than she likes me.*)

(2) *Who* and *Whom*

The case of the pronouns *who* and *whom* depends on their function *within their own clause*. When a pronoun serves as the subject of its clause, use *who* or *whoever*; when it functions as an object, use *whom* or *whomever*.

> The Salvation Army gives food and shelter to <u>whoever</u> is in need. (*Whoever* is the subject of the dependent clause *whoever is in need.*)

> I wonder <u>whom</u> jazz musician Miles Davis influenced. (*Whom* is the object of *influenced* in the dependent clause *whom jazz musician Miles Davis influenced.*)

Close-up: Pronoun Case in Questions

To determine whether to use subjective case (*who*) or objective case (*whom*) in a question, use a personal pronoun to answer the question. If the personal pronoun is the subject, use *who*; if the personal pronoun is the object, use *whom*.

> <u>Who</u> wrote *The Age of Innocence*? <u>She</u> wrote it. (subject)

> <u>Whom</u> do you support for mayor? I support <u>her</u>. (object)

---

(3) Appositives

An <u>appositive</u> is a noun or noun phrase that identifies or renames an adjacent noun or pronoun. The case of a pronoun in an appositive depends on the function of the word the appositive identifies or renames.

ESL
55c4

> We heard two Motown recording artists, Smokey Robinson and <u>him</u>. (*Artists* is the object of the verb *heard*, so the pronoun in the appositive *Smokey Robinson and him* takes the objective case.)

> Two Motown recording artists, <u>he</u> and Smokey Robinson, had contracts with Motown Records. (*Artists* is the subject of the sentence, so the pronoun in the appositive *he and Smokey Robinson* takes the subjective case.)

(4) *We* and *Us* before a Noun

When a first-person plural pronoun directly precedes a noun, the case of the pronoun depends on how the noun functions in the sentence.

> <u>We</u> women must stick together. (*Women* is the subject of the sentence, so the pronoun *we* must be in the subjective case.)

> Teachers make learning easy for <u>us</u> students. (*Students* is the object of the preposition *for*, so the pronoun *us* must be in the objective case.)

34c   Revising Pronoun Reference Errors

An **antecedent** is the word or word group to which a pronoun refers. The connection between a pronoun and its antecedent should always be clear. If the **pronoun reference** is not clear, you will need to revise the sentence.

ESL
55c1

(1) Ambiguous Antecedent

Sometimes it is not clear to which antecedent a pronoun—for example, *this, that, which,* or *it*—refers. In such cases, eliminate the ambiguity by substituting a noun for the pronoun.

> The accountant took out his calculator and completed the tax return. Then, he put ~~it~~ the calculator into his briefcase. (The pronoun *it* can refer either to *calculator* or to *tax return*.)

(2) Remote Antecedent

If a pronoun is far from its antecedent, readers will have difficulty making a connection between them. To eliminate this problem, replace the pronoun with a noun.

During the mid-1800s, many Czechs began to immigrate to America. By 1860, about 23,000 Czechs had left their country; by 1900, 13,000 Czech immigrants were coming to ~~its~~ *America's* shores each year.

(3) Nonexistent Antecedent

Sometimes a pronoun—for example, *this*—refers to an antecedent that does not exist. In such cases, add a word that identifies the unstated antecedent.

Some one-celled organisms contain chlorophyll yet are considered animals. This *paradox* illustrates the difficulty of classifying single-celled organisms. (Exactly what does *this* refer to?)

NOTE: Colloquial expressions such as "*It* says in the paper" and "*He* said on the news," which refer to unidentified antecedents, are not acceptable in college writing. Substitute an appropriate noun for the unclear pronoun: "The *article* in the paper says . . ." and "In his commentary, *Ted Koppel* observes. . . ."

(4) *Who, Which*, and *That*

In general, *who* refers to people or to animals that have names. *Which* and *that* refer to things or to unnamed animals. When referring to an antecedent, be sure to choose the appropriate pronoun (*who, which*, or *that*).

David Henry Hwang, <u>who</u> wrote the Tony Award-winning play *M. Butterfly*, also wrote *Family Devotions* and *FOB*.

The spotted owl, <u>which</u> lives in old growth forests, is in danger of extinction.

Houses <u>that</u> are built today are usually more energy efficient than those built thirty years ago.

Never use *that* to refer to a person.

The man ~~that~~ *who* holds the world record for eating hot dogs is my neighbor.

NOTE: Be sure to use *which* in nonrestrictive clauses, which are always set off with commas. In most cases, use *that* in restrictive clauses, which are not set off with commas. *Who* may be used in both restrictive clauses and nonrestrictive clauses.

See
44d1

CHAPTER 35

Using Adjectives and Adverbs

Adjectives modify nouns and pronouns. **Adverbs** modify verbs, adjectives, or other adverbs—or entire phrases, clauses, or sentences.

The function of a word, not its form, determines whether it is an adjective or an adverb. Although many adverbs (such as *immediately* and *hopelessly*) end in *-ly*, others (such as *almost* and *very*) do not. Moreover, some words that end in *-ly* (such as *lively*) are adjectives.

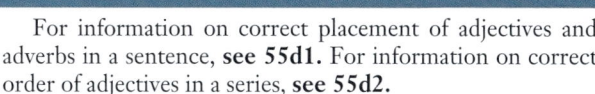

ESL Tip

For information on correct placement of adjectives and adverbs in a sentence, **see 55d1.** For information on correct order of adjectives in a series, **see 55d2.**

35a Using Adjectives

Be sure to use an adjective, not an adverb, as a subject complement. A **subject complement** is a word that follows a linking verb and modifies the sentence's subject, not its verb. A **linking verb** does not show physical or emotional action. *Seem, appear, believe, become, grow, turn, remain, prove, look, sound, smell, taste, feel,* and the forms of the verb *be* are or can be used as linking verbs.

> Michelle seemed <u>brave</u>. (*Seemed* shows no action and is therefore a linking verb. Because *brave* is a subject complement that modifies the noun *Michelle,* it takes the adjective form.)

> Michelle smiled <u>bravely</u>. (*Smiled* shows action, so it is not a linking verb. *Bravely* modifies *smiled,* so it takes the adverb form.)

NOTE: Sometimes the same verb can function as either a linking verb or an action verb: He remained <u>stubborn</u>. (He was still stubborn.) He remained <u>stubbornly</u>. (He remained, in a stubborn manner.)

35b Using Adverbs

Be sure to use an **adverb**, not an adjective, to modify verbs, adjectives, or other adverbs—or entire phrases, clauses, or sentences.

Most students did _∧~~great~~ *very well* on the midterm.

My friends dress a lot more conservative_∧*ly* than I do.

411

See
B2

> **Close-up: Using Adjectives and Adverbs**
>
> In informal speech, adjective forms such as *good, bad, sure, real, slow, quick,* and *loud* are often used to modify verbs, adjectives, and adverbs. Avoid these informal modifiers in college writing.
>
> The program ran ~~real good~~ *really well* the first time we tried it, but the new system performed ~~bad~~ *badly*.

35c Using Comparative and Superlative Forms

Most adjectives and adverbs have **comparative** and **superlative** forms that can be used with nouns to indicate degree.

	Comparative and Superlative Forms	
Form	**Function**	**Example**
Positive	Describes a quality; indicates no comparisons	big
Comparative	Indicates comparisons between *two* qualities (greater or lesser)	bigger
Superlative	Indicates comparisons among *three or more* qualities (greatest or least)	biggest

(1) Regular Comparative Forms

To form the comparative, all one-syllable adjectives and many two-syllable adjectives (particularly those that end in *-y, -ly, -le, -er,* and *-ow*) add *-er:* slow<u>er</u>, funni<u>er</u>. (Note that a final *y* becomes *i* before *-er* is added.)

Other two-syllable adjectives and all long adjectives form the comparative with *more:* <u>more</u> famous, <u>more</u> incredible.

Adverbs ending in *-ly* also form the comparative with *more:* <u>more</u> slowly. Other adverbs use the *-er* ending to form the comparative: soon<u>er</u>.

All adjectives and adverbs indicate a lesser degree with *less:* <u>less</u> lovely, <u>less</u> slowly.

(2) Regular Superlative Forms

Adjectives that form the comparative with *-er* add *-est* to form the superlative: nic<u>est</u>, funni<u>est</u>. Adjectives that indicate the comparative with *more* use *most* to indicate the superlative: <u>most</u> famous, <u>most</u> challenging.

The majority of adverbs use *most* to indicate the superlative: <u>most</u> quickly. Others use the *-est* ending: soon<u>est</u>.

All adjectives and adverbs use *least* to indicate the least degree: <u>least</u> interesting, <u>least</u> willingly.

Close-up: Using Comparatives and Superlatives

- Never use both *more* and *-er* to form the comparative or both *most* and *-est* to form the superlative.

  Nothing could have been ~~more~~ easier.
  Jack is the ~~most~~ meanest person in town.

- Never use the superlative when comparing only two things.

  older
  Stacy is the ∧~~oldest~~ of the two sisters.

- Never use the comparative when comparing more than two things.

  earliest
  We chose the ∧~~earlier~~ of the four appointments.

---

(3) Irregular Comparatives and Superlatives

Some adjectives and adverbs have irregular comparative and superlative forms. Instead of adding a word or an ending to the positive form, they use different words to indicate the comparative and the superlative.

Irregular Comparatives and Superlatives

	Positive	Comparative	Superlative
Adjectives:	good	better	best
	bad	worse	worst
	a little	less	least
	many, some, much	more	most
Adverbs:	well	better	best
	badly	worse	worst

35d Avoiding Illogical Comparatives and Superlatives

Many adjectives can logically exist only in the positive degree. For example, words like *perfect, unique, excellent, impossible, parallel, empty,* and *dead* cannot have comparative or superlative forms.

I read ~~the most~~ ^an^ excellent story.

The vase in her collection was ~~very~~ unique.

These words can, however, be modified by words that suggest approaching the absolute state—*nearly* or *almost*, for example.

He revised until his draft was <u>almost perfect</u>.

NOTE: Some adverbs, particularly those indicating time, place, and degree (*almost, very, here, yesterday, immediately*), do not have comparative or superlative forms.

PART 9

Improving Sentence Style

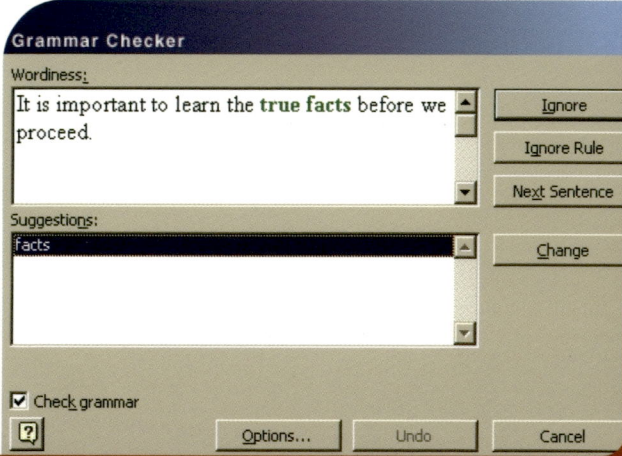

PART 9

Improving Sentence Style

CHAPTER 36

Writing Varied Sentences

Varying the way you construct your sentences can make your writing lively and interesting. This strategy can also help you emphasize the most important ideas in your sentences.

36a Using Compound, Complex, and Compound-Complex Sentences

Paragraphs that mix simple, compound, and complex sentences are more varied—and therefore more interesting—than those that do not.

(1) Compound Sentences

A **compound sentence** consists of two or more independent clauses joined with *coordinating conjunctions, transitional words and phrases, correlative conjunctions, semicolons,* or *colons.*

Coordinating Conjunctions

The pianist made some mistakes, <u>but</u> the concert was a success.

NOTE: Use a comma before a coordinating conjunction—*and, or, nor, but, for, so,* and *yet*—that joins two <u>independent clauses</u>.

See 44a

Transitional Words and Phrases

Exercise can help lower blood pressure; <u>however</u>, those with high blood pressure should still limit salt intake.

The saxophone does not belong to the brass family; <u>in fact</u>, it is a member of the woodwind family.

NOTE: Use a semicolon—not a comma—before a transitional word or phrase that joins two independent clauses. Frequently used <u>transitional words and phrases</u> include conjunctive adverbs like *consequently, finally, still,* and *thus* as well as expressions like *for example, in fact,* and *for instance.*

See 7b2

Correlative Conjunctions

Diana <u>not only</u> passed the exam, <u>but</u> she <u>also</u> received the highest grade in the class.

<u>Either</u> he left his coat in his locker, <u>or</u> he left it on the bus.

Semicolons

Alaska is the largest state; Rhode Island is the smallest.

Colons

He got his orders: he was to leave for Iraq on Sunday.

(2) Complex Sentences

A **complex sentence** consists of one independent clause and at least one dependent clause. A **subordinating conjunction** or **relative pronoun** links the independent and dependent clauses and indicates the relationship between them.

(dependent clause)   (independent clause)
[After the town was evacuated], [the hurricane began].

(independent clause)   (dependent clause)
[Officials watched the storm] [that threatened the town].

Sometimes a dependent clause may be embedded within an independent clause.

(dependent clause)
Town officials, [who were very concerned], watched the storm.

Frequently Used Subordinating Conjunctions

after	before	until
although	if	when
as	once	whenever
as if	since	where
as though	that	wherever
because	unless	while

Relative Pronouns

that	whatever	who (whose, whom)
what	which	whoever (whomever)

---

(3) Compound-Complex Sentences

A **compound-complex sentence** consists of two or more independent clauses and at least one dependent clause.

(dependent clause)
[When small foreign imports began dominating the US
(independent clause)
automobile industry], [consumers were very responsive], but
(independent clause)
[American autoworkers were concerned].

36b   Combining Choppy Simple Sentences

Strings of short simple sentences can be tedious—and sometimes hard to follow, as the following paragraph illustrates.

> John Peter Zenger was a newspaper editor. He waged and won an important battle for freedom of the press in America. He criticized the policies of the British governor. He was charged with criminal libel as a result. Zenger's lawyers were disbarred by the governor. Andrew Hamilton defended him. Hamilton convinced the jury that Zenger's criticisms were true. Therefore, the statements were not libelous.

You can revise choppy sentences like these by using *coordination*, *subordination*, or *embedding* to combine them with adjacent sentences.

(1) Using Coordination

Coordination pairs similar elements—words, phrases, or clauses—giving equal weight to each.

> John Peter Zenger was a newspaper editor. He waged and won an important battle for freedom of the press in America. <u>He criticized the policies of the British governor, and he was charged with criminal libel as a result.</u> Zenger's lawyers were disbarred by the governor. Andrew Hamilton defended him. Hamilton convinced the jury that Zenger's criticisms were true. Therefore, the statements were not libelous.

Two choppy sentences linked with and, *creating a compound sentence*

ESL Tip

   Some ESL students rely on simple sentences and coordination in their writing because they are afraid of making sentence structure errors. The result is a monotonous style. To add variety, try using **subordination** and **embedding** (explained below) in your sentences.

---

(2) Using Subordination

Subordination places the more important idea in an independent clause and the less important idea in a dependent clause.

> <u>John Peter Zenger was a newspaper editor who waged and won an important battle for freedom of the press in America.</u> He criticized the policies of the British governor, and he was charged with criminal libel as a result. <u>When Zenger's lawyers were disbarred by the governor, Andrew Hamilton defended him,</u> Hamilton convinced the jury that Zenger's criticisms were true. Therefore, the statements were not libelous.

Complex sentence

Complex sentence

(3) Using Embedding

Embedding is the working of additional words and phrases into sentences.

The sentence Hamilton convinced the jury. . . . becomes the phrase convincing the jury   John Peter Zenger was a newspaper editor who waged and won an important battle for freedom of the press in America. He criticized the policies of the British governor, and he was charged with criminal libel as a result. <u>When Zenger's lawyers were disbarred by the governor, Andrew Hamilton defended him, convincing the jury that Zenger's criticisms were true.</u> Therefore, the statements were not libelous.

This final revision of the original paragraph's choppy sentences is interesting and readable because it is composed of varied and logically linked sentences. The final short, simple sentence has been retained for emphasis.

36c Breaking Up Strings of Compound Sentences

When you write, try to avoid creating an unbroken series of compound sentences. A string of compound sentences can be extremely monotonous; moreover, if you connect clauses only with coordinating conjunctions, you may find it difficult to indicate exactly how ideas are related and which idea is most important.

All Compound Sentences: A volcano that is erupting is considered *active*, but one that may erupt is designated *dormant*, and one that has not erupted for a long time is called *extinct*. Most active volcanoes are located in "The Ring of Fire," a belt that circles the Pacific Ocean, and they can be extremely destructive. Italy's Vesuvius erupted in AD 79, and it destroyed the town of Pompeii. In 1883, Krakatoa, located between the Indonesian islands of Java and Sumatra, erupted, and it caused a tidal wave, and more than 36,000 people were killed. Martinique's Mont Pelée erupted in 1902, and its hot gas and ash killed 30,000 people, and this completely wiped out the town of St. Pierre.

Varied Sentences: A volcano that is erupting is considered *active*. (**simple sentence**) One that may erupt is designated *dormant*, and one that has not erupted for a long time is called *extinct*. (**compound sentence**) Most active volcanoes are located in "The Ring of Fire," a belt that circles the Pacific Ocean. (**simple sentence with modifier**) Active volcanoes can be extremely destructive. (**simple sentence**) Erupting in AD 79, Italy's Vesuvius destroyed the town of Pompeii. (**simple sentence with modifier**) When Krakatoa, located between the Indonesian islands of Java and Sumatra, erupted in 1883, it caused a tidal wave

that killed 36,000 people. (**complex sentence with modifier**)
The eruption of Martinique's Mont Pelée in 1902 produced hot gas and ash that killed 30,000 people, completely wiping out the town of St. Pierre. (**complex sentence with modifier**)

36d   Varying Sentence Openings

Rather than beginning every sentence with the subject (*I* or *It*, for example), try beginning with a modifying *word*, *phrase*, or *clause*.

Words

<u>Proud</u> and <u>relieved</u>, they watched their daughter receive her diploma. (adjectives)

<u>Hungrily</u>, he devoured his lunch. (adverb)

Phrases

<u>For better or worse</u>, credit cards are now widely available to college students. (prepositional phrase)

<u>Located on the west coast of Great Britain</u>, Wales is part of the United Kingdom. (participial phrase)

<u>His interest widening</u>, Picasso designed ballet sets and illustrated books. (absolute phrase)

Clauses

<u>After Woodrow Wilson was incapacitated by a stroke</u>, his wife unofficially performed many presidential duties. (adverb clause)

Grammar Checker: Coordinating Conjunctions and Fragments

If you begin a sentence with a coordinating conjunction, use your grammar checker to make sure that it is a complete sentence and not a **fragment**.

See Ch. 28

Spelling and Grammar: English (U.S.)	? X
Fragment:	
And then the speaker.	Ignore
	Ignore Rule
	Next Sentence
Suggestions:	
Fragment (consider revising)	Change

CHAPTER 37

Writing Emphatic Sentences

In speaking, we emphasize certain ideas and deemphasize others with intonation and gestures; in writing, we convey **emphasis**—the relative importance of ideas—through the selection and arrangement of words.

37a Conveying Emphasis through Word Order

Because readers tend to focus on the beginning and end of a sentence, you should place the most important information there.

(1) Beginning with Important Ideas

Placing key ideas at the beginning of a sentence stresses their importance. The unedited version of the following sentence emphasizes the study, not those who conducted it or those who participated in it. Editing shifts this focus and puts the emphasis on the researcher, not on the study.

~~In a landmark study of alcoholism,~~ Dr. George Vaillant of Harvard followed *, in a landmark study of alcoholism,* two hundred Harvard graduates and four hundred inner-city, working-class men from the Boston area.

Situations that demand a straightforward presentation—laboratory reports, memos, technical papers, business correspondence, and the like—call for sentences that present vital information first and qualifiers later.

Treating cancer with interferon has been the subject of a good deal of research. (emphasizes the treatment, not the research)

Dividends will be paid if the stockholders agree. (emphasizes the dividends, not the stockholders)

Close-up: Writing Emphatic Sentences

Placing an empty phrase like *there is* or *there are* at the beginning of a sentence generally weakens the sentence.

MIT places
~~There is~~ heavy emphasis ~~placed~~ on the development of computational skills ~~at MIT.~~

(2) Ending with Important Ideas

Placing key elements at the end of a sentence is another way to convey their importance.

Using a Colon or a Dash   A colon or a dash can emphasize an important word or phrase by isolating it at the end of a sentence.

> Beth had always dreamed of owning one special car: a 1953 Corvette.

> The elderly need a good deal of special attention—and they deserve that attention.

Close-up: Placing Transitional Expressions

When they are placed at the end of a sentence, conjunctive adverbs or other transitional expressions lose their power to indicate the relationship between ideas. Placed earlier in the sentence, **transitional words and phrases** can link ideas and add emphasis.

See
7b2

Smokers do have rights; *however,* they should not try to impose their habit on others, ~~however.~~

Using Climactic Word Order   **Climactic word order,** the arrangement of a series of items from the least to the most important, places emphasis on the last item in the series.

> Binge drinking can lead to vandalism, car accidents, and even death. (*Death* is the most serious consequence.)

(3) Experimenting with Word Order

ESL
55f

In English sentences, the most common **word order** is subject-verb-object (or subject-verb-complement). When you depart from this expected word order, you call attention to the word, phrase, or clause you have relocated.

> More modest and less inventive than Turner's paintings are John Constable's landscapes.

Here the writer calls special attention to the modifying phrase *more modest and less inventive than Turner's paintings* by inverting word order, placing the complement and the verb before the subject.

37b   Conveying Emphasis through Sentence Structure

As you write, try to construct sentences that emphasize more important ideas and deemphasize less important ones.

(1) Using Cumulative Sentences

A **cumulative sentence** begins with an independent clause, followed by the additional words, phrases, or clauses that expand or develop it.

> She holds me in strong arms, arms that have chopped cotton, dismembered trees, scattered corn for chickens, cradled infants, shaken the daylights out of half-grown upstart teenagers. (Rebecca Hill, *Blue Rise*)

Because it presents its main idea first, a cumulative sentence tends to be clear and straightforward. (Most English sentences are cumulative.)

(2) Using Periodic Sentences

A **periodic sentence** moves from supporting details, expressed in modifying phrases and dependent clauses, to the sentence's key idea, which is placed in the independent clause at the end of the sentence.

> Unlike World Wars I and II, which ended decisively with the unconditional surrender of US enemies, the war in Vietnam did not end when American troops withdrew.

NOTE: In some periodic sentences, the modifying phrase or dependent clause comes between subject and the predicate: Columbus, after several discouraging and unsuccessful voyages, finally reached America.

37c Conveying Emphasis through Parallelism and Balance

See 39a
Parallelism can help you emphasize information by reinforcing the similarity between grammatical elements.

> We seek an individual who is a self-starter, who owns a late-model automobile, and who is willing to work evenings. (classified advertisement)

> Do not pass go; do not collect $200. (instructions)

> The Faust legend is central in Benét's *The Devil and Daniel Webster*, in Goethe's *Faust*, and in Marlowe's *Dr. Faustus*. (exam answer)

A **balanced sentence** is neatly divided between two parallel structures—for example, two independent clauses in a compound sentence. The symmetrical structure of a balanced sentence adds emphasis by highlighting similarities or differences between the ideas in the two clauses.

In the 1950s, the electronic miracle was the television, but in the 1980s, the electronic miracle was the computer.

Alive, the elephant was worth at least a hundred pounds; dead, he would only be worth the value of his tusks, five pounds, possibly. (George Orwell, "Shooting an Elephant")

37d Conveying Emphasis through Repetition

<u>Unnecessary repetition</u> makes sentences dull and monotonous as well as wordy.

> He had a good arm and <u>also</u> could field well, and he was <u>also</u> a fast runner.

Effective repetition, however, can emphasize key words or ideas.

> They decided to begin again: <u>to begin</u> hoping, <u>to begin</u> trying to change, <u>to begin</u> working toward a goal.

> During those years when I was just learning to speak, my mother and father addressed me only <u>in Spanish;</u> <u>in Spanish</u> I learned to reply. (Richard Rodriguez, *Aria: A Memoir of a Bilingual Childhood*)

37e Conveying Emphasis through Active Voice

The <u>active voice</u> is generally more emphatic than the <u>passive voice</u>.

> **Passive:** The prediction that oil prices will rise is being made by economists.

> **Active:** Economists are predicting that oil prices will rise.

Notice that the passive voice focuses readers' attention on the action or on its recipient rather than on who is performing it. The recipient of the action is the subject of a passive sentence, so the actor fades into the background (*by economists*) or is omitted entirely (*the prediction . . . is being made*). The active voice, however, places the emphasis where it belongs: on the actor or actors (*Economists*).

Sometimes, of course, you *want* to stress the action rather than the actor, so you intentionally use the passive voice.

> **Passive:** The West was explored by Lewis and Clark. (stresses the exploration of the West, not who explored it)

> **Active:** Lewis and Clark explored the West. (stresses the contribution of the explorers)

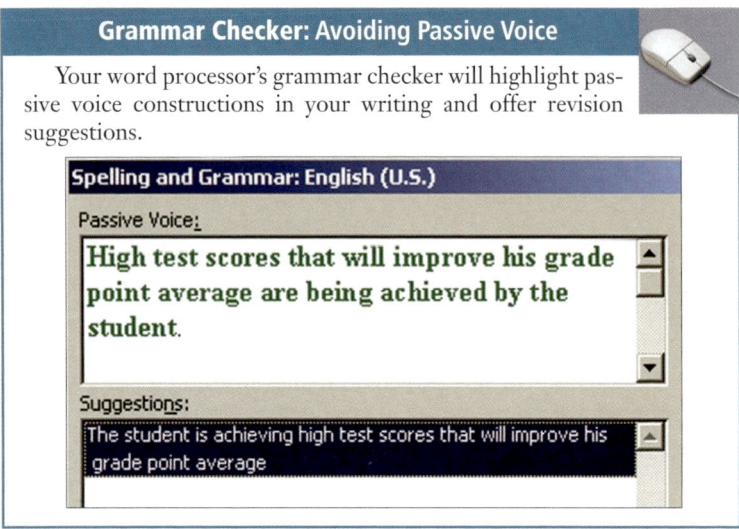

Grammar Checker: Avoiding Passive Voice

Your word processor's grammar checker will highlight passive voice constructions in your writing and offer revision suggestions.

Spelling and Grammar: English (U.S.)

Passive Voice:

> **High test scores that will improve his grade point average are being achieved by the student.**

Suggestions:

> The student is achieving high test scores that will improve his grade point average

NOTE: Passive voice is also used when the identity of the person performing the action is irrelevant or unknown (*The course was canceled*). For this reason, the passive voice is frequently used in scientific and technical writing: *The beaker was filled with a saline solution.*

Grammar Checker: Using Passive Voice

Sometimes the clearest way to express your ideas is by using passive verbs. For example, the use of passive voice in the sentence below is necessary for clarity. The grammar checker's suggestion is awkward—and incorrect.

Spelling and Grammar: English (U.S.)

Passive Voice:

> **The spreadsheet is sorted by number.**

Suggestions:

> Number sorts the spreadsheet

CHAPTER 38

Writing Concise Sentences

A sentence is not concise simply because it is short; a **concise** sentence contains only the words necessary to make its point.

38a Eliminating Nonessential Words

A good way to find out which words are essential in a sentence is to underline the key words. Look carefully at the remaining words so you can see which are unnecessary and then eliminate wordiness by deleting them.

> It seems to me that it does not make sense to allow any <u>bail</u> to be <u>granted</u> to <u>anyone</u> who has ever been <u>convicted</u> of a <u>violent</u> <u>crime</u>.

The underlining shows you immediately that none of the words in the long introductory phrase are essential. The following revision includes just the words necessary to convey the key ideas:

> Bail should not be granted to anyone who has ever been convicted of a violent crime.

Whenever possible, delete nonessential words—*deadwood*, *utility words*, and *circumlocution*—from your writing.

(1) Eliminating Deadwood

The term **deadwood** refers to unnecessary phrases that take up space and add nothing to meaning.

> *Many*
> ~~There were many~~ ∧factors ~~that~~ influenced his decision to become a priest.

> The two plots are ~~both~~ similar in ~~the way~~ that they trace the characters' increasing rage.

> Shoppers ~~who are~~ looking for bargains often go to outlets.

> *an exhausting*
> They played ∧a racquetball game ~~that was exhausting~~.

> *This*
> ~~In this~~ ∧article ~~it~~ discusses lead poisoning.

> *is*
> The most tragic character in *Hamlet* ∧~~would have to be~~ Ophelia.

427

Deadwood also includes unnecessary statements of opinion, such as *I feel*, *it seems to me*, and *in my opinion*.

~~I think the~~ *The* characters seem undeveloped.

~~As far as I'm concerned, this~~ *This* course looks interesting.

(2) Eliminating Utility Words

Utility words act as filler and contribute nothing to the meaning of a sentence. Utility words include nouns with imprecise meanings (*factor, situation, type, aspect*, and so on); adjectives so general that they are almost meaningless (*good, bad, important*); and common adverbs denoting degree (*basically, actually, quite, very, definitely*). Often you can just delete the utility word; if you cannot, replace it with a more precise word.

~~The registration situation~~ *Registration* was disorganized.

The scholarship ~~basically~~ offered Fran *an* ~~a good~~ opportunity to study Spanish.

It was ~~actually~~ a worthwhile book, but I didn't ~~completely~~ finish it.

(3) Avoiding Circumlocution

Circumlocution is taking a roundabout way to say something (using ten words when five will do). Instead of complicated constructions, use concise, specific words and phrases that come right to the point.

~~It is not unlikely that the~~ *The* trend toward lower consumer spending will *probably* continue.

Joe was in the army *while* ~~during the same time that~~ I was in college.

Close-up: Revising Wordy Phrases	

A wordy phrase can almost always be replaced by a more concise, more direct term.

Wordy	Concise
at the present time	now
at this point in time	now
for the purpose of	for
due to the fact that	because
on account of the fact that	because
until such time as	until

Wordy	Concise
in the event that	if
by means of	by
in the vicinity of	near
have the ability to	be able to

38b Eliminating Unnecessary Repetition

Repetition can make your writing more <u>emphatic</u>, but unnecessary repetition and **redundant** word groups (repeated words or phrases that say the same thing, such as *free gift* and *unanticipated surprise*) can obscure your meaning. Correct unnecessary repetition by using one of the following strategies.

See 37d

(1) Deleting Redundancy

People's clothing ~~attire~~ can reveal a good deal about their personalities.

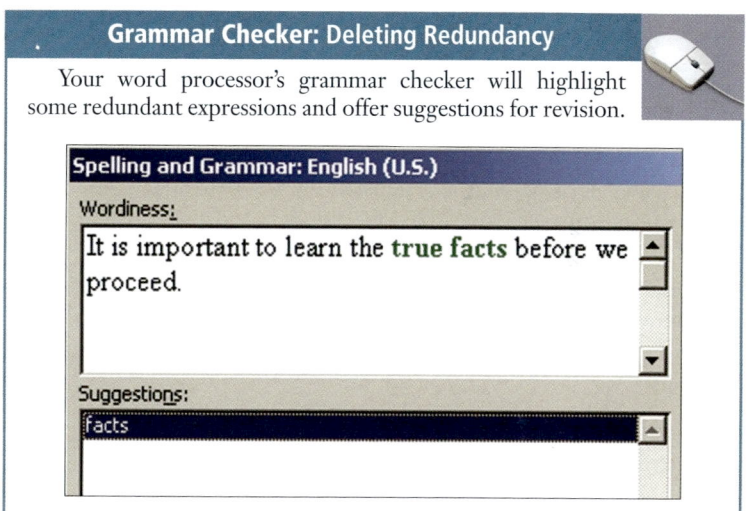

Grammar Checker: Deleting Redundancy

Your word processor's grammar checker will highlight some redundant expressions and offer suggestions for revision.

Spelling and Grammar: English (U.S.)

Wordiness:

It is important to learn the **true facts** before we proceed.

Suggestions:

facts

(2) Substituting a Pronoun

Fictional detective Miss Marple has solved many crimes. *The Murder at the Vicarage* was one of ~~Miss Marple's~~ her most challenging cases.

(3) Creating an Appositive

Red Barber, ~~was~~ a sportscaster. He was known for his colorful expressions.

(4) Creating a Compound

John F. Kennedy was the youngest man ever elected president,
and
,He was the first Catholic to hold this office.

(5) Creating a Complex Sentence

, which
Americans value freedom of speech,, ~~Freedom of speech~~ is guaranteed by the First Amendment.

38c Tightening Rambling Sentences

The combination of nonessential words, unnecessary repetition, and complicated syntax creates **rambling sentences.** Revising rambling sentences frequently requires extensive editing.

(1) Eliminating Excessive Coordination

When you string a series of clauses together with coordinating conjunctions, you create a rambling, unfocused compound sentence. To revise such sentences, first identify the main idea, and then subordinate supporting details to that main idea.

Wordy: Puerto Rico is a large island in the Caribbean, and it is very mountainous, and it has steep slopes, and they fall to gentle plains along the coast.

Concise: A large island in the Caribbean, Puerto Rico is very mountainous, with steep slopes falling to gentle plains along the coast. (Puerto Rico's mountainous terrain is the sentence's main idea.)

(2) Eliminating Adjective Clauses

A series of <u>adjective clauses</u> is also likely to produce a rambling sentence. To revise, substitute concise modifying words or phrases for adjective clauses.

Wordy: *Moby-Dick*, <u>which is a novel about a white whale</u>, was written by Herman Melville, <u>who was friendly with Nathaniel Hawthorne</u>, <u>who urged him to revise the first draft</u>.

Concise: *Moby-Dick*, a novel about a white whale, was written by Herman Melville, who revised the first draft at the urging of his friend Nathaniel Hawthorne.

(3) Eliminating Passive Constructions

Excessive use of the **passive voice** can create rambling sentences. Correct this problem by changing passive to active voice.

See 33d

ESL 55a6

~~Water rights are being fought for in court by~~ Indian tribes like

are fighting in court for water rights.

the Papago in Arizona and the Pyramid Lake Paiute in Nevada~~,~~⌃

(4) Eliminating Wordy Prepositional Phrases

When you revise, substitute adjectives or adverbs for wordy **prepositional phrases**.

See B3.1

dangerous   *exciting*

The trip was⌃~~one of danger~~ but also⌃~~one of excitement~~.

confidently   *authoritatively*

He spoke⌃~~in a confident manner~~ and⌃~~with a lot of authority~~.

(5) Eliminating Wordy Noun Constructions

Substitute strong verbs for wordy **noun phrases**.

See B3.1

decided

We have⌃~~made the decision~~ to postpone the meeting until ~~the~~

appear

~~appearance of~~ all the board members⌃.

CHAPTER 39

Using Parallelism

  Parallelism—the use of matching words, phrases, clauses, or sentence structures to express equivalent ideas—adds unity, balance, and force to your writing. Effective parallelism can help you write clearer sentences, but faulty parallelism can create awkward sentences that obscure your meaning and confuse readers.

39a Using Parallelism Effectively

 Parallelism highlights the correspondence between *items in a series*, *paired items*, and elements in *lists* and *outlines*.

(1) With Items in a Series

Eat, drink, and be merry.

Baby food consumption, toy production, and school construction are likely to decline as the US population ages.

Three factors influenced his decision to seek new employment: his desire to relocate, his need for greater responsibility, and his dissatisfaction with his current job.

NOTE: For information on punctuating items in a series, **see 44b** and **45b.**

(2) With Paired Items

The thank-you note was short but sweet.

Roosevelt represented the United States, and Churchill represented Great Britain.

Ask not what your country can do for you; ask what you can do for your country. (John F. Kennedy)

Paired elements linked by **correlative conjunctions** (such as *not only/but also, both/and, either/or, neither/nor,* and *whether/or*) should always be parallel.

The design team paid close attention not only to color but also to texture.

Either repeat physics or take calculus.

432

Parallelism also highlights the contrast between paired elements linked by *than* or *as*.

Richard Wright and James Baldwin chose <u>to live in Paris</u> rather than <u>to remain in the United States</u>.

Success is as much <u>a matter of hard work</u> as <u>a matter of luck</u>.

(3) In Lists and Outlines

Elements in a <u>list</u> should be parallel.

See
24c

The Irish potato famine had four major causes:
1. The establishment of the landlord-tenant system
2. The failure of the potato crop
3. The reluctance of England to offer adequate financial assistance
4. The passage of the Corn Laws

Elements in an <u>outline</u> should also be parallel.

See
12h

39b Revising Faulty Parallelism

Faulty parallelism occurs when elements that have the same function in a sentence are not presented in parallel terms.

Many people in developing countries suffer because the countries lack sufficient housing, sufficient food, and ~~their~~ *sufficient* health-care facilities ~~are also insufficient.~~

To correct faulty parallelism, match nouns with nouns, verbs with verbs, and phrases or clauses with similarly constructed phrases or clauses.

Popular exercises for men and women include yoga, weight ~~lifters~~ *lifting*, and jogging.

I look forward to hearing from you and to ~~have~~ *having* an opportunity to tell you more about myself.

<table>
<tr><td colspan="2">**Close-up: Repeating Key Words**</td></tr>
</table>

Although the use of similar grammatical structures may sometimes be enough to convey parallelism, sentences are often clearer if certain key words (for example, prepositions that introduce items in a series) are also parallel. In the following sentence,

(continued)

Repeating key words (continued)

repeating the preposition *by* makes it clear that *not* applies only to the first phrase.

Computerization has helped industry by not allowing labor
costs to skyrocket, ᵇʸ increasing the speed of production, and ᵇʸ improving efficiency.

Grammar Checker: Revising Faulty Parallelism

Grammar checkers are not very useful for identifying faulty parallelism. Although your grammar checker may highlight some nonparallel constructions, it may miss others.

PART 10

Using Words Effectively

Using Words Effectively
437–458

objection.
ex·cep′tion·a·ble.
exceptionable.
ex·cep′tion·a·bly
manner.
ex·cep′tion·al, *a*.
ception; out of t
uncommon;   ex
talent.

PART 10
Using Words Effectively

CHAPTER 40

Choosing Words

40a Choosing an Appropriate Level of Diction

Diction, which comes from the Latin word for *say,* refers to the choice and use of words. Different audiences and situations call for different levels of diction.

(1) Formal Diction

Formal diction is grammatically correct and uses words familiar to an educated audience. A writer who uses formal diction sometimes maintains emotional distance from the audience by using the impersonal *one* rather than the more personal *I* and *you.* In addition, the tone of the writing—as determined by word choice, sentence structure, and choice of subject—is dignified and objective.

> We learn to perceive in the sense that we learn to respond to things in particular ways because of the contingencies of which they are a part. We may perceive the sun, for example, simply because it is an extremely powerful stimulus, but it has been a permanent part of the environment of the species throughout its evolution, and more specific behavior with respect to it could have been selected by contingencies of survival (as it has been in many other species). (B. F. Skinner, *Beyond Freedom and Dignity*)

(2) Informal Diction

Informal diction is the language that people use in conversation and in personal letters and informal emails. You should use informal diction in your college writing only to reproduce speech or dialect or to give a paper a conversational tone.

> ### ESL Tip
>
> Some of the expressions you learn from other students or from television are too informal for use in college writing. When you hear new expressions, pay attention to the contexts in which they are used.

Colloquial Diction **Colloquial diction** is the language of everyday speech. Contractions—*isn't, I'm*—are typical colloquialisms, as are

clipped forms—for example, *phone* for *telephone* and *dorm* for *dormitory*. Other colloquialisms include placeholders like *kind of* and utility words like *nice* for *acceptable*, *funny* for *odd*, and *great* for almost anything. Colloquial English also includes expressions like *get across* for *communicate*, *come up with* for *find*, and *check out* for *investigate*.

Slang **Slang,** language that calls attention to itself, is used to establish or reinforce identity within a group—urban teenagers or rock musicians, for example. One characteristic of slang vocabulary is that it is usually relatively short-lived, coming into existence and fading out much more quickly than other words do. Because slang terms can emerge and disappear so quickly, no dictionary—even a dictionary of slang—can list all or even most of the slang terms currently in use. Some slang words, however, eventually lose their slang status and become accepted as part of the language.

Regionalisms **Regionalisms** are words, expressions, and idiomatic forms that are used in particular geographical areas but may not be understood by a general audience. In eastern Tennessee, for example, a paper bag is a *poke*, and empty soda bottles are *dope bottles*. And New Yorkers stand *on line* for a movie, whereas people in most other parts of the country stand *in line*.

Nonstandard Diction **Nonstandard diction** refers to words and expressions not generally considered a part of standard English—words like *ain't*, *nohow*, *anywheres*, *nowheres*, *hisself*, and *theirselves*.

No absolute rules distinguish standard from nonstandard usage. In fact, some linguists reject the idea of nonstandard usage altogether, arguing that this designation relegates both the language and those who use it to second-class status.

NOTE: Keep in mind that colloquial expressions, slang, regionalisms, and nonstandard diction are almost always inappropriate in your college writing.

Grammar Checker: Setting the Writing Style Level

Your word processor's grammar checker offers different writing style levels but defaults to the "standard" level. To increase your grammar checker's ability to detect awkward or incorrect constructions in your college writing, you can change the writing style level to Formal or Technical.

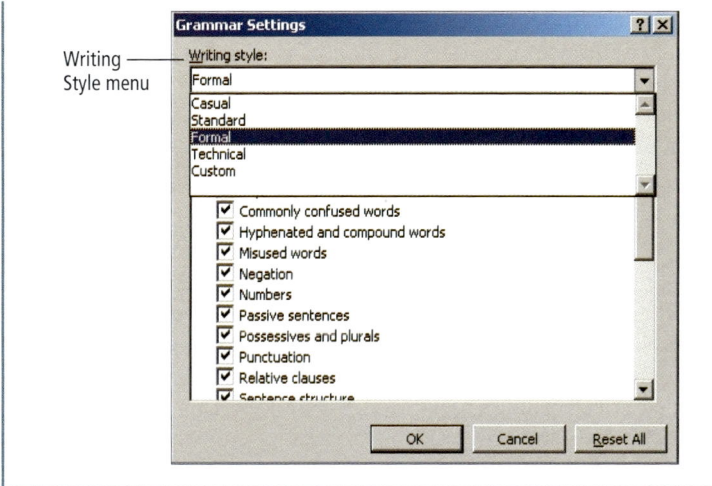

Writing Style menu

(3) College Writing

The level of diction appropriate for college writing depends on your assignment and your audience. A personal experience essay may require a somewhat informal style, but a research paper, an exam, or a report requires a more formal vocabulary and a more objective tone. In general, most college writing falls somewhere between formal and informal English, using a conversational tone but maintaining grammatical correctness and using a specialized vocabulary when the situation requires it. (This is the level of diction that is used in this book.)

http://kirsznermandell.wadsworth.com

Computer Tip: Diction and Electronic Communication

In email and instant messages, writers commonly use **emoticons**—typed characters, such as :-) or ;-), that indicate emotions or feelings—and **acronyms,** such as BTW (by the way) or LOL (laughing out loud). Although these typographical devices are common in informal electronic communication, they are inappropriate in formal electronic or print situations, such as academic essays or emails to professors or supervisors.

40b Choosing the Right Word

Choosing the right word to use in a particular context is important. If you use the wrong word—or even *almost* the right one—you run the risk of misrepresenting your ideas.

(1) Denotation and Connotation

A word's **denotation** is its basic dictionary meaning, what it stands for without any emotional associations. A word's **connotations** are the emotional, social, and political associations it has in addition to its denotative meaning.

Word	Denotation	Connotation
politician	someone who holds a political office	opportunist; wheeler-dealer

Selecting a word with the appropriate connotation isn't always easy. For example, words and expressions like *mentally ill, insane, neurotic, crazy, psychopathic,* and *emotionally disturbed,* although similar in meaning, have different emotional, social, and political connotations that affect people's responses. If you use terms without considering their connotations, you run the risk of confusing and possibly angering your readers.

ESL Tip

Dictionary entries sometimes give a word's connotations as well as its denotations. You can also figure out a word's connotations from the context in which the word appears.

---

(2) Euphemisms

A **euphemism** is a polite term used in place of a blunt or harsh term for something many people consider offensive or unpleasant. College writing is no place for euphemisms. Say what you mean—*pregnant,* not *expecting; died,* not *passed away;* and *strike,* not *work stoppage.*

(3) Specific and General Words

Specific words refer to particular persons, items, or events; **general** words denote entire classes or groups. For example, *Queen Elizabeth II* is more specific than *monarch, jeans* is more specific than *clothing,* and *SUV* is more specific than *vehicle.* You can use general words to describe entire classes of items, but you must use specific words to clarify such generalizations.

(4) Abstract and Concrete Words

Abstract words—*beauty, truth, justice,* and so on—refer to ideas, qualities, or conditions that cannot be perceived by the senses. **Concrete** words name things that readers can see, hear, taste, smell, or touch. As with general and specific words, whether a word is abstract or concrete is relative. The more concrete your words and phrases, the more vivid the image you evoke in the reader.

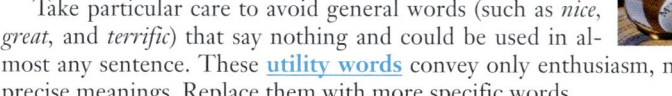

Close-up: Using Specific Words

Take particular care to avoid general words (such as *nice*, *great*, and *terrific*) that say nothing and could be used in almost any sentence. These <u>utility words</u> convey only enthusiasm, not precise meanings. Replace them with more specific words.

See 38a2

40c   Using Figures of Speech

Writers often use **figures of speech** (such as *similes* and *metaphors*) to go beyond the literal meanings of words. By doing so, they make their writing more vivid and more interesting.

Close-up: Commonly Used Figures of Speech

- A **simile** is a comparison between two essentially unlike things on the basis of a shared quality. A simile is introduced by *like* or *as*.

  Like travelers with exotic destinations on their minds, the graduates were remarkably forgetful. (Maya Angelou, *I Know Why the Caged Bird Sings*)

- A **metaphor** also compares two essentially dissimilar things, but instead of saying that one thing is *like* another, it *equates* them.

  Perhaps it is easy for those who have never felt the stings and darts of segregation to say, "Wait." (Martin Luther King Jr., "Letter from Birmingham Jail")

- An **analogy** explains an unfamiliar item or concept by comparing it to a more familiar one.

  According to Robert Frost, writing free verse is like playing tennis without a net.

- **Personification** gives an idea or inanimate object human attributes, feelings, or powers.

  Truth strikes us from behind, and in the dark, as well as from before in broad daylight. (Henry David Thoreau, *Journals*)

- **Hyperbole** (or overstatement) is intentional exaggeration for emphasis. For example, Jonathan Swift uses hyperbole in his essay "A Modest Proposal" when he suggests that eating Irish babies would help alleviate famine.

- **Understatement** intentionally downplays the seriousness of a situation or sentiment by saying less than is really meant.

  According to Mao Tse-tung, a revolution is not a tea party.

40d Avoiding Inappropriate Language

(1) Jargon

Jargon, the specialized or technical vocabulary of a trade, a profession, or an academic discipline, is useful for communicating in the field for which it was developed. Outside that field, however, it may be confusing. For example, business executives may want departments to *interface* effectively, and sociologists may identify the need for *perspectivistic thinking* to achieve organizational goals. If they are addressing other professionals in their respective fields, these terms can facilitate communication. If, however, they are addressing a general audience, such terms should be avoided.

(2) Neologisms

Neologisms are newly coined words that are not part of standard English. New situations call for new words, and frequently such words become a part of the language—*email, carjack,* and *outsource,* for example. Others, however, may never become part of standard English. For example, questionable neologisms are created when the suffix *-wise* is added to existing words—creating nonstandard words like *weatherwise, sportswise, timewise,* and *productwise*.

(3) Pretentious Diction

Good writing is clear and direct, not pompous or flowery. Revise to eliminate **pretentious diction,** inappropriately elevated and wordy language.

> As I fell ~~into slumber~~, I ~~cogitated~~ about my day ~~ambling~~ through ~~the splendor of~~ the Appalachian Mountains.
>
> *asleep*   *thought*   *hiking*

Close-up: Using Pretentious Diction

Frequently, pretentious diction is formal diction used in an informal situation. In such a context, it is always out of place. For every pretentious word, there is usually a clear, direct alternative.

Pretentious	Clear	Pretentious	Clear
ascertain	discover	reside	live
commence	start	terminate	end
implement	carry out	utilize	use
minuscule	small	individual	person

---

(4) Clichés

Figures of speech, such as metaphors and similes, stimulate thought by calling up vivid images in a reader's mind. When overused, however, figures of speech lose their power and become **clichés**—pat, meaningless phrases.

off the beaten path	a shot in the arm
free as a bird	smooth sailing
spread like wildfire	fit like a glove
Herculean efforts	fighting like cats and dogs

In your college writing, also avoid the temptation to use clichés. Take the time to think of original expressions that will give your writing the impact and appeal your ideas deserve.

ESL Tip

Many ESL students have learned a long list of English idioms. Some of these, however, have become clichés. Although becoming familiar with these idioms can help you understand them when you encounter them, university instructors discourage students from using clichés in their writing, preferring language that is more original and more precise.

40e Avoiding Offensive Language

Because the language we use not only expresses our ideas but also shapes our thinking, you should avoid using words that insult or degrade others.

(1) Stereotypes

Racial and Ethnic When referring to any racial, ethnic, or religious group, use words with neutral connotations or words that the group uses in *formal* speech or writing to refer to itself—for example, *African American*, *Native American*, *Asian*, or *Latino/Latina*.

Age Avoid potentially offensive labels relating to age. Many older people like to call themselves *senior citizens* or *seniors*, and these terms are commonly used by the media and the government.

Class Do not demean certain jobs because they are low paying or praise others because they have impressive titles. Similarly, do not use words—*hick*, *cracker*, *redneck*, or *trailer-park trash*, for example—that denigrate people based on their social class.

Sexual Orientation Use neutral terms (such as *gay* and *lesbian*). In addition, do not mention a person's sexual orientation unless it is relevant to your discussion.

(2) Sexist Language

Be careful to avoid **sexist language,** language that promotes gender stereotyping. Sexist language entails much more than the use of derogatory words, such as *hunk* and *chick*. Assuming that some professions are exclusive to one gender—for instance, that *nurse* denotes only women and that *doctor* denotes only men—is also sexist. So is the use of outdated job titles, such as *mailman* for *letter carrier, fireman* for *firefighter,* and *stewardess* for *flight attendant.*

Sexist language also occurs when a writer fails to apply the same terminology to both men and women. For example, refer to two scientists with PhDs not as Dr. Sagan and Mrs. Yallow, but as Dr. Sagan and Dr. Yallow. Refer to two writers as James and Wharton, or Henry James and Edith Wharton, not James and Mrs. Wharton.

In your writing, always use *women*—not *girls, gals,* or *ladies*—when referring to adult females. Use *Ms.* as the form of address when a woman's marital status is unknown or irrelevant. Finally, avoid using the generic *he* or *him* when your subject could be either male or female. Use the third-person plural (*they*) or the phrase *he or she* (not *he/she*) instead.

Sexist: Before boarding, each passenger should make certain that <u>he</u> has <u>his</u> ticket.

Revised: Before boarding, <u>passengers</u> should make certain that they have <u>their</u> tickets.

Revised: Before boarding, each <u>passenger</u> should make certain that <u>he or she</u> has a ticket.

NOTE: When trying to avoid sexist use of *he* and *him* in your writing, be careful not to use the plural pronoun *they* or *their* to refer to a singular antecedent.

Drivers
_∧~~Any driver~~ caught speeding should have their driving privileges suspended.

Close-up: Eliminating Sexist Language

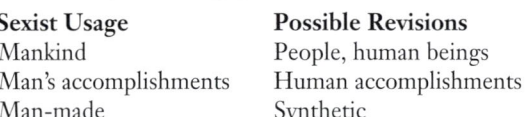

For every sexist usage, there is a nonsexist alternative.

Sexist Usage	Possible Revisions
Mankind	People, human beings
Man's accomplishments	Human accomplishments
Man-made	Synthetic
Female engineer/lawyer/ accountant, and so on; male model	Engineer/lawyer/accountant, and so on; model
Policeman/woman	Police officer
Salesman/woman/girl	Salesperson, clerk
Businessman/woman	Businessperson, executive
<u>Everyone</u> should complete <u>his</u> application by Tuesday.	<u>Everyone</u> should complete <u>his or her</u> application by Tuesday. <u>All students</u> should complete <u>their</u> applications by Tuesday.

CHAPTER 41

Using a Dictionary

Every writer should own a **desk dictionary**—such as *The American Heritage Dictionary, The Concise Oxford Dictionary, The Random House College Dictionary,* or *Webster's New World College Dictionary.*

To fit a lot of information into a small space, dictionaries use a system of symbols, abbreviations, and typefaces (see Figure 41.1). Consult the preface of your dictionary to determine how its system operates.

Entry word   Pronunciation guide   Usage labels

cou•ple (kŭp′əl), *n.* **1.** Two items of the same kind; a pair. **2.** Something that joins or connects two things together; a link. **3.** *(used with a sing. or pl. verb)* **a.** Two people united, as by betrothal or marriage. **b.** Two people together. **4.** *Informal* A few; several: *a couple of days.* **5.** *Physics* A pair of forces of equal magnitude acting in parallel but opposite directions, capable of causing rotation but not translation. ❖ *v.* **-pled, -pling, -ples** —*tr.* **1.** To link together; connect: *coupled her refusal with an explanation.* **2a.** To join as spouses; marry. **b.** To join in sexual union. **3.** *Electricity* To link (two circuits or currents) as by magnetic induction. —*intr.* **1.** To form pairs; join. **2.** To unite sexually; copulate. **3.** To join chemically. ❖ *adj. Informal* Two or few: *"Every couple years the urge strikes, to . . . haul off to a new site"* (Garrison Keillor). [Middle English, from Old French, from Latin *cōpula,* bond, pair.]

Grammatical functions

Part-of-speech labels

Meanings

Quotation

Etymology

Usage Note When used to refer to two people who function socially as a unit, as in *a married couple,* the word *couple* may take either a singular or a plural verb, depending on whether the members are considered individually or collectively: *The couple were married last week. Only one couple was left on the dance floor.* When a pronoun follows, *they* and *their* are more common than *it* and *its: The couple decided to spend their* (less commonly *its*) *vacation in Florida.* Using a singular verb and a plural pronoun, as in *The couple wants their children to go to college,* is widely considered to be incorrect. Care should be taken that the verb and pronoun agree in number: *The couple want their children to go to college.* • Although the phrase *a couple of* has been well established in English since before the Renaissance, modern critics have sometimes maintained that *a couple of* is too inexact to be appropriate in formal writing. But the inexactitude of *a couple of* may serve a useful purpose, suggesting that the writer is indifferent to the precise number of items involved. Thus the sentence *She lives only a couple of miles away* implies not only that the distance is short but that its exact measure is unimportant. This usage should be considered unobjectionable on all levels of style. • The *of* in the phrase *a couple of* is often dropped in speech, but this omission is usually considered a mistake, especially in formal contexts. Three-fourths of the Usage Panel finds the sentence *I read a couple books over vacation* to be unacceptable; however, another 20% of the Panel finds the sentence to be acceptable in informal speech and writing.

Usage note

Figure 41.1 Entry from *The American Heritage Dictionary of the English Language*.

Entry Word and Pronunciation Guide The **entry word,** which appears in boldface at the beginning of the entry, gives the spelling of a word and indicates how the word is divided into syllables.

> **col • or** *n.* Also chiefly British **col • our**

The **pronunciation guide** appears in parentheses or between slashes after the main entry. Dictionaries use symbols to represent sounds, and an explanation of these symbols usually appears at the bottom of each page or across the bottom of facing pages throughout the alphabetical listing.

Part-of-Speech Label Abbreviations called **part-of-speech labels** indicate parts of speech and grammatical forms.

See
33a

If a verb is regular, the entry provides only the base form of the verb. If a verb is irregular, the part-of-speech label indicates the irregular principal parts of the verb.

> **with • draw** . . . *v.* -drew, -drawn, -drawing

In addition, the label indicates whether a verb is transitive (*tr.*), intransitive (*intr.*), or both.

Part-of-speech labels also indicate the plural form of irregular nouns. (When the plural form is regular, it is not shown.)

> **child** . . . *n. pl.* chil · dren

See
35c

Finally, part-of-speech labels indicate the comparative and superlative forms of both regular and irregular adjectives and adverbs.

Etymology The **etymology** of a word—its history and its evolution over the years—appears in brackets either before or after the list of meanings.

Meanings Some dictionaries give the most common meaning first and then list less common ones. Others begin with the oldest meaning and then move to the most current ones. Check the preface of your dictionary to find out how its entries are arranged.

Synonyms and Antonyms A dictionary entry often lists synonyms (and occasionally antonyms) in addition to definitions. **Synonyms** are words that have similar meanings, such as *well* and *healthy.* **Antonyms** are words that have opposite meanings, such as *courage* and *cowardice.*

Idioms Dictionary entries often show how certain words are used in set expressions called **idioms.** The meaning of such phrases cannot

http://kirsznermandell.wadsworth.com

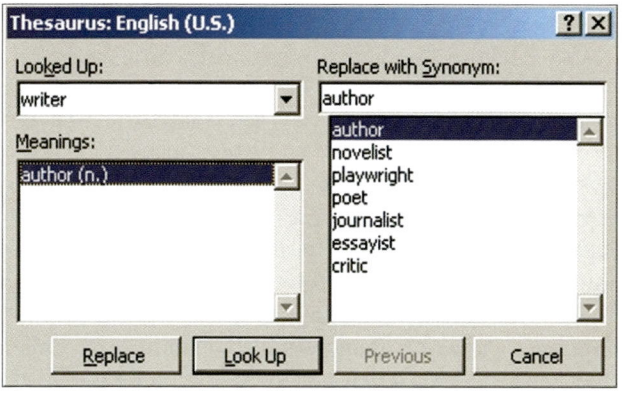

Computer Tip: Using an Electronic Thesaurus

FAQs
link

A good way to find synonyms is to use the Thesaurus tool in your word-processing program. Remember, however, that no two words have exactly the same meaning. Use synonyms carefully, making sure the connotation of the synonym is very close to that of the original word.

always be determined from the words alone. For example, why do we say "catch a cold" or "take a walk"?

Dictionaries also indicate the idiomatic use of **prepositions**. For example, we do not say that we *abide with* a decision; we say *abide by*.

ESL
55e2

Usage Labels Dictionaries use **usage labels** to indicate in what contexts words are acceptable. Among these labels are *nonstandard* (in wide use but not considered standard usage); *informal/colloquial* (part of the language of conversation and acceptable in informal writing); *slang* (appropriate only in extremely informal situations); *dialect/regional* (limited to a certain geographical area); *obsolete* (no longer in use); *archaic/rare* (once common but now seldom used); and *poetic* (common only in poetry).

ESL Tip

A number of special dictionaries are designed to help ESL writers. Two useful dictionaries are *Heinle's Newbury House Dictionary of American English*, 4th edition (available online at http://nhd.heinle.com) and *Heinle's Basic Newbury House Dictionary of American English*, 2nd edition.

CHAPTER 42

A Glossary of Usage

This glossary of usage lists words and phrases that writers often find troublesome.

a, an   Use *a* before words that begin with consonants and words with initial vowels that sound like consonants: *a* person, *a* historical document, *a* one-horse carriage, *a* uniform. Use *an* before words that begin with vowels and words that begin with a silent *h: an* artist, *an* honest person.

accept, except   *Accept* is a verb that means "to receive"; *except* as a preposition or conjunction means "other than" and as a verb means "to leave out": The auditors will *accept* all your claims *except* the last two. Some businesses are *excepted* from the regulation.

advice, advise   *Advice* is a noun meaning "opinion or information offered"; *advise* is a verb that means "to offer advice to": The broker *advised* her client to take his attorney's *advice*.

affect, effect   *Affect* is a verb meaning "to influence"; *effect* can be a verb or a noun (as a verb it means "to bring about," and as a noun it means "result"): We know how the drug *affects* patients immediately, but little is known of its long-term *effects*. The arbitrator tried to *effect* a settlement between the parties.

all ready, already   *All ready* means "completely prepared"; *already* means "by or before this or that time": I was *all ready* to help, but it was *already* too late.

all right, alright   Although the use of *alright* is increasing, current usage calls for *all right*.

allusion, illusion   An *allusion* is a reference or hint; an *illusion* is something that is not what it seems: The poem makes an *allusion* to the Pandora myth. The shadows created an optical *illusion*.

a lot   *A lot* is always two words.

among, between   *Among* refers to groups of more than two things; *between* refers to just two things: The three parties agreed *among* themselves to settle the case. There will be a brief intermission *between* the two acts. (Note that *amongst* is British, not American, usage.)

amount, number   *Amount* refers to a quantity that cannot be counted; *number* refers to things that can be counted: Even a

small *amount* of caffeine can be harmful. Seeing their comman-
der fall, a large *number* of troops ran to his aid.

an, a   See **a, an.**

and/or   In business or technical writing, use *and/or* when either or
both of the items it connects can apply. In college writing, however, avoid the use of *and/or.*

as . . . as . . .   In such constructions, *as* signals a comparison; therefore, you must always use the second *as:* John Steinbeck's *East of
Eden* is *as* long *as* his *The Grapes of Wrath.*

as, like   *As* can be used as a conjunction (to introduce a complete
clause) or as a preposition; *like* should be used as a preposition
only: In *The Scarlet Letter,* Hawthorne uses imagery *as* (not *like*)
he does in his other works. After classes, Amy works *as* a manager of a fast-food restaurant. Writers *like* Carl Sandburg appear
once in a generation.

at, to   Many people use the prepositions *at* and *to* after *where* in conversation: *Where* are you working *at? Where* are you going *to?*
This usage is redundant and should not appear in college writing.

awhile, a while   *Awhile* is an adverb; *a while,* which consists of an article and a noun, is used as the object of a preposition: Before we
continue, we will rest *awhile.* (modifies the verb *rest*); Before we
continue, we will rest for *a while.* (object of the preposition *for*)

bad, badly   *Bad* is an adjective, and *badly* is an adverb: The school
board decided that *Huckleberry Finn* was a *bad* book. American
automobile makers did not do *badly* this year. After verbs that
refer to any of the senses or after any other linking verb, use the
adjective form: He looked *bad.* He felt *bad.* It seemed *bad.*

being as, being that   These awkward phrases add unnecessary
words and weaken your writing. Use *because* instead.

beside, besides   *Beside* is a preposition meaning "next to"; *besides* can
be either a preposition meaning "except" or "other than" or an
adverb meaning "as well": *Beside* the tower was a wall that ran
the length of the city. *Besides* its industrial uses, laser technology
has many other applications. Edison invented not only the light-
bulb but the phonograph *besides.*

between, among   See **among, between.**

bring, take   *Bring* means "to transport from a farther place to a
nearer place"; *take* means "to carry or convey from a nearer
place to a farther one": *Bring* me a souvenir from your trip. *Take*
this message to the general, and wait for a reply.

can, may   *Can* denotes ability, and *may* indicates permission: If you
can play, you *may* use my piano.

capital, capitol   *Capital* refers to a city that is an official seat of government; *capitol* refers to a building in which a legislature meets: Washington, DC, is the *capital* of the United States. When we were there, we visited the *Capitol* building.

center around   This imprecise phrase is acceptable in speech and informal writing but not in college writing. Use *center on* instead.

cite, site   *Cite* is a verb meaning "to quote as an authority or example"; *site* is a noun meaning "a place or setting": Jeff *cited* five sources in his research paper. The builder cleared the *site* for the new bank.

climactic, climatic   *Climactic* means "of or related to a climax"; *climatic* means "of or related to climate": The *climactic* moment of the movie occurred unexpectedly. If scientists are correct, the *climatic* conditions of Earth are changing.

coarse, course   *Coarse* is an adjective meaning "inferior" or "having a rough, uneven texture"; *course* is a noun meaning "a route or path," "an area on which a sport is played," or "a unit of study": *Coarse* sandpaper is used to smooth the surface. The *course* of true love never runs smoothly. Last semester I had to drop a *course*.

complement, compliment   *Complement* means "to complete or add to"; *compliment* means "to give praise": A double-blind study would *complement* their preliminary research. My instructor *complimented* me on my improvement.

conscious, conscience   *Conscious* is an adjective meaning "having one's mental faculties awake"; *conscience* is a noun that means the moral sense of right and wrong: The patient will remain *conscious* during the procedure. His *conscience* would not allow him to lie.

continual, continuous   *Continual* means "recurring at intervals"; *continuous* refers to an action that occurs without interruption: A pulsar is a star that emits a *continual* stream of electromagnetic radiation. (It emits radiation at regular intervals.) A small battery allows the watch to run *continuously* for five years. (It runs without stopping.)

could of, should of, would of   The contractions *could've, should've,* and *would've* are often misspelled as the nonstandard constructions *could of, should of,* and *would of.* Use *could have, should have,* and *would have* in college writing.

council, counsel   A *council* is "a body of people who serve in a legislative or advisory capacity"; *counsel* means "to offer advice or guidance": The city *council* argued about the proposed ban on smoking. The judge *counseled* the couple to settle their differences.

couple of   *Couple* means "a pair," but *couple of* is often used colloquially to mean "several" or "a few." In your college writing, specify "four points" or "two examples" rather than using "a couple of."

criterion, criteria *Criteria*, from the Greek, is the plural of *criterion*, meaning "standard for judgment": Of all the *criteria* for hiring graduating seniors, class rank is the most important *criterion*.

data *Data* is the plural of the Latin *datum*, meaning "fact." In everyday speech and writing, *data* is often used as the singular as well as the plural form. In college writing, use *data* only for the plural: The *data* discussed in this section *are* summarized in Table 1.

different from, different than *Different than* is widely used in American speech. In college writing, use *different from*.

discreet, discrete *Discreet* means "careful or prudent"; *discrete* means "separate or individually distinct": Because Madame Bovary was not *discreet*, her reputation suffered. Atoms can be broken into hundreds of *discrete* particles.

disinterested, uninterested *Disinterested* means "objective" or "capable of making an impartial judgment"; *uninterested* means "indifferent or unconcerned": The American judicial system depends on *disinterested* jurors. Finding no treasure, Hernando de Soto was *uninterested* in going farther.

don't, doesn't *Don't* is the contraction of *do not; doesn't* is the contraction of *does not*. Do not confuse the two: My dog *doesn't* (not *don't*) like to walk in the rain.

effect, affect See **affect, effect.**

e.g. *E.g.* is an abbreviation for the Latin *exempli gratia*, meaning "for example" or "for instance." In college writing, do not use *e.g.* Instead, use its English equivalent.

emigrate from, immigrate to To *emigrate* is "to leave one's country and settle in another"; to *immigrate* is "to come to another country and reside there." The noun forms of these words are *emigrant* and *immigrant*: My great-grandfather *emigrated from* Warsaw along with many other *emigrants* from Poland. Many people *immigrate* to the United States for economic reasons, but such *immigrants* still face great challenges.

eminent, imminent *Eminent* is an adjective meaning "standing above others" or "prominent"; *imminent* means "about to occur": Oliver Wendell Holmes Jr. was an *eminent* jurist. In ancient times, a comet signaled *imminent* disaster.

enthused *Enthused*, a colloquial form of *enthusiastic*, should not be used in college writing.

etc. *Etc.*, the abbreviation of *et cetera*, means "and the rest." Do not use it in your college writing. Instead, say "and so on"—or, better yet, specify exactly what *etc.* stands for.

everyday, every day   *Everyday* is an adjective that means "ordinary" or "commonplace"; *every day* means "occurring daily": In the Gettysburg Address, Lincoln used *everyday* language. She exercises almost *every day*.

everyone, every one   *Everyone* is an indefinite pronoun meaning "every person"; *every one* means "every individual or thing in a particular group": *Everyone* seems happier in the spring. *Every one* of the packages had been opened.

except, accept   See **accept, except.**

explicit, implicit   *Explicit* means "expressed or stated directly"; *implicit* means "implied" or "expressed or stated indirectly": The director *explicitly* warned the actors to be on time for rehearsals. Her *implicit* message was that lateness would not be tolerated.

farther, further   *Farther* designates distance; *further* designates degree: I have traveled *farther* from home than any of my relatives. Critics charge that welfare subsidies encourage *further* dependence.

fewer, less   Use *fewer* with nouns that can be counted: *fewer* books, *fewer* people, *fewer* dollars. Use *less* with quantities that cannot be counted: *less* pain, *less* power, *less* enthusiasm.

firstly (secondly, thirdly, . . .)   Archaic forms meaning "in the first . . . second . . . third place." Use *first, second, third*.

further, farther   See **farther, further.**

good, well   *Good* is an adjective, never an adverb: She is a *good* swimmer. *Well* can function as an adverb or as an adjective. As an adverb, it means "in a good manner": She swam *well* (not *good*) in the race. *Well* is used as an adjective with verbs that denote a state of being or feeling. Here *well* can mean "in good health": I feel *well*.

got to   *Got to* is not acceptable in college writing. To indicate obligation, use *have to, has to*, or *must*.

hanged, hung   Both *hanged* and *hung* are past participles of *hang*. *Hanged* is used to refer to executions; *hung* is used to mean "suspended": Billy Budd was *hanged* for killing the master-at-arms. The stockings were *hung* by the chimney with care.

he, she   Traditionally *he* has been used in the generic sense to refer to both males and females. To acknowledge the equality of the sexes, however, avoid the generic *he*. Use plural pronouns whenever possible. **See 40e2.**

hopefully   The adverb *hopefully*, meaning "in a hopeful manner," should modify a verb, an adjective, or another adverb. Do not use *hopefully* as a sentence modifier meaning "it is hoped." Rather than "*Hopefully*, scientists will soon discover a cure for AIDS," write "*Everyone hopes* scientists will soon discover a cure for AIDS."

i.e. The abbreviation *i.e.* stands for the Latin *id est*, meaning "that is." In college writing, do not use *i.e.* Instead, use its English equivalent.

if, whether When asking indirect questions or expressing doubt, use *whether:* He asked *whether* (not *if*) the flight would be delayed. The flight attendant was not sure *whether* (not *if*) it would be delayed.

illusion, allusion See **allusion, illusion.**

immigrate to, emigrate from See **emigrate from, immigrate to.**

implicit, explicit See **explicit, implicit.**

imply, infer *Imply* means "to hint" or "to suggest"; *infer* means "to conclude from": Mark Antony *implied* that the conspirators had murdered Caesar. The crowd *inferred* his meaning and called for justice.

infer, imply See **imply, infer.**

inside of, outside of *Of* is unnecessary when *inside* and *outside* are used as prepositions: He waited *inside* (not *inside of*) the coffee shop. *Inside of* is colloquial in references to time: He could run a mile in *under* (not *inside of*) eight minutes.

irregardless, regardless *Irregardless* is a nonstandard version of *regardless.* Use *regardless* instead.

is when, is where These constructions are faulty when they appear in definitions: A playoff *is* (not *is when*) an additional game played to establish the winner of a tie.

its, it's *Its* is a possessive pronoun; *it's* is a contraction of *it is:* It's no secret that the bank is out to protect *its* assets.

kind of, sort of *Kind of* and *sort of,* when used to mean "rather" or "somewhat," are colloquial and should not appear in college writing: It is well known that Napoleon was *rather* (not *kind of*) short.

lay, lie See **lie, lay.**

leave, let *Leave* means "to go away from" or "to let remain"; *let* means "to allow" or "to permit": *Let* (not *leave*) me give you a hand.

less, fewer See **fewer, less.**

let, leave See **leave, let.**

lie, lay *Lie* is an intransitive verb (one that does not take an object) meaning "to recline." Its principal forms are *lie, lay, lain, lying:* Each afternoon she would *lie* in the sun and listen to the surf. *As I Lay Dying* is a novel by William Faulkner. By 1871, Troy had *lain* undisturbed for two thousand years. The painting shows a nude *lying* on a couch.

Lay is a transitive verb (one that takes an object) meaning "to put" or "to place." Its principal forms are *lay, laid, laid, laying:* The Federalist Papers *lay* the foundation for American conservatism. In October 1781, the British *laid* down their arms and surrendered. He had *laid* his money on the counter before leaving. We watched the stonemasons *laying* a wall.

like, as   See **as, like.**

loose, lose   *Loose* is an adjective meaning "not rigidly fastened or securely attached"; *lose* is a verb meaning "to misplace": The marble facing of the building became *loose* and fell to the sidewalk. After only two drinks, most people *lose* their ability to judge distance.

lots, lots of, a lot of   These words are colloquial substitutes for *many, much*, or *a great deal of.* Avoid their use in college writing: This point of view has many (not *lots of* or *a lot of*) advantages.

man   Like the generic pronoun *he, man* has been used in English to denote members of both sexes. This usage is being replaced by *human beings, people*, or similar terms that do not specify gender. **See 40e2.**

may, can   See **can, may.**

may be, maybe   *May be* is a verb phrase; *maybe* is an adverb meaning "perhaps": She *may be* the smartest student in the class. *Maybe* her experience has given her an advantage.

media, medium   *Medium*, meaning a "means of conveying or broadcasting something," is singular; *media* is the plural form and requires a plural verb: The *media* have distorted the issue.

might have, might of   *Might of* is a nonstandard spelling of *might've*, the contraction of *might have.* Use *might have* in college writing.

number, amount   See **amount, number.**

OK, O.K., okay   All three spellings are acceptable, but this term should be avoided in college writing. Replace it with a more specific word or words: The lecture was *adequate* (not *okay*), if uninspiring.

outside of, inside of   See **inside of, outside of.**

passed, past   *Passed* is the past tense of the verb *pass; past* means "belonging to a former time" or "no longer current": The car must have been going eighty miles per hour when it *passed* us. In the envelope was a bill marked *past* due.

percent, percentage   *Percent* indicates a part of a hundred when a specific number is referred to: "Ten *percent* of his salary." *Percentage* is used when no specific number is referred to: "a *percentage* of next year's receipts."

phenomenon, phenomena   A *phenomenon* is a single observable fact or event. It can also refer to a rare or significant occurrence.

Phenomena is the plural form and requires a plural verb: Many supposedly paranormal *phenomena* are easily explained.

plus   As a preposition, *plus* means "in addition to." Avoid using *plus* as a substitute for *and:* Include the principal, *plus* the interest, in your calculations. Your quote was too high; moreover (not *plus*), it was inaccurate.

precede, proceed   *Precede* means "to go or come before"; *proceed* means "to go forward in an orderly way": Robert Frost's *North of Boston* was *preceded* by an earlier volume. In 1532, Francisco Pizarro landed at Tumbes and *proceeded* south.

principal, principle   As a noun, *principal* means "a sum of money (minus interest) invested or lent" or "a person in the leading position"; as an adjective, it means "most important"; *principle* is a noun meaning a rule of conduct or a basic truth: He wanted to reduce the *principal* of the loan. The *principal* of the high school is a talented administrator. Women are the *principal* wage earners in many American households. The Constitution embodies certain fundamental *principles.*

quote, quotation   *Quote* is a verb. *Quotation* is a noun. In college writing, do not use *quote* as a shortened form of *quotation:* Scholars attribute these *quotations* (not *quotes*) to Shakespeare.

raise, rise   *Raise* is a transitive verb, and *rise* is an intransitive verb—that is, *raise* takes an object, and *rise* does not: My grandparents *raised* a large family. The sun will *rise* at 6:12 this morning.

real, really   *Real* means "genuine" or "authentic"; *really* means "actually." In your college writing, do not use *real* as an adjective meaning "very."

reason is that, reason is because   *Reason* should be used with *that* and not with *because*, which is redundant: The *reason* he left *is that* (not *is because*) you insulted him.

regardless, irregardless   See **irregardless, regardless.**

respectably, respectfully, respectively   *Respectably* means "worthy of respect"; *respectfully* means "giving honor or deference"; *respectively* means "in the order given": He skated quite *respectably* at his first Olympics. The seminar taught us to treat others *respectfully.* The first- and second-place winners were Tai and Kim, *respectively.*

rise, raise   See **raise, rise.**

set, sit   *Set* means "to put down" or "to lay." Its principal forms are *set* and *setting:* After rocking the baby to sleep, he *set* her down carefully in her crib. After *setting* her down, he took a nap. *Sit* means "to assume a sitting position." Its principal forms are *sit*, *sat*, and *sitting:* Many children *sit* in front of the television five to six hours a day. The dog *sat* by the fire. We were *sitting* in the airport when the flight was canceled.

shall, will *Will* has all but replaced *shall* to express future action.

should of See **could of, should of, would of.**

since Do not use *since* for *because* if there is any chance of confusion. In the sentence "*Since* President Nixon traveled to China, trade between China and the United States has increased," *since* could mean either "from the time that" or "because." To be clear, use *because*.

sit, set See **set, sit.**

so Avoid using *so* alone as a vague intensifier meaning "very" or "extremely." Follow *so* with *that* and a clause that describes the result: She was *so* pleased with their work *that* she took them out to lunch.

sometime, sometimes, some time *Sometime* means "at some time in the future"; *sometimes* means "now and then"; *some time* means "a period of time": The president is planning to address Congress *sometime* next week. All automobiles, no matter how reliable, *sometimes* need repairs. It has been *some time* since I read that book.

sort of, kind of See **kind of, sort of.**

stationary, stationery *Stationary* means "staying in one place"; *stationery* means "materials for writing" or "letter paper": The communications satellite appears to be *stationary* in the sky. The office manager supplies each department with *stationery*.

supposed to, used to *Supposed to* and *used to* are often misspelled. Both verbs require the final *d* to indicate past tense.

take, bring See **bring, take.**

than, then *Than* is a conjunction used to indicate a comparison; *then* is an adverb indicating time: The new shopping center is bigger *than* the old one. He did his research; *then*, he wrote a report.

that, which, who Use *that* or *which* when referring to a thing; use *who* when referring to a person: It was a speech *that* inspired many. The movie, *which* was a huge success, failed to impress her. Anyone *who* (not *that*) takes the course will benefit.

their, there, they're *Their* is a possessive pronoun; *there* indicates place and is also used in the expressions *there is* and *there are*; *they're* is a contraction of *they are*: Watson and Crick did *their* DNA work at Cambridge University. I love Los Angeles, but I wouldn't want to live *there*. *There* is nothing we can do to resurrect an extinct species. When *they're* well treated, rabbits make excellent pets.

themselves, theirselves, theirself   *Theirselves* and *theirself* are non-standard variants of *themselves*.

then, than   See **than, then.**

till, until, 'til   *Till* and *until* have the same meaning, and both are acceptable. *Until* is preferred in college writing. *'Til*, a contraction of *until*, should be avoided.

to, at   See **at, to.**

to, too, two   *To* is a preposition that indicates direction; *too* is an adverb that means "also" or "more than is needed"; *two* expresses the number 2: Last year we flew from New York *to* California. "Tippecanoe and Tyler, *too*" was William Henry Harrison's campaign slogan. The plot was *too* complicated for the average reader. Just north of *Two* Rivers, Wisconsin, is a petrified forest.

try to, try and   *Try and* is the colloquial equivalent of the more formal *try to*: He decided to *try to* (not *try and*) do better. In college writing, use *try to*.

-type   Deleting this empty suffix eliminates clutter and clarifies meaning: Found in the wreckage was an *incendiary* (not *incendiary-type*) device.

uninterested, disinterested   See **disinterested, uninterested.**

unique   Because *unique* means "the only one," not "remarkable" or "unusual," never use constructions like "the most unique" or "very unique."

until   See **till, until, 'til.**

used to   See **supposed to, used to.**

utilize   In most cases, replace *utilize* with *use* (*utilize* often sounds pretentious).

wait for, wait on   To *wait for* means "to defer action until something occurs." To *wait on* means "to act as a waiter": I am *waiting for* (not *on*) dinner.

weather, whether   *Weather* is a noun meaning "the state of the atmosphere"; *whether* is a conjunction used to introduce an alternative: The *weather* outside is frightful, but the fire inside is delightful. It is doubtful *whether* we will be able to ski tomorrow.

well, good   See **good, well.**

were, we're   *Were* is a verb; *we're* is the contraction of *we are*: The Trojans *were* asleep when the Greeks attacked. We must act now if *we're* going to succeed.

whether, if   See **if, whether.**

which, who, that   See **that, which, who.**

who, whom When a pronoun serves as the subject of its clause, use *who* or *whoever;* when it functions in a clause as an object, use *whom* or *whomever:* Sarah, *who* is studying ancient civilizations, would like to visit Greece. Sarah, *whom* I met in France, wants me to travel to Greece with her.

who's, whose *Who's* means "who is"; *whose* indicates possession: *Who's* going to take calculus? The writer *whose* book was in the window was autographing copies.

will, shall See **shall, will.**

would of See **could of, should of, would of.**

your, you're *Your* indicates possession; *you're* is the contraction of *you are:* You can improve *your* stamina by jogging two miles a day. *You're* certain to be the winner.

PART 11

Understanding Punctuation

**Punctuation
461–490**

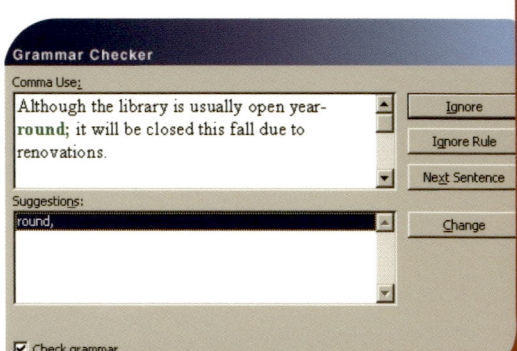

Grammar Checker

Comma Use:

Although the library is usually open year-**round**; it will be closed this fall due to renovations.

Ignore
Ignore Rule
Next Sentence

Suggestions:

round,

Change

☑ Check grammar

PART 11

Understanding Punctuation

FREQUENTLY ASKED QUESTIONS

OVERVIEW OF SENTENCE PUNCTUATION: COMMAS, SEMICOLONS, COLONS, DASHES, PARENTHESES

(Further explanations and examples are located in the sections listed in parentheses after each example.)

SEPARATING INDEPENDENT CLAUSES

With a Comma and a Coordinating Conjunction
The House approved the bill, but the Senate rejected it. **(44a)**

With a Semicolon
Paul Revere's *The Boston Massacre* is traditional American protest art; Edward Hicks's paintings are socially conscious art with a religious strain. **(45a)**

With a Semicolon and a Transitional Word or Phrase
Thomas Jefferson brought two hundred vanilla beans and a recipe for vanilla ice cream back from France; thus, he gave America its all-time favorite ice-cream flavor. **(45a)**

With a Colon
A *U.S. News & World Report* survey has revealed a surprising fact: Americans spend more time at malls than anywhere else except at home and at work. **(48a2)**

SEPARATING ITEMS IN A SERIES

With Commas
Chipmunk, raccoon, and *Mugwump* are Native American words. **(44b)**

With Semicolons
Laramie, Wyoming; Wyoming, Delaware; and Delaware, Ohio were three of the places they visited. **(45b)**

SETTING OFF EXAMPLES, EXPLANATIONS, OR SUMMARIES

With a Colon
She had one dream: to play professional basketball. **(48a2)**

With a Dash
"Study hard," "Respect your elders," "Don't talk with your mouth full"—Sharon had often heard her parents say these things. **(48b2)**

SETTING OFF NONESSENTIAL MATERIAL

With a Single Comma
His fear increasing, he waited to enter the haunted house. **(44d3)**

With a Pair of Commas
Mark McGwire, not Sammy Sosa, was the first to break Roger Maris's home run record. **(44d3)**

With Dashes
Neither of the boys—both nine-year-olds—had any history of violence. **(48b1)**

With Parentheses
In some European countries (notably Sweden and France), high-quality day care is offered at little or no cost to parents. **(48c1)**

CHAPTER 43

Using End Punctuation

43a Using Periods

(1) Ending a Sentence

Use a period to signal the end of a statement, a mild command or polite request, or an indirect question.

> Something is rotten in Denmark. (statement)
>
> Be sure to have the oil checked before you start out. (mild
> command)
>
> When the bell rings, please exit in an orderly fashion. (polite
> request)
>
> They wondered whether the water was safe to drink. (indirect
> question)

(2) Marking an Abbreviation

Use periods in most abbreviations.

> Mr. Spock   Aug.   Dr. Dolittle
>
> 9 p.m.   etc.   1600 Pennsylvania Ave.

If an abbreviation ends the sentence, do not add another period.

> He promised to be there at 6 a.m./

However, add a question mark if the sentence is a question.

> Did he arrive at 6 p.m.?

If the abbreviation falls *within* a sentence, use normal punctuation
after the period.

> He promised to be there at 6 p.m., but he forgot.

Close-up: Abbreviations without Periods	

Abbreviations composed of all capital letters do not usually
require periods unless they stand for initials of people's names
(E. B. White).

> MD   RN   BC

Familiar abbreviations of names of corporations or government
agencies and abbreviations of scientific and technical terms do not require periods.

CD-ROM   NYU   DNA   EPA   HBO

Acronyms—new words formed from the initial letters or first few letters of a series of words—do not include periods.

modem   op-ed   scuba   radar
OSHA   AIDS   NAFTA   CAT scan

Clipped forms (commonly accepted shortened forms of words, such as *gym*, *dorm*, *math*, and *fax*) do not use periods.

Postal abbreviations do not include periods.

TX   CA   MS   PA   FL   NY

(3) Marking Divisions in Dramatic, Poetic, and Biblical References

Use periods to separate act, scene, and line numbers in plays; book and line numbers in long poems; and chapter and verse numbers in biblical references. (Do not space between the periods and the elements they separate.)

Dramatic Reference: *Hamlet* 2.2.1–5

Poetic Reference: *Paradise Lost* 7.163–67

Biblical Reference: Judges 4.14

NOTE: In **MLA parenthetical references**, titles of literary and biblical works are often abbreviated: (<u>Ham</u>. 2.2.1-5); (Judg. 4.14).

See
17a1

(4) Marking Divisions in Electronic Addresses

Periods, along with other punctuation marks (such as slashes and colons), are also used in electronic addresses (URLs).

http://kirsznermandell.wadsworth.com

NOTE: When you type a URL, do not end it with a period or add spaces after periods within the address.

43b Using Question Marks

(1) Marking the End of a Direct Question

Use a question mark to signal the end of a direct question.

Who was that masked man?

(2) Marking Questionable Dates and Numbers

Use a question mark in parentheses to indicate uncertainty about a date or number.

Aristophanes, the Greek playwright, was born in 448 (?) BC and died in 380 (?) BC.

(3) Editing Misused Question Marks

Use a period, not a question mark, with an **indirect question** (a question that is not reproduced word for word).

The personnel officer asked whether he knew how to type?.

Do not use a question mark to convey sarcasm. Instead, suggest your attitude through your choice of words.

I refused his ^not very^ generous (?) offer.

43c Using Exclamation Points

Use an exclamation point to signal the end of an emotional or emphatic statement, an emphatic interjection, or a forceful command.

Remember the *Maine*!

"No! Don't leave!" he cried.

NOTE: Except for recording dialogue, exclamation points are almost never appropriate in college writing. Even in informal writing, use exclamation points sparingly.

http://kirsznermandell.wadsworth.com

Computer Tip: Replacing Punctuation Marks

Microsoft Word's Find and Replace tool allows you to search for certain punctuation marks and replace them with others. Select Find from the Edit menu, click the Replace tab, type a punctuation mark into the Find What box, and then type the replacement mark into the Replace With box. Clicking Replace will replace this punctuation mark one time; clicking Replace All will replace it each time it appears in your document.

Find and Replace	? X
Find Replace Go To	
Find what:	?
Replace with:	.
More ∓ Replace Replace All Find Next Cancel	

CHAPTER 44

Using Commas

44a Setting Off Independent Clauses

Use a comma when you form a compound sentence by linking two independent clauses with a <u>coordinating conjunction</u> or a pair of <u>correlative conjunctions</u>.

> **See A7**

> The House approved the bill, <u>but</u> the Senate rejected it.

> <u>Either</u> the hard drive is full, <u>or</u> the modem is too slow.

NOTE: You may omit the comma if the two independent clauses are very short: Love it <u>or</u> leave it.

44b Setting Off Items in a Series

Use commas between items in a series of three or more **coordinate elements** (words, phrases, or clauses joined by a coordinating conjunction).

> *Chipmunk,* *raccoon,* and *Mugwump* are Native American words.

> You may pay <u>by check,</u> <u>with a credit card,</u> or in <u>cash.</u>

> <u>Brazilians speak Portuguese,</u> <u>Colombians speak Spanish,</u> and Haitians speak French and Creole.

NOTE: To avoid ambiguity, always use a comma before the *and* (or other coordinating conjunction) that separates the last two items in a series: The downtown area includes a bakery, a florist, a small supermarket with an excellent butcher, and a bookstore.

Do not use a comma to introduce or to close a series.

> Three important criteria are, fat content, salt content, and taste.

> The provinces Quebec, Ontario, and Alberta, are in Canada.

NOTE: If a phrase or clause in a <u>series</u> already contains commas, separate the items with semicolons.

> **See 45b**

Use a comma between items in a series of two or more **coordinate adjectives**—adjectives that modify the same word or word group—unless they are joined by a conjunction.

> She brushed her <u>long,</u> <u>shining</u> hair.

> The baby was <u>tired</u> and <u>cranky</u> and <u>wet</u>. (no commas required)

Checklist: Punctuating Adjectives in a Series

☐ If you can reverse the order of the adjectives or insert *and* between the adjectives without changing the meaning, the adjectives are coordinate, and you should use a comma.

She brushed her long, shining hair.

She brushed her shining, long hair.

She brushed her long [and] shining hair.

☐ If you cannot reverse the order of the adjectives or insert *and*, the adjectives are not coordinate, and you should not use a comma.

Ten red balloons fell from the ceiling.

Red ten balloons fell from the ceiling.

Ten [and] red balloons fell from the ceiling.

NOTE: Numbers—such as *ten*—are not coordinate with other adjectives.

ESL Tip

For more information on the correct order of adjectives in a series, **see 55d2.**

44c Setting Off Introductory Elements

(1) Dependent Clauses

An introductory dependent clause is generally set off from the rest of the sentence by a comma.

> Although the CIA used to call undercover agents *penetration agents,* they now routinely refer to them as *moles.*

> When war came to Baghdad, many victims were children.

If the dependent clause is short and designates time, you may omit the comma—provided the sentence will be clear without it.

> When I exercise I drink plenty of water.

NOTE: Do not use a comma to set off a dependent clause at the *end* of a sentence.

(2) Verbal and Prepositional Phrases

See B3.1

An introductory **verbal phrase** is generally set off by a comma.

> Thinking that this might be his last chance, Peary struggled toward the North Pole. (participial phrase)

To write well, one must read a lot. (infinitive phrase)

> ### Close-up: Using Commas with Verbal Phrases
>
> A verbal phrase that serves as a subject is *not* set off by a comma.
>
> Laughing out loud can release tension. (gerund phrase)
>
> To know him is to love him. (infinitive phrase)

An introductory **prepositional phrase** is also usually set off by a comma.

During the Depression, movie attendance rose.

However, if an introductory prepositional phrase is short and no ambiguity is possible, you may omit the comma.

After lunch I took a four-hour nap.

(3) Transitional Words and Phrases

When a **transitional word or phrase** begins a sentence, it is usually set off with a comma.

See 7b2

However, any plan that is enacted must be fair.

In other words, we cannot act hastily.

44d Setting Off Nonessential Material

Sometimes words, phrases, or clauses *contribute* to the meaning of a sentence but are not *essential* for conveying the sentence's main point or emphasis. Use commas to set off such **nonessential** material whether it appears at the beginning, in the middle, or at the end of a sentence.

(1) Nonrestrictive Modifiers

Use commas to set off **nonrestrictive modifiers,** which supply information that is not essential to the meaning of the word or word group they modify. (Do *not* use commas to set off **restrictive modifiers,** which supply information essential to the meaning of the word or word group they modify.)

Nonrestrictive (commas required): Actors, who have inflated egos, are often insecure. (*All* actors—not just those with inflated egos—are insecure.)

Restrictive (no commas): Actors who have inflated egos are often insecure. (Only those actors with inflated egos—not all actors—are insecure.)

In the following examples, commas set off only nonrestrictive modifiers—those that supply nonessential information—but not restrictive modifiers, which supply essential information.

Adjective Clauses

Nonrestrictive: He ran for the bus, which was late as usual.

Restrictive: Speaking in public is something that most people fear.

Prepositional Phrases

Nonrestrictive: The clerk, with a nod, dismissed me.

Restrictive: The man with the gun demanded their money.

Verbal Phrases

Nonrestrictive: The marathoner, running his fastest, beat his previous record.

Restrictive: The candidates running for mayor have agreed to a debate.

Appositives

Nonrestrictive: *Citizen Kane,* Orson Welles's first film, made him famous.

Restrictive: The film *Citizen Kane* made Orson Welles famous.

Checklist: Restrictive and Nonrestrictive Modifiers

To determine whether a modifier is restrictive or nonrestrictive, ask yourself these questions:

☐ Is the modifier essential to the meaning of the noun it modifies (*The man with the gun,* not just any man)? If so, it is restrictive.
☐ Is the modifier introduced by *that* (*something that most people fear*)? If so, it is restrictive. *That* cannot introduce a nonrestrictive clause.
☐ Can you delete the relative pronoun without causing ambiguity or confusion (*something [that] most people fear*)? If so, the clause is restrictive.
☐ Is the appositive more specific than the noun that precedes it (*the film Citizen Kane*)? If so, it is restrictive.

Close-up: Using Commas with *That* and *Which*

That introduces only restrictive clauses, which are not set off by commas.

I bought a used car that cost $2,000.

Which can introduce both restrictive and nonrestrictive clauses.

> **Restrictive** (no comma): I bought a used car <u>which</u> cost $2,000.
>
> **Nonrestrictive** (commas needed): The used car I bought, <u>which</u> cost $2,000, broke down after a week.

Many writers, however, prefer to use *which* only to introduce non-restrictive clauses.

Grammar Checker: *That* or *Which*

Your word processor's grammar checker may label *which* as an error when it introduces a restrictive clause. It will prompt you to add commas (using *which* to introduce a nonrestrictive clause) or to change *which* to *that*. Carefully consider the meaning of your sentence, and revise accordingly.

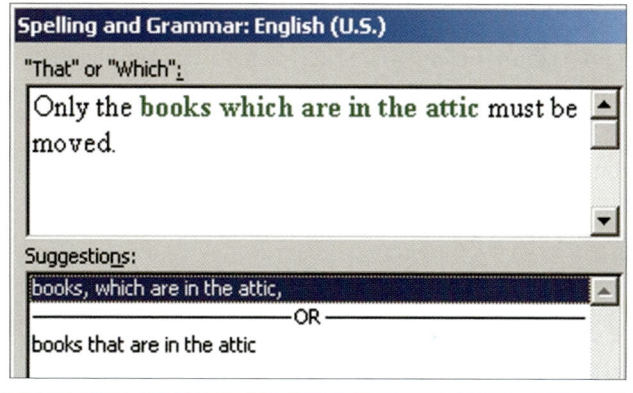

Spelling and Grammar: English (U.S.)

"That" or "Which":

Only the **books which are in the attic** must be moved.

Suggestions:

books, which are in the attic,

——————————OR——————————

books that are in the attic

---

(2) Transitional Words and Phrases

See 7b2

Transitional words and phrases—which include conjunctive adverbs like *however, therefore, thus,* and *nevertheless* as well as expressions like *for example* and *on the other hand*—qualify, clarify, and make connections. However, they are not essential to a sentence's meaning. For this reason, they are always set off by commas when they interrupt a clause or when they begin or end a sentence.

The Outward Bound program<u>, for example,</u> is extremely safe.

<u>In fact,</u> Outward Bound has an excellent reputation.

Other programs are not so safe<u>, however</u>.

Close-up: Transitional Words and Phrases

When a transitional word or phrase joins two independent clauses, it must be preceded by a semicolon and followed by a comma.

> Laughter is the best medicine<u>; of course,</u> penicillin also comes in handy sometimes.

(3) Contradictory Phrases and Absolute Phrases

A phrase that expresses a **contradiction** is usually set off by commas.

This medicine is taken after meals, never on an empty stomach.

Mark McGwire, not Sammy Sosa, was the first to break Roger Maris's home run record.

An **absolute phrase,** which usually consists of a noun plus a participle, is always set off by commas from the sentence it modifies.

His fear increasing, he waited to enter the haunted house.

Many soldiers were lost in Southeast Asia, their bodies never recovered.

(4) Miscellaneous Nonessential Elements

Other nonessential elements usually set off by commas include tag questions, names in direct address, mild interjections, and *yes* and *no.*

This is your first day on the job, isn't it?

I wonder, Mr. Honeywell, whether Mr. Albright deserves a raise.

Well, it's about time.

Yes, that's what I thought.

44e Using Commas in Other Conventional Contexts

(1) With Direct Quotations

In most cases, use commas to set off a direct quotation from the **identifying tag**—the phrase that identifies the speaker (*he said, she answered,* and so on).

Emerson said, "I greet you at the beginning of a great career."

"I greet you at the beginning of a great career," Emerson said.

"I greet you," Emerson said, "at the beginning of a great career."

When the identifying tag comes between two complete sentences, however, the tag is introduced by a comma but followed by a period.

"Winning isn't everything," Coach Vince Lombardi once said. "It's the only thing."

If the first sentence of an interrupted quotation ends with a question mark or an exclamation point, do not use commas.

"Should we hold the front page?" she asked. "It's a slow news day."

"Hold the front page!" he cried. "There's breaking news!"

(2) With a Title or Degree That Follows a Name

Hamlet, Prince of Denmark, is Shakespeare's most famous character.

Michael Crichton, MD, wrote *Jurassic Park*.

(3) In Addresses and Dates

When a date or an address falls within a sentence, use a comma after the last element.

On August 30, 1983, the space shuttle *Challenger* was launched.

Do not use a comma to separate the street number from the street or the state name from the ZIP code.

Her address is 600 West End Avenue, New York, NY 10024.

NOTE: Do not use a comma to separate the month from the year: August 1983.

44f Using Commas to Prevent Misreading

In some cases, you need a comma to avoid ambiguity. For example, consider the following sentence.

Those who can, sprint the final lap.

Without the comma, *can* appears to be an auxiliary verb ("Those who <u>can sprint</u>. . . ."), and the sentence seems incomplete. The comma tells readers to pause, thereby preventing confusion.

Also use a comma to acknowledge the omission of a repeated word, usually a verb, and to separate words repeated consecutively.

Pam carried the box; Tim, the suitcase.

Everything bad that could have happened, happened.

44g Editing Misused Commas

Do not use commas in the following situations.

(1) To Set Off Restrictive Modifiers

Do not use commas to set off restrictive elements. Commas are only used to set off <u>nonrestrictive modifiers</u>.

See
44d1

The film, *Malcolm X*, was directed by Spike Lee.

They planned a picnic, in the park.

(2) Between Inseparable Grammatical Constructions

Do not place a comma between grammatical elements that cannot be logically separated: a subject and its predicate, a verb and its complement or direct object, a preposition and its object, or an adjective and the word or phrase it modifies.

A woman with dark red hair, opened the door. (comma incorrectly placed between subject and predicate)

Louis Braille developed, an alphabet of raised dots for the blind. (comma incorrectly placed between verb and object)

They relaxed somewhat during, the last part of the obstacle course. (comma incorrectly placed between preposition and object)

Wind-dispersed weeds include the well-known and plentiful, dandelions, milkweed, and thistle. (comma incorrectly placed between adjective and words it modifies)

(3) Between a Verb and an Indirect Quotation or Indirect Question

Do not use a comma between a verb and an indirect quotation or between a verb and an indirect question.

General Douglas MacArthur vowed, that he would return. (comma incorrectly placed between verb and indirect quotation)

The landlord asked, if we would sign a two-year lease. (comma incorrectly placed between verb and indirect question)

(4) In Compounds That Are Not Composed of Independent Clauses

 Do not use commas before coordinating conjuctions like *and* and *but* when they join two elements of a compound subject, predicate, object, or complement.

During the 1400s plagues, and pestilence were common. (compound subject)

Many women thirty-five and older are returning to college, and tend to be good students. (compound predicate)

Mattel has marketed a lab coat, and an astronaut suit for its Barbie doll. (compound object)

People buy bottled water because it is pure, and fashionable. (compound complement)

(5) Before a Dependent Clause at the End of a Sentence

A comma is not generally used before a dependent clause that falls at the end of a sentence.

Jane Addams founded Hull House, because she wanted to help Chicago's poor.

CHAPTER 45

Using Semicolons

A semicolon is used only between items of equal grammatical rank: two independent clauses, two phrases, and so on.

45a Separating Independent Clauses

Use a semicolon between closely related independent clauses that convey parallel or contrasting information but are not joined by a coordinating conjunction.

> Paul Revere's *The Boston Massacre* is traditional American protest art; Edward Hicks's paintings are socially conscious art with a religious strain.

NOTE: Using only a comma or no punctuation at all between independent clauses creates a <u>comma splice</u> or <u>fused sentence</u>. **See Ch. 29**

Use a semicolon before a <u>transitional word or phrase</u> that joins two independent clauses (the transitional element is followed by a comma). **See 7b2**

> Thomas Jefferson brought two hundred vanilla beans and a recipe for vanilla ice cream back from France; thus, he gave America its all-time favorite ice cream flavor.

45b Separating Items in a Series

Use semicolons between items in a series when one or more of these items include commas.

> Three papers are posted on the bulletin board outside the building: a description of the exams; a list of appeal procedures for students who fail; and an employment ad from an automobile factory, addressed specifically to candidates whose appeals are turned down. (Andrea Lee, *Russian Journal*)

> Laramie, Wyoming; Wyoming, Delaware; and Delaware, Ohio, were three of the places they visited.

45c Editing Misused Semicolons

Do not use semicolons in the following situations.

(1) Between a Phrase and a Clause

Use a comma, not a semicolon, between a phrase and a clause.

> Increasing rapidly; computer crime poses a challenge for business and government.

(2) Between a Dependent and an Independent Clause

Use a comma, not a semicolon, between a dependent and an independent clause.

> Because drugs can now suppress the body's immune reaction; fewer organ transplants are rejected.

(3) To Introduce a List

See
24c

Use a colon, not a semicolon, to introduce a list.

> Despite the presence of CNN and Fox News, the evening news remains a battleground for the three major television networks; CBS, NBC, and ABC.

See
48a

NOTE: Always introduce a list with a complete sentence followed by a colon.

(4) To Introduce a Quotation

See
47a

Do not use a semicolon to introduce quoted speech or writing.

> Marie Antoinette may not have said; "Let them eat cake."

CHAPTER 46

Using Apostrophes

Use an apostrophe to form the possessive case, to indicate omissions in contractions, and to form certain plurals.

46a Forming the Possessive Case

The possessive case indicates ownership. In English, the possessive case of nouns and indefinite pronouns is indicated either with a phrase that includes the word *of* (the hands *of* the clock) or with an apostrophe and, in most cases, an *s* (the clock's hands).

(1) Singular Nouns and Indefinite Pronouns

To form the possessive case of singular nouns and indefinite pronouns, add *-'s*.

> "The Monk's Tale" is one of Chaucer's *Canterbury Tales.*

> When we would arrive was anyone's guess.

(2) Singular Nouns Ending in *-s*

To form the possessive case of singular nouns that end in *-s*, add *-'s* in most cases.

> Reading Henry James's *The Ambassadors* was not Maris's idea of fun.

> The class's time was changed to 8 a.m.

NOTE: With some singular nouns that end in *-s*, pronouncing the possessive ending as a separate syllable can sound awkward. In such cases, it is acceptable to use just an apostrophe: Crispus Attucks' death, Aristophanes' *Lysistrata.*

(3) Plural Nouns

To form the possessive case of regular plural nouns (those that end in *-s* or *-es*), add only an apostrophe.

> Laid-off employees received two weeks' severance pay and three months' medical benefits.

> The Lopezes' three children are triplets.

To form the possessive case of nouns that have irregular plurals, add *-'s*.

> *The Children's Hour* is a play by Lillian Hellman.

(4) Compound Nouns or Groups of Words

To form the possessive case of **compound nouns** (nouns formed from two or more words) or of word groups, add -'s to the last word.

the Secretary of State's resignation

someone else's responsibility

(5) Two or More Items

To indicate individual ownership of two or more items, add -'s to each item.

Ernest Hemingway's and Gertrude Stein's writing styles have some similarities.

To indicate joint ownership, add -'s only to the last item.

We studied Lewis and Clark's expedition.

46b   Indicating Omissions in Contractions

(1) Omitted Letters

Apostrophes replace omitted letters in **contractions** that combine a pronoun and a verb (*he* + *will* = *he'll*) or the elements of a verb phrase (*do* + *not* = *don't*).

Frequently Used Contractions

couldn't (could not)	they're (they are)
don't (do not)	we'd (we would)
he's (he is, he has)	we'll (we will)
I'm (I am)	we're (we are)
isn't (is not)	we've (we have)
it's (it is, it has)	who's (who is, who has)
let's (let us)	won't (will not)
she's (she is, she has)	wouldn't (would not)
they'd (they had)	you'd (you would)

NOTE: Contractions are generally too informal for use in college writing.

Grammar Checker: Revising Contractions

If you set your word processor's writing style to Formal or Technical, the grammar checker will highlight contractions and offer suggestions for revision.

Spelling and Grammar: English (U.S.)

Contraction Use:

You'll want to be sure to bring your laptop and external DVD drive.

Suggestions:

You will

Close-up: Using Apostrophes

Be careful not to confuse contractions (which always include apostrophes) with the possessive forms of personal pronouns (which never include apostrophes).

Contractions	Possessive Forms
Who's on first?	Whose book is this?
They're playing our song.	Their team is winning.
It's raining.	Its paws were muddy.
You're a real pal.	Your résumé is impressive.

(2) Omitted Numbers

In informal writing, an apostrophe may also be used to represent the century in a year: Class of '03, the '60s. In college writing, however, write out the number in full: 2003, 1960s.

46c Forming Plurals

In a few special situations, add -'s to form plurals.

Forming Plurals with Apostrophes

Plurals of Letters
The Italian language has no *i*'s or *k*'s.

Plurals of Words Referred to as Words
The supervisor would accept no *if*'s, *and*'s, or *but*'s.

NOTE: Elements spoken of as themselves (letters, numerals, or words) are set in italic type; the plural ending, however, is not.

See
51c

NOTE: Apostrophes are not used in plurals of abbreviations (including acronyms) or numbers.

DVDs   PACs   1960s

46d Editing Misused Apostrophes

Do not use apostrophes with plural nouns that are not possessive.

The Thompson's are not at home.

Down vest's are very warm.

The Philadelphia Seventy Sixer's have had good years and bad.

Do not use apostrophes to form the possessive case of personal pronouns.

This ticket must be your's or her's.

The next turn is their's.

Her doll had lost it's right eye.

The next great moment in history is our's.

NOTE: Be careful not to confuse the possessive forms of personal pronouns with <u>contractions</u>.

See 46b1

CHAPTER 47

Using Quotation Marks

Use quotation marks to set off brief passages of quoted speech or writing, to set off titles, and to set off words used in special ways. Do not use quotation marks when quoting long passages of prose or poetry.

47a Setting Off Quoted Speech or Writing

When you quote a word, phrase, or brief passage of someone's speech or writing, enclose the quoted material in a pair of quotation marks.

> Gloria Steinem observed, "We are becoming the men we once hoped to marry."

> Galsworthy writes that Aunt Juley is "prostrated by the blow" (329). (Note that in this example from a student paper, the end punctuation follows the parenthetical documentation.)

Close-up: Using Quotation Marks with Dialogue

When you record **dialogue** (conversation between two or more people), enclose the quoted words in quotation marks. Begin a new paragraph each time a new speaker is introduced.

When you are quoting several paragraphs of dialogue by one speaker, begin each new paragraph with quotation marks. However, use closing quotation marks only at the end of the *entire quoted passage*, not at the end of each paragraph.

Special rules govern the punctuation of a quotation when it is used with an **identifying tag,** a phrase (such as *he said*) that identifies the speaker or writer. Punctuation guidelines for various situations involving identifying tags are outlined below.

(1) Identifying Tag in the Middle of a Quoted Passage

Use a pair of commas to set off an identifying tag that interrupts a quoted passage.

> "In the future," pop artist Andy Warhol once said, "everyone will be world famous for fifteen minutes."

If the identifying tag follows a completed sentence but the quoted passage continues, place the period after the identifying tag, and begin the new sentence with a capital letter and quotation marks.

"Be careful," Erin warned. "Reptiles can be tricky."

(2) Identifying Tag at the Beginning of a Quoted Passage

Use a comma after an identifying tag that introduces quoted speech or writing.

The Raven repeated, "Nevermore."

See 48a3 Use a colon instead of a comma before a quotation if the identifying tag is a complete sentence.

She gave her final answer: "No."

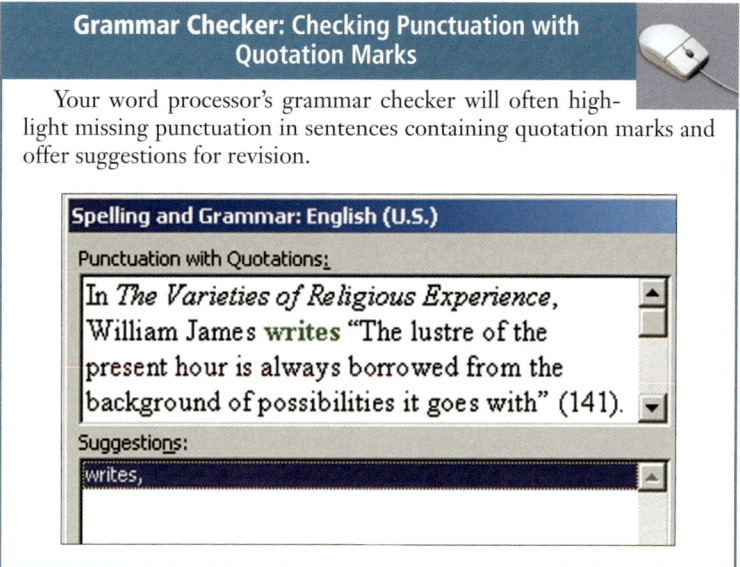

Grammar Checker: Checking Punctuation with Quotation Marks

Your word processor's grammar checker will often highlight missing punctuation in sentences containing quotation marks and offer suggestions for revision.

Spelling and Grammar: English (U.S.)

Punctuation with Quotations:

In *The Varieties of Religious Experience,* William James **writes** "The lustre of the present hour is always borrowed from the background of possibilities it goes with" (141).

Suggestions:

writes,

(3) Identifying Tag at the End of a Quoted Passage

Use a comma to set off a quotation from an identifying tag that follows it.

"Be careful out there," the sergeant warned.

If the quotation ends with a question mark or an exclamation point, use that punctuation mark instead of the comma. In this situation, the identifying tag begins with a lowercase letter even though it follows end punctuation.

"Is Ankara the capital of Turkey?" she asked.

"Oh, boy!" he cried.

NOTE: Commas and periods are always placed *inside* quotation marks. For information on placement of other punctuation marks with quotation marks, **see 47e**.

47b Setting Off Long Prose Passages and Poetry

(1) Long Prose Passages

Do not enclose a **long prose passage** (a passage of more than four lines) in quotation marks. Instead, set it off by indenting the entire passage one inch (or ten spaces) from the left-hand margin. Treat the quoted passage like regular text: double-space above and below it, and double-space between lines within it. Introduce the passage with a colon, and place parenthetical documentation one space after the end punctuation.

The following portrait of Aunt Juley illustrates several of the devices Galsworthy uses throughout <u>The Forsyte Saga</u>, such as a journalistic detachment that is almost cruel in its scrutiny, a subtle sense of the grotesque, and an ironic stance:

> Aunt Juley stayed in her room, prostrated by the blow. Her face, discoloured by tears, was divided into compartments by the little ridges of pouting flesh which had swollen with emotion. . . . At fixed intervals she went to her drawer, and took from beneath the lavender bags a fresh pocket-handkerchief. Her warm heart could not bear the thought that Ann was lying there so cold. (329)

Many similar portraits of characters appear throughout the novel.

Close-up: Quoting Long Prose Passages

When you quote a long prose passage that is a single paragraph, do not indent the first line. When quoting two or more paragraphs, however, indent the first line of each paragraph (including the first) *three* additional spaces. If the first sentence of the quoted passage does not begin a paragraph in the source, do not indent it—but do indent the first line of each subsequent paragraph. If the passage you are quoting includes material set in quotation marks, reproduce those quotation marks.

NOTE: <u>APA guidelines</u> differ from those set forth here, which conform to MLA style.

See 18b

(2) Poetry

Treat one line of poetry like a short prose passage: enclose it in quotation marks, and run it into the text. If you quote two or three lines of poetry, separate the lines with **slashes**, and run the quotation into the text. (Leave one space before and one space after the slash.)

> See
> 48e

> Alexander Pope writes, "True Ease in Writing comes from Art,
>
> not Chance, / As those move easiest who have learned to dance."

> See
> 47b1

If you quote more than three lines of poetry, set them off like a **long prose passage**. (For special emphasis, you may set off fewer lines in this manner.) Be sure to reproduce punctuation, spelling, capitalization, and indentation of the quoted lines *exactly* as they appear in the poem.

> Wilfred Owen, a poet who was killed in action in World
>
> War I, expressed the horrors of war with vivid imagery:
>
> > Bent double, like old beggars under sacks,
> >
> > Knock-kneed, coughing like hags, we cursed through
> >
> > > sludge.
> >
> > Till on the haunting flares we turned our backs
> >
> > And towards our distant rest began to trudge.
> >
> > > (lines 1-4)

47c Setting Off Titles

> See
> 51a

Titles of short works and titles of parts of long works are enclosed in quotation marks. Other titles are **italicized**.

NOTE: MLA style recommends underlining to indicate italics.

Titles Requiring Quotation Marks

Articles in Magazines, Newspapers, and Professional Journals
"Why Johnny Can't Write"

Essays, Short Stories, Short Poems, and Songs
"Fenimore Cooper's Literary Offenses"
"Flying Home"
"The Road Not Taken"
"The Star-Spangled Banner"

Chapters or Sections of Books
"Miss Sharp Begins to Make Friends" (Chapter 10 of *Vanity Fair*)

Episodes of Radio or Television Series
"Lucy Goes to the Hospital" (*I Love Lucy*)

47d   Setting Off Words Used in Special Ways

Enclose a word used in a special or unusual way in quotation marks. (If you use *so-called* before an unusual usage, do not use quotation marks as well.)

> It was clear that adults approved of children who were "readers," but it was not at all clear why this was so. (Annie Dillard)

Also enclose a **coinage**—an invented word—in quotation marks.

> After the twins were born, the minivan became a "babymobile."

47e   Using Quotation Marks with Other Punctuation

Place quotation marks *after* the comma or period at the end of a quotation.

> Many, like the poet Robert Frost, think about "the road not taken," but not many have taken "the one less traveled by."

Place quotation marks *before* a semicolon or colon at the end of a quotation.

> Students who do not pass the test receive "certificates of completion"; those who pass are awarded diplomas.

> Taxpayers were pleased with the first of the candidate's promised "sweeping new reforms": a balanced budget.

If a question mark, exclamation point, or dash is part of the quotation, place the quotation marks *after* the punctuation.

> "Who's there?" she demanded.

> "Stop!" he cried.

> "Should we leave now, or—" Vicki paused, unable to continue.

If a question mark, exclamation point, or dash is *not* part of the quotation, place the quotation marks *before* the punctuation.

> Did you finish reading "The Black Cat"?

> Whatever you do, don't yell "Uncle"!

> The first story—Updike's "*A & P*"—provoked discussion.

Close-up: Quotations within Quotations

FAQs link

Use *single* quotation marks to enclose a quotation within a quotation.

> Claire noted, "Liberace always said, 'I cried all the way to the bank.' "

(continued)

Quotations within quotations (continued)

Also use single quotation marks within a quotation to indicate a title that would normally be enclosed in double quotation marks.

I think what she said was, "Play it, Sam. Play 'As Time Goes By.' "

See
47b1
Use *double* quotation marks around quotations or titles within a <u>long prose passage</u>.

47f Editing Misused Quotation Marks

Do not use quotation marks in the following situations.

(1) To Set Off Indirect Quotations

Do not use quotation marks to set off **indirect quotations** (someone else's written or spoken words that are not quoted exactly).

Freud wondered ~~"~~what women wanted.~~"~~

(2) To Set Off Slang or Technical Terms

Do not use quotation marks to set off slang or technical terms. (Note that slang is not appropriate in college writing.)

Dawn is ~~"~~into~~"~~ running.

~~"~~Biofeedback~~"~~ is sometimes used to treat migraines.

Close-up: Titles of Your Own Papers	
Do not use quotation marks (or italics) to set off the titles of your own papers.	

CHAPTER 48

Using Other Punctuation Marks

48a Using Colons

The **colon** is a strong punctuation mark that points readers ahead to the rest of the sentence. When a colon introduces a list or series, explanatory material, or a quotation, it must be preceded by a complete sentence.

(1) Introducing Lists or Series

Use colons to set off lists or series, including those introduced by phrases like *the following* or *as follows.*

> Waiting tables requires three skills**:** memory, speed, and balance.

(2) Introducing Explanatory Material

Use a colon to introduce material that explains, exemplifies, or summarizes. Frequently, such material is presented in the form of an **appositive,** a word group that identifies or renames an adjacent noun or pronoun.

> Diego Rivera painted a controversial mural**:** the one commissioned for Rockefeller Center in the 1930s.

> She had one dream**:** to play professional basketball.

Sometimes a colon separates two independent clauses, the second illustrating or explaining the first.

> A *U.S. News & World Report* survey has revealed a surprising fact**:** Americans spend more time at shopping malls than anywhere else except at home and at work.

Close-up: Using Colons

When a complete sentence follows a colon, the sentence may begin with either a capital or a lowercase letter. However, if the sentence is a quotation, the first word is always capitalized (unless it was not capitalized in the source).

---

(3) Introducing Quotations

When you quote a <u>long prose passage</u>, always introduce it with a colon. Also use a colon before a short quotation when it is introduced by a complete sentence.

FAQs

See
47b1

With dignity, Bartleby repeated the familiar words: "I prefer not to."

Other Conventional Uses of Colons

To Separate Titles from Subtitles
Family Installments: Memories of Growing Up Hispanic

To Separate Minutes from Hours
6:15 a.m.

See 26a

After Salutations in business letters
Dear Dr. Evans:

See 17a2

To Separate Place of Publication from Name of Publisher in an MLA works-cited list
Boston: Wadsworth, 2006.

---

(4) Editing Misused Colons

Do not use colons after expressions such as *namely, for example, such as*, or *that is.*

> The Eye Institute treats patients with a wide variety of conditions, such as/ myopia, glaucoma, and cataracts.

Do not place colons between verbs and their objects or complements or between prepositions and their objects.

> James Michener wrote/ *Hawaii, Centennial, Space,* and *Poland.*

> Hitler's armies marched through/ the Netherlands, Belgium, and France.

48b Using Dashes

(1) Setting Off Nonessential Material

See 44d

Like commas, **dashes** can set off nonessential material, but unlike commas, dashes call attention to the material they set off. Indicate a dash with two unspaced hyphens (which your word-processing program will automatically convert to a dash).

For emphasis, you may use dashes to set off explanations, qualifications, examples, definitions, and appositives.

> Neither of the boys—both nine-year-olds—had any history of violence.

> Too many parents learn the dangers of swimming pools the hard way—after a toddler has drowned.

(2) Introducing a Summary

Use a dash to introduce a statement that summarizes a list or series before it.

"Study hard," "Respect your elders," "Don't talk with your mouth full"—Sharon had often heard her parents say these things.

(3) Indicating an Interruption

In dialogue, a dash may indicate a hesitation or an unfinished thought.

"I think—no, I know—this is the worst day of my life," Julie sighed.

(4) Editing Overused Dashes

Too many dashes can make a passage seem disorganized and out of control, so be careful not to overuse them.

. Most
Registration was a nightmare,—most of the courses I wanted to take—geology and conversational Spanish, for instance—met at inconvenient times—or were closed by the time I tried to sign up for them.

48c   Using Parentheses

(1) Setting Off Nonessential Material

Use parentheses to enclose material that expands, clarifies, illustrates, or supplements.

In some European countries (notably Sweden and France), high-quality day care is offered at little or no cost to parents.

When a complete sentence enclosed in parentheses falls within another sentence, it should not begin with a capital letter or end with a period.

The area is so cold (temperatures average in the low twenties) that it is virtually uninhabitable.

If the parenthetical sentence does *not* fall within another sentence, however, it must begin with a capital letter and end with appropriate punctuation.

The region is very cold. (Temperatures average in the low twenties.)

(2) Using Parentheses in Other Situations

Use parentheses around letters and numbers that identify points on a list, dates, cross-references, and documentation.

All reports must include the following components: (1) an opening summary, (2) a background statement, and (3) a list of conclusions.

Russia defeated Sweden in the Great Northern War (1700–1721).

Other scholars also make this point (see p. 54).

One critic has called the novel "puerile" (Arvin 72).

NOTE: Punctuation never precedes an opening parenthesis (although punctuation may follow a closing parenthesis).

48d Using Brackets

(1) Setting Off Comments within Quotations

Brackets within quotations tell readers that the enclosed words are yours and not those of your source. You can bracket an explanation, a clarification, a correction, or an opinion.

> "Even at Princeton he [F. Scott Fitzgerald] felt like an outsider."

If a quotation contains an error, indicate that the error is not yours by following the error with the Latin word *sic* ("thus") in brackets.

> "The octopuss [sic] is a cephalopod mollusk with eight arms."

NOTE: Use brackets to indicate changes that you make in order to fit a **quotation** smoothly into your sentence.

See 15d1

(2) Replacing Parentheses within Parentheses

When one set of parentheses falls within another, use brackets in place of the inner set.

> In her study of American education (*The Troubled Crusade* [New York: Basic, 1963]), Diane Ravitch addresses issues like educational reforms and campus unrest.

48e Using Slashes

(1) Separating One Option from Another

> The either/or fallacy is a common error in logic.
>
> Writer/director M. Night Shyamalan spoke at the film festival.

Notice that in this situation there is no space before or after the slash.

(2) Separating Lines of Poetry Run into the Text

> The poet James Schevill writes, "I study my defects / And learn how to perfect them."

In this situation, leave one space before and one space after the slash.

48f Using Ellipses

Use ellipses in the following situations.

(1) Indicating an Omission in Quoted Prose

Use an **ellipsis**—three *spaced* periods—to indicate that you have omitted words from a prose quotation. Note that an ellipsis in the middle of a quoted passage can indicate the omission of a word, a sentence or two, or even a whole paragraph or more. When deleting material from a quotation, be very careful not to change the meaning of the original passage.

> **Original:** "When I was a young man, being anxious to distinguish myself, I was perpetually starting new propositions." (Samuel Johnson)

> **With Omission:** "When I was a young man, ... I was perpetually starting new propositions."

Note that when you delete words immediately after an internal punctuation mark (such as the comma in the above example), you retain the punctuation before the ellipsis.

When you delete material at the end of a sentence, place the sentence's period or other end punctuation before the ellipsis.

> According to humorist Dave Barry, "from outer space Europe appears to be shaped like a large ketchup stain. ..." (period followed by ellipses)

NOTE: Never begin a quoted passage with an ellipsis.

When you delete material between sentences, any punctuation should precede the ellipsis.

> **Deletion from Middle of One Sentence to End of Another**
> According to Donald Hall, "Everywhere one meets the idea that reading is an activity desirable in itself. ... People surround the idea of reading with piety and do not take into account the purpose of reading." (period followed by ellipses)

> **Deletion from Middle of One Sentence to Middle of Another**
> "When I was a young man, ... I found that generally what was new was false." (Samuel Johnson) (comma followed by ellipses)

NOTE: If a quoted passage already contains an ellipsis, MLA recommends that you enclose your own ellipses in brackets to distinguish them from those that appear in the original quotation.

Close-up: Using Ellipses

If a quotation ending with an ellipsis is followed by parenthetical documentation, the final punctuation *follows* the documentation.

As Jarman argues, "Compromise was impossible ..." (161).

(2) Indicating an Omission in Quoted Poetry

Use an ellipsis when you omit a word or phrase from a line of poetry. When you omit one or more lines of poetry, use a line of spaced periods. (The length may be equal either to the line above it or to the missing line—but it should not be longer than the longest line of the poem.)

Original:

Stitch! Stitch! Stitch!
In poverty, hunger, and dirt,
And still with a voice of dolorous pitch,
Would that its tone could reach the Rich,
She sang this "Song of the Shirt!"

(Thomas Hood)

With Omission:

Stitch! Stitch! Stitch!
In poverty, hunger, and dirt,
. . . .
She sang this "Song of the Shirt!"

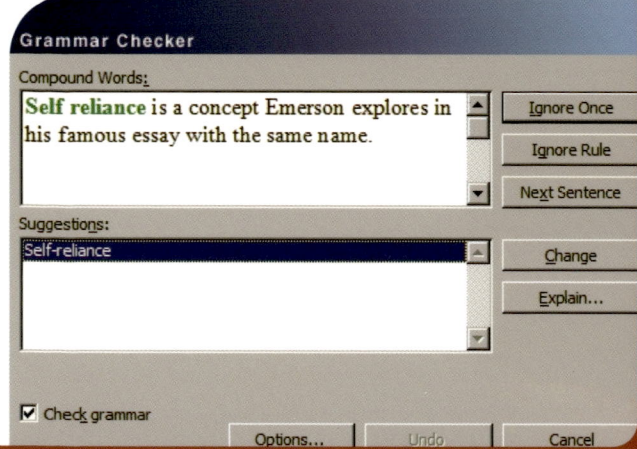

Grammar Checker

Compound Words:

Self reliance is a concept Emerson explores in his famous essay with the same name.

Ignore Once

Ignore Rule

Next Sentence

Suggestions:

Self-reliance

Change

Explain...

☑ Check grammar

Options...   Undo   Cancel

Understanding Spelling and Mechanics

FREQUENTLY ASKED QUESTIONS

CHAPTER 49

Improving Spelling

Most people can spell even difficult words "almost" correctly; usually only a letter or two are wrong. For this reason, memorizing a few rules and their exceptions and learning the correct spelling of the most commonly misspelled words can help you become a better speller.

49a Understanding Spelling and Pronunciation

Because pronunciation in English often provides few clues to spelling, you must memorize the spellings of many words and use a dictionary and a spell checker regularly.

(1) Vowels in Unstressed Positions

Many unstressed vowels sound exactly alike. For instance, it is hard to tell from pronunciation alone that the *i* in *terrible* is not an *a*. In addition, the unstressed vowels *a*, *e*, and *i* are impossible to distinguish in the suffixes *-able* and *-ible*, *-ance* and *-ence*, and *-ant* and *-ent*.

comfort<u>a</u>ble	brilli<u>a</u>nce	serv<u>a</u>nt
compat<u>i</u>ble	excell<u>e</u>nce	independ<u>e</u>nt

(2) Silent Letters

Some English words contain silent letters, such as the *b* in *climb* and the *t* in *mortgage*.

ai<u>s</u>le	depo<u>t</u>	<u>p</u>neumonia
clim<u>b</u>	kni<u>g</u>ht	sil<u>h</u>ouette
condem<u>n</u>	mor<u>t</u>gage	sovereign

(3) Words That Are Often Pronounced Carelessly

Words like the following are often misspelled because they are pronounced carelessly in everyday speech. Consequently, we may leave out, add, or transpose letters when we spell them.

can<u>d</u>idate	lib<u>r</u>ary	reco<u>g</u>nize
environ<u>m</u>ent	light<u>n</u>ing	speci<u>f</u>ic
Feb<u>r</u>uary	nuc<u>l</u>ear	suppose<u>d</u> to
govern<u>m</u>ent	per<u>f</u>orm	sur<u>p</u>rise
hund<u>r</u>ed	quan<u>t</u>ity	use<u>d</u> to

(4) American and British Spellings

Some words are spelled one way in the United States and another way in Great Britain.

American	British
color	colour
defense	defence
judgment	judgement
theater	theatre
toward	towards
traveled	travelled

(5) Homophones

Homophones are words—such as *accept* and *except*—that are pronounced alike but spelled differently.

accept	to receive
except	other than
affect	to have an influence on (*verb*)
effect	result (*noun*); to cause (*verb*)
its	possessive of *it*
it's	contraction of *it is*
principal	most important (*adjective*); head of a school (*noun*)
principle	a basic truth; rule of conduct

For a full list of these and other homophones, along with their meanings and sentences illustrating their use, **see Chapter 42.**

Close-up: One Word or Two?

Some words may be written as one word or two, depending on meaning.

any way vs. anyway
The early pioneers made the trip west *any way* they could.
It began to rain, but the game continued *anyway*.

every day vs. everyday
Every day brings new opportunities.
John thought of his birthday as an *everyday* event.

Other words are frequently misspelled because people are not sure whether they are one word or two.

One Word	Two Words
already	a lot
cannot	all right
classroom	even though
overweight	no one

Consult a dictionary if you have any doubts about whether a word is written as one word or two.

http://kirsznermandell.wadsworth.com

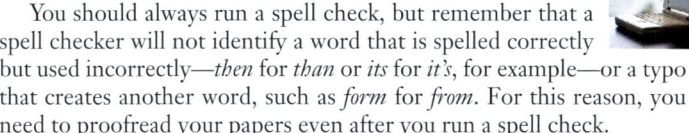

Computer Tip: Running a Spell Check

   You should always run a spell check, but remember that a spell checker will not identify a word that is spelled correctly but used incorrectly—*then* for *than* or *its* for *it's*, for example—or a typo that creates another word, such as *form* for *from*. For this reason, you need to proofread your papers even after you run a spell check.

49b   Learning Spelling Rules

Knowing a few reliable rules can help you overcome problems caused by the inconsistency between pronunciation and spelling.

(1) The *ie/ei* Combinations

Use *i* before *e* except after *c* or when pronounced *ay*, as in *neighbor*.

   i before *e:* belief, chief, niece, friend

   ei after *c:* ceiling, deceit, receive

   ei pronounced *ay:* weigh, freight, eight

Exceptions: *either, neither, foreign, leisure, weird,* and *seize.* In addition, if the *ie* combination is not pronounced as a unit, the rule does not apply: *atheist, science.*

(2) Doubling Final Consonants

The only words that double their consonants before a suffix that begins with a vowel (*-ed* or *-ing*) are those that pass the following three tests:

1. They have one syllable or are stressed on the last syllable.
2. They contain only one vowel in the last syllable.
3. They end in a single consonant.

The word *tap* satisfies all three conditions: it has only one syllable, it contains only one vowel (*a*), and it ends in a single consonant (*p*). Therefore, the final consonant doubles before a suffix beginning with a vowel (*tapped, tapping*).

The word *relent*, however, meets only two of the three conditions: it is stressed on the last syllable, and it has one vowel in the last syllable, but it does not end in a single consonant. Therefore, its final consonant is not doubled (*relented, relenting*).

(3) Prefixes

The addition of a prefix never affects the spelling of the root (*mis + spell = misspell*). Some prefixes can cause spelling problems, however, because they are pronounced alike although they are not spelled alike: *ante-/anti-, en-/in-, per-/pre-,* and *de-/di-*.

antebellum	antiaircraft
encircle	integrate
perceive	prescribe
deduct	direct

(4) Silent e before a Suffix

When a suffix that begins with a consonant is added to a word ending in a silent *e*, the *e* is generally kept: *hope/hopeful; lame/lamely; bore/boredom.* **Exceptions:** *argument, truly, ninth, judgment,* and *acknowledgment.*

When a suffix that begins with a vowel is added to a word ending in a silent *e*, the *e* is generally dropped: *hope/hoping; trace/traced; grieve/grievance; love/lovable.* **Exceptions:** *changeable, noticeable,* and *courageous.*

(5) y before a Suffix

When a word ends in a consonant plus *y*, the *y* generally changes to an *i* when a suffix is added (*beauty + ful = beautiful*). The *y* is kept, however, when the suffix *-ing* is added (*tally + ing = tallying*) and in some one-syllable words (*dry + ness = dryness*).

When a word ends in a vowel plus *y*, the *y* is kept (*joy + ful = joyful; employ + er = employer*). **Exception:** *day + ly = daily.*

(6) *seed* Endings

Endings with the sound *seed* are nearly always spelled *cede*, as in *precede, intercede, concede,* and so on. **Exceptions:** *supersede, exceed, proceed,* and *succeed.*

(7) -able, -ible

If the root of a word is itself a word, the suffix *-able* is most commonly used. If the root of a word is not a word, the suffix *-ible* is most often used.

comfort<u>able</u>	compat<u>ible</u>
agree<u>able</u>	incred<u>ible</u>
dry<u>able</u>	plaus<u>ible</u>

(8) Plurals

Most nouns form plurals by adding *-s: savage/savages, tortilla/tortillas, boat/boats.* There are, however, a number of exceptions.

Words Ending in -f or -fe Some words ending in *-f* or *-fe* form plurals by changing the *f* to *v* and adding *-es* or *-s: life/lives, self/selves.* Others add just *-s: belief/beliefs, safe/safes.* Words ending in *-ff* take *-s* to form plurals: *tariff/tariffs.*

Words Ending in -y Most words that end in a consonant followed by *y* form plurals by changing the *y* to *i* and adding *-es: baby/babies.* **Exceptions:** proper nouns such as *Kennedys* (never *Kennedies*).

    Words that end in a vowel followed by a *y* form plurals by adding *-s: monkey/monkeys.*

Words Ending in -o Words that end in a vowel followed by *o* form the plural by adding *-s: radio/radios, stereo/stereos, zoo/zoos.* Most words that end in a consonant followed by *o* add *-es* to form the plural: *tomato/tomatoes, hero/heroes.* **Exceptions:** *silo/silos, piano/pianos, memo/memos, soprano/sopranos.*

Words Ending in -s, -ss, -sh, -ch, -x, and -z These words form plurals by adding *-es: Jones/Joneses, mass/masses, rash/rashes, lunch/lunches, box/boxes, buzz/buzzes.* **Exceptions:** Some one-syllable words that end in *-s* or *-z* double their final consonants when forming plurals: *quiz/quizzes.*

Compound Nouns   **Compound nouns**—nouns formed from two or more words—usually form the plural with the last word in the compound construction: *welfare state/welfare states; snowball/snowballs.* However, compound nouns whose first element is more important than the others form the plural with the first element: *sister-in-law/sisters-in-law, attorney general/attorneys general, hole in one/holes in one.*

Foreign Plurals Some words, especially those borrowed from Latin or Greek, keep their foreign plurals.

Singular	Plural
criterion	criteria
datum	data
larva	larvae
medium	media
memorandum	memoranda
stimulus	stimuli

http://kirsznermandell.wadsworth.com

Computer Tip: Spelling an Unfamiliar Word

Most spell checkers suggest corrections for misspelled words in your documents. Often, the word you meant to use is included in the list of possible words the spell checker generates; sometimes, however, you must determine the correct spelling yourself.

CHAPTER 50

Knowing When to Capitalize

> **Computer Tip: Revising Capitalization Errors**
>
> In *Microsoft Word*, the AutoCorrect tool will automatically capitalize certain words—such as the first word of a sentence or the days of the week. You can also designate additional words to be automatically capitalized for you as you type. To do this, select Auto-Correct from the Tools menu, and type in the words you want to capitalize. Be sure to proofread your documents after using the AutoCorrect tool, though, since it may introduce capitalization errors into your writing.

50a Capitalizing the First Word of a Sentence

Capitalize the first word of a sentence, including a sentence of quoted speech or writing.

As Shakespeare wrote, "Who steals my purse steals trash."

Do not capitalize a sentence set off within another sentence by dashes or parentheses.

Finding the store closed—it was a holiday—they went home.

The candidates are Frank Lester and Jane Lester (they are not related).

> **Close-up: Using Capital Letters in Poetry**
>
> Remember that the first word of a line of poetry is generally capitalized. If the poet uses a lowercase letter to begin a line, however, follow that style when you quote the line.

50b Capitalizing Proper Nouns

Proper nouns—the names of specific persons, places, or things—are capitalized, and so are adjectives formed from proper nouns.

499

ESL Tip
Do not capitalize a word simply because you want to emphasize its importance. If you are not sure whether a noun should be capitalized, look it up in a dictionary.

(1) Specific People's Names

Eleanor Roosevelt   Medgar Evers

Capitalize a title when it precedes a person's name (<u>S</u>enator <u>O</u>lympia Snowe) or is used instead of the name (<u>D</u>ad). Do not capitalize titles that *follow* names (Olympia Snowe, the <u>s</u>enator from Maine) or those that refer to the general position, not the particular person who holds it (a stay-at-home <u>d</u>ad).

You may, however, capitalize titles that indicate very high-ranking positions even when they are used alone or when they follow a name: the <u>P</u>ope; George W. Bush, <u>P</u>resident of the United States. Never capitalize a title denoting a family relationship when it follows an article or a possessive pronoun (an <u>u</u>ncle, his <u>m</u>om).

Capitalize titles that represent academic degrees or abbreviations of those degrees even when they follow a name: <u>D</u>r. Benjamin Spock; Benjamin Spock, <u>MD</u>.

(2) Names of Particular Structures, Special Events, Monuments, and So On

the *Titanic*	the World Series
the Brooklyn Bridge	Mount Rushmore

(3) Places and Geographical Regions

Saturn	the Straits of Magellan
Budapest	the Western Hemisphere

Capitalize *north*, *east*, *south*, and *west* when they denote particular geographical regions, but not when they designate directions.

There are more tornadoes in Kansas than in the <u>East</u>. (*East* refers to a specific region.)

Turn <u>west</u> at Broad Street and continue <u>north</u> to Market. (*West* and *north* refer to directions, not specific regions.)

(4) Days of the Week, Months, and Holidays

Saturday	Rosh Hashanah
January	Cinco de Mayo

(5) Historical Periods, Documents, and Names of Legal Cases

the Reformation   the Treaty of Versailles
the Battle of Gettysburg   *Brown v. Board of Education*

NOTE: Names of court cases are italicized (or underlined to indicate italics) in the text of your papers but not in works-cited entries.

(6) Philosophic, Literary, and Artistic Movements

Naturalism   Neoclassicism
Romanticism   Expressionism

(7) Races, Ethnic Groups, Nationalities, and Languages

African American   Korean
Latino/Latina   Dutch

NOTE: When the words *black* and *white* refer to races, they have tra-ditionally not been capitalized. Current opinion is divided on whether to capitalize *black*.

(8) Religions and Their Followers; Sacred Books and Figures

Jews   the Talmud   Buddha
Islam   God   the Bible

(9) Specific Organizations

the New York Yankees   the American Bar Association
the Democratic Party   the Anti-Defamation League

(10) Businesses, Government Agencies, and Other Institutions

General Electric
the Environmental Protection Agency
Lincoln High School
the University of Maryland

(11) Brand Names and Words Formed from Them

Coke   Astroturf   Rollerblades   Post-it   Velcro

NOTE: In general, use generic references, not brand names, in college writing—*photocopy*, not *Xerox*, for example. These generic names are not capitalized.

(12) Specific Academic Courses and Departments

Sociology 201   English Department

NOTE: Do not capitalize a general subject area (sociology, zoology) unless it is the name of a language (French).

(13) Adjectives Formed from Proper Nouns

Keynesian economics   Elizabethan era

Freudian slip   Shakespearean sonnet

When words derived from proper nouns have lost their specialized meanings, do not capitalize them: *china bowl, french fries.*

Grammar Checker: Checking Proper Nouns

Your word processor's spell checker may not recognize many of the proper nouns you use in your documents, particularly those that require irregular capitalization, such as *Leonardo da Vinci*, and therefore will identify these nouns as spelling errors. To solve this problem, click Ignore once to instruct the spell checker to ignore the word one time and Ignore All to instruct the spell checker to ignore all uses of the word in your document.

Spelling and Grammar: English (U.S.)

The Last Supper is one of Leonardo **da** Vinci's masterpieces

Suggestions:
ad
day
dad
dam
dab
dap

- Ignore Once
- Ignore All
- Add to Dictionary
- Change
- Change All
- AutoCorrect

☑ Check grammar

Options...   Undo   Cancel

50c   Capitalizing Important Words in Titles

In general, capitalize all words in titles with the exception of articles (*a*, *an*, and *the*), prepositions, coordinating conjunctions, and the *to* in infinitives. If an article, preposition, or coordinating conjunction is the *first* or *last* word in the title, however, do capitalize it.

"Dover Beach"	*On the Waterfront*
The Declaration of Independence	*A Man and a Woman*
Across the River and into the Trees	"What Friends Are For"

50d   Capitalizing the Pronoun *I*, the Interjection *O*, and Other Single Letters in Special Constructions

Always capitalize the pronoun *I*, even if it is part of a contraction (*I'm, I'll, I've*).

Always capitalize the interjection *O*.

Give us peace in our time, <u>O</u> Lord.

However, capitalize the interjection *oh* only when it begins a sentence.

NOTE: Many other single letters are capitalized in certain usages: an A in history, vitamin B, C major. Check your dictionary to determine whether to use a capital letter.

50e   Editing Misused Capitals

Do not use capital letters for emphasis or as an attention-getting device. If you are not certain whether a word should be capitalized, consult your dictionary.

(1) Seasons

Do not capitalize the names of the seasons—summer, fall, winter, spring—unless they are personified, as in *Old Man Winter*.

(2) Centuries and Loosely Defined Historical Periods

Do not capitalize the names of centuries or of general historical periods.

seventeenth-century poetry   the automobile age

Do, however, capitalize the names of specific historical, anthropological, and geological periods.

the Renaissance   Iron Age   Paleozoic Era

(3) Diseases and Other Medical Terms

Do not capitalize names of diseases or medical tests or conditions unless a proper noun is part of the name or unless the disease is an acronym.

See 43a2

smallpox   Apgar test   AIDS
Lyme disease   mumps   SIDS

CHAPTER 51

Using Italics

51a Setting Off Titles and Names

Use italics for the categories of titles and names listed in the box below. All other titles are set off with quotation marks.

Titles and Names Set in Italics

Books: *David Copperfield, The Bluest Eye*

Newspapers: the *Washington Post*, the *Philadelphia Inquirer* (According to MLA style, the word *the* is not italicized in titles of newspapers.)

Magazines and Journals: *Rolling Stone, Scientific American*

Online Magazines and Journals: *salon.com, theonion.com*

Web Sites or Home Pages: *urbanlegends.com, movie-mistakes.com*

Pamphlets: *Common Sense*

Films: *The Matrix, Citizen Kane*

Television Programs: *60 Minutes, The Apprentice, Fear Factor*

Radio Programs: *All Things Considered, A Prairie Home Companion*

Long Poems: *John Brown's Body, The Faerie Queen*

Plays: *Macbeth, A Raisin in the Sun*

Long Musical Works: *Rigoletto, Eroica*

Software Programs: *Microsoft Word, PowerPoint*

Search Engines and Web Browsers: *Google, Netscape Communicator*

Databases: *Academic Search Premier, Expanded Academic ASAP Plus*

Paintings and Sculpture: *Guernica, Pietà*

Ships: *Lusitania*, U.S.S. *Saratoga* (S.S. and U.S.S. are not italicized.)

Trains: *City of New Orleans, The Orient Express*

Aircraft: *The Hindenburg, Enola Gay* (Only particular aircraft, not makes or types such as Piper Cub or Boeing 757, are italicized.)

Spacecraft: *Challenger, Enterprise*

NOTE: Names of sacred books, such as the Bible and the Koran, and well-known documents, such as the Constitution and the Declaration of Independence, are neither italicized nor placed within quotation marks.

> **Close-up: Using Italics**
>
> MLA guidelines recommend that you underline to indicate italics. However, you may italicize if your instructor prefers. (Note that style guides in other disciplines may require italics.)

51b Setting Off Foreign Words and Phrases

Italics are often used to set off foreign words and phrases that have not become part of the English language.

> "*C'est la vie*," Madeleine said when she saw the long line for the concert.
>
> *Spirochaeta plicatilis* is a corkscrew-like bacterium.

If you are not sure whether a foreign word has been assimilated into English, consult a dictionary.

51c Setting Off Elements Spoken of as Themselves and Terms Being Defined

Use italics to set off letters, numerals, and words that refer to the letters, numerals, and words themselves.

> Is that a *p* or a *g*?
>
> I forget the exact address, but I know it has a *3* in it.
>
> Does *through* rhyme with *cough*?

Also use italics to set off words and phrases that you go on to define.

> A *closet drama* is a play meant to be read, not performed.

NOTE: When you quote a dictionary definition, put the word you are defining in italics and the definition itself in quotation marks.

> To *infer* means "to draw a conclusion"; to *imply* means "to suggest."

51d Using Italics for Emphasis

Italics can occasionally be used for emphasis.

> Initially, poetry might be defined as a kind of language that says *more* and says it *more intensely* than does ordinary language. (Lawrence Perrine, *Sound and Sense*)

However, overuse of italics is distracting. Instead of italicizing, try to indicate emphasis through word choice and sentence structure.

CHAPTER 52

Using Hyphens

Hyphens have two conventional uses: to break a word at the end of a line and to link words in certain compounds.

52a Breaking a Word at the End of a Line

A computer will not automatically break a word at the end of a line; if the full word will not fit, it is brought down to the next line. Sometimes, however, you will want to break a word with a hyphen—for example, to fill in space at the end of a line. When you break a word at the end of a line, divide it only between syllables, consulting a dictionary if necessary. Never divide a word at the end of a page, and never hyphenate a one-syllable word. In addition, never leave a single letter at the end of a line or carry only one or two letters to the next line.

See 52b

If you divide a *compound word* at the end of a line, put the hyphen between the elements of the compound (*snow-mobile*, not *snowmo-bile*).

http://kirsznermandell.wadsworth.com

> **Computer Tip: Dividing Electronic Addresses (URLs)**
>
>
>
> Never insert a hyphen to divide an electronic address (URL) at the end of a line. (Readers might think the hyphen is part of the address.) MLA style recommends that you break the URL after a slash. If this is not possible, break it in a logical place—after a period, for example—or avoid the problem altogether by moving the entire URL to the next line.

52b Dividing Compound Words

A compound word is composed of two or more words. Some familiar compound words are always hyphenated: *no-hitter, helter-skelter.* Other compounds are always written as one word: *peacetime, fireplace.* Finally, some compounds are always written as two separate words: *labor relations, bunk bed.* Your dictionary can tell you whether a particular compound requires a hyphen.

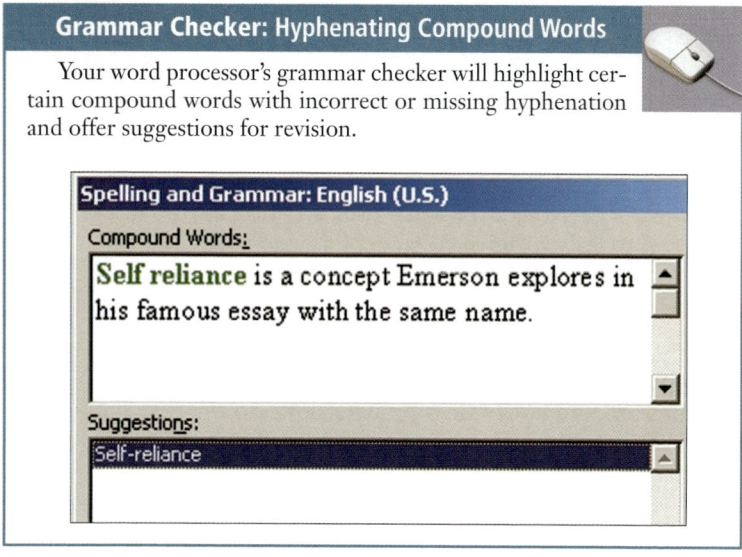

Grammar Checker: Hyphenating Compound Words

Your word processor's grammar checker will highlight certain compound words with incorrect or missing hyphenation and offer suggestions for revision.

> **Spelling and Grammar: English (U.S.)**
>
> Compound Words:
>
> **Self reliance** is a concept Emerson explores in his famous essay with the same name.
>
> Suggestions:
>
> Self-reliance

Hyphens are generally used in the following compounds.

(1) In Compound Adjectives

A compound adjective is a series of two or more words that function together as an adjective. When a compound adjective *precedes* the noun it modifies, use hyphens to join its elements.

> The research team tried to use nineteenth-century technology to design a space-age project.

When a compound adjective *follows* the noun it modifies, do not use hyphens to join its elements.

> The three government-operated programs were run smoothly, but the one that was not government operated was short of funds.

NOTE: A compound adjective formed with an adverb ending in *-ly* is not hyphenated even when it precedes the noun: Many upwardly mobile families are on tight budgets.

Use **suspended hyphens**—hyphens followed by a space or by appropriate punctuation and a space—in a series of compounds that modify the same word.

> Graduates of two- and four-year colleges were eligible for the grants.

> The exam called for sentence-, paragraph-, and essay-length answers.

(2) With Certain Prefixes or Suffixes

Use a hyphen between a prefix and a proper noun or proper adjective.

mid-July   pre-Columbian

Use a hyphen to connect the prefixes *all-*, *ex-*, *half-*, *quarter-*, *quasi-*, and *self-* and the suffix *-elect* to a noun.

ex-senator   self-centered

quarter-moon   president-elect

NOTE: The words *selfhood*, *selfish*, and *selfless* do not include hyphens because in these cases, *self* is the root, not a prefix.

(3) In Compound Numerals and Fractions

Hyphenate compounds that represent numbers below one hundred (even if they are part of a larger number).

the twenty-first century   three hundred sixty-five days

Also hyphenate the written form of a fraction when it modifies a noun.

a two-thirds share of the business

(4) For Clarity

Hyphenate to prevent readers from misreading one word for another.

In order to reform criminals, we must re-form our ideas about prisons.

Hyphenate to avoid certain hard-to-read combinations, such as two *i*'s (*semi-illiterate*) or more than two of the same consonant (*shell-less*).

In most cases, hyphenate between a capital initial and a word when the two combine to form a compound: *A-frame, T-shirt, D-day.*

(5) In Coined Compounds

A **coined compound,** one that uses a new combination of words as a unit, requires hyphens.

He looked up with a who-do-you-think-you-are expression.

CHAPTER 53

Using Abbreviations

See
Ch. 22

Generally speaking, **abbreviations** are not appropriate in college writing except in tables, charts, and works-cited lists. Some abbreviations are acceptable in scientific, technical, or business writing, or only in a particular <u>discipline</u>. If you have questions about the appropriateness of a particular abbreviation, check the style manual of the field for which you are writing.

http://kirsznermandell.wadsworth.com

Computer Tip: Shorthand and Text Messaging

Like emoticons and acronyms, which are popular in email and instant messages, shorthand abbreviations and symbols—such as GR8 (great) and 2NITE (tonight)—are common in text messages between mobile phones and in other forms of electronic communication. Although such abbreviations are acceptable in informal electronic communication, they are not appropriate in college writing or in business communications.

53a Abbreviating Titles

Titles before and after proper names are usually abbreviated.

Mr. Homer Simpson   Rep. Chaka Fattah
Henry Kissinger, PhD   Dr. Martin Luther King, Jr.

Do not, however, use an abbreviated title without a name.

The ~~Dr.~~ *doctor* diagnosed hepatitis.

53b Abbreviating Organization Names and Technical Terms

See
43a2

You may refer to well-known businesses and to government, social, and civic organizations by capitalized initials. These <u>abbreviations</u> fall into two categories: those in which the initials are pronounced as separate units (MTV) and **acronyms**, in which the initials are pronounced as words (FEMA).

Close-up: Abbreviations in MLA Documentation

See
17a

MLA documentation style requires abbreviations of publishers' company names—for example, Columbia UP for *Columbia University Press*—in the works-cited list. Do not, however, use such abbreviations in the body of your paper.

   MLA style also permits the use of abbreviations that designate parts of written works (ch. 3, sec. 7)—but only in the works-cited list and parenthetical documentation.

   Finally, MLA recommends abbreviating literary works and books of the Bible in the works-cited list: Oth. (Othello), Exod. (Exodus). These words should not be abbreviated in the text of your paper.

   To save space, you may also use accepted abbreviations for complex technical terms that are not well known, but be sure to spell out the full term the first time you mention it, followed by the abbreviation in parentheses.

> Citrus farmers have been using ethylene dibromide (EDB), a chemical pesticide, for more than twenty years. Now, however, EDB has contaminated water supplies.

53c   Abbreviating Dates, Times of Day, and Temperatures

Dates, times of day, and temperatures are often abbreviated.

50 BC (*BC* follows the date)	AD 432 (*AD* precedes the date)
3:03 p.m.	180° F (Fahrenheit)

Always capitalize *BC* and *AD*. (The alternatives *BCE*, for "before the Common Era," and *CE*, for "Common Era," are also capitalized.) Use lowercase letters for a.m. and p.m., but use these abbreviations only when they are accompanied by numbers.

   I'll see you in the ~~a.m.~~ *morning.*

NOTE: Avoid the abbreviation *no.* (written either *no.* or *No.*), except in technical writing, and then use it only before a specific number: *The unidentified substance was labeled no. 52.*

53d   Editing Misused Abbreviations

In college writing, abbreviations are not used in the following cases.

(1) Names of Days, Months, or Holidays

Do not abbreviate days of the week, months, or holidays.

On ∧Sat., Dec. 23, I started my ∧Xmas shopping.
  Saturday, December   *Christmas*

(2) Names of Streets and Places

In general, do not abbreviate names of streets and places.

He lives on Riverside ∧Dr. in ∧NYC.∕
                     Drive   *New York City.*

Exceptions: The abbreviation *US* is often acceptable (*US Coast Guard*), as is *DC* in *Washington, DC*. Also permissible are *Mt.* before the name of a mountain (*Mt. Etna*) and *St.* in a place name (*St. Albans*).

(3) Names of Academic Subjects

Do not abbreviate names of academic subjects.

∧Psych. and English ∧lit. are required courses.
  Psychology   *literature*

(4) Names of Businesses

Write company names exactly as the firms themselves write them: *AT & T, Charles Schwab & Co., Inc.* Abbreviations for *company, corporation*, and the like are used only along with a company name.

The ∧corp. merged with a ∧co. in Ohio.
    corporation   *company*

(5) Latin Expressions

Abbreviations of the common Latin phrases *i.e.* ("that is"), *e.g.* ("for example"), and *etc.* ("and so forth") are not appropriate in college writing.

Other musicians (∧e.g. Bruce Springsteen) have also been influenced by Bob Dylan.
              for example,

Poe wrote "The Raven," "Annabel Lee," ∧etc.
                                    and other poems.

(6) Units of Measurement

In technical and business writing, some units of measurement are abbreviated when they are preceded by a numeral.

The hurricane had winds of 35 mph.
One new hybrid car gets over 50 mpg.

MLA style, however, requires that you write out units of measurement and spell out words such as *inches, feet, years, miles, pints, quarts*, and *gallons.*

(7) Symbols

The symbols =, +, and # are acceptable in technical and scientific writing but not in nontechnical college writing. The symbols % and $ are acceptable only when used with **numerals** (15%, $15,000), not with spelled-out numbers.

See
54b4, 7

CHAPTER 54

Using Numbers

Convention determines when to use a **numeral** (22) and when to spell out a number (twenty-two). Numerals are commonly used in scientific and technical writing and in journalism, but they are used less often in the humanities.

NOTE: The guidelines in this chapter are based on the *MLA Handbook for Writers of Research Papers*, 6th ed. (2003). APA style, however, requires that all numbers below ten be spelled out if they do not represent specific measurements and that numbers ten and above be expressed in numerals.

54a Spelled-Out Numbers versus Numerals

 Unless a number falls into one of the categories listed in **54b,** spell it out if you can do so *in one or two words*.

The Hawaiian alphabet has only <u>twelve</u> letters.

Class size stabilized at <u>twenty-eight</u> students.

The subsidies are expected to total about <u>two</u> million dollars.

Numbers *more than two words* long are expressed in figures.

The dietitian prepared <u>125</u> sample menus.

The developer of the community purchased <u>300,000</u> doorknobs and <u>153,000</u> faucets.

Never begin a sentence with a numeral. If necessary, reword the sentence.

Faulty: 250 students are currently enrolled in World History 106.

Revised: Current enrollment in World History 106 is 250 students.

NOTE: When one number immediately precedes another in a sentence, spell out the first, and use a numeral for the second: *five 3-quart containers.*

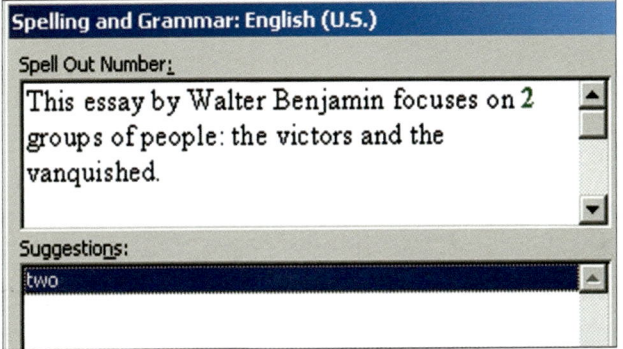

> ## Grammar Checker: Spelled-Out Numbers versus Numerals
>
> Your word processor's grammar checker will often highlight numerals in your writing and suggest that you spell them out. Before making a change, be sure that the number does not fall into one of the categories listed in **54b**.

Spelling and Grammar: English (U.S.)

Spell Out Number:

This essay by Walter Benjamin focuses on 2 groups of people: the victors and the vanquished.

Suggestions:

two

54b Conventional Uses of Numerals

(1) Addresses

111 Fifth Avenue, New York, NY 10003

(2) Dates

January 15, 1929   1914–1919

(3) Exact Times

9:16   10 a.m. (or 10:00 a.m.)

Exceptions: Spell out times of day when they are used with *o'clock: eleven o'clock*, not *11 o'clock*. Also spell out times expressed as round numbers: *They were in bed by ten*.

(4) Exact Sums of Money

$25.11 $6,752.00

NOTE: Always use a numeral (not a spelled-out number) with a $ symbol. You may spell out a round sum of money if you use sums infrequently in your paper, provided you can do so in two or three words: *five dollars; two thousand dollars*.

(5) Divisions of Written Works

Use arabic (not roman) numerals for chapter and volume numbers; for acts, scenes, and lines of plays; for chapters and verses of the Bible; and for line numbers of long poems.

(6) Measurements before an Abbreviation or Symbol

12″	55 mph
32°	15 cc

(7) Percentages and Decimals

80%   3.14

NOTE: You may spell out a percentage (*eighty percent*) if you use percentages infrequently in your paper, provided the percentage can be expressed in two or three words. Always use a numeral (not a spelled-out number) with a % symbol.

(8) Ratios, Scores, and Statistics

See Ch. 18 In a paper that follows **APA** style, use numerals for numbers presented as a comparison.

Children preferred Fun Flakes over Graino by a ratio of 20 to 1.
The Orioles defeated the Phillies 6 to 0.
The median age of the voters was 42; the mean age was 40.

(9) Identification Numbers

Route 66   Track 8   Channel 12

NOTE: When writing out large numbers, insert a comma every three digits from the right, beginning after the third digit.

3,000   25,000   6,751,098

Do not, however, use commas in four-digit page and line numbers, addresses, or year numbers.

page 1202   3741 Laurel Ave.   1968

PART 13

Resources for Bilingual and ESL Writers

PART 13

Resources for Bilingual and ESL Writers

FREQUENTLY ASKED QUESTIONS

CHAPTER 55

Understanding Grammar and Usage

For ESL writers (as for many native English writers), grammar can be a persistent problem. Grammatical knowledge in a second language usually develops slowly, with time and practice, and much about English is idiomatic (not subject to easy-to-learn rules). This chapter is designed to provide you with the tools you will need to address some of the most common grammatical problems ESL writers face.

55a Solving Verb-Related Problems

(1) Subject-Verb Agreement

English **verbs** change their form according to person, number, and tense. The verb in a sentence must **agree** with the subject in both person and number. Person refers to *who* or *what* is performing the action of the verb (for example, *I, you,* or someone else), and number refers to *how many* people or things are performing the action (one or more than one).

See A3

In English, the rules for **subject-verb agreement** are very important. Unless you use the correct person and number in the verbs in your sentences, you will confuse your English-speaking audience by communicating meanings you do not intend.

See 30a

(2) Tense

See 33b

Tense refers to *when* the action of the verb takes place. One problem that many nonnative speakers of English have with English verb tenses results from the large number of **irregular verbs** in English. For example, the first-person singular present tense of *be* is not "I be" but "I am," and the past tense is not "I beed" but "I was."

See 33a

Close-up: Choosing the Simplest Verb Forms

Some nonnative English speakers use verb forms that are more complicated than they need to be. They may do this because their native language uses more complicated verb forms than English does or because they "overcorrect" their verbs into complicated forms. Specifically, nonnative speakers tend to use progressive

(continued)

> *Choosing the simplest verb forms (continued)*
>
> and perfect verb forms instead of simple verb forms. To communicate your ideas clearly to an English-speaking audience, choose the simplest possible verb form.

(3) Auxiliary Verbs

The **auxiliary verbs** (also known as **helping verbs**) *be, have,* and *do* are used to create some present, past, and future forms of verbs in English: "Julio is taking a vacation"; "I have been tired lately"; "He does not need a license." The auxiliary verbs *be, have,* and *do* change form to reflect the time frame of the action or situation and to agree with the subject; however, the main verb remains in simple present or simple past form.

> ### Close-up: Auxiliary Verbs
>
> Only auxiliary verbs, not the verbs they "help," change form to indicate person, number, and tense.
>
> **Present:** We <u>have</u> to eat.
>
> **Past:** We <u>had</u> to eat. (*not* "We had to ate.")
>
> Modal auxiliaries (such as *can* and *should*) do not change form to indicate tense, person, or number.

See A3

(4) Negative Verbs

The meaning of a verb may be made negative in English in a variety of ways, chiefly by adding the words *not* or *does not* to the verb (is, is *not*; can ski, *can't* ski; drives a car, *does not* drive a car).

> ### Close-up: Correcting Double Negatives
>
> A **double negative** occurs when the meaning of a verb is negated not just once but twice in a single sentence.
>
> Henry doesn't have ~~no~~ ^{*any*} friends. (*or* Henry ~~doesn't have~~ ^{*has*} no friends.)
>
> I looked for articles in the library, but there weren~~'t~~ none. (*or* I looked for articles in the library, but there weren't ~~none~~ ^{*any*}.)

(5) Phrasal Verbs

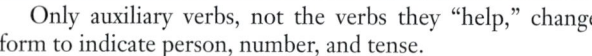

FAQs Many verbs in English are composed of two or more words—for example, *check up on, run for, turn into,* and *wait on*. These verbs are called **phrasal verbs.** It is important to become familiar with phrasal verbs and their definitions so you will recognize these verbs as phrasal verbs (instead of as verbs that are followed by prepositions).

Sometimes the words that make up a phrasal verb can be separated from each other by a direct object. In these **separable phrasal verbs,** the object can come either before or after the preposition. For example, "<u>Ellen</u> <u>turned</u> <u>down</u> the job offer" and "<u>Ellen</u> <u>turned</u> the job offer <u>down</u>" are both correct. However, when the object is a pronoun, the pronoun must come before the preposition. Therefore, "<u>Ellen</u> <u>turned</u> *it* <u>down</u>" is correct, but "<u>Ellen</u> <u>turned</u> <u>down</u> *it*" is incorrect.

Close-up: Separable Phrasal Verbs		
Verb	**Definition**	
call off	cancel	
carry on	continue	
cheer up	make happy	
clean out	clean the inside of	
cut down	reduce	
figure out	solve	
fill in	substitute	
find out	discover	
give back	return something	
give up	stop doing something or stop trying	
leave out	omit	
pass on	transmit	
put away	place something in its proper place	
put back	place something in its original place	
put off	postpone	
start over	start again	
talk over	discuss	
throw away/out	discard	
touch up	repair	

However, some phrasal verbs—such as *look into, make up for,* and *break into*—consist of words that can never be separated. With these **inseparable phrasal verbs,** you do not have a choice about where to place the object; the object must always follow the preposition. For example, "<u>Anna</u> <u>cared for</u> her niece" is correct, but "<u>Anna</u> <u>cared</u> her niece <u>for</u>" is incorrect.

Close-up: Inseparable Phrasal Verbs		
Verb	**Definition**	
come down with	develop an illness	
come up with	produce	

(continued)

Inseparable phrasal verbs (continued)

Verb	Definition
do away with	abolish
fall behind in	lag
get along with	be congenial with
get away with	avoid punishment
keep up with	maintain the same achievement or speed
look up to	admire
make up for	compensate
put up with	tolerate
run into	meet by chance
see to	arrange
show up	arrive
stand by	wait or remain loyal to
stand up for	support
watch out for	beware of or protect

(6) Voice

See 33d

Verbs may be in either active or passive <u>voice</u>. When the subject of a sentence performs the action of the verb, the verb is in **active voice.** When the action of the verb is performed on the subject, the verb is in **passive voice.**

> Karla and Miguel <u>purchased</u> the tickets. (active voice)

> <u>The tickets</u> <u>were purchased</u> by Karla and Miguel. (passive voice)

Because your writing will usually be clearer and more concise if you use the active voice, you should use the passive voice only when you have a good reason to do so.

(7) Transitive and Intransitive Verbs

Many nonnative English speakers find it difficult to decide whether or not a verb needs an object and in what order direct and indirect objects should appear in a sentence. Learning the difference between transitive verbs and intransitive verbs can help you with such problems.

A **transitive verb** is a verb that has a direct object: "<u>My father asked</u> a question" (subject + verb + direct object). In this example, *asked* is a transitive verb; it needs an object to complete its meaning.

An **intransitive verb** is a verb that does not take an object: "<u>The doctor smiled</u>" (subject + verb). In this example, *smiled* is an intransitive verb; it does not need an object to complete its meaning.

A transitive verb may be followed by a direct object or by both an indirect object and a direct object. (An indirect object answers the question "To whom?" or "For whom?") The indirect object may come before or after the direct object. If the indirect object follows the direct object, the preposition *to* or *for* must precede the indirect object.

    s   v   do

<u>Keith</u> <u>wrote</u> a letter. (subject + verb + direct object)

    s   v   io   do

<u>Keith</u> <u>wrote</u> his friend a letter. (subject + verb + indirect object + direct object)

    s   v   do   io

<u>Keith</u> <u>wrote</u> a letter *to* his friend. (subject + verb + direct object + *to/for* + indirect object)

Some verbs in English look similar and have similar meanings, except that one is transitive and the other is intransitive. For example, *lie* is intransitive, *lay* is transitive; *sit* is intransitive, *set* is transitive; *rise* is intransitive, *raise* is transitive. Knowing whether a verb is transitive or intransitive will help you with troublesome verb pairs like these and will help you place words in the correct order.

NOTE: It is also important to know whether a verb is transitive or intransitive because only transitive verbs can be used in the **passive voice**. To determine whether a verb is transitive or intransitive—that is, to determine whether or not it needs an object—consult the example phrases in a dictionary.

See 33d

55b   Solving Noun-Related Problems

A **noun** names things: people, animals, objects, places, feelings, ideas. If a noun names one thing, it is singular; if a noun names more than one thing, it is plural.

See A1

(1) Recognizing Noncount Nouns

Some English nouns do not have a plural form. These are called **noncount nouns** because what they name cannot be counted.

Close-up: Noncount Nouns

The following commonly used nouns are noncount nouns. These words have no plural forms. Therefore, you should never add *-s* to them.

advice	homework
clothing	information
education	knowledge
equipment	luggage
evidence	merchandise
furniture	revenge

(2) Using Articles with Nouns

English has two kinds of **articles,** indefinite and definite.

Use an **indefinite article** (*a* or *an*) with a noun when readers are not familiar with the noun you are naming—when you are introducing the noun for the first time, for example. To say, "Jatin entered *a* building," signals to the audience that you are introducing the idea of the building for the first time. The building is indefinite, or not specific, until it has been identified.

The indefinite article *a* is used when the word following it (which may be a noun or an adjective) begins with a consonant or with a consonant sound: *a tree, a onetime offer.* The indefinite article *an* is used if the word following it begins with a vowel (*a, e, i, o,* or *u*) or with a vowel sound: *an apple, an honor.*

Use the **definite article** (*the*) when the noun you are naming has already been introduced, when the noun is already familiar to readers, or when the noun to which you refer is specific. To say, "Jatin entered *the* building," signals to readers that you are referring to the same building you mentioned earlier. The building has now become specific and may be referred to by the definite article.

> ### Close-up: Using Articles with Nouns
>
> There are two exceptions to the rules governing the use of articles with nouns:
>
> 1. **Plural** nouns do not require **indefinite articles:** "I love horses," not "I love <u>a</u> horses." (Plural nouns do, however, require definite articles: "I love <u>the</u> horses in the national park near my house.")
>
> 2. **Noncount nouns** may not require articles: "Love conquers all," not "<u>A</u> love conquers all" or "<u>The</u> love conquers all."

(3) Using Other Determiners with Nouns

ESL
55d
Determiners are words that function as <u>adjectives</u> to limit or qualify the meaning of nouns. In addition to articles, **demonstrative pronouns, possessive nouns and pronouns, numbers** (both **cardinal** and **ordinal**), and other words indicating number and order can function in this way.

> ### Close-up: Using Other Determiners with Nouns
>
> • **Demonstrative pronouns** (*this, that, these, those*) communicate
>
>   1. the relative nearness or farness of the noun from the speaker's position (*this* and *these* for things that are *near; that* and *those* for

things that are *far*): *this* book on my desk, *that* book on your desk; *these* shoes on my feet, *those* shoes in my closet.

2. the number of things indicated (*this* and *that* for *singular* nouns, *these* and *those* for *plural* nouns): *this* (or *that*) flower in the vase, *these* (or *those*) flowers in the garden.

- **Possessive nouns** and **possessive pronouns** (*Ashraf's, his, their*) show who or what the noun belongs to: *Maria's* courage, *everybody's* fears, the *country's* natural resources, *my* personality, *our* groceries.

- **Cardinal** numbers (*three, fifty, a thousand*) indicate how many of the noun you mean: *seven* continents. **Ordinal** numbers (*first, tenth, thirtieth*) indicate in what order the noun appears among other items: *third* planet.

- Words other than numbers may indicate **amount** (*many, few*) and **order** (*next, last*) and function in the same ways as cardinal and ordinal numbers: *few* opportunities, *last* chance.

55c Using Pronouns

Any English noun may be replaced by a <u>pronoun</u>. Pronouns enable you to avoid repeating a noun over and over. For example, *doctor* may be replaced by *he* or *she*, *books* by *them*, and *computer* by *it*.

See A2

(1) Pronoun Reference

<u>Pronoun reference</u> is very important in English sentences, where the noun the pronoun replaces (the **antecedent**) must be easily identified. In general, you should place the pronoun as close as possible to the noun it replaces so the noun to which the pronoun refers is clear. If this is impossible, use the noun itself instead of replacing it with a pronoun.

See 34c

> **Unclear:** When Tara met Emily, she was nervous. (Does *she* refer to Tara or to Emily?)
>
> **Clear:** When Tara met Emily, <u>Tara</u> was nervous.

> **Unclear:** Stefano and Victor love his DVD collection. (Whose DVD collection—Stefano's, Victor's, or someone else's?)
>
> **Clear:** Stefano and Victor love <u>Emilio's</u> DVD collection.

(2) Pronoun Placement

Never use a pronoun immediately after the noun it replaces. For example, do not say, "Most of my classmates they are smart"; instead, say, "Most of my classmates are smart." The only exception to this rule occurs with an **intensive pronoun**, which ends in *-self* and emphasizes the preceding noun or pronoun: Marta <u>herself</u> was eager to hear the results.

(3) Indefinite Pronouns

Unlike **personal pronouns** (*I, you, he, she, it, we, they, me, him, her, us, them,* and so on), **indefinite pronouns** do not refer to a particular person, place, or thing. Therefore, an indefinite pronoun does not require an antecedent. **Indefinite pronoun subjects** (*anybody, nobody, each, either, someone, something, all, some*), like personal pronouns, must <u>agree</u> in number with the sentence's verb.

See 30a

Nobody _∧~~have~~ failed the exam. (*Nobody* is a singular subject and requires a singular verb.)

has appears above "have"

(4) Appositives

Appositives are nouns or noun phrases that identify or rename an adjacent noun or pronoun. An appositive usually follows the noun it explains or modifies but can sometimes precede it.

My parents, Mary and John, live in Louisiana. (*Mary and John* identifies *parents*.)

See 34a

NOTE: The <u>case</u> of a pronoun in an appositive depends on the case of the word it identifies.

If an appositive is *not* essential to the meaning of the sentence, use commas to set off the appositive from the rest of the sentence. If an appositive *is* essential to the meaning of the sentence, do not use commas.

His aunt Trang is in the hospital. (*Trang* is necessary to the meaning of the sentence because it identifies which aunt is in the hospital.)

Akta's car, a 1997 Jeep, broke down last night, so she had to walk home. (*a 1997 Jeep* is not essential to the meaning of the sentence.)

(5) Pronouns and Gender

A pronoun must agree in **gender** with the noun to which it refers.

My sister sold <u>her</u> old car.

Your uncle is walking <u>his</u> dog.

NOTE: In English, most nonhuman nouns are referred to as *it* because they do not have grammatical gender. However, exceptions are sometimes made for pets, ships, and countries. Pets are often referred to as *he* or *she*, depending on their sex, and ships and countries are sometimes referred to as *she*.

55d Using Adjectives and Adverbs

Adjectives and adverbs are words that **modify** (describe, limit, or qualify) other words.

See Ch. 35, A4–5

(1) Position of Adjectives and Adverbs

Adjectives in English usually appear *before* the nouns they modify. A native speaker of English would not say, "*Cars red and black* are involved in more accidents than *cars blue or green*" but would say instead, "*Red and black cars* are involved in more accidents than *blue or green cars.*"

However, adjectives may appear *after* linking verbs ("The name seemed *familiar*"), *after* direct objects ("The coach found them *tired* but *happy.*"), and *after* indefinite pronouns ("Anything *sad* makes me cry.")

Adverbs may appear before or after the verbs they describe, but they should be placed as close to the verb as possible: not "I *told* John that I couldn't meet him for lunch *politely*," but "I *politely* told John that I couldn't meet him for lunch" or "I *told* John *politely* that I couldn't meet him for lunch." When an adverb describes an adjective or another adverb, it usually comes *before* that adjective or adverb: "The essay has *basically* sound logic"; "You must express yourself *absolutely* clearly." Never place an adverb between the verb and the direct object.

Incorrect: Rolf drank *quickly* the water.

Correct: Rolf drank the water *quickly* (or, Rolf *quickly* drank the water).

Incorrect: Suong took *quietly* the test.

Correct: Suong *quietly* took the test (or, Suong took the test *quietly*).

(2) Order of Adjectives

A single noun may be modified by more than one adjective, perhaps even by a whole list of adjectives. Given a list of three or four adjectives, most native speakers would arrange them in a sentence in the same order. If, for example, shoes are to be described as *green* and *big*, numbering *two*, and of the type worn for playing *tennis*, a native speaker would say "two big green tennis shoes." Generally, the adjectives that are most important in completing the meaning of the noun are placed closest to the noun.

Close-up: Order of Adjectives

1. Articles (*a, the*), demonstratives (*this, those*), and possessives (*his, our, Maria's, everybody's*)
2. Amounts (*one, five, many, few*), order (*first, next, last*)
3. Personal opinions (*nice, ugly, crowded, pitiful*)
4. Sizes and shapes (*small, tall, straight, crooked*)
5. Age (*young, old, modern, ancient*)
6. Colors (*black, white, red, blue, dark, light*)
7. Nouns functioning as adjectives to form a unit with the noun (*soccer* ball, *cardboard* box, *history* class)

55e Using Prepositions

See
A6

In English, **prepositions** (such as *to, from, at, with, among, between*) give meaning to nouns by linking them with other words and other parts of the sentence. Prepositions convey several different kinds of information:

- Relations to **time** (*at* nine o'clock, *in* five minutes, *for* a month)
- Relations of **place** (*in* the classroom, *at* the library, *beside* the chair) and **direction** (*to* the market, *onto* the stage, *toward* the freeway)
- Relations of **association** (go *with* someone, the tip *of* the iceberg)
- Relations of **purpose** (working *for* money, dieting *to* lose weight)

(1) Commonly Used Prepositional Phrases

In English, the use of prepositions is often idiomatic rather than governed by grammatical rules. In many cases, therefore, learners of English as a second language need to memorize which prepositions are used in which phrases.

In English, some prepositions that relate to time have specific uses with certain nouns, such as days, months, and seasons:

- *On* is used with days and specific dates: *on* Monday, *on* September 13, 1977.
- *In* is used with months, seasons, and years: *in* November, *in* the spring, *in* 1999.
- *In* is also used when referring to some parts of the day: *in* the morning, *in* the afternoon, *in* the evening.

- *At* is used to refer to other parts of the day: *at* noon, *at* night, *at* seven o'clock.

> ### Close-up: Difficult Prepositional Phrases
>
> The following phrases (accompanied by their correct prepositions) sometimes cause difficulties for ESL writers:
>
> | | | |
> |---|---|---|
> | according *to* | *at* least | relevant *to* |
> | apologize *to* | *at* most | similar *to* |
> | appeal *to* | refer *to* | subscribe *to* |
> | different *from* | | |

(2) Commonly Confused Prepositions

The prepositions *to*, *in*, *on*, *into*, and *onto* are very similar to one another and are therefore easily confused.

> ### Close-up: Using Common Prepositions
>
> - *To* is the basic preposition of direction. It indicates movement toward a physical place: "She went *to* the restaurant"; "He went *to* the meeting." *To* is also used to form the infinitive of a verb: "He wanted *to deposit* his paycheck before noon"; "Irene offered *to drive* Maria to the baseball game."
>
> - *In* indicates that something is within the boundaries of a particular space or period of time: "My son is *in* the garden"; "I like to ski *in* the winter"; "The map is *in* the car."
>
> - *On* indicates position above or the state of being supported by something: "The toys are *on* the porch"; "The baby sat *on* my lap"; "The book is *on* top of the magazine."
>
> - *Into* indicates movement to the inside or interior of something: "She walked *into* the room"; "I threw the stone *into* the lake"; "He put the photos *into* the box." Although *into* and *in* are sometimes interchangeable, note that usage depends on whether the subject is stationary or moving. *Into* usually indicates movement, as in "I jumped *into* the water." *In* usually indicates a stationary position relative to the object of the preposition, as in "Mary is swimming *in* the water."
>
> - *Onto* indicates movement to a position on top of something: "The cat jumped *onto* the chair"; "Crumbs are falling *onto* the floor." Both *on* and *onto* can be used to indicate a position on top of something (and therefore they can sometimes be used interchangeably), but *onto* specifies that the subject is moving to a place from a different place or from an outside position.

> ### Close-up: Prepositions in Idiomatic Expressions
>
> | Common Nonnative Speaker Usage | Native Speaker Usage |
> |---|---|
> | according *with* | according *to* |
> | apologize *at* | apologize *to* |
> | appeal *at* | appeal *to* |
> | believe *at* | believe *in* |
> | different *to* | different *from* |
> | *for* least, *for* most | *at* least, *at* most |
> | refer *at* | refer *to* |
> | relevant *with* | relevant *to* |
> | similar *with* | similar *to* |
> | subscribe *with* | subscribe *to* |

55f   Understanding Word Order

In English, word order is extremely important, contributing a good deal to the meaning of a sentence.

(1) Standard Word Order

Like Chinese, English is an "SVO" language, or one in which the most typical sentence pattern is "subject-verb-object." (Arabic, by contrast, is an example of a "VSO" language.)

(2) Word Order in Questions

Word order in questions can be particularly troublesome for speakers of languages other than English, partly because there are so many different ways to form questions in English.

> ### Close-up: Word Order in Questions
>
> 1. To create a **yes/no question** from a statement using the verb *be*, simply invert the order of the subject and the verb:
>
>   <u>Rasheem</u> <u>is</u> researching the depletion of the ozone layer.
>
>   <u>Is</u> <u>Rasheem</u> researching the depletion of the ozone layer?
>
> 2. To create a **yes/no question** from a statement using a verb other than *be*, use a form of the auxiliary verb *do* before the sentence without inverting the subject and verb:
>
>   <u>Does</u> <u>Rasheem</u> want to research the depletion of the ozone layer?
>
>   <u>Do</u> Rasheem's <u>friends</u> want to help him with his research?
>
>   <u>Did</u> Rasheem's <u>professors</u> approve his research proposal?

3. You can also form a question by adding a **tag question**—such as *won't he?* or *didn't I?*—to the end of a statement. If the verb of the main statement is *positive*, then the verb of the tag question is *negative*; if the verb of the main statement is *negative*, then the verb of the tag question is *positive*:

   <u>Rasheem</u> <u>is</u> researching the depletion of the ozone layer, <u>isn't he</u>?

   <u>Rasheem</u> <u>doesn't</u> intend to write his dissertation about the depletion of the ozone layer, <u>does</u> he?

4. To create a **question asking for information, use interrogative** words (*who, what, where, when, why, how*), and invert the order of the subject and verb (note that *who* functions as the subject of the question in which it appears):

   <u>Who</u> <u>is</u> researching the depletion of the ozone layer?

   What <u>is</u> <u>Rasheem</u> researching?

   Where <u>is</u> <u>Rasheem</u> researching the depletion of the ozone layer?

PART 14

Appendixes

Appendixes
535–546

Parts of Speech

The eight basic **parts of speech**—the building blocks for all English sentences—are *nouns, pronouns, verbs, adjectives, adverbs, prepositions, conjunctions,* and *interjections.* How a word is classified depends on its function in a sentence.

A1   Using Nouns

<u>Nouns</u> name people, animals, places, things, ideas, actions, or qualities.

ESL
55b

A **common noun** names any of a class of people, places, or things: *artist, judge, building, event, city.*

A **proper noun,** always capitalized, refers to a particular person, place, or thing: *Mary Cassatt, Crimean War.*

A **count noun** names something that can be counted: *five dogs, two dozen grapes.*

A **noncount noun** names a quantity that is not countable: *time, dust, work, gold.* Noncount nouns generally have only a singular form.

A **collective noun** designates a group thought of as a unit: *committee, class, family.* Collective nouns are generally singular unless the members of the group are referred to as individuals.

An **abstract noun** refers to an intangible idea or quality: *love, hate, justice, anger, fear, prejudice.*

A2   Using Pronouns

<u>Pronouns</u> are words used in place of nouns or other pronouns. The word for which a pronoun stands is its **antecedent.**

ESL
55c

If you use a <u>quotation</u> in your paper, you must document <u>it</u>.

NOTE: Although different types of pronouns may have exactly the same form, they are distinguished from one another by their function in a sentence.

A **personal pronoun** stands for a person or thing: *I, me, we, us, my, mine, our, ours, you, your, yours, he, she, it, its, him, his, her, hers, they, them, their, theirs.*

The firm made Debbie an offer, and <u>she</u> couldn't refuse <u>it</u>.

535

An **indefinite pronoun** does not refer to any particular person or thing, and so it does not require an antecedent. Indefinite pronouns include *another, any, each, few, many, some, nothing, one, anyone, everyone, everybody, everything, someone, something, either,* and *neither.*

<u>Many</u> are called, but <u>few</u> are chosen.

A **reflexive pronoun** ends with *-self* and refers to a recipient of the action that is the same as the actor: *myself, yourself, himself, herself, itself, oneself, themselves, ourselves, yourselves.*

They found <u>themselves</u> in downtown Pittsburgh.

An **intensive pronoun** emphasizes a preceding noun or pronoun. Intensive pronouns have the same form as reflexive pronouns.

Darrow <u>himself</u> was sure his client was innocent.

A **relative pronoun** introduces an adjective or noun clause in a sentence. Relative pronouns include *which, who, whom, that, what, whose, whatever, whoever, whomever,* and *whichever.*

Gandhi was the man <u>who</u> led India to independence. (introduces adjective clause)

<u>Whatever</u> happens will be a surprise. (introduces noun clause)

An **interrogative pronoun** introduces a question. Interrogative pronouns include *who, which, what, whom, whose, whoever, whatever,* and *whichever.*

<u>Who</u> was that masked man?

A **demonstrative pronoun** points to a particular thing or group of things. *This, that, these,* and *those* are demonstrative pronouns.

<u>This</u> is one of Shakespeare's early plays.

A **reciprocal pronoun** denotes a mutual relationship. The reciprocal pronouns are *each other* and *one another. Each other* indicates a relationship between two individuals; *one another* denotes a relationship among more than two.

Cathy and I respect <u>each other</u> for our differences.

Many of our friends do not respect <u>one another</u>.

A3 Using Verbs

ESL
55a A <u>verb</u> may express either action or a state of being.

He <u>ran</u> for the train. (physical action)

He <u>thought</u> about taking the bus. (emotional action)

Jen <u>became</u> ill after dinner. (state of being)

Verbs can be classified into two groups: *main verbs* and *auxiliary verbs.*

Main Verbs   **Main verbs** carry most of the meaning in a sentence or clause. Some main verbs are action verbs.

Emily Dickinson <u>wrote</u> innovative poetry.

Other main verbs are linking verbs. A **linking verb** does not show any physical or emotional action. Its function is to link the subject to a **subject complement,** a word or phrase that renames or describes the subject. Linking verbs include *be, become,* and *seem* and verbs that describe sensations—*look, appear, feel, taste, smell,* and so on.

Carbon disulfide <u>smells</u> bad.

Auxiliary Verbs   **Auxiliary verbs** (also called **helping verbs**), such as *be* and *have,* combine with main verbs to form **verb phrases.** Auxiliary verbs indicate tense, voice, or mood.

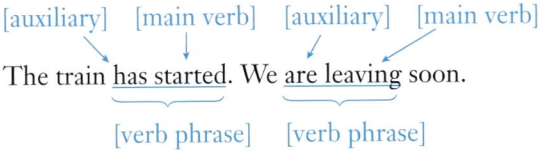

Certain auxiliary verbs, known as **modal auxiliaries,** indicate necessity, possibility, willingness, obligation, or ability.

Modal Auxiliaries			
can	might	ought [to]	will
could	must	shall	would
may	need [to]	should	

Verbals   **Verbals,** such as *known* or *running* or *to go,* are verb forms that act as adjectives, adverbs, or nouns. A verbal can never serve as a sentence's main verb unless it is used with one or more auxiliary verbs (*is going*). Verbals include *participles, infinitives,* and *gerunds.*

Participles   Virtually every verb has a **present participle,** which ends in *-ing* (*loving, learning*), and a **past participle,** which usually ends in *-d* or *-ed* (*agreed, learned*). Some verbs have <u>**irregular**</u> past participles (*gone, begun, written*). Participles may function in a sentence as adjectives or as nouns.

See 33b

Twenty brands of <u>running</u> shoes were on display. (Present participle serves as adjective modifying *shoes.*)

The <u>wounded</u> were given emergency first aid. (Past participle serves as subject.)

Infinitives An **infinitive** is made up of *to* and the base form of the verb (*to defeat*). An infinitive may function as an adjective, as an adverb, or as a noun.

Ann Arbor was clearly the place <u>to be</u>. (Infinitive serves as adjective modifying *place*.)

Carla went outside <u>to think</u>. (Infinitive serves as adverb modifying *went*.)

<u>To win</u> was everything. (Infinitive serves as subject.)

Gerunds **Gerunds,** which like present participles end in *-ing*, always function as nouns.

<u>Seeing</u> is <u>believing</u>. (Gerunds serve as subject and subject complement.)

Andrew loves <u>skiing</u>. (Gerund is direct object of verb *loves*.)

A4   Using Adjectives

ESL
55d
<u>Adjectives</u> describe, limit, qualify, or in some other way modify nouns or pronouns.

Descriptive adjectives name a quality of the noun or pronoun they modify.

After the game, they were <u>exhausted</u>.

They ordered a <u>chocolate</u> soda and a <u>butterscotch</u> sundae.

When articles, pronouns, numbers, and the like function as adjectives, limiting or qualifying nouns or pronouns, they are referred to as **determiners**.

A5   Using Adverbs

ESL
55d1
<u>Adverbs</u> describe the action of verbs or modify adjectives or other adverbs (or complete phrases, clauses, or sentences). They answer the questions "How?" "Why?" "Where?" "When?" "Under what conditions?" and "To what extent?"

He walked <u>rather hesitantly</u> toward the front of the room. (walked *how?*)

Let's meet <u>tomorrow</u> for coffee. (meet *when?*)

Adverbs that modify adjectives or other adverbs limit or qualify the words they modify.

He pitched an <u>almost perfect</u> game yesterday.

Interrogative Adverbs The **interrogative adverbs** (*how*, *when*, *why*, and *where*) introduce questions.

<u>Why</u> did the compound darken?

Conjunctive Adverbs **Conjunctive adverbs** act as <u>transitional words</u>, joining and relating independent clauses.

See 7b2

Frequently Used Conjunctive Adverbs			
accordingly	furthermore	meanwhile	similarly
also	hence	moreover	still
anyway	however	nevertheless	then
besides	incidentally	next	thereafter
certainly	indeed	nonetheless	therefore
consequently	instead	now	thus
finally	likewise	otherwise	undoubtedly

A6   Using Prepositions

ESL 55e

A <u>preposition</u> introduces a noun or pronoun (or a phrase or clause functioning in the sentence as a noun), linking it to other words in the sentence. The word or word group that the preposition introduces is its **object**.

prep   obj   prep   obj

They received a postcard <u>from</u> Bobby telling <u>about</u> his trip.

Frequently Used Prepositions			
about	beneath	inside	since
above	beside	into	through
across	between	like	throughout
after	beyond	near	to
against	by	of	toward
along	concerning	off	under
among	despite	on	underneath
around	down	onto	until
as	during	out	up
at	except	outside	upon
before	for	over	with
behind	from	past	within
below	in	regarding	without

A7   Using Conjunctions

Conjunctions connect words, phrases, clauses, or sentences.

Coordinating Conjunctions **Coordinating conjunctions** (*and, or, but, nor, for, so, yet*) connect words, phrases, or clauses of equal weight.

> Should I order chicken <u>or</u> fish? (*Or* links two nouns.)

> Thoreau wrote *Walden* in 1854, <u>and</u> he died in 1862. (*And* links two independent clauses.)

Correlative Conjunctions Always used in pairs, **correlative conjunctions** also link items of equal weight.

> <u>Both</u> Hancock <u>and</u> Jefferson signed the Declaration of Independence. (Correlative conjunctions link nouns.)

> <u>Either</u> I will renew my lease, <u>or</u> I will move. (Correlative conjunctions link independent clauses.)

Correlative Conjunctions	
both . . . and	neither . . . nor
either . . . or	not only . . . but also
just as . . . so	whether . . . or

Subordinating Conjunctions Words such as *since, because,* and *although* are **subordinating conjunctions**. They introduce adverb clauses and thus connect the sentence's independent (main) clause to a dependent (subordinate) clause to form a complex sentence.

> <u>Although</u> people may feel healthy, they can still have medical problems.

> It is best to diagram your garden <u>before</u> you start to plant.

A8   Using Interjections

Interjections are words used as exclamations to express emotion: *Oh! Ouch! Wow! Alas! Hey!* They may be set off in a sentence by commas, or (for greater emphasis) they may be followed by an exclamation point.

Sentence Review

B1 Basic Sentence Elements

A **sentence** is an independent grammatical unit that contains a subject and a predicate and expresses a complete thought.

The quick brown fox jumped over the lazy dog.

It came from outer space.

A **simple subject** is a noun or pronoun (*fox*, *it*) that tells who or what the sentence is about. A **simple predicate** is a verb or verb phrase (*jumped*, *came*) that tells or asks something about the subject. The **complete subject** of a sentence includes the simple subject plus all its modifiers (*the quick brown fox*). The **complete predicate** includes the verb or verb phrase and all the words associated with it—such as modifiers, objects, and complements (*jumped over the lazy dog*, *came from outer space*).

B2 Basic Sentence Patterns

A **simple sentence** consists of at least one subject and one predicate. Simple sentences conform to one of five patterns.

Subject + Intransitive Verb (s + v)

> s   v
> The price of gold rose.

> s   v
> Stock prices may fall.

Here, the verbs *rose* and *may fall* are **intransitive**—that is, they do not need an object to complete their meaning.

Subject + Transitive Verb + Direct Object (s + v + do)

> s   v   do
> Van Gogh created *The Starry Night*.

> s   v   do
> Caroline saved Jake.

Here, the verbs *created* and *saved* are **transitive**—they require an object to complete their meaning. In each case, a **direct object** indicates where the verb's action is directed and who or what is affected by it.

Subject + Transitive Verb + Direct Object + Object Complement (s + v + do + oc)

This pattern includes an object complement that describes or renames the direct object.

> s   v   do   oc
> I <u>found</u> the exam easy. (Object complement *easy* describes direct object *exam.*)

>   s   v   do   oc
> <u>The class</u> <u>elected</u> Bridget treasurer. (Object complement *treasurer* renames direct object *Bridget.*)

Subject + Linking Verb + Subject Complement (s + v + sc)

>   s   v   sc
> <u>The injection</u> <u>was</u> painless.

>   s   v   sc
> <u>Tony Blair</u> <u>became</u> prime minister.

See A3

Here, a **linking verb** (*was, became*) connects a subject to a **subject complement** (*painless, prime minister*), a word or phrase that describes or renames the subject. In the first sentence, the complement is a **predicate adjective** that describes the subject; in the second, the complement is a **predicate nominative** that renames the subject. The linking verb is like an equal sign, equating the subject with its complement (*Tony Blair = prime minister.*)

Subject + Transitive Verb + Indirect Object + Direct Object (s + v + io + do)

The **indirect object** tells to whom or for whom the verb's action was done.

>   s   v   io   do
> <u>Cyrano</u> <u>wrote</u> Roxanne a poem. (Cyrano wrote a poem for Roxanne.)

>   s   v io   do
> <u>Hester</u> <u>gave</u> Pearl a kiss. (Hester gave a kiss to Pearl.)

B3 Phrases and Clauses

(1) Phrases

A **phrase** is a group of related words that lacks a subject or predicate or both and functions as a single part of speech. It cannot stand alone as a sentence.

A **verb phrase** consists of a **main verb** and all its auxiliary verbs. (Time *is flying*.) A **noun phrase** includes a noun or pronoun plus all related modifiers. (I'll climb *the highest mountain*.)

A **prepositional phrase** consists of a <u>preposition</u>, its object, and any modifiers of that object.

> See A6

They discussed the ethical implications <u>of the animal studies</u>.

He was last seen heading <u>into the sunset</u>.

A **verbal phrase** consists of a <u>verbal</u> and its related objects, modifiers, or complements. A verbal phrase may be a **participial phrase,** a **gerund phrase,** or an **infinitive phrase.**

> See A3

<u>Encouraged by the voter turnout</u>, the candidate predicted a victory. (participial phrase)

<u>Taking it easy</u> always makes sense. (gerund phrase)

The jury recessed <u>to evaluate the evidence</u>. (infinitive phrase)

An **absolute phrase** usually consists of a noun and a participle, accompanied by modifiers. It modifies an entire independent clause rather than a particular word or phrase.

<u>Their toes tapping</u>, they watched the auditions.

(2) Clauses

A **clause** is a group of related words that includes a subject and a predicate. An **independent** (main) **clause** may stand alone as a sentence, but a **dependent** (subordinate) **clause** cannot. It must always be combined with an independent clause to form a complex sentence.

[Lucretia Mott was an abolitionist]. [She was also a pioneer for women's rights.] (two independent clauses)

[Lucretia Mott was an abolitionist] [who was also a pioneer for women's rights]. (independent clause, dependent clause)

[Although Lucretia Mott was known for her support of women's rights], [she was also a prominent abolitionist]. (dependent clause, independent clause)

Dependent clauses may be *adjective, adverb,* or *noun* clauses.

Adjective clauses, sometimes called **relative clauses,** modify nouns or pronouns and always follow the nouns or pronouns they modify. They are introduced by relative pronouns—*that, what, which, who,* and so forth—or by the adverbs *where* and *when.*

> Celeste's grandparents, <u>who were born in Romania</u>, speak little English. (Adjective clause modifies the noun *grandparents.*)

> The Pulitzer Prizes are prestigious awards <u>that are presented for excellence in journalism</u>. (Adjective clause modifies the noun *awards.*)

> *Sophie's Choice* is a novel set in Brooklyn, <u>where the narrator lives in a pink house</u>. (Adjective clause modifies the noun *Brooklyn.*)

Adverb clauses modify verbs, adjectives, adverbs, entire phrases, or independent clauses. They are always introduced by subordinating conjunctions.

> Mark will go <u>wherever there's a party</u>. (Adverb clause modifies *will go,* telling *where* Mark will go.)

> <u>Because 75 percent of its exports are fish products</u>, Iceland's economy is heavily dependent on the fishing industry. (Adverb clause modifies independent clause, telling *why* the fishing industry is so important.)

Noun clauses function as subjects, objects, or complements. A noun clause may be introduced by a relative pronoun or by *whether, when, where, why,* or *how.*

> <u>What you see</u> is <u>what you get</u>. (Noun clauses are subject and subject complement.)

> They wondered <u>why it was so quiet</u>. (Noun clause is direct object.)

> To <u>whom it may concern</u>: (Noun clause is object of preposition.)

B4   Types of Sentences

(1) Simple, Compound, Complex, and Compound-Complex Sentences

A **simple sentence** is a single independent clause. A simple sentence may consist of just a subject and a predicate.

> <u>Jessica</u> <u>fell</u>.

Or, a simple sentence can be expanded with different kinds of modifying words and phrases.

Jessica fell hopelessly in love with the very mysterious Henry Goodyear.

A **compound sentence** consists of two or more simple sentences (independent clauses) linked by a coordinating conjunction (preceded by a comma), by a semicolon (alone or with a transitional word or phrase), by correlative conjunctions, or by a colon.

See 36a1

       independent clause   independent clause
[The moon rose in the sky], <u>and</u> [the stars shone brightly].

                independent clause
[José wanted to spend a quiet afternoon fishing and reading];
                 independent clause
<u>however</u>, [his friends surprised him with a new set of plans].

A **complex sentence** consists of an independent clause along with one or more dependent clauses.

See 36a2

     independent clause   dependent clause
[It was hard for us to believe] [that anyone could be so cruel].

             dependent clause
[Because the program had been so poorly attended in the past],
     independent clause   dependent clause
[the committee wondered] [whether it should be funded this year].

A **compound-complex sentence** is a compound sentence—made up of at least two independent clauses—that also includes at least one dependent clause.

See 36a3

         dependent clause   independent
[Because driving a cab can be so dangerous], [my mother always
clause   dependent clause   independent
worried] [when my father had to work late], and [she could rarely
clause
sleep more than a few minutes at a time].

(2) Declarative, Interrogative, Imperative, and Exclamatory Sentences

Sentences can also be classified according to their function.

    Declarative sentences, the most common type, make statements: *World War II ended in 1945.*

    Interrogative sentences pose questions, usually by inverting standard subject-verb order (often with an interrogative word) or adding a form of *do: Is Maggie at home? Where is Maggie? Does Maggie live here?*

Imperative sentences express commands or requests, using the second-person singular of the verb and generally omitting the pronoun subject *you: Go to your room. Please believe me. Stop that.*

Exclamatory sentences express strong emotion and end with an exclamation point: *The killing must stop now!*

CREDITS

Text and Illustrations

Photos

Part Openers

p. 1: © Keith Brofsky/PhotoDisc/Getty Images

p. 77: © John Giustina/Iconica/Getty Images

p. 107: © PhotoDisc/Getty Images

p. 175: © John Coletti Photography

p. 225: © John Coletti Photography

p. 291: © Christoph Wilhelm/Taxi/Getty Images

p. 435: © Royalty-Free/Corbis

p. 517: NASA Goddard Space Flight Center. Image by Reto Stockli. Enhancement by Robert Simmon

Icons

Computer tips: © Keith Brofsky/PhotoDisc/Getty Images

Grammar checkers: © Siede Preis/PhotoDisc/Getty Images

Checklists: © John Coletti

Close-up: © PhotoDisc/Getty Images

ESL tips: NASA Goddard Space Flight Center. Image by Reto Stockli. Enhancement by Robert Simmon

Interior Photos

p. 14 left: © MAPS.com/Corbis

p. 14 right: © Jeff Greenberg/Lonely Planet Images/Getty Images

p. 15 top left: *Profile of a Woman Wearing a Jabot* (pastel on paper), Cassatt, Mary Stevenson (1844–1926) Private Collection © Christie's Image/Bridgeman Art Library

p. 15 top right: Photo courtesy of Mercedes-Benz USA, LLC

p. 15 bottom right: © Don Bishop/PhotoDisc Green/Getty Images

p. 16: Figure 3.1. "The Whole World is Watching . . . Member of Marine honor guard passes the Vietnam memorial on which names of casualties of the war are inscribed" from *Philadelphia Inquirer*, November 14, 1982. Reprinted by permission of Philadelphia Newspapers.

p. 56: © The Thomson Corporation/Heinle Image Resource Bank

p. 99: U.S. Department of Transportation

p. 101: Figure 10.4. © Chris Hamilton/Aurora Photos

p. 102: Figures 10.5 and 10.6. © Bettmann/Corbis

p. 105: Figure 11.1. Reprinted by permission of Carl Steadman

p. 113: Figure 12.1. Reprinted by permission of © Google Inc.

p. 113: Figure 12.2. Screen shot from InfoTrac® by Gale Group. Reprinted by permission of The Gale Group.

p. 127: Figure 12.3. Reprinted by permission of © Google Inc.

p. 133: Figure 13.1. Southeastern Louisiana University

p. 134: Figure 13.2. Southeastern Louisiana University

p. 136: Figure 13.3. Southeastern Louisiana University

p. 137: Figure 13.4. "The Supply Side of the Digital Divide: Is There Equality in the Broadband Internet Access Market" by James E. Prieger from *Economy Inquiry*, April 2003, Vol. 41, No. 2, p. 346. Reprinted by permission of Oxford University Press.

p. 140: Figure 13.5. Provided courtesy of The General Libraries, The University of Texas at Austin

p. 148: Figure 14.1. © 2005 Netscape Communications Corporation. Screen shot used with permission.

p. 150: Figure 14.2. Reproduced with permission of Yahoo! Inc. © 2005 by Yahoo! Inc. *Yahoo!* and the *Yahoo!* logo are trademarks of Yahoo! Inc.

p. 151: Figure 14.3. Reprinted by permission of © Google Inc.

p. 169: "The Red Wheelbarrow" by William Carlos Williams from *Collected Poems: 1909–1939, Volume 1*, copyright 1938 by New Directions Publishing Corp. Reprinted by permission of New Directions Publishing Corp.

p. 241: © Microsoft Corporation

p. 311: Figure 22.1. © Joseph Sohm/Corbis

p. 312: Figure 22.3. © Cloud Hill Imaging Ltd/Corbis

p. 331: Figure 24.1. © Microsoft Corporation

p. 337: Figure 24.5. Home page of website from Lyric Opera of Waco. Reprinted by permission of Lyric Opera of Waco, Education Department

p. 341: Figure 25.1. © Chris Rusu

p. 343: Figure 25.3. Screen shot reprinted with permission from National Family, Career & Community Leaders of America, Inc.

p. 344: Figure 25.4. Reprinted by permission of School of Music, Northern Illinois University, DeKalb, IL

p. 349: © Microsoft Corporation

p. 354: © Microsoft Corporation

p. 356: Figure 26.1. © Yue Li

p. 357: Figure 26.2. © Yue Li

p. 365: Figure 27.2. © Microsoft Corporation

p. 375: Figure 28.1. © Orange Glo International

p. 439: © Microsoft Corporation

p. 447: © Microsoft Corporation

p. 464: © Microsoft Corporation

INDEX

Note: Page numbers in blue indicate definitions.

Con tents

Frequently Asked Questions